ON THE JOHN U

The path to higher education OTJU *sta*

U.S. HISTORY

ON THE JOHN UNIVERSITY™

The path to higher education OTJU *starts with a good sit down.*

U.S. HISTORY

SWEETWATER
PRESS

SWEETWATER
PRESS

On the John University: U.S. History

Copyright © 2008 Sweetwater Press

Produced by arrangement with Cliff Road Books

ISBN-13: 978-1-58173-741-7

Book design by Miles G. Parsons
Cover design by Ford Wiles
Contributors: Jim Dunn, Rita Doughty

Printed in the U.S.

EXPLORATION BEFORE COLUMBUS

Contrary to what we learned from Porky Pig and Looney Tunes, Christopher Columbus was not the first European to reach the Americas.

Vikings from Scandinavia had crossed the North Atlantic and reached Iceland as early as the ninth century. Erik the Red led the Norsemen even farther west, settling Greenland in 986.

Sometime after the year 1000, Erik's son Leif finally reached the northeastern shore of North America. He called the place Vinland (modern-day Newfoundland) and spent the winter there before returning to Greenland. Later, other Vikings founded a colony in Vinland, but abandoned the settlement after spending several years fighting off hostile Indians.

The Vikings were followed by small independent fishermen from ports all along the Atlantic coast: Portugal, France, England, and Norway. Trying to avoid a large fishing monopoly that prevented them from fishing in the North Sea, they traveled further to unclaimed waters.

The fishermen built sturdy fishing ships to withstand the dangerous northern seas as they tracked schools of cod. The fishermen followed the cod around Greenland all the way down to Cape Cod. By the time Columbus sailed, thousands of Spaniards, Portuguese, Frenchmen, Englishmen, and other western Europeans had found their way to the shores of Newfoundland and probably the North American mainland.

These fishermen did not have many resources to found colonies, and they cared even less about doing so. They simply landed on beaches in sheltered coves along the Newfoundland and New England coast to clean, dry, and salt their catch.

While the fishermen prepared their fish for the trip back to Europe, curious Indians approached them. They traded small items for the fur capes the Indians were wearing and brought the capes back to Europe. This was the beginning of the fur trading business.

THE SEARCH IS ON

Who can't imagine searching for gold? But, what if you couldn't pick up a five-pound bag of sugar at the grocery store on your way home from work?

In the fifteenth century, sugar was an expensive luxury that only the very rich could afford. Even Spain's Queen Isabella saved it for a special Christmas gift for her children. In fact, Europeans used gold to buy sugar from the Mediterranean.

They used so much of their gold to pay for sugar and other luxuries, like silks and spices, that they worried about running out. Logically, they thought of finding more gold and then of setting up their own sugar-growing operations closer to home.

Europeans had heard stories of gold in Africa and wanted to search there while looking for land to grow sugarcane cheaply. Native Africans were not happy to see the foreigners and defended their land fiercely.

So, Portugal's Prince Henry took to the sea, sailing south along the African coast to find islands where he could grow sugarcane. Portugal set up a trading station on the Gold Coast to import gold, and they established sugar plantations in the Azores, Madeira, and the Cape Verde islands. Sugar became a major commercial enterprise.

A young man named Christopher Columbus was one of many sailors who transported sugar from the islands to western Europe. In the Azores, Columbus worked for a leading trader and even married his daughter. From those islands, he could see the things that washed ashore, and he assumed there was another land beyond the open sea. More importantly, he noticed the headwinds blowing toward the Azores that made it almost impossible to sail westward. The time Columbus spent in the Azores helped him understand that to sail west, he would need to travel south first.

Crash Course
Accidental Discoveries

Most of the discoveries in the New World were based on trial-and-error. On any good trip, you start out with an itinerary and a map. So did the earliest explorers, setting off with a plan and an idea of where they wanted to go.

However, many of them were, quite simply, wrong. Lucky for us, they were the kind of men who made the best of the situation, no matter where they landed.

(Actually, the more probable explanation is that they were afraid to return home without something to show for all the money their supporters had put up to pay for the trips. So, they gathered information and anything that they could take back, trying to show that their trip had been worthwhile, after all.)

In any event, we can thank the following Europeans, among many others, for their persistence that literally "put us on the map."

Explorer	Date	Looking for	Found
Christopher Columbus	1492	India	Bahamas
John Cabot	1497	northwest passage to the Orient	Newfoundland, Nova Scotia
Pedro Cabral	1500	India	Brazil
Sebastian Cabot	1509	northwest passage to the Orient	North American coast
Sebastian Cabot	1512	Spice Island in the Orient	Paraguay
Juan Ponce de León	1513	Fountain of Youth on Bimini	Florida
Ferdinand Magellan	1519	Spice Island in the Orient	Buenos Aires
Giovanni da Verrazano	1524	northwest passage to the Orient	New York Harbor, Rhode Island
Jacques Cartier	1535	passage to the Orient	Montreal
Hernando de Soto	1540	riches of Seven Cities of Cibola	the Mississippi River
Samuel de Champlain	1603	northwest passage to the Pacific	the Great Lakes
Henry Hudson	1609	northwest passage to the Pacific	Hudson River

A CAPE TO GIVE SAILORS HOPE

The Cape of Good Hope is a rocky point of land extending out into the Atlantic on the southernmost coast of South Africa. It is about 90 miles north of the southern tip of Africa.

For years, Europeans had searched for a sea route that would take them to India and Asia. By sailing straight there, they could trade directly with the Oriental merchants and cut out the expensive middlemen of the Middle East who monopolized their trade on land. This obsessive search for a path to the Orient ultimately led to the accidental discovery of the Americas.

By the time of Columbus's day, Europeans already knew that there was a way to get around the southern tip of Africa. That's because they had seen old Chinese, Arabian, and Indian maps showing a rough picture of the trip around Africa.

In 1487, John II of Portugal sent navigator Bartolomeu Dias to study the discoveries that had already been made and explore farther. In 1488, Dias was the first European to round the Cape of Good Hope, which he called *Cabo das Tormentas*, or the "Cape of Storms." When Dias rounded of Cape in 1488, he opened the road to India. Establishing a sea route to the Far East was a major psychological and geographic milestone for the Portuguese.

King John Has the Last Word

King John II renamed the cape *Cabo da Boa Esperança*, or "Cape of Good Hope," because it was so exciting to find a sea route to India and the East. Sailors think of it as a point of "Good Hope," because it is where the rough seas let up for the first time anywhere south of the equator.

COLUMBUS SAILED THE OCEAN BLUE

Most schoolchildren learn the first two or four lines of the "1492 Poem:"

> *In fourteen hundred ninety-two*
> *Columbus sailed the ocean blue.*
>
> *He had three ships and left from Spain;*
> *He sailed through sunshine, wind and rain.*

Honestly, the poem covers the story of Columbus' voyages in a concise—but quite elementary—narrative. Columbus departed from Spain on August 3, 1492, with three ships: the Niña, the Pinta, and the Santa María. He stopped at the Canary Islands and restocked, sailing on September 6. Then he arrived at the Bahamas on October 12, where he named each island. Columbus arrived back in Spain on March 15, 1493.

Read the rest of the poem:

> *He sailed by night; he sailed by day;*
> *He used the stars to find his way.*
>
> *A compass also helped him know*
> *How to find the way to go.*
>
> *Ninety sailors were on board;*
> *Some men worked while others snored.*
>
> *Then the workers went to sleep;*
> *And others watched the ocean deep.*
>
> *Day after day they looked for land;*
> *They dreamed of trees and rocks and sand.*
>
> *October 12 their dream came true,*
> *You never saw a happier crew!*

"Indians! Indians!" Columbus cried;
His heart was filled with joyful pride.

But "India" the land was not;
It was the Bahamas, and it was hot.

The Arakawa natives were very nice;
They gave the sailors food and spice.

Columbus sailed on to find some gold
To bring back home, as he'd been told.

He made the trip again and again,
Trading gold to bring to Spain.

The first American? No, not quite.
But Columbus was brave, and he was bright.

Cristoforo Colombo

Christopher Columbus's actual name was Cristoforo Colombo. Although we think of him as being Italian, he was born in Genoa, which was an independent city-state at that time. He was well educated and was fluent in Ligurian (the native language of Genoa), Latin, Portuguese, and Spanish.

Voyage 1: Columbus Travels to Parts Unknown

Christopher Columbus outfitted two small, light sailing ships, the *Pinta* and the *Santa Clara* (also known as the *Niña)* A third small, round ship with a large hold was Columbus's flagship. It was called the *Santa María.*

On August 3, 1492, the three ships, with about a hundred men, left for parts unknown. After stopping at the Canary Islands, the voyagers departed the known world on September 6, 1492, traveling primarily westward. Ushered along by the strong Canaries Current, Columbus had made a good choice to sail from the Canary Islands.

Two hours past midnight on the morning of October 12, 1492, a lookout on the *Pinta* yelled, "Tierra! Tierra!" ("Land! Land!"). Later that day, Columbus and the excited but tired voyagers set foot on land after thirty-six days of sailing. They really thought they had landed in the Orient. Columbus claimed the island for Spain, naming it San Salvador ("Holy Savior"), which may or may not be the actual San Salvador that we know today.

Curious but cautious, the islanders approached. They greeted the explorers, willing to trade for anything: balls of spun cotton, parrots, and spears for the sailors' glass beads, red caps, and trinkets. The sailors called them Taínos, part of a larger native family called the Arawak. The Taínos were not scared of the Spanish and their swords. (They had never seen swords before, and cut themselves when handling them.)

The explorers were very interested to see that the islanders had small pieces of gold pierced in their noses. Excitement built when they told Columbus that neighbors on countless other islands wore gold arm and leg bands. Believing they had arrived in the Indies, the Spaniards called the islanders "Indians."

On the third day, Taíno guides took Columbus to explore other islands. By the end of October, Columbus reached Cuba. The guides told him it was an island. But he sailed north and south along its coast, convinced it was part of China.

To the east of Cuba, Columbus sailed to La Isla Española, or Hispaniola. As he cruised the coast, the *Santa María* struck a reef and grounded. The crew salvaged what they could and built a fort from the lumber. Thirty-nine men stayed behind. Named Villa de la Navidad, "Christmas Town," this was the first European settlement in the Americas.

In January the *Pinta* and the *Niña* headed home. Columbus again enjoyed the good fortune of an ocean current. Entering the Gulf Stream, his ships sailed far enough north to catch the westerly winds. But as the ships neared Europe, they ran into a hurricane and were separated. On March 15, 1493, the *Niña* returned to the same port harbor it had departed from 32 weeks earlier, rejoining the *Pinta*.

Columbus met with King Ferdinand and Queen Isabella in Barcelona, presenting exotic islanders and colorful parrots and telling tales of the voyage and of the islands with their scenic beauty and curious natives. He showed the gold he had brought back: gold crowns, gold masks, gold ornaments, gold nuggets, and gold dust.

Ferdinand and Isabella honored Columbus and rewarded him with the title "Admiral of the Ocean Seas," along with 1,000 doubloons. The King and Queen—and Columbus, too—truly believed that Columbus had accomplished what he had set out to do: find a sea route to China. Promising gold, spices, and other luxuries, Columbus had no problem at all convincing Ferdinand and Isabella to pay for a second voyage as soon as possible.

Columbus Remembered

Americans have found many ways to honor the memory of Columbus's voyage. The District of Columbia, Columbus, Ohio, and Columbia, South Carolina, and Columbia University are all named for him. Hundreds of schools use his name and there is a statue of him at Columbus Circle in New York.

THE THORN IN COLUMBUS'S SIDE

Martín Alonso Pinzón, a Spanish sea captain, played a big part in getting Columbus's first voyage underway. He built the three vessels for the voyage, and he helped persuade local sailors to join the expedition. Pinzón, who made it clear that he had much more experience than Columbus, commanded the *Pinta*.

Throughout the crossing, Pinzón was "difficult." He always sailed in advance of the other ships and refused to obey Columbus's orders. Clearly, Pinzón viewed himself as Columbus's rival, if not superior.

On the third day after reaching land, Columbus sailed to explore Cuba. Not long after that, Pinzón suddenly sailed off in the *Pinta*. Several theories still float around about why Pinzón separated from the others. The natives said he wanted to take all the treasures for himself.

Similarly, historians guess that he was looking for gold. Others think he was hoping to be the first to discover the imaginary golden island of Osabeque. Based on his course, some scholars believe he was first to discover Puerto Rico. We do know that Pinzón was the first to discover Hispaniola, now called Haiti, and the river where he landed was called the River of Martin Alonso for a long time.

When he rejoined the expedition, he told Columbus he was stressed out from the weather, and Columbus accepted this excuse, whether or not he actually believed it.

The explorers set off to return to Spain. Off the coast of the Azores, Pinzón deserted again, sailing full speed ahead in hopes of beating Columbus back to King Ferdinand and Queen Isabella. In a nice example of "what goes around, comes around," he was blown off course by a hurricane.

Very sick, probably of syphilis caught during the voyage, Pinzón died before he had a chance to report to the king.

VOYAGE 2: COLUMBUS BRINGS EVERYTHING BUT THE KITCHEN SINK

The second voyage departed on September 25, 1493. This time, Columbus did not pack light; he brought 17 ships and about 1,200 men, including his brothers, Bartholomew and Diego. First, they were going to relieve the men left behind on La Navidad in Hispaniola, then settle more colonists on the islands, and explore and claim other islands.

King Ferdinand and Queen Isabella were more than happy to pay for whatever supplies Columbus wanted. He brought horses, cattle, donkeys, sheep, goats, pigs, dogs, cats, chickens, grain, and seed. But that's not all he packed. He also brought equipment and tools for sailing, defending against attacks, building settlements, and setting up an administration overseas.

The fleet stopped at the Canary Islands to replenish provisions, then took a more southerly route this time. Land was sighted twenty-one days later, on November 2. On this trip, they had reached a new group of smaller islands, the Lesser Antilles, which were south and east of Cuba and Hispaniola (also known as in the Greater Antilles).

Moving on toward Hispaniola, Columbus claimed the islands of Guadeloupe and Puerto Rico along the way, coming to La Navidad at the end of November. The sailors fired a cannon to announce their arrival, and waited to hear the answering boom. But no salute was returned. They were horrified to discover the entire settlement massacred, the site burned, and a mass grave of Spaniards.

As with many settlements that disappeared in the New World, no one will ever know for sure what happened at La Navidad. Many believe that local islanders got sick and tired of the Europeans' greed and laziness and destroyed the settlement out of disgust.

Columbus built a new settlement, Isabela, near La Navidad. Unfortunately, the settlers did not learn anything from the La Navidad destruction. They were more interested in finding gold than working to establish the village. To keep the peace, Columbus organized a gold-searching expedition, which only made matters worse. Not much gold was found, and the settlers grew even more restless. Although it turned out to offend the queen, Columbus instituted a policy of forced labor, enslaving the natives to work on the settlement.

The explorers began to wear out their welcome with the Indians, raiding the native villages for gold. The longer they didn't find gold, the unhappier they were. Many of them sailed back to Spain or sent letters complaining about the conditions and the leadership. In October 1495, a Spanish official arrived from Ferdinand and Isabella to investigate the charges they had heard.

Even with forced labor, the searches for gold on Hispaniola were not successful until 1496, when they finally collected about 22 pounds of loose gold. That year, Columbus first found Jamaica and explored more of Cuba. He was desperate to prove that Cuba was part of Asia, even forcing his men to swear an oath that it was a cape of Asia.

On March 10, 1496, Columbus had no choice but to return home to defend himself against the complaints. He named Francisco Roldán to be mayor of Isabela and left his brothers behind.

Ferdinand and Isabella welcomed him warmly and were interested in his discovery of new islands with great potential. They were grateful and still honored him, and even cleared him of any charges, but they were not quite so quick to approve a third voyage.

Far East Trade

What were the Europeans so desperate to bring back from India? Through the ages, they had seen all manner of exotic riches arriving over the land route, the Silk Road. Some of the items they wanted from Silk Road trade included:
- Silks: cultivated silk, wild silk
- Spices: cloves, nutmeg, mace
- Jewels: lapis lazuli, jade, rubies, soapstone, pearls
- Resources: Lebanese cedar, gold, bronze, myrrh

VASCO DA GAMA TRADES FOR SPICES

A Portuguese navigator, Vasco da Gama was the first European to successfully journey by sea to India. Supported by Portugal's King Manuel I, da Gama left Lisbon in July 1497 with four ships. He sailed around the Cape of Good Hope, passed the easternmost point reached by Bartolomeu Dias, and continued up Africa's east coast to Kenya.

Then da Gama crossed the Indian Ocean, reaching Calcutta in May 1498. This was significant because he had opened up a way for Europe to reach the Indies. More importantly, the new ocean trade routes that da Gama discovered led to tremendous growth in spice trade commerce.

When he returned to Portugal in 1499, da Gama's ships carried exotic spices. This voyage brought an age of European domination in the Far East. Portugal immediately gained great riches from the spice trade, and a struggle began among European nations to gain control of trade along the spice routes. From Vasco da Gama's discovery, the Portuguese Empire grew.

In 1502 da Gama led a second India voyage, helping establish Portuguese power in Indian waters. He treated chiefs on the African coast with cruelty to force them to submit to Portugal. As the first to discover a route to India, da Gama was honored with many titles and a lot of money. In 1524 he returned to India as viceroy, but he died soon after his arrival.

Da Gama: The Man

Vasco da Gama was born in Sines, Province of Alemtejo, Portugal, to a noble family. His father was a famous soldier who had connections to royalty. Due to his status, da Gama was well educated and studied several languages, physics, geometry, mathematics, and astronomy.

CRASH COURSE
JOHN CABOT

It is important to know about John Cabot because England's claims in North America were based on his discoveries. Also, he was unintentionally responsible for the halt of English exploration, which wasn't resumed until more than seventy-five years later.

An Italian native (his Italian name was Giovanni Caboto), English explorer John Cabot apparently shared Christopher Columbus's belief that it would be easiest to reach the rich trade of East Asia by sailing west.

Supported by England's Henry VII, in 1497 Cabot sailed north from Bristol toward the New World in search of a passage to Asia. Five weeks later, his crew of eighteen men sighted land. Even though the distance was shorter than Columbus's trips from Spain to the Bahamas, it took longer because the northern winds and stormy North Atlantic waters were not as favorable.

Instead of the Orient, what Cabot had discovered was the North American coast, with its rich fishing grounds. He called the land "New Found Land," which could have actually been present-day Newfoundland or even Cape Breton Island in Nova Scotia. Cabot reported back to Henry about the great fishing potential of the area, which the English took advantage of for a long time before establishing any permanent colonies.

In 1498, Cabot again sailed for America to explore the coast, this time with four ships and about three hundred men. The fate of the expedition is unknown. He never returned, and was believed lost as sea, although some reports show that the expedition did reach America and that some of its members did return to England.

Considering the fate of Cabot's second trip, Henry VII refused to finance further voyages for England. English exploration was halted until Elizabeth I sent an expedition in 1576.

EXTRA CREDIT: John Cabot had a son named Sebastian Cabot.

VOYAGE 3: COLUMBUS FACES REBELLION AND ARREST

Columbus sailed on May 30, 1498, this time with six ships. They split up, one group heading toward Hispaniola. He sailed further south, hoping to discover new islands.

Columbus's good-sailing-weather luck ran out. He sailed into the doldrums, an unbearably hot, dead space in the ocean where wind and currents die. A week went by, then a breeze finally pushed them on, toward an island he named Trinidad. Columbus spent weeks sailing into the Gulf of Paria, near Venezuela, and the coast of South America, discovering the mouth of the Orinoco River.

In Hispaniola, Bartholomew Columbus had moved the Isabela settlement. His reasons: Isabela had a poor water supply, and the new site, Santo Domingo, was close to gold mines. Arriving in August, Columbus found the situation had gone downhill since he left. The lazy and disheartened settlers were rebelling.

One group stayed loyal to the Columbus family. The rebels followed Isabela mayor Francisco Roldán. Columbus spent two years trying to restore order. To calm everyone down, he finally gave the rebels each a plot of land and the islanders living on it.

Things didn't get better. Columbus asked the king and queen for someone to deal with the situation. They sent Francisco de Bobadilla. This was not quite what Columbus had asked for. Unfortunately, Bobadilla stripped Columbus of his titles, appointed himself governor, seized Columbus's possessions, arrested the three Columbus brothers, and shipped them back to Spain in chains.

On December 17, 1500, Columbus appeared before the king and queen. They returned his possessions but did not reinstate his titles. They did, however, replace Bobadilla with Nicolás de Ovando.

In the meantime, Portuguese sailor Vasco da Gama found a route to Asia; he went around Africa to India. To keep up with Portugal, Spain agreed to Columbus's suggestion of another voyage.

CLAIMING THE ALREADY-DISCOVERED BRAZIL

In 1500, Portugal's King Manuel I outfitted another expedition to India, this one commanded by Pedro Cabral. Manuel instructed Cabral and his thirteen ships to closely follow Vasco da Gama's earlier route to India. However, winds and currents pushed the ships off-course—actually, way off-course—and they sailed much farther to the west, all the way to South America.

On April 22, 1500, Cabral's fleet discovered Brazil. Even though Spanish sailor Vicente Yáñez Pinzón (Martín Alonso's brother) had visited Brazil earlier, Cabral claimed the land for Portugal.

Then Cabral turned and headed east, passing the Cape of Good Hope in late May. After that, he continued right along da Gama's route to India. Along the way, he fought with middle-east spice traders who were threatened by the competition from the Europeans. He finally arrived in January 1501 and was again successful in trading for spices in Portugal's name.

So, the Portuguese claimed Brazil, but they did not rush to colonize the land. The first permanent settlement, called São Vicente (near current-day São Paulo), was not established until thirty years later, in 1532. At that time, the natives taught the explorers how to grow corn, make hammocks, and use dugout canoes.

Brazil

When Cabral sighted Brazil in 1500, he named it "Island of the True Cross." King Manuel I renamed the land "Holy Cross." The name was changed one more time, this time to *Brazil*, from the Portuguese word for the red color of brazilwood (*brasa* means "glowing coal"), a kind of dyewood found there. The wood of the tree was used to color clothes and fabrics.

Voyage 4: Columbus Gets Very Specific Instructions

Before Columbus left, Ferdinand and Isabella specifically stated the voyage's purpose: search for gold, silver, precious stones, and spices. They were equally specific forbidding him to return to Hispaniola, for fear of making matters worse in the colony.

Sailing on May 9, 1502, with four ships and 150 men, Columbus was 50 years old and in bad health. He could not captain a ship, but a crew of loyal seamen served the admiral once again.

After stops in the Canarie Islands and on Martinique for supplies, Columbus headed directly for Hispaniola, reaching Santo Domingo on June 29. Even though it had been forbidden, one ship needed repair, and a hurricane was coming. Columbus sent a message to Governor Ovando asking to enter port and advising against ships departing.

Ovando refused permission to enter port. He also did not take the advice. Columbus rode out the storm in a small harbor nearby, but Ovando's fleet sailed and was almost entirely destroyed. Surely Columbus gloated a little, because Bobadilla and Roldán died at sea.

After the hurricane, Columbus traveled to Central America. The seas were rough, especially on the ships; one wrecked on Panama's coast, and sea worms destroyed another. The crews crowded onto the two remaining, rickety ships.

By December, disappointed over not finding an Asian passage and concerned about damaged ships, Columbus turned toward Jamaica, where the ships were beached, and the men were marooned for more than a year.

Two sailors volunteered to cross the open channel to Hispaniola, which was almost one hundred miles, by canoe and arrived five days later. Ovando waited seven months to send a ship to Jamaica. The rescue ship delivered the sailors to Santo Domingo on August 13, 1504. One month later, Columbus took his last voyage across the Atlantic Ocean.

COLUMBUS: THE MAN

Who was Christopher Columbus, this Italian who labored so hard to bring riches to the King and Queen of Spain? He was a skilled navigator, a sailor who boldly dared to go where no man had gone before.

For better insight into Columbus's all-consuming quest for fame and fortune, consider what happened when land was first sighted on his first voyage. Queen Isabella had offered a reward of a pension of 10,000 maravedis per year to the sailor who saw land first. (This was a pretty penny in those days — an able seaman could earn about 12,000 maravedis per year.) Early on the morning of October 12, 1492, a lookout on the *Pinta* cried "Land! Land!" Did Columbus congratulate him and hand over the money? No! He claimed that he had seen several lights the night before, and kept it for himself.

There is no doubt Columbus was highly intelligent, with coping skills for any situation. While marooned in Jamaica on his fourth trip, he encountered a potentially devastating problem. The islanders had reached their limit for the Spaniards' greed and control, and they refused to provide any more food. Fortunately, Columbus had an almanac, which he consulted. Expecting a lunar eclipse on February 29, 1504, he threatened to punish the islanders by taking light away from the Moon. When the Moon began to disappear, the frightened natives reestablished trade with his crew.

No one can deny Christopher Columbus's place in history. He claimed more land for Spain than they ever imagined, and he discovered, by his own count, 1,700 islands. Columbus died in 1506, still believing he had found a western route to Asia.

CRASH COURSE
THE UNITED STATES OF COLUMBUS?

Ever wonder why the New World wasn't named for Christopher Columbus? After all, he is the man who discovered it. Well, it's a topic that can still spark heated arguments. How did the land we live in come to be called *America*?

Yes, Columbus found the new world. But, he died still thinking he had discovered Asia. It was another Italian, Amerigo Vespucci, who actually recognized the land as a new world.

Between 1497 and 1504, Vespucci made his own voyages across the Atlantic, exploring the Gulf of Mexico and the coast from Virginia to South America and giving mapmakers 3,300 more miles to chart on the maps. He also made significant improvements in navigational techniques and predicted the earth's circumference to within fifty miles.

After he returned, Vespucci reviewed his notes to determine where he had been. He realized that he had not been exploring Asia, at all (as Columbus had thought), but an entirely new continent. His notes were published, and Vespucci became very famous.

So, was Vespucci so vain that he decided to name the new continent after himself? No, not at all. A German mapmaker, Martin Waldseemüller, read Vespucci's notes. Waldseemüller reasoned that, since Vespucci was the one to recognize the new continent, it should be named after him. He changed the name to *America* because he wanted the word to end with *a*, like *Asia* and *Africa*. Waldseemüller printed the name on a map, and it caught on.

The question still remains: should the New World have been named for the man who made the geographical discovery (Columbus)? Or should it have been named for the man who recognized it for what it was (Vespucci)? Either way, Amerigo Vespucci deserves credit for knowing that he had found a new continent.

NATIVE AMERICAN LIFE

Contrary to later descriptions of the natives as "savages," newcomers to the Americas found them living in well-organized societies, healthy and happy. They were the first to show a good dose of that famous "Southern hospitality," eager to help strangers and share the best of what they had.

Other than dogs, the early Americans did not have animals like goats, sheep, horses, donkeys, camels, or elephants that the Europeans were used to employing. Without any beasts of burden, naturally, they did not have any plows. They used wood implements such as a pointed stick to punch holes in the ground to drop seeds; something that looked like a hoe for weeding; and a spade-like tool to dig. Their strength and skill using these primitive tools impressed the Europeans.

The Europeans were astonished to see that the Indians had already taught themselves a lot about edible plants and what could be used for medicine. Their biggest crop was corn, which the Europeans noticed grew in almost every different climate and environment. Most importantly, the Indians knew how to make the best of it. They used corn to make bread, boiled corn for gruel, and made corn hominy. They also ate potatoes, gourds, pumpkins, squash, lima beans, and kidney beans.

Agriculture—planting, weeding, harvesting, and cooking—was considered women's work. The men took care of the hunting and fishing, bringing home deer, bear, beaver, otters, and fish. With such a varied diet of fruits, vegetables, and protein, the Indians were healthy and physically striking.

Indian men, who averaged 5-foot-7-inches, were about an inch taller than Englishmen and the Indian women were sometimes a full two inches taller than Englishwomen. In contrast to the English, who considered bathing unhealthy and would go months without even taking off their clothes, the Indians bathed every morning and were noted for their cleanliness. It's not hard to guess which group suffered from lice and other pests, and which group enjoyed a plague-free existence.

When they wore clothes, the Native American dress was simple. The men wore a fur mantle and a loincloth. Children wore nothing at all, and women only wore a loincloth "variation." An exception to this dress was when women were picking fruit or working in a cornfield, they dispensed with the loincloth and wore nothing.

Like their dress, the Indian houses were simple but effective. They were built like arbors with a wood frame covered with mats and tree bark or thatch. Shivering in their hand-built homes, the Europeans often noted how warm and toasty the Indian houses were, holding in heat from their fire and insulating against the cold weather.

Because East Coast Indians were farmers, they tended to settle and plant the land. Their houses were built to last for about ten years. In that time, they would be ready to move to another site for fertile land, sort of like reverse crop rotation.

Native American government was a form of democracy. While they did have a chief, he couldn't make decisions on his own without discussing everything with his council, on threat of punishment or death. They believed in collective ownership, that the land belonged to the whole group and was not sectioned out to each individual family.

The Bering Strait Land Bridge

Many scientists theorize that Native Americans arrived to the contitent 40,000 years ago via the Bering Strait land bridge between Asia and Alaska. This bridge was created during the Ice Age when receding water levels exposed a large section of land. It is believed that the first Americans followed herds of animals, most likely woolly mammoths, which they hunted for food.

MAYAS, AZTECS, AND INCAS: THE TRIBE HAS SPOKEN

Thanks to cruise ships offering shore excursions to ancient Mayan and Aztec ruins, many travelers have been fortunate to get a real feel for life in Central and South America before the Europeans arrived. Even more of us have seen the commercials, or, better yet, watched episodes of a very popular survival reality show that has filmed seasons in Panama, Guatemala, and the Pearl Islands.

The people who populated Central and South America before the days of Columbus's arrival were part of highly developed societies of intelligent and resourceful citizens.

The Maya

- The intellectually-gifted Maya ruled from southern Mexico to northern Belize until about the tenth century.

- The Mayan population dwindled as the Aztec empire strengthened around that time.

- Superior mathematicians and astronomers, they invented positional notation, developed the concept of zero, and predicted solar eclipses.

- The Maya built massive stone pyramids, temples, and sculptures.

- The Maya created an accurate solar calendar based on 365 days. Later, the Aztecs would base their own 365-day calendar on Mayan astronomical discoveries.

- Classical Mayan religion was based on a number of nature gods with elaborate rituals that included bloodletting and self-mutilation as well as human and animal sacrifices.

- Mayan art was the most highly developed among the old American cultures. What we know of their history comes from their complicated hieroglyphics, which archaeologists still continue to interpret.

The Aztecs

- The Aztec people were originally hunters and gatherers who settled in the area around Mexico City.

- The Aztec capital was the largest city in the world of its time, featuring a temple complex, a royal palace, and numerous canals.

- Their expertise in irrigation and reclaiming swampland made their nation rich and populous.

- The Aztec fashioned jewelry using gold, silver, copper, emerald, turquoise, and jade.

- Aztecs were also known as the Mexica.

- At its peak, the Aztec empire controlled as many as five hundred small states and six million people.

- Montezuma, their particularly harsh king, routinely sacrificed his subjects to the supreme Aztec deity.

The Incas

- The Incan empire included the western South American coast, from the Pacific shoreline to the Andes Mountains.

- They built a road system that ranged 2,250 miles through Chile from Quito to Santiago. Using a sophisticated system, couriers could run messages along this road at about 150 miles a day.

- The Inca built rope suspension bridges across the steep mountain valleys of the Andes. Some of these rope bridges were nearly 330 feet in length.

- At its height, the Incan empire had about 12 million subjects.

- The Inca system of government was among the most complex political organizations of any Native American people.

- The Inca were caught in the middle of a civil war when Spaniards arrived in 1531. The newcomers were able to play sides against each other to defeat the entire nation and take its hoard of gold and silver.

NATIVE AMERICAN TRIBES

In studying the Indians, historians have identified at least 580 different languages spoken by natives in North and South America. This means that there were at least 580 different groups or tribes already in the New World before the Europeans arrived.

Some of the known tribes in North America are listed below with a general present-day geographical description of where they were located.

Along the Saint Lawrence River	Algonquians
Near Lake Ontario	5 nations of Iroquis: Kaniengebaga (or Mohawks), Oneidas, Onandagas, Cayugas, and Senecas
Carolinas	Cherokee and Tuscarora
Piedmont area southward from Maryland	Catawba, Saponi, Tutelo, Occaneechee, Cheraw
Maryland	Yoacomaco
Georgia	Creek
Gulf Coast, Georgia to the Mississippi River	Muskhogean: Chatot, Chitimacha, Biloxi, Mobile
Minnesota	Ojibwa
West of Lake Michigan	Menomini, Sauk Fox, Kickapoo, Winnebago
South of Lake Michigan	Miami
Between Lakes Michigan and Huron	Potawatomi
North of Lake Huron	Ottawa
Between Lakes Huron and Erie	Tobacco
South of Lake Erie	Erie
North of Lake Ontario	Huron
New Brunswick	Malecite and Micmac
Maine	Abnaki
New Hampshire	Pennacook
New York	Mohican
Delaware	Delaware
Pennsylvania/ West Virginia	Susquehanna
Kentucky	Shawnee
Along the Tennessee River	Yuchi
Illinois	Illinois

Iowa	Iowa
Missouri	Missouri, Osage
Alabama and Mississippi	Chickasaw, Choctaw
Florida	Timucua, Clausa
Louisiana and Mississippi	Natchez, Caddo
Arkansas	Quapaw
Cuba	Ciboney, Subtaino

With that many different people, it's no wonder they were often at war with one another. There was always a struggle to defend their land or enlarge their territory. In fact, while the European explorers did their best to exploit the Indians for food, shelter, and labor, the Indians were at the same time trying to enlist the foreigners in their wars to gain an edge over their opponents.

Indian State Names

Many state names were derived from Native American words. Here's a short list:

Connecticut: Quinnehtukqut word meaning "beside the long tidal river"

Illinois: Algonquin word for "tribe of superior men"

Kansas: From a Sioux word meaning "people of the south wind"

Kentucky: From an Iroquoian word "Ken-tah-ten" meaning "land of tomorrow"

Mississippi: From an Indian word meaning "Father of Waters"

Nebraska: From an Oto Indian word meaning "flat water"

North Dakota: From a Sioux word meaning "allies"

Ohio: From an Iroquoian word meaning "great river"

Oklahoma: From two Choctaw Indian words meaning "red people"

Texas: From an Indian word meaning "friends"

Wyoming: From the Delaware Indian word, meaning "mountains and valleys alternating"

EARLY ATTEMPTS AT CONVERTING NATIVES

The push to the New World brought more than explorers looking for gold and a passage to China. Missionaries and priests hurried to America to convert the natives to Christianity and save their souls.

From the time Columbus returned from his first voyage, his benefactor Queen Isabella encouraged the Catholic Church to bring the natives to Christ. On Columbus's second voyage in 1493, Isabella sent Catholic priests to convert as many barbarians as possible. Although they were threatened with death or enslavement, the natives resisted strongly, even killing the Catholic priests. This made it easier for the explorers to justify their horrific treatment of the natives, taking their land, food, and women.

In 1567, Jesuits tried to establish their first missions in Florida. The friars realized that they could not control Indians as long as they lived in what they called "a state of nature." So, the missionaries implemented a plan to "reduce" the Indians into something similar to Europeans. "Reduction" meant relocating Indians into new settlements grouped around churches.

First, the friars discovered that the settlements had to be self-sustaining. They imported European tools and animals. To Indians used to planting with stick-tools, the ox-drawn plow was revolutionary, and they were amazed by other livestock, too: cattle, donkeys, horses, sheep, and goats.

The priests taught the natives farming and blacksmithing. But most of all, the priests were concerned about covering the natives' nudity—a lot more concerned about that than about teaching them to read or write. The Indians learned how to weave, and a textile market grew with the settlements.

Indians seeking refuge from marauding explorers flocked to the missions. Unfortunately, they were put to work at hard labor and confined to the boundaries of the settlements, both physically and economically.

SQUANTO: A REAL LIFESAVER

Even young schoolchildren can tell you about one character in their history books: Squanto. But, children don't always get the whole story about *how* Squanto came to speak English.

When Squanto was a young man, in 1614 an English captain kidnapped twenty Indians to sell in the Spanish slave market. Spanish monks bought Squanto and treated him well. He learned a lot about European culture and language, but he was homesick.

Squanto found that his knowledge would be invaluable to sailors planning transatlantic trips, and managed to sail with a 1619 scouting expedition. Obviously, the explorers planned to use Squanto as a guide and interpreter in the New World. But as soon as they landed, Squanto bolted to go home. Unfortunately, he found his village deserted and in ruins. He later learned that an epidemic disease had destroyed his tribe about two years earlier. So, he joined a nearby Wampanoag tribe.

The Pilgrims came along and built Plymouth town on the site of Squanto's village in December 1620. In spring, Squanto introduced himself to the Pilgrims. The colonists were amazed by his grasp of the English language. They were also excited about his potential value to their success. They invited Squanto to join their community, and he did.

Squanto helped the Pilgrims recover from their first difficult winter by teaching them how to fish and when and how to plant corn. He also helped them to build warmer houses to survive in cold New England. He literally was a lifesaver Squanto also established friendly relations between the Pilgrims and the Wampanoags, acted as interpreter, and introduced them to the fur trade. He stayed with the Pilgrims until his death in 1622.

EXTRA CREDIT: Stevie Wonder mentions Squanto in the lyrics to his song "Black Man" on the album *Songs in the Key of Life*.

DISEASE: A NEW ENEMY

Native American tribes often went to war over arguments about land. For fighting in battle, the Indians had developed effective weapons and strategies to win their side. Then, with the arrival of the Europeans came a new enemy against which the Indians did not have any defense. Native immune systems were not prepared for Old World infections, and Indian tribes were vulnerable to them. Early explorers and then colonists brought disease-causing organisms—to which they were already immune—that decimated the Native Americans who had built up no immunity. Many natives died outright, and those who survived found themselves alone and on their own.

Transmitted through traded goods or a single infected person, a host of diseases annihilated entire communities: measles, smallpox, bubonic plague, cholera, typhoid fever, scarlet fever, pleurisy, mumps, diphtheria, pneumonia, whooping cough, malaria, yellow fever, and sexually transmitted infections.

This obliteration was a powerful tool in defeating people who the Europeans considered "savage." For example, smallpox is credited for Spanish explorer Hernán Cortés' victory over the Aztecs in 1521 with fewer than 500 men. Smallpox killed almost 3 million Aztecs, one-third of the population. The Europeans even thought that God had sent these epidemics to prove their moral superiority over the natives.

Some believe that 90 to 95 percent of the native population was reduced by death caused from Old World diseases. For example,

- Disease killed the entire native population of the Canary Islands in the sixteenth century.

- Measles killed 2 million Mexican natives in the 1600s.

- Smallpox killed half of the Taíno people on Hispaniola.

- Smallpox killed 100,000 Incas in Cuzco (60–90 percent of the population).

- The American Southwest Pueblo population fell 90–95 percent by 1850.

- Smallpox killed 30 percent of the West Coast Native Americans in 1770s.

ECONOMICS 101
FROM WAMPUM TO COIN

Indians used money in the form of seashells. Northeast coastal Indians had more access to shells, and therefore had better money stores. Indians divided their "money" into value ratings: *wompompeag* was worth three times as much as the common Roanoke. Whelk shells were used to make the white variety and quahog shells for the dark purple or black variety.

Many tribes used *wampum,* cylindrical beads fashioned from the central column of seashells. The beads were woven into strings, belts, sashes, headbands, and other items. The value of wampum increased as it moved farther from its place of manufacture.

Wampum was more of a symbolic value; most trade was by barter. In the seventeenth century, however, wampum drew the attention of Europeans. With metal coins scarce in New England, wampum soon became an accepted currency. Not only did colonists use the shells in their trade with Native Americans, but wampum was legal tender among whites in New England for small sums. The New Amsterdam Dutch settlers even quoted prices in "wampum," along with silver and beaver skins.

In the fur trade, Europeans found wampum to be an important medium of exchange. Indians increased their wampum production so they could buy goods from Dutch and English traders. The traders, on the other hand, turned around and used the wampum to buy furs from other groups. By the nineteenth, Europeans had perfected the wampum market, going so far as to establish wampum factories on Long Island and in New Jersey to mass-produce wampum for trade.

CROSSING THE ATLANTIC: THE VESSELS

With today's mammoth oceanliners and Coast Guard rescues, you must switch your mental gears to understand what explorers saw when they boarded ships for the New World. Many fifteenth- and sixteenth-century boats were as small as modern sailboats—thirty tons and thirty feet in length.

Few ships displaced more than 150 tons; at seventy-five feet long, the *Santa María* displaced about one hundred tons. The ninety-foot *Mayflower* was 180 tons, and the first settlers to Maryland took the 350-ton *Ark*. In comparison, the *Titanic* measured 882 feet and 46,328 tons. If you can't picture that, consider that one cruise line's smallest ship today boasts 728 feet and 46,052 tons.

Length of the passage depended entirely on the weather. While Columbus cruised to the Bahamas in four sunny weeks, one 1731 voyage took twenty-four weeks, and two-thirds of the passengers starved to death.

Traveling the southern route, from Spain, through the Canarie Islands, then northward, the last part of the trip was known as a ship killer. Where the Gulf Stream's warm waters met colder waters off Cape Hatteras, North Carolina, storms were often violent enough to dismantle ships. In the eighteenth century, explorers began taking a northerly route, northwest from the British Isles to Iceland, then southwest past Nova Scotia and south along the New England coast.

With no accurate maps yet, sailors navigated by the seats of their pants, not knowing locations of reefs, rocks, or sandbars. They used crude instruments (compass, sand glass, and log line) for rough longitude estimates and dead reckonings.

Even if they actually figured out where they were going, ships were always the target of privateers and pirates. As the Atlantic was contested among the British, French, Dutch, and Spanish navies, any protection at all depended on the latest war or peace.

CROSSING THE ATLANTIC: THE PASSENGERS

Crossing the Atlantic to reach the New World was not for the faint of heart. Conditions on board were unimaginable to us today.

First, consider the provisions. Meat was a luxury; the only way to preserve beef or pork was to soak it in saltwater, and it rotted anyway. Biscuits were the staple, and you can bet they weren't tasty, even before they became moldy and soggy, sloshed by seawater in the hold. Even worse, the food was gnawed by rats and infested by worms. When food ran out, passengers resorted to eating any of those same rats that they could catch.

Packed with people, their belongings, equipment, and animals, the boats had room for little else. No matter how long the trip ended up taking, they could only bring a certain amount of food and drink. The 1,500 gallons of water they brought was questionable at best, drawn from a source near the port where all kinds of waste and garbage had collected. Stored in barrels onboard, it stagnated, and slime gathered on top. So, the people chose to drink beer instead. Crew and passengers of an average-size ship on a three-month trip brought along 3,500 gallons of beer.

Passengers stayed in the area known as 'tween-decks, between the hold and the deck, which was only four to five feet high. It could only be aired out in fair weather, as the hatch was battened down in rough seas to avoid flooding. There was no way to bathe or wash clothes; lice and other pests were everywhere. Even worse, because no one wanted to face a fire at sea, no candles or lanterns were permitted, so the quarters were pitch-black.

Such descriptions can't help but make you wonder, just how desperate were people to leave the motherland?

Privateers and Pirates

First, let's talk about the difference between "privateer" and "pirate." While their actions were quite similar, the consequences were very different.

A privateer was an armed ship or crew commissioned by a government to fight or harass enemy ships. As payment for their work, privateers were given part of the captured ship's fortune. A pirate was a person or crew who robbed or committed illegal violence at sea or on the sea shores. While pirates kept all of their loot, they were severely punished if caught. Because of this, privateers were quick to deny acts of piracy.

When England and Spain, or France and Spain, were at war, anything on the ocean was a target. During the first half of the eighteenth century, about five thousand pirates were active in the Atlantic. They did not care about geography, ethnicity, society, or law. Even law-abiding merchant ship captains sometimes "subsidized" their legitimate income with a little piracy on the side.

Privateers and pirates kept up their game, even in peacetime. Actually, *especially* in peacetime: There were more pirates around then. As navies discharged after a war's end, the veterans often turned to piracy.

When Spaniards captured pirates, they were whipped and enslaved. Or, if they were Protestant, turned over to the Inquisition, where they were put on the rack or marched to the gallows. British-captured pirates were either killed immediately or brought back to London for public execution, an unsettlingly popular spectator event.

However, most pirates got away. They had scoped out hideouts where shallow waters or reefs prevented larger warships from following. They even set up their own republics on various Caribbean islands. Some of the best-known were New Providence in the Bahamas, the island of Tortuga, and Port Royal, Jamaica.

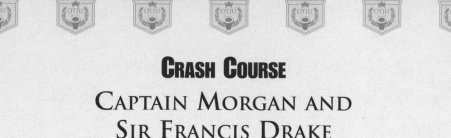

CRASH COURSE
CAPTAIN MORGAN AND SIR FRANCIS DRAKE

Other than a certain spiced adult beverage, what do you know about Captain Morgan?

First of all, Henry Morgan was not a pirate. He was, however, one of the most famous of all privateers. A Welsh buccaneer commissioned by the governor of Jamaica for aggression against the Spanish, Morgan captured and ransacked settlements in Cuba, Panama, and Venezuela. He was known to be exceedingly cruel to his captors, torturing them to get information about treasure, and even using priests as human shields. Although he was reprimanded for some of his actions, he was always protected by Jamaica's governor, Sir Thomas Modyford.

In 1672 Morgan was tried in England for plundering Panama City after a treaty had already been signed between England and Spain. He argued that he was unaware of the treaty. Convinced of his loyalty, King Charles II knighted Morgan and appointed him lieutenant governor of Jamaica.

Sir Francis Drake was probably the most famous British privateer, especially because he had such close contact with the throne. Queen Elizabeth commissioned Drake, who set out for the Caribbean. On land, he ambushed a Spanish mule train carrying a shipment of silver from Peru. He delivered his treasure to Elizabeth, who rewarded him by naming him head of an expedition to sail around the world.

The first English captain to see the Pacific Ocean, he seized Spanish treasure and attacked Spanish settlements as he went. When he returned to England in 1580, Spain demanded that he be executed as a pirate. Queen Elizabeth instead knighted Drake and allowed him to continue his raids on Spanish America. He was later instrumental in defending England from attacks by the Spanish Armada. Drake died a natural death and was buried at sea.

THE REAL PIRATES OF THE CARIBBEAN

No, there wasn't really a Captain Jack Sparrow. But there really were pirates and they really were in the Caribbean.

Captain William Kidd was a Scottish sailor executed for piracy, although he protested until the end that he acted only as a privateer. He was commissioned by New York's governor to attack all those associated with pirates and any enemy French ships. Kidd took an Armenian boat whose English captain had purchased French East India Company passes that promised protection of the French Crown. Kidd's crew felt the capture was perfectly legal, as Kidd was commissioned to take French ships, and an Armenian ship with French passes counted as French. For this and other offenses, Kidd was tried by English Parliament, found guilty on charges of murder and piracy, and hanged.

Edward Teach, or "Blackbeard," was an English pirate who also probably began as a privateer for Britain. His reputation preceded him, and he captured most of his booty based on fear alone. Rumor has it that he wove hemp and lighted matches into his black beard during battle. Teach shared his treasure with North Carolina's governor in exchange for his pardon. Virginia's governor did not like having the retired pirate living nearby and sent a party to hunt down and destroy Blackbeard. Teach gave a valiant chase, but after a bloody fight was killed and his head delivered to the Virginia governor.

Bartholomew Roberts was a Welsh pirate who raided the waters around the Americas and West Africa. He was the most successful pirate, capturing far more ships than even Blackbeard or Captain Kidd. Roberts was killed during a ship battle and was buried at sea by his crew. He is also known as Black Bart, but this name was never used in his lifetime.

John Cabot's Son, Sebastian

Accomplished mapmaker and navigator Sebastian Cabot made exploratory voyages both under English and Spanish flags. In 1509, he sailed on a northern route to discover a Northwest Passage. He expected to find a strait to the Orient.

Instead, his crew threatened mutiny, and Sebastian Cabot headed back to England. He was certain he'd found a Northwest Passage to the East, which was probably the Hudson Bay. On his way back, he explored the coast of North America.

In 1512, Sebastian Cabot entered Spanish service. From Spain, in 1526 he sailed toward southern South America, heading toward Spice Island. However, he ended up spending several years exploring the Paraguay, Río de la Plata, and Paraná rivers. Apparently, he did not behave any better than the explorers before him, because the natives were hostile to his expedition. That, coupled with lack of food, forced him to return to Spain in 1530.

Sebastian Cabot rejoined the English navy. Still hoping to find a trade route to China, in 1553, he organized another trip to seek a Northwest Passage. The expedition reached the White Sea on Russia's northwest coast. There, they negotiated a treaty with Russia, breaking the monopoly that had thwarted independent fishermen for years.

There Were TWO Cabot Explorers

Note: Sebastian Cabot was the son of John Cabot. This is important for two reasons:

- Sebastian more than likely sailed with his father in 1497, and even 1498, and therefore grew up around the life of a sailor and explorer.
- Past historians and scholars somehow managed to confuse the two Cabots, and tried to attribute all of their adventures to one person. Understandably, this did not make sense, so for a long time, students tried to meld Sebastian's records into John's by changing dates to match John's voyages.

Juan Ponce de León Does Not Discover the Fountain of Youth

You may have already heard of Juan Ponce de León and his quest throughout Florida for the Fountain of Youth. Well, there's a little more to the story than that.

First of all, Ponce de León had sailed with Columbus on his second voyage. After that, he was appointed governor of Puerto Rico. It was during his time in the New World that he heard tales from the natives about a beautiful island called Bimini, where healing waters flowed that would restore old men to their younger life.

Ponce de León set out in 1513 to find this island. Instead, he found Florida in the first known European expedition there. Claiming the land for Spain, Ponce de León named it *Pascua Florida*, which means "Feast of Flowers," or Easter. Some say that even though he landed on Easter, he named the area for its beautiful flowers and scenery, and not specifically for the day.

Starting around present-day St. Augustine, Ponce de León sailed all along the Florida coast, charting the rivers and naming the areas as he passed: Cape Canaveral (which means "Cape of Currents") the Florida Keys, Florida's west coast, and Cape Romano. Although he almost sailed the entire length of Florida's Atlantic coast and a good part of the west coast, he didn't quite go far enough. Ponce de León thought that Florida was another island.

Ponce de León was commissioned to colonize the Island of Florida. Eight years later, he returned in 1521 establish a settlement. He brought two hundred men, including priests, farmers, and craftsmen; fifty horses and other domestic animals; and farm tools. They landed near Charlotte Harbor. But the native Calusa Indians attacked the colonists immediately and chased them away. Fatally wounded by a poisoned arrow, Ponce de León died on the return voyage to Cuba. His death brought Spanish exploration to a temporary halt.

Whether or not he was actually searching for the Fountain of Youth, he will always be known for discovering Florida.

Hands-on History
The Fountain of Youth

Stories of healing waters that could restore an old man's youth were passed down in both the Old and New Worlds long before Ponce de León came along. But his name will forever be associated with the legend of Florida's Fountain of Youth.

Indian stories about a special spring included a mythical land called Beemeenee. The natives in Hispaniola, Cuba, and Puerto Rico all told the Spanish explorers about this land of wealth and beauty located somewhere north, pointing toward the Bahamas.

The story of Ponce de León's search for the Fountain of Youth actually was not associated with him until after he died. Some historians claimed he was looking for the youthful waters of Bimini to cure his impotence.

To further confuse the issue, the city of St. Augustine, Florida, does have a Fountain of Youth National Archaeological Park. The park is located at the spot where they believe Ponce de León landed as a tribute to his part in the city's history.

Extra Credit: St. Augustine, Florida, calls itself "The Nation's Oldest City." Established in 1565, it is the oldest continuously occupied European-established city in the continental United States.

From Stowaway to Famous Explorer

Vasco Núñez De Balboa was the first European to see the Pacific Ocean, which historians consider to be the second most important event of Spanish exploration, after Columbus's discovery in 1492.

Balboa stowed away— with his dog— on an expedition headed for Colombia. The unfriendly natives there attacked. The Spaniards prayed to the *Virgen de la Antigua* for help, vowing to name a settlement after her. So, in 1510 Balboa founded Santa María la Antigua del Darién in Panama, the first permanent European settlement on the mainland of the Americas.

Searching for gold, he sailed west along Panama's coastline, taking care to befriend the natives. He found them very helpful in his quest.

He met a tribe who first spoke of "the other sea," where tribes had gold plates and goblets. This was doubly intriguing, and of course Balboa had to check it out. He started across the Isthmus of Panama, reaching a mountain summit on September 25, 1513. He saw the water on the horizon—the undiscovered sea.

They rushed down to the coast. Once there, Balboa walked into the ocean and claimed the new sea and all adjoining lands in the name of King Ferdinand and Queen Isabella. He named it *Mar del Sur*, or South Sea, since they had traveled south to reach it.

Other explorers, jealous of his findings, accused Balboa of treason and had him beheaded in 1519. Today, streets, parks, and buildings throughout the Americas honor Balboa. For one, the fabulous San Diego Zoo is located in Balboa Park, the nation's largest urban cultural park, with fifteen major museums, performing arts venues, and beautiful gardens.

Extra Credit: In 1520, Ferdinand Magellan renamed the sea the Pacific Ocean, meaning "peaceful," because of its calm waters.

CIRCUMNAVIGATION

Circumnavigation: It's a long, bulky word that simply means "go all the way around."

In September 1519, working for Spain's Charles I, Portuguese explorer Ferdinand Magellan (also called Fernão de Magalhães) sailed with five ships and about 265 men. Like Columbus, Magellan wanted to reach the Far East, specifically Spice Island, by sailing west.

First, he headed toward Brazil in South America. Looking for a suspected passage, he visited Rio de Janeiro and the Río de la Plata in modern-day Buenos Aires. He spent the winter months in Patagonia. Remember, in the southern hemisphere, winter is opposite from in North America, so he actually spent March through August 1520 in Patagonia. During that time, Magellan put down a mutiny led by two Spanish captains.

In August he sailed south from Puerto San Julián. On October 21, 1520, more than a year after leaving Spain, Magellan finally discovered and entered the strait that would take him East.
A month later, his three remaining ships emerged from the strait into the Pacific Ocean.

Magellan had finally found the westward route that European explorers had been searching for. His crew later reported that he broke down and cried when he realized this. Crossing the Pacific, they didn't see any land for almost two months, and didn't refresh their supplies for three.

Finally, on March 6, Magellan arrived at Guam, and discovered the Philippines ten days later. He stayed in the Philippines for the rest of his life. On April 27, 1521, Magellan was killed on the island of Mactan while supporting one group of natives against another.

Following his death, another boat was destroyed. The remaining two vessels reached Borneo and finally the Moluccas (now called Maluku), Spice Island, their destination.

One boat sailed for Panama but was wrecked. The one remaining ship, commanded by Juan del Cano, sailed across the Indian Ocean, rounded the Cape of Good Hope, and finally, with only eighteen men, reached Spain in September 1522. The crew had just completed the first circumnavigation of the world.

Although he did not survive the trip, Magellan's skill and determination achieved one of the greatest navigational feats, taking ships over an unknown part of the globe. His voyage proved beyond a doubt that the Earth is round, it introduced the relative proportions of land and water, and it confirmed that the Americas are a new world, and certainly not Asia.

The Strait of Magellan

- The most important natural passage between the Pacific and Atlantic Oceans.
- Located south of Chile, South America, and north of Isla Grande de Tierra del Fuego.
- Only two and one-half miles wide at its narrowest point.
- Considered a difficult route to navigate because of bad climate and the narrow width.
- First named Estrecho de Todos los Santos, or "Strait of All Saints" because Magellan entered it on All Saint's Day.
- The Spanish king renamed it Estrecho de Magallanes in honor of Magellan.
- Other early explorers: Pedro Sarmiento de Gamboa, Sir Thomas Cavendish, Francis Drake.

TIMELINE:
HERNÁN CORTÉS CONQUERS MEXICO

Hernán(do) Cortés Pizarro, was a Spanish conquistador who made his name in Mexico, conquering the Aztec Empire in the name of Spain's King Charles V. He began the first phase of the Spanish colonization of the Americas.

In his lifetime (1485-1547), Cortés accomplished many victories and achievements. The following timeline highlights his impact on Mexico:

1502
- Cortés joins a West Indies expedition led by Nicolás de Ovando with Diego Velázquez.

1506
- Cortés takes part in the conquest of Hispaniola and Cuba, receiving a large estate of land and Indian slaves for his efforts.

1510
- Diego Columbus, the new governor of Hispaniola, selects Velázquez as commander of an expedition to conquer the island of Cuba.
- Cortés is chosen to join the Velázquez expedition. Cuba is quickly conquered.

1513
- The town of Bayamo on Cuba is established.

1514
- The towns of Trinidad, Santo Espiritu, Puerto Principe, and Santiago de Cuba are founded.

1518
- May 1 — A fleet under Juan de Grijalva leaves Santiago to explore the coast of Mexico and sends back favorable reports to Velázquez.
- Velázquez chooses Cortés and to captain an exploratory expedition to establish a colony in Mexico.

1519
Cortés is elected captain of the third expedition to the mainland.

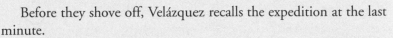

Before they shove off, Velázquez recalls the expedition at the last minute.

- February 19 — Cortés ignores Velázquez's order, and with a force of six hundred men and twenty horses, sets sail for Mexico. This is an act of open mutiny.
- Cortés lands on the Yucatan Peninsula.
- March — Cortés lands in Mexico, claiming it for Spain.
- March — Cortés and suppresses the town of Tabasco. The natives give him a woman called Malinche, who becomes his mistress, guide, and interpreter.
- July — Cortés establishes the town of La Villa Rica de la Vera Cruz. By doing this, Cortés dismisses the authority of the governor of Cuba and places himself directly under the orders of Charles V. To prevent any possibility of desertion and retreat he burns all of his boats.
- August — Cortés marches inland toward Tenochtitlan, bringing four hundred men, fifteen horsemen, fifteen cannons, and hundreds of native carriers and warriors.
- August — On the way to Tenochtitlan, Cortés makes alliances with native Americans such as the Nahuas, the Tlaxcaltec, and the Totonacs.
  Cortés learns about the fabulous riches of the Aztec Empire and marches his troops inland to discover the land of the Aztecs.
- October — Cortés and his men, accompanied by about three thousand Tlaxcalteca, march to Cholula, the second largest city in central Mexico. Cortés massacres thousands of unarmed members of the nobility gathered at the central plaza and partially burns down the city. He did this in response to a trap he noticed was being set for him.
- Cortés forges an alliance with the Aztec Indians of Tlaxcala and learns about their customs, culture, and religion.
- Cortés learns of Quetzalcoatl of Aztec legend. This "Winged God / Feather Serpent" was a light skinned, bearded God-King of civilization revered by the Aztecs. His arrival coincides with Quetzalcoatl's predicted return.
- Cortés heads further inland and reaches the Aztec capital of

Tenochtitlan. The Aztecs believe that Cortes could be Quetzalcoatl their light skinned, bearded God-King

- November — Aztec king Montezuma II the peacefully receives Cortés into Tenochtitlan, the Aztec capital and home to thousands of Aztecs.
- Montezuma deliberately lets Cortés enter the heart of the Aztec Empire, hoping to get to know his weaknesses better and to crush him later.
- Montezuma gives lavish gifts of gold to the Spaniards. This confirms their search for gold and spurs them on to steal huge amounts of the precious metal.
- Cortés meets no resistance and establishes headquarters inside Tenochtitlan.

1520

- Cortés learns that Spaniards on the coast have been attacked. To assert his authority, he takes Montezuma hostage and forces him to swear allegiance to King Charles.
- April — Velázquez sends more than one thousand soldiers to arrest Cortés.
- April — Cortés quickly leaves Tenochtitlan to fight the soldiers from Velázquez. Cortés defeats the soldiers and persuades them to join him.
- April — While Cortés is dealing with the soldiers, one of his lieutenants in Mexico slaughters six hundred Aztec nobles in the Main Temple, which triggers a local rebellion.
- Cortés is attacked by thousands of Aztec warriors on his return to Tenochtitlan.
- June 30– July 1— Cortés and his soldiers flee from Tenochtitlan. Many are killed. Cortés also loses most of the treasure he had looted and his artillery.
- July 1 — Cortés quickly returns to Mexico to do damage control. He tries to calm the Aztecs by releasing Montezuma. But, the Aztecs stone Montezuma to death.

1521

- Cortés returns to Tenochtitlan with reinforcements from Cuba.
- Cortés begins a "blockade" of the island city of Tenochtitlan. He cuts off supplies and contact with their allies.
- August — Plague strikes the Aztec population. Tenochtitlan falls to Cortés.
- August 13 —Cortés captures Cuauhtémoc, the ruler of Tenochtitlan, and the Aztec Empire disappears. Cortés had conquered five million Aztecs with less than one thousand soldiers.

1521-1524

- Cortés personally governs Mexico. He initiates the construction of Mexico City, destroying Aztec temples and buildings, then rebuilding on the Aztec ruins. Mexico City soon becomes the most important European city in the Americas.

1528

- Cortés returns to Spain and is given the title, "Marques del Valle de Oaxaca."

1530

- Cortés returns to the New World and settles in Cuernavaca, Mexico.

1536

- Cortés makes his final expedition and discovers Baja California.

1539

- Francisco de Ulloa discovers the Sea of Cortés, now called the Gulf of California.

1540

- Cortés returns home to Spain for the last time.

1541

- Spain fears the power that Cortés has in the New World. He is denied any government post in Mexico and his reputation is smeared by rumors.
- Cortés receives permission to join Charles' fleet in the great, but unsuccessful, expedition against Algiers in the Barbary Coast.

GIOVANNI DA VERRAZANO SAILS INTO NEW YORK BAY

Sent by French King François I, Giovanni da Verrazano set out in 1524 to reach Asia. His goal was to find a passage to the Pacific Ocean. Verrazano first arrived near present-day Cape Fear, North Carolina. He didn't find a place to land, so he turned south. A day or so later, still looking for a good place to land, he doubled back to the north to modern-day Virginia. He wrote about a large body there which he thought might be the opening to the Asian passage, but it turned out to be a massive bay, more than likely Chesapeake Bay. He encountered natives here, which he thought were Chinese. They were friendly and receptive to Verrazano's party, probably the first Europeans they had ever seen.

Traveling farther northward, Verrazano found the Narrows and the mouth of what is now known as the Hudson River. In fact, Giovanni da Verrazano was the first European explorer to sail into New York Harbor. Verrazano also explored New York Bay and Block Island and Narragansett Bay, both in Rhode Island. By the time he reached Rhode Island, Verrazano began to notice that the natives, who had more than likely already experienced European trading, were less receptive.

Verrazano continued northward, exploring the eastern seaboard of North America. Rounding Cape Cod, the explorers met openly hostile Indians, who had no doubt already had their fill of Europeans. Verrazano traveled as far as Nova Scotia before returning to France. Verrazano's trip established a substantial French claim to North America, calling the area Terre Francesca.

Today, when you travel to New York City, you fly over the Verrazano-Narrows Bridge, which spans the Narrows of New York Harbor from Brooklyn to Staten Island.

SAN MIGUEL DE GUADALUPE: SPAIN'S FIRST FAILURE

With Spanish backing, Lucas Vázquez de Ayllón led an expedition to Santa Elena, about halfway between modern-day Charleston and Savannah. Not finding gold or anything that they thought was valuable to take back, the sailors instead kidnapped Indians to sell as slaves.

Ayllón took the Indians to Hispaniola and kept several to teach Spanish so they could serve as guides and translators on later trips. Then in July 1526, Ayllón with his men, captors, tools, and horses, returned to the Chesapeake area to start a colony. They ran aground near present-day Cape Fear in North Carolina, and the Indians escaped. This left Ayllón's crew all but stranded, with no knowledge of the area or the native language.

The Spaniards got on their horses and surveyed the land, settling on an island offshore from what we now call Georgetown, South Carolina. The settlement, San Miguel de Guadalupe, was Spain's first attempt to create a colony in North America. It was not a success.

Ayllón had sailed from Hispaniola with five hundred men. In addition to the guides who fled, many of the San Miguel de Guadalupe colonists died of fever. By the time Ayllón died, the number was down to 150 men. They gave up and sailed back to Hispaniola.

Although with San Miguel de Guadalupe, Spain's attempt to colonize North America failed, it was the first European colony in America. San Miguel de Guadalupe was settled almost one hundred years before Jamestown or the Pilgrims at Plymouth Rock, and almost forty years before St. Augustine (the first successful colony).

CABEZA DE VACA TAKES THE LONG WAY

Planning a cross-country trip, you know to allow a few hours for the flight. But, what if you knew it would take eight years?

Spaniard Pánfilo Narváez brought four hundred men and eighty horses to the Tampa Bay area in 1528. His group was so focused on finding gold that they moved inland and got lost. They tried to work with the Indians, but did not treat them fairly, repaying the native's friendliness with stealing and harassment. Quite naturally, the Indians retaliated, killing many of the party. Others died of fever. One of the few survivors was Álvar Núñez Cabeza de Vaca, who set out on an eight-year journey toward Mexico to meet other Spaniards there.

During his wanderings from tribe to tribe, he began to see the local natives as people and not barbarians. He acted as a medicine man, healing their sick. Word spread among the tribes. Not only was his survival guaranteed, but he developed a large following of native "groupies" who joined his trek across the American Southwest and Northern Mexico. Cabeza de Vaca wrote about his experiences in a report for Charles V, *La Relación* (The Report). This report is considered a colonial literature classic, offering descriptions that anthropologists would not otherwise have.

On the way, his small group endured hardships from lack of food to being enslaved by various tribes. Traveling on foot, Cabeza de Vaca explored what is now Texas, and parts of New Mexico and Arizona. He walked along the Texas coast, up the Rio Grande, down the Pacific coast, eventually reaching Mexico City.

Cabeza de Vaca hoped to be named governor of Florida. However, Charles V had already appointed Hernando de Soto to lead the next expedition, so he declined to join the group.

JACQUES CARTIER, EXPLORER
(NOT JEWELER)

Frenchman Jacques Cartier sailed in 1534 to claim land for France's King François I. He was successful—a good portion of the French claim to Canada is based on Cartier's explorations.

Cartier encountered: Newfoundland, the Strait of Belle Isle, Labrador, the etire Gulf of St. Lawrence, Prince Edward Island, New Brunswick, Chaleur Bay, the Gaspé Peninsula, and the St. Lawrence River estuary.

On the Gaspé Peninsula, he met a number of Indians, and kidnapped two to take back to France. He did not see anything resembling the "great quantities of gold" the king expected. But he returned and reported that there was hope.

Based on that report, Cartier planned a new venture the following year to find out if the Saint Lawrence was the route to the "South Sea." Using his two kidnapped Indians as guides, he went almost one thousand miles up the Saint Lawrence River until reaching rapids at Montreal.

Caught completely unprepared for the cold Canadian winter, half of Cartier's crew died. To try and help, the Iroquois Indians shared what they had, which was not a lot. So, Cartier's men simply took what they didn't share. This affected their relationship with the Iroquois, and not in a good way. In fact, it laid early groundwork for the struggles between the French and the Iroquois to come.

Six years later, in 1541, Cartier returned, this time with plans to establish the colony of Charlesbourg-Royal in Quebec. It was ultimately not successful and abandoned after two years. But while the men were there, they discovered diamonds and gold, which they collected to take back to France. But, alas, the minerals turned out to be only quartz crystals and iron pyrites, or "fool's gold." The business of jewels would have to wait for another man named Cartier.

CRASH COURSE
HERNANDO DE SOTO

The King of Spain commissioned Hernando de Soto to colonize Florida, and he landed in Charlotte Harbor in June 1539. Prepared to settle, they brought: clothing and trade goods; shields, armor, helmets, cross-bows, guns, and black powder; nails, tools, seeds, and plows; horses, long-legged pigs, bloodhounds, and mules.

One month later he marched his army inland then spent that winter in north Florida. De Soto continued to explore the southeastern United States, looking for gold and jewels. Instead, he found hostile Indians. Most significant was the discovery he made on May 21, 1540—the Mississippi River.

In his explorations, de Soto visited what would become at least twelve different states: Florida, Alabama, Georgia, the Carolinas, Tennessee, Kentucky, Indiana, Illinois, Missouri, Arkansas, and Louisiana.

Get out your U.S. map, and follow along de Soto's route over the next two years:

Spring 1540: Through Alabama and Georgia, up to the Carolinas, then west through Tennessee, and south back through Georgia and Alabama.

October 1540: Headed down to meet his ships at Mobile Bay. Chief Tuscaloosa's tribe ambushed the group about 100 miles from the port. de Soto won the skirmish but retreated northward, beyond the Tennessee River.

Spring 1541: Turned due north through Kentucky and Indiana, reaching Lake Michigan, then southwestward through Illinois and Missouri.

Winter 1541: Camped in Arkansas.

May 21, 1542: Died of fever near present-day Ferriday, Louisiana. His companions sank his body in the Mississippi River, which he would forever be known for discovering.

FRANCISCO VÁSQUEZ DE CORONADO

What do you do when the "cities of gold" turn out to be dirt? How about leave behind a legacy of descriptions? That's what Spanish explorer Francisco Vásquez de Coronado did for us, providing valuable images of the southwestern United States.

Marrying into wealth, Coronado received political appointments in Mexico, where everyone had heard Cabeza de Vaca's stories of gold from his years trekking across the land. They also heard rumors of the Seven Cities of Cíbola, filled with gold.

Coronado left Mexico in February 1540 to find the Seven Cities somewhere in the northeastern part of New Spain. He never found any gold. But Coronado's party was the first to see several exciting phenomena, including the Grand Canyon and a herd of buffalo.

1540

- Started north along the western slope of the Sierra Madre Occidental, keeping close to the Gulf of California.
- Veered inland along the Sonora and San Pedro rivers.
- Crossed the White Mountains in eastern Arizona.
- Reached Cíbola in July. Cíbola was a great disappointment, merely communities of Zuni pueblos with no treasures at all.
- Headed northwest, finding that the Hopi pueblos were just as poor.
- Headed far to the west, coming to the Grand Canyon, but could not get to the bottom.
- Spent the winter in the Rio Grande valley near Albuquerque, New Mexico.

1541

- Set out east searching Quivira, rumored to be rich.
- Crossed the Great Plains of northern Texas.
- Turned north into Kansas, found a hostile village of Wichita Indians.

1542

- Returned home to Mexico in bad health, with no wealth.

THE FATHER OF NEW FRANCE

There's no wonder Samuel de Champlain is known as "The Father of New France." Consider all he accomplished there: produced the first accurate chart of the Atlantic coast from Newfoundland to Cape Cod; mapped the St. Lawrence Valley and Great Lakes Basin; wrote notes on the native's language and actions that were valuable to settlers who followed. He also kicked off the French and Indian War.

In 1603 King Henry IV sent Champlain on a fur-trading mission to the Gulf of St. Lawrence. Five years later, he returned with a group of colonists and founded Québec. This was the first permanent white settlement in Canada, and today it is the oldest city in the western hemisphere north of St. Augustine, Florida.

Québec's early success is purely because of its founder's common sense and prior knowledge. Champlain had earlier spent a couple of years in the Caribbean with the Spanish fleet. This experience gave him an opportunity to observe and study a European colony before trying to found one.

The Huron Indians, clearly unacquainted with Europeans in this remote area, met them with dancing and a feast. Champlain was no idiot, though, and he realized they would expect something in return for this warm welcome. The Hurons and their Algonquin allies were at war with the Iroquois, and they hoped these newcomers would take their side. Being that he was sitting at their feast, and all, Champlain sided with the Hurons. In June 1609, Champlain joined the Huron, Montagnais, and Algonquin Indians when they invaded the hunting grounds of a longtime enemy, the Iroquois, by Lake Champlain. This marked the beginning of warfare between the French and the Iroquois Indians that lasted off and on for ninety years.

After 1612, Champlain split his time between France and Québec. He used the settlement as a base of operation from which to carry out his life goals, which were to explore and map the continent, find a water route to the Pacific, and convert the natives to Christianity. Such aims cost money, but he knew how to earn good money from the fur trade with his local allies.

In his explorations, Champlain visited and/or mapped:

- Saguenay River
- St. Lawrence River
- Montréal Island
- Richelieu River
- Hudson Bay
- The Great Lakes
- Acadia, now New Brunswick
- The Bay of Fundy
- The Saint-Jean River, now the St. John River
- St. Croix River
- Port Royal
- Cape Cod
- Lake Champlain
- Ottawa River
- Allumette Island

Using information from his Indian allies, Champlain discovered what turned out to be the Great Lakes. This western body of water was so huge that he believed it must connect with the Pacific Ocean, and it must be the much-sought Northwest Passage through the continent.

In fact, Champlain was so convinced that he was "this close" to finding the Northwest Passage, he began, literally, banking on it. In 1618, he reported to the king his plan for supporting the Québec colony: 1) increase the fortifications and staffing; 2) take advantage of marketing the land's resources of fish, timber, copper, iron, silver, and precious stones; 3) levy tolls to other European nations wanting to use the short water route to China, once this route was discovered. (Yes, I'm sure you saw the major flaw in the third part of that plan right away.)

In 1629 disaster struck. Anglo-Scots privateers demanded the surrender of Québec and seized the company's reinforcements and supplies. Without enough men to defend it, Champlain turned over the settlement.

FUR TRADERS AND
COUREURS DE BOIS

The society of New France differed markedly from that of New Spain. While the Spanish mentality led them to conquer and plunder for gold, the French focused their efforts on a different kind of money-making venture: the fur trade. It was, undoubtedly, very lucrative for New France.

Because they couldn't trap the fur-bearing animals themselves, they let the natives do the dirty work and then traded things for the furs. This meant they had to stay on good terms with the Indians. If they had taken the route of plundering and imprisoning the natives, which the Spanish had so quickly fallen into, the natives, in turn, wouldn't have really cared so much to trade with them. Instead, the French offered the Indians trade goods they had purchased cheaply in exchange for pelts that they would sell for a high price.

Many colonists risked a dangerous journey through hostile Iroquois territory to the "upper country" around the Great Lakes to find native trappers to trade with. It wasn't long before a new kind of Frenchman, the *coureur de bois*, emerged.

A coureur des bois was an unlicensed fur trader in Canada. Like the Spaniards looking for gold and adventure, these guys were lured by the opportunity of wealth. These young men left their families, became trappers, and traded with the Indians illegally. They eventually moved into the Indian villages, living in Indian houses, speaking the Indian languages, dressing in Indian clothing—some even married into the tribes.

Some illicit traders later caused problems by trading alcohol for furs. (But, introducing alcohol to the Indians brings up a whole different story that's better saved for later. . . .)

Economics 101
Dutch West India Company

When you think about the high-power deals that go down each day in New York City, you know that it's fitting for that huge metropolis to have been founded by an entire company.

The Dutch West India Company was a trading and colonizing company for the Netherlands. Basically, they prevented any citizens of the Netherlands from doing business almost anywhere in the New World without going through them.

In the early 1600s, they were busy in North America, building Fort Orange, now Albany, New York; Fort Nassau on the Delaware River; Fort Good Hope, now Hartford, Connecticut; and Fort Amsterdam on the southern tip of Manhattan Island. All of these settlements were on land that England had claimed. But England was at war with France and Spain, and really couldn't take on the Netherlands, too, so they let it go.

We all know the legend of how Manhattan was bought from the Canarsee Indians for 60 guilders, about $24, in trinkets in 1626. The colony was successful, and other immigrants joined them. Germans, Swiss, Moravians, French, English, and Portuguese moved in, and New Amsterdam grew rapidly, becoming a cosmopolitan center. At least eighteen different languages were being spoken in the city as early as 1650.

The Dutch period ended in 1664 when four English warships arrived in the harbor on August 18. The citizens surrendered. The English renamed the community New York in honor of the Duke of York.

Extra Credit: In 1652, the Dutch West India Company established the first European settlement in South Africa on the Cape of Good Hope.

HENRY HUDSON LOOKS FOR A NORTHWEST PASSAGE

English navigator Henry Hudson was a single-minded explorer, with one goal: to find a Northwest Passage. His stubborn pursuit ultimately led to his death.

Hudson made four voyages, all of them with the purpose of finding a Northwest Passage. He certainly wasn't successful in reaching the Pacific Ocean from New York, but he did discover both a river and a bay in North America, which are now named for him.

- *First Voyage — 1607 — Employed by the English Muscovy Company*
  Gambling that the Northwest Passage could be by way of the Arctic Ocean to East Asia, Hudson reached Greenland and the Svalbard islands, midway between Norway and the North Pole.

- *Second Voyage — 1608 — Employed by the English Muscovy Company*
  Hudson again looked to the north for the elusive Passage, sailing to the Russian islands of Novaya Zemlya in the Barents Sea, an arm of the Arctic Ocean.

- *Third Voyage — 1609 — Employed by the Dutch East India Company*
  Hudson went back to Novaya Zemlya. But it was severely cold, and his crew mutinied. So Hudson headed west and south past Nova Scotia and down the North American coast, looking for a narrow strip of land. In September 1609 he entered New York Bay, and he spent a month exploring the Hudson River to about Albany.

- *Fourth Voyage — 1610 — Employed by a company of English gentlemen*
  Hudson sailed into Hudson Bay. He spent three months exploring the eastern islands and shores. Unfortunately, he lingered too long, and the ship was frozen in for the winter. A very cold and unhappy crew mutinied. In June 1611 they put Hudson adrift in a small boat, and he was never seen again.

HUDSON'S BAY COMPANY, FURRIERS FROM 1670 TO 1991

From its charter in 1670 to the closing of retail stores in 1991, Hudson's Bay Company has been involved in the fur business for more than three hundred years. Chartered by England's Charles II for trading and settling in North America as well as finding the Northwest Passage to Asia, the Hudson's Bay Company virtually held a monopoly over fur trade in the Hudson Bay area.

The Hudson's Bay Company had all rights to fur trade in the region drained by rivers flowing into Hudson Bay. (That's an awfully long description, but it's fitting for the size of the area it covered.) Called the Great Company, they also, in effect, had the power to govern the land.

Although it was part of their purpose, Hudson's Bay Company only made a minimal effort to explore for the Northwest Passage. One expedition led by Samuel Hearne to the mouth of Canada's Coppermine River in the Arctic Ocean definitely proved that there was no short Northwest Passage out of Hudson Bay.

In the eighteenth century, a rival, the North West Company, gained some power and threatened Hudson's Bay's position. The two corporations sometimes fought bitterly for dominance, but eventually merged in 1821, keeping the name Hudson's Bay Company. Their combined territory stretched to the Arctic Ocean on the north and the Pacific Ocean on the west. Hudson's Bay Company was, indeed, a vast empire.

During World War I, the Hudson's Bay Company operated a steamship line that transported food and arms for the French and Belgian governments. Today, it is best known for a chain of department stores in Canada called Hudson's Bay. The company still ran retail fur salons until pressure from animal rights activists convinced them to close the stores in 1991.

Rene-Robert Cavelier de La Salle Honors King Louis XIV

We owe Louisiana to René-Robert Cavelier de La Salle. He claimed the entire Mississippi Valley, including all the land drained by the river, for France and named the region to honor King Louis XIV.

La Salle arrived in the New World in 1666, and made his living as a Canadian trader. He explored the wilderness south of Lakes Ontario and Erie and learned the natives' languages and traditions. He also claims discovering the Ohio River in 1671.

La Salle hatched a plan to investigate farther west. He set out in 1679. Along the way, he established forts on the Saint Joseph and Illinois Rivers. In February 1680, he began surveying the upper Mississippi River and ultimately sailed its entire length to the Gulf of Mexico, which he reached on April 9, 1682.

La Salle returned to France to report to the king. Next, he wanted to go straight from France to the mouth of the Mississippi River to establish a colony. He sailed in 1684. But when he reached the Gulf of Mexico, he couldn't find the Mississippi River. It turns out he overshot it, and landed at Matagorda Bay, Texas. He thought the bay was an outlet of the river, but after he looked farther on land for the river's mouth, La Salle realized his mistake.

During all this searching, his group ran out of supplies. So, in January 1687 La Salle decided to head back to Canada to restock from the forts there. His men had already been through too much: disease, hostile Indians, mosquitoes, poisonous snakes, deadly buffalo. They mutinied before they ever left Texas and killed him near the Trinity River.

THE BELLE

One of La Salle's ships, the *Belle*, sank in 1686 during a fierce storm. It was discovered in Matagorda Bay in 1995.

Needless to say, archaeologists were very excited about the find and what we can learn about the French at the time. Studying the excavation gave us new information about the seventeenth century, from the lives of the people on board, to ship construction, to French trade and the items they thought were necessary to establish a colony.

Fortunately for us, the ship was remarkably well preserved. Gooey gray mud had encased the Belle, in essence sealing it from decay. In this amazing "time capsule," scientists found:

• a cannon
• pewter plates
• well-preserved rows of wooden barrels
• pottery
• bronze clothespins
• small bells used for falconry
• glass beads
• wooden handles of tools
• wooden boxes jammed with trade goods
• casks lined with muskets
• miles of woven rope

Many of these items were still in the same place where the French put them before the wreck. Even the ship's hull and timbers were intact, still looking a lot like they did when La Salle last saw them. Excavators could even still read the original numbers scratched into each timber piece to help the ship's builders put the *Belle* together.

Today, a statue of La Salle overlooks Matagorda Bay.

LATER ATTEMPTS AT
CONVERTING THE NATIVES

European missionaries to North America did not have an easy time of converting Indian souls. For one, they were competing with the natives' own tribal holy men.

Many tribes welcomed help from the missionaries because it provided them with much-needed service, but they had no intention of changing their customs or their lifestyle. One group, the Society of Jesus, launched an all-out assault in New France on what they called native paganism and superstition. These Jesuits risked their lives and limbs seeking converts in native villages.

The Huron tribes of southern Ontario allowed the Jesuits to live in their villages and learn their language and culture. They still resisted the missionaries' attempts to change their beliefs, though. But, the Jesuits used the advantages of their European background to persuade thousands of Hurons to accept Christianity. First, the Jesuits had developed immunity against the epidemic diseases that could wipe out entire tribes, then they demonstrated an ability to predict eclipses, and finally, they flaunted their mysterious power of literacy.

Members of the Iroquois Confederation, however, were not as accepting of the missionaries' message. They would kidnap Jesuits and submit them to horrible tortures before burning them at the stake. One surviving missionary wrote of having his fingernails pulled out and his fingers burned down to the knuckles with lit pipes. In the midst of inflicting this excruciating pain, the Iroquois urged him to sing a kind of surrender song to acknowledge his helplessness. The missionary said it was too hard to sing the song, because he couldn't stop screaming in agony.

POP QUIZ #1

1) What are the first two lines of the "1492 Poem?"

2) English explorer John Cabot discovered the fishing potential off the coast of the land he called "New Found Land," which we now know as _____.

3) Who was the new world named after?

4) What do these words all have in common: Biloxi, Mobile, Erie, Huron, Illinois, Missouri, Natchez, Iroquis, and Mohawks?

5) Besides European coins, what Native American shell became accepted legal tender in New England?

6) Regarding privateers and pirates, which group was in danger of punishment for their actions?

7) The first European colony in America, San Miguel de Guadalupe, was located near present-day Georgetown, South Carolina. Did Spain's first attempt to colonize North America succeed?

8) Henry Hudson discovered what river and what bay in North America?

ANSWERS:

1) "In fourteen hundred ninety-two, Columbus sailed the ocean blue."
2) Newfoundland
3) Amerigo Vespucci
4) These are some of the 580 different Native American tribes already in the New World before the Europeans arrived.
5) Wampum
6) Privateers received part of a captured ship's fortune for their payment. A pirate, on the other hand, would be severely punished if caught.
7) No
8) Hudson River and Hudson Bay

THE OLDEST CITY

After a number of failed attempts and against the best wishes of the Native Americans, in 1565 the Spanish established a permanent settlement in Florida.

On August 28, the Feast Day of St. Augustine, Don Pedro Menendez de Aviles first sighted the coast of Florida. Several days later, on September 8, he stepped ashore, planted the Spanish flag, and, with the soldiers and settlers who had traveled with him, Menendez founded St. Augustine.

The settlers went through the same problems that all colonists in America endured: wars with the British, French, and Native Americans; starvation; disease; and hurricanes. But they held their ground.

Now known as "The Oldest City," St. Augustine is the oldest permanent European settlement in North America. Through its long tenancy, St. Augustine has seen a lot of history:

- English navigator Sir Francis Drake burned and sacked it in 1586.
- Spain's Queen Mariana directed the residents to begin building military fortress Castillo de San Marcos in 1672 to protect against attacks by the British Empire.
- The Spanish sold Florida to the United States in 1821 and ceded St. Augustine.
- The city's military involvement during the Seminole war of the late 1830s helped the town prosper.
- Union forces captured the city in 1862 during the Civil War.

A Modern Old City

Today, St. Augustine still has the distinctive plan of a sixteenth-century Spanish Colonial walled town. A walk through the old heart of the city will give you a living history lesson, with architecture from 1703 to 1898, including the Government House (1713), the Basilica Cathedral of St. Augustine (1797), and Trinity Episcopal Church (1825). The Oldest House is a traditional Spanish Colonial residence built around 1706 and the oldest surviving residence in the city's history.

Slavery Comes to America

As the Spanish continued to settle the new world, they needed more and more labor to help their colonies prosper. At first, they captured Indians and enslaved them. The Indian slaves were put to work in the mines digging for precious metals, farming the land (which was once theirs, but the Spanish had now claimed), and tending Spanish livestock.

By introducing disease to the Americas, the Europeans were themselves responsible for wiping out their own enslaved labor force. The Spanish quickly replaced the lost Indian labor with hundreds of thousands of imported African slaves.

Europeans found that they preferred Africans to Indians. The Africans had already been exposed to European diseases at home, and therefore had developed immunity. They also had agricultural experience, unlike many Indians.

It wasn't long before the use of African slave labor expanded. Almost as soon as the Jamestown settlers discovered they could grow tobacco on the land, they also discovered a need for help tending the crop. The first few Africans arrived in Jamestown in 1619 as indentured servants. While the Virginia tobacco growers at first were too poor to purchase the slaves, Africans and their offspring soon were a main source of farm labor.

Indentured Servants

An indentured servant was often a person (usually a young man) who, in exchange for free transportation to a colony, was obligated to work on a plantation for a certain number of years. Usually, the transportation was paid for by wealthy plantation owners, who quickly caught on that the more indentured servants they sponsored in passage, the more land they would accumulate.

COLONIES: CORPORATE, ROYAL, AND PROPRIETARY

Every English colony received its identity and its authority to operate from a charter by the reigning king or queen (depending on who was on the throne at the time). Each charter described in general terms the relationship that was supposed to exist between the colony and the crown.

Over time, three types of charters developed. This, in turn, meant that three kinds of English colonies were established:

- Corporate colonies were operated by joint-stock companies, at least during the colonies' early years. Jamestown, Massachusetts Bay, Plymouth, Rhode Island, and Connecticut were corporate colonies.

- Royal colonies were to be under the direct authority/control and rule of the king's or queen's government. Virginia was England's first royal colony. Other royal colonies were New Hampshire, the Carolinas, New York, New Jersey, and Georgia.

- Proprietary colonies were under the authority of individuals granted charters of ownership by the king. Maryland, Pennsylvania, and Delaware were proprietary colonies.

Joint-Stock Companies

The English came up with a simple and practical way to finance the founding of new colonies. *Joint-stock companies* are jointly owned by different people who receive shares of stock in exchange for investing their own money. English joint-stock companies pooled the savings of people of moderate income. That money supported trading ventures that could potentially turn a big profit for all involved. The first joint-stock companies to try out their plan in the Americas were the Virginia Company of London and the Virginia Company of Plymouth, which collectively became known as the Virginia Company.

SIR WALTER RALEIGH'S ROANOKE ATTEMPTS

First Try: Sir Walter Raleigh pays for navigators Philip Amadas and Arthur Barlowe to scout out a suitable place for a colony. In 1584, they found Roanoke Island in present-day North Carolina.

Second Try: Raleigh gets a grant from Queen Elizabeth I and sends out a colonizing expedition. They land at Roanoke in 1585, but tension grows with Native Americans when the colonists suffer serious food shortages and attempt to forcibly secure supplies from the natives. They abandon the colony and return to England in 1586.

Third Try: Raleigh sends an expedition to establish a permanent English colony in America. Commanded by John White, more than one hundred colonists arrive at Roanoke Island in 1587. White returns to England for more supplies, but is delayed and cannot return until 1590. There is no sign of the colonists: no houses, no bodies. All White found were the letters *CRO* carved in a tree near the beach and the word *Croatoan* on a post.

The Lost Colony of Roanoke

What happened to the Colony of Roanoke is a much-debated mystery. Disease, Native American attacks, or even a hurricane may have killed the settlers, but no evidence that they actually died on Roanoke Island has been found. White had told the colonists that if they had to leave, to carve a message somewhere to let him know their destination. He also told them to carve a Maltese cross if they were leaving in distress.

Because there was no cross carved next to the word they found, a widely held belief is that the colonists left the island with friendly Croatan Native Americans. Just to muddy things up, recently an analysis of the growth rings of nearby cypress trees suggests that the colonists disappeared during one of the worst droughts since the thirteenth century.

Virginia Dare

John White traveled with Walter Raleigh's third expedition to North America. White brought along his pregnant daughter Elenora and her husband, Ananias Dare, who was White's assistant. About a month after the colonists settled on Roanoke Island, on August 18, 1587, Elenora gave birth to Virginia Dare, the first child born to English parents in America. The colony of Virginia was named in honor of Elizabeth, the virgin queen, and so the baby was named *Virginia Dare.*

Her baptism on Sunday after her birth was the second recorded Christian rite in North America. (The first baptism a few days earlier was of Manteo, an Indian chief who was rewarded for his service by being christened and named "Lord.")

White returned to England for more supplies but was unable to return until 1590. When he finally got back, he found the settlement deserted. No trace of any of the colonists, including Elenora and Virginia, was ever found.

Legend of the White Doe

An Indian legend called newborn Virginia Dare *White Fawn.* Because her family had come from across the sea, she stared wistfully in that direction. If one could shoot the white doe with a silver arrowhead, this would restore her to mortal form.

Many hunters pursued the white doe. But as many found it impossible to shoot their arrow once it was aimed. Finally, a great deer hunt was assembled, and one special hunter hit her with his silver-tipped arrow. The beautiful doe leapt, heart pierced, into the air and sank to the ground. Running to her side, the hunter looked into the dying eyes, and saw, suddenly, the face of a pretty young woman, who whispered her name, "Virginia Dare," and died.

CRASH COURSE
THE WILD LIFE OF JOHN SMITH

Even before he traveled to America, John Smith had lived a life of adventure. At the age of twenty, he fought in Hungary against the Turks, who captured him and sold him into slavery.

Smith escaped and returned to England in 1604.

John Smith was a mercenary with the London Company's expedition to Virginia. Apparently he was a troublemaker on the voyage over, because he was not popular with the Jamestown settlers. When he proposed to go on a food-finding expedition for the starving colony, the group agreed, figuring it would work out either way—if he came back with food, they would have something to eat, and if he never came back, they wouldn't miss him.

Smith did come back, having established a fragile peace with the local Indians and bringing food. He was elected Jamestown's governor and imposed his stern leadership. Smith insisted that all the colonists work, saying that whoever did not work would not eat. The colony survived, but Smith's strict control did not make him popular with the colonists, especially those who were not used to hard labor.

After his return from Jamestown in late 1609, Smith sailed to the New World two more times, with the Plymouth Company. On a 1614 voyage he mapped New England's coastline. On a 1615 voyage, he was captured by French pirates off the Azores, and escaped three months later, but never saw North America after that.

Smith's books about his adventures in North America left us with vivid descriptions of the land and people: *Map of Virginia with a Description of the Country* (1612) and *The Generall Historie of Virginia, New England, and the Summer Isles* (1624).

EXTRA CREDIT: John Smith named the Northern coastal region New England.

THE POWER OF THE POWHATAN CONFEDERACY

Chief Powhatan led the Powhatan Confederacy of Algonquian tribes of Native North Americans. This confederacy consisted of about thirty tribes, with nine thousand members in about two hundred settlements in the tidewater Virginia and Chesapeake Bay eastern shore areas.

Powhatan's authority in North America could be compared to an English king. He proved to be an intelligent, capable leader, but also a cruel one.

Fighting between the Native Americans and colonists arose soon after the settlers arrived. The Jamestown colonists began taking lands belonging to the Algonquians, especially sacred hunting grounds. This did not sit well with Powhatan. So, when John Smith headed out on an expedition to gather food for the starving Jamestown colonists, he was captured.

Powhatan could have killed Smith, but instead decided to toy with him. Powhatan thought Smith might eventually be a potential ally against tribes that opposed his rule. Smith did a little dog-and-pony show, which fortunately amused Powhatan, and he was allowed to return to Jamestown.

The English continued to rely on the Indians for food. When the Indians would not share their corn, the English seized the best lands and burned villages to get it anyway. Powhatan quickly retaliated and cut off Indian trading with the English. He ordered the tribes of his confederacy to stop trading with the whites, knowing that they would starve without the Indian corn.

The colonists stepped up their "powers of persuasion" with the Indians to get corn. Powhatan responded in kind, and there was a lot of death and bloodshed for several years. A fragile peace agreement was reached when Powhatan's daughter married one Jamestown settler.

POCAHONTAS BRINGS PEACE AND TOBACCO

Background to remember:

- John Smith returned to England in 1609.
- The great Algonquian chief Powhatan controlled most of the Indian trade with the settlers of Jamestown.
- Jamestown's Captain Samuel Argall came across an opportunity for leverage in trading with the Indians when he kidnapped Powhatan's daughter Pocahontas and brought her to Jamestown in 1613. While ransom negotiations dragged on for more than a year, she became accustomed to life among the English, converted to Christianity, and was baptized. In April 1614, she even married John Rolfe. Powhatan reluctantly accepted the marriage but did not attend the wedding. This union brought with it a long truce between the whites and the Indians, but it mainly served the interests of the whites so that they could expand their settlement without resistance.
- John Rolfe and Pocahontas developed a new variety of tobacco, which became very popular in Europe and brought prosperity to the Jamestown colony.
- When John Smith learned that Pocahontas (now Rebecca Rolfe) would be visiting England in 1616, he jumped on the opportunity. By this time, Rebecca lived the life of an English woman, speaking the language well and carrying herself like a lady.
- Smith wrote a letter to Queen Anne telling a story that had never been told before, although he had already had plenty of opportunity. In this story, Smith said that during a 1607 encounter with Powhatan, twelve-year-old Pocahontas had saved his life, literally putting herself between Smith and her tribesmen as they prepared to kill him.
- Whether or not the story was true, Queen Anne and James I did accept Pocahontas at court, and she was popular throughout England. In 1617, as she prepared to return to Jamestown with her husband and son, Pocahontas got smallpox and died in England.

GEOGRAPHY 101
COLONISTS NAME A SETTLEMENT AFTER KING JAMES I

In 1603, England's King James I took the throne. Eager to expand to North America, he chartered a joint-stock company, the Virginia Company. This group established the first permanent English colony in America in 1607.

The colonists sailed to Virginia, into the Chesapeake Bay, and up a river they named the James. The Jamestown settlers suffered from Indian attacks, famine, and disease—and their own misinformation. The settlement's location in a swampy area along the James River made the settlers prone to dysentery and malaria, diseases that killed many.

Even more crippling, many of the colonists were gentlemen who had never done any physical labor, while others were gold-seeking adventurers who refused to hunt or farm. Food supplies dwindled to almost nothing, and the colonists nearly starved.

Through the stern leadership of Captain John Smith and the establishment of the tobacco industry by John Rolfe, the Jamestown colony survived. The growing of tobacco in Jamestown's plantations required a large labor force. At first, the Virginia Company tried to meet that need by sending indentured servants to the colony. A few Africans arrived in Jamestown in 1619 and became indentured servants. After that, the Virginia tobacco growers began to use a combination of both forced labor (slavery) and free labor (indentured servitude).

Although it made profits from tobacco sales, the Virginia Company made bad decisions and fell into debt. King James I revoked the bankrupt company's charter in 1624, and the colony was renamed Virginia and came under the direct control of King James I.

EXTRA CREDIT: The James River and Jamestown were both named after England's adventuresome new king, James I.

THOMAS WEST, THOMAS GATES, AND THOMAS DALE

Jamestown saw some changes when King James I issued a new charter to form a colonial governing body. Before the first governor, Thomas West, baron De La Warr could sail, the Virginia Company sent Thomas Gates as a temporary placement.

Gates arrived in Jamestown in 1610 to a settlement all but decimated by starvation. The colonists had been reduced to eating rats, cats and dogs, and horsehide. Some were even accused of cannibalism.

With a purpose of survival, Gates established a harsh government. When West arrived with supplies and food, he backed Gates' strict rules. They were called Dale's Code after the marshal who enforced them, Thomas Dale.

Dale's Code required obedience of the Sabbath, no immodest dress, and no laziness. Punishments were severe, from being burned at the stake, hanged or shot, to being broken on the wheel. Some "crimes" and their consequences:

- Killing an animal without permission – death
- Washing filthy items near the village well = whipping
- Cursing and fighting = hands and feet tied together every night for a month

By the time he was appointed Governor, Dale saw that cruelty alone would not be enough to motivate the settlers to want to farm and grow food. He did two things to raise morale.

First, Dale arranged to bring women from England for the men to marry. As unromantic as it sounds, the men were happy to see any females, no matter how they looked, who their family was, or how little money they had.

Second, Dale assigned three-acre plots to the older settlers to farm privately. The settlers agreed to provide to the general community one month's work each year and two and a half barrels of corn. This eventually expanded into the "headright" system of awarding one hundred-acre plots to new settlers.

Puritans and the Massachusetts Bay Company

First of all, let's settle a point of some confusion: Contrary to some belief, the Puritans and Pilgrims were not two separate groups of people. The Pilgrims were a certain group of Puritans.

With that said, let's get to the Pilgrims later, and discuss the Puritans in general now.

They were a group of English Protestants who were interested in "purifying" the Church of England. They believed that God guides those who are to be saved.

England's king was not happy about the Puritans' take on his religion, and he arrested and jailed these worshipers. They wanted to have more religious freedom than that, so they decided to ask the king for a royal charter to colonize North America. The king granted the Puritans a charter to establish the Massachusetts Bay Company.

The Puritans traveled to the New World for religious reasons, not for adventure and wealth. In 1630, John Winthrop sailed for the Massachusetts shore with about one thousand Puritans. He settled Boston and several other towns. The Massachusetts Bay colony experienced an unexpected population growth when a civil war in England broke out shortly afterwards. About 15,000 more English fled to the Massachusetts Bay colony settlement. Quite unimaginatively, this was called the *Great Migration.*

The Massachusetts Bay Colony established a representative government, which means they engaged in yearly elections and a representative assembly.

EXTRA CREDIT: Massachusetts Bay united with Plymouth Colony, Martha's Vineyard, Nantucket, the Province of Maine, and what is now Nova Scotia to form the Province of Massachusetts Bay in 1692.

PILGRIMS, THE MAYFLOWER, AND PLYMOUTH COLONY

The Pilgrims were a group of Puritans who were so disgusted with the Church of England that instead of simply "purifying" the church, they chose to organize a completely separate church. They are known as *Separatists*.

The Separatists left England looking for the freedom to practice their own religion. First, they went to Holland, but they didn't fit in with the culture or economy there. So, they thought outside the Old World box, and decided to settle in a new colony in America operated by the Virginia Company.

About ten years before the Massachusetts Bay Company headed to North American shores, a small group of Pilgrims sailed for Virginia in 1620. You know this story from kindergarten, but here it is one more time:

About half of the fifty passengers on the *Mayflower* were Pilgrims. The rest were people hoping for economic gain from the trip. After sixty-five days, they missed their target of Virginia, and reached the Massachusetts coast instead. The Pilgrims landed at a place they called Plymouth Rock and established Plymouth Colony.

Like many other colonies in the new world, the Pilgrims had a hard time at first. Many of them died during the first winter. Luckily, friendly Indians taught them how to catch game and grow crops in this new land. They celebrated a good harvest at a feast, which we all know as the first Thanksgiving.

One more thing: The Pilgrims drew up and signed an important document that established self-government and a form of written constitution, called the Mayflower Compact.

Maryland Is a Colony of Tolerance, For a While

King Charles I rewarded George Calvert (Lord Baltimore) for his loyal service to the crown by granting Calvert control of a chartered colony located on either side of Chesapeake Bay. George Calvert began making plans for his own great wealth while also providing a haven for fellow Catholics, but he died.

King Charles passed control of the charter to George's son, Cecil Calvert—the second Lord Baltimore—who set about implementing his father's plan in 1633. The colony was located near the mouth of the Potomac River. The Maryland Colony was able to learn from the Jamestown Colony experiences and did not suffer as badly as some of the earlier settlements.

Many wealthy English Catholics joined Calvert in his avoidance of Puritans' intolerance and persecution and immigrated to Maryland. The Catholics established large colonial plantations but were quickly outnumbered by Protestant farmers.

Soon, Protestants held a majority in Maryland's representative assembly. In 1649, Calvert persuaded the assembly to adopt the Act of Religious Toleration, the first colonial statute granting religious freedom to all Christians. (Before you sing, "We Are the World," however, you should know that the statute also called for the death of anyone who denied Jesus.)

Plus, it didn't really work, after all. In the late 1600s, the Protestants and Catholics got into a brief civil war. The Protestants came out ahead, and the Act of Toleration was repealed. Catholics lost their right to vote in elections for the Maryland assembly. Baltimore regained control of the Colony, and Maryland remained a state of greater tolerance of religious diversity among different Protestant sects.

EXTRA CREDIT: Cecil Calvert named the colony Maryland after King Charles's wife, Queen Henrietta Maria.

Roger Williams Offers Religious Freedom in Rhode Island

While Maryland offered religious tolerance to Protestant settlers, the best place for all kinds of religious differences was Rhode Island. Catholics, Quakers, and Jews could worship freely here.

Puritan minister Roger Williams first went to Boston in 1631. He believed that any authority could not control an individual's conscience. Other Puritan leaders disagreed and banished him from the Massachusetts Bay colony. Williams headed south to Narragansett Bay, where he founded a settlement in 1636. The colony was named Providence, to thank God for his divine intervention in bringing Williams and his followers to this place.

At first, Williams did not have a colonial charter. So, he wrote a government compact that allowed all residents of Providence to vote regardless of religious affiliations. This was, in essence, the first government providing for the separation of church and state. The new colony was also unique in recognizing the rights of the Native Americans. Instead of the usual way of taking land from the Indians, Williams purchased it from them.

In 1644, English Parliament granted Williams a charter joining Providence, Newport, and nearby Portsmouth into a single colony, Rhode Island.

How Did Rhode Island Get Its Name?

There are two different explanations of where *Rhode Island* came from. The first is what the state officially claims: *Rhode Island* is the English version of *Roodt Eylandt*, which the Dutch settlers called it for the red clay on the island's shore.

Early explorers to the area said that Block Island was about the size of Rhodes in the Mediterranean.

Either way, we do know that Williams named other islands in the Narragansett Bay after virtues: Patience Island, Prudence Island, and Hope Island.

THE LONDON COMPANY
OF VIRGINIA

Bear with us here, and we'll try to make this as un-boring as we can. Really, it's interesting reading, especially if you're an entrepreneurial type.

The London Company of Virginia, later known as the Virginia Company, was established to pay for North American colonization. First of all, the company got a tax break; it did not have to pay any customs (a fancy word for taxes) until the colony turned a profit. Second, the company was given free reign to rule the colony any way it wanted to, and it was backed by the king. Finally, to raise initial money, the company ran a national lottery, the only time that it truly made any money. (Note that the company never paid taxes because it never yielded return on the initial investment of £50,000. Today, we would say they did not have a good business plan.)

As soon as they reached the New World, the settlers began sending back what resources they could. They had expected to find silver and gold but quickly saw that these precious metals were not growing on trees. They do get points for being able to see the forest for the trees.

Even before the Jamestown settlement was finished, the colonists sent a shipment of cedar to England. It was probably the first timber exported from America. The settlers also exported beaver and otter skins, and, eventually, smoking tobacco to England.

As a way to solve the problem of labor on the new tobacco plantations, in 1618 the company began offering two "headrights," or one hundred acres, to newcomers. This land ownership provided an incentive to work the plantations and make them as profitable as possible. As you would expect, wealthy sponsors figured out how to work the system to collect multiple headrights into vast plantations.

HANDS-ON HISTORY
COLONIAL-ERA CLOTHING

Clothing wasn't always t-shirts and blue jeans. Colonial Americans might outfit themselves in everything from spatterdashes to stomachers, while changing a baby's clout or fastening the buttons on a skeleton suit. Herewith, a few fashion terms of the Colonial era:

- *Banyan*: A loose-fitting gown worn at home by men of the era.
- *Brunswick*: A two-piece woman's gown composed of a high-necked, hip-length jacket with a hood, and a matching petticoat. The Brunswick was popular for traveling.
- *Clout*: Colonial American for *diaper*.
- *Engageantes*: Fancy false sleeves worn by ladies.
- *Leading strings*: In effect reins for children, leading strings were sewn to the shoulders of children's clothes so that the parents could control them and prevent falls.
- *Mob cap*: A woman's dust bonnet.
- *Panniers*: Hoops that extended a skirt's width at the sides. Apparently, sporting cartoonishly large hips was a good thing at the time.
- *Pattens*: Overshoes worn by men and women that lifted the shoes off the ground. A good thing to have when mud, and other substances better left unmentioned, were common obstacles.
- *Pudding cap*: A padded cap placed on toddler's heads that protected them when they fell.
- *Skeleton suit*: A tight-fitting suit worn by boys in which the top and bottom were buttoned together.
- *Spatterdashes*: Long gaiters that covered the lower legs of men. The term was later shortened to "spats."
- *Stomacher*: A triangular piece of cloth, usually highly ornamented, that covered the chest and stomach. Although it was only worn by Colonial American women, the stomacher started out in the fifteenth century as both male and female ornamentation.
- *Undress*: Predating George Orwell's *Big Brother* "un" language by a couple of centuries, this term referred to everyday clothes.

ANNE HUTCHINSON: A WOMAN
DARES TO SPEAK PUBLICLY

Anne Hutchinson was another who questioned the doctrines of the Puritan authorities. Growing up the daughter of an English clergyman who himself often challenged the Church of England's religious authority, Hutchinson had learned a great deal about Christian doctrine and scripture.

Hutchinson immigrated in 1634 to the Massachusetts Bay Colony. She organized meetings among the Boston women to share and discuss her beliefs in antinomianism—the idea that faith alone is necessary for salvation. The Bay Colony leaders felt threatened that this belief would spread. They worried that if colonists thought salvation was through God's grace (and not by obeying their laws), there might be a challenge to their authority. The leaders said Hutchinson's teachings were an attack on their moral and legal codes and on their authority.

In 1637 Hutchinson was tried for "traducing (slandering) the ministers." She defended every charge, quoting scripture from the same Bible that the Puritans used to prosecute her. When the lawyers even said that the scriptures did not fit her case exactly, she responded, "Must I shew my name written therein?"

Hutchinson was found guilty, anyway, and banished from the Bay colony. She moved with her family and founded the town of Portsmouth, Rhode Island, not far from the Providence colony. After her husband died, Hutchison settled in today's Pelham Bay, New York. She was killed in an Indian attack in 1643.

Aside: Now, we don't want to sound like bra-burners, but ... If Anne Hutchinson had been a man, preaching these same beliefs would still have upset the colony's leaders. But a man would not have offended them as much as a woman saying the same things did. The Puritans thought Hutchinson had overstepped her bounds as a wife, who was expected to obey her husband.

CRIMINAL JUSTICE 101
COLONIAL LAW

Besides beginning and then following through with that split from the mother country, the nascent nation had to form a system of laws. While it could use English law as a guideline, those laws were one of the reasons they had left that country in the first place, so some tweaking was in order.

In *Law and People in Colonial America*, Peter Charles Hoffer describes colonial law thusly:

> Colonial criminal law followed the contours of English criminal law but was never as severe. In the early colonies labor was always scarce and thus greatly valued. No colony ever duplicated the severity of punishment for crime on the English statute books, for no colony could afford to lose any of its laborers.

According to Hoffer, the first Quaker colonies reserved the death penalty for murder, and early New Englanders only considered burglary and robbery capital offenses if the defendant was a repeat offender.

Befitting a country that breathed freedom like oxygen, colonial law gave greater standing to the individual. Hoffer writes:

> Going beyond the English practice, colonial law codes stipulated that criminal defendants had a right to be represented by lawyers, a signal advantage not extended to English felony suspects until 1836. Provisions in the Massachusetts Body of Liberties and Connecticut's Fundamental Laws implied that there was a right to counsel.

Not that everything was equal tea and crumpets:

> The daughters of respectable parents were no longer called to account for a premarital pregnancy, but poor women, servants, and others without patrons still had to bear the shame and the civil penalties of bearing a child out of wedlock.

COLONIAL LAWYERS

Just as the colonial system of law was in its formative stages, so was the training of lawyers. Perhaps because of their negative experiences with British law both in their home country and in the colonies, the colonists didn't take to lawyers very well. Considering the quality of education those lawyers received, the mistrust may have been well-founded.

Albert James Harno's book *Legal Education in the United States* says,

> There was no conceptual legal system in early Colonial America, and no legal profession. The Colonists' feelings toward lawyers was not merely negative; they viewed lawyers with suspicion and distrust.

Colonial law schools weren't the models of protracted training modern Americans are used to, either. "Preparation for the practice of law in early Colonial America was desultory," Harno writes.

> What colleges there were did not offer courses in law and there were no independent law schools....The colleges had no law books and only the more affluent lawyers possessed libraries, consisting of reports and texts, of from fifty to one hundred volumes. A common reading assignment for the young apprentice was [Sir Edward] Coke's Institutes, a work well characterized as that 'disorderly mass of crabbed pedantry that Coke poured forth as institutes of English law.'

Timeline of Major American Colleges and Universities

- University of Pennsylvania, Philadelphia (1740)
- Princeton University, New Jersey (1746)
- Columbia University, New York City (1754)
- Dartmouth College, Hanover, New Hampshire (1754)
- Brown University, Providence, Rhode Island (1764)
- Rutgers, The State University of New Jersey, (1766)
- Cornell University, Ithaca, New York (1865)
- Johns Hopkins University, Baltimore (1876)

American Literature
Anne Bradstreet, First Colonial Poet

Anne Bradstreet was an English-born writer and the first significant woman author in the American colonies. More importantly, she was the first notable American poet.

Anne Bradstreet came to Massachusetts during the Great Migration in 1630 with her father, Thomas Dudley, and her new husband Simon Bradstreet; both men later became governors of the Massachusetts Bay Colony.

An educated Puritan housewife who raised eight children, she found time to write poetry while her husband was away on political business. Bradstreet's poetry leaves readers today an excellent glimpse into early colonial life, including the hardships of a new land as well as the struggles of a Puritan wife and colonial women in general. In her poetry, Bradstreet asserted women's right to education and expression of thought, and many label her an early feminist.

Anne's poems were published in 1650 as *The Tenth Muse Lately Sprung Up in America*. This is considered the first book of original poetry written in colonial America. In 1678, she produced another volume, *Several Poems*, which included her thoughts about the early deaths of her grandchildren; her place in the natural world ("Contemplations"); the conflict she felt between living a pleasant life and living a Christian life ("The Flesh and the Spirit"); and her doubts about Puritanism ("Meditations Divine and Moral").

Lines from *"To My Dear and Loving Husband"*

If ever two were one, then surely we.
If ever man were lov'd by wife, then thee;
If ever wife was happy in a man,
Compare with me ye women if you can.
I prize thy love more than whole Mines of gold,
Or all the riches that the East doth hold.

HOOKER AND DAVENPORT
IN CONNECTICUT

Settlers unhappy with the Massachusetts authorities soon spread out to the Connecticut River Valley.

- In 1634 English trader John Oldham brought a large party to settle at Wethersfield.
- John Winthrop established Saybrook in 1635 at the mouth of the Connecticut River.
- Roger Ludlow led colonists to establish their own settlement at Windsor.
- The Reverend Thomas Hooker led about one hundred Boston Puritan colonists into the Connecticut River Valley and founded the colony of Hartford in 1636.
- In 1638, Puritan minister John Davenport established a trading colony on the former Pequot lands. First called Quinnipiac, it was renamed New Haven in 1640.
- In 1665, New Haven merged with the colony of Connecticut by royal charter from Charles II.

The Fundamental Orders of Connecticut

In 1638 and 1639, representatives of Hartford, Windsor, and Wethersfield met to discuss plans to unite into a single colony. On January 14, 1639, the colony of Connecticut was formed, and the colonists formally adopted a basic set of laws known as the Fundamental Orders of Connecticut.

This was the first written constitution based on the consent of the governed in American history. The Fundamental Orders established a representative government consisting of a legislature elected by popular vote and a governor chosen by that legislature. Two general assemblies, one legislative and the other judicial, were set up, and representatives were chosen from each town.

Political Science 101
Navigation Acts (1651 to 1673)

The English government imposed its mercantilism policy on the American colonies with Navigation Acts passed between 1651 and 1673. These acts established rules for colonial trade:

- Goods imported to or exported from the colonies could be carried only by English or colonial-built ships, operated only by English or colonial crews.
- All goods imported into the colonies (except some perishables) could pass only through British ports.
- Only specific or "enumerated" goods from the colonies could be exported. Tobacco was the first enumerated good, but over the years other colonial products, such as sugar, rice, indigo, and cotton, joined the list.

Positive Impact on the Colonies:

- American shipbuilding in New England prospered.
- Chesapeake tobacco had a monopoly in England.
- English military forces protected the colonies from attacks by the French and Spanish.
- Producers of most of the enumerated goods had a stable market in England.

Negative Impact on the Colonies:

- Colonial manufacturing was severely limited.
- Farmers received low prices for their crops.
- Colonists had to pay high prices for English manufactured goods.

In hindsight, these acts were redundant; the colonies would have traded with England anyway for the same advantages that the acts allowed. So, the disadvantages were more strongly felt and led to hard feelings against Britain. This was the beginnings of what eventually ended with the American Revolution.

Like a slow leak, resentment spread against the regulations, ending in defiance. The colonists began smuggling goods from other countries. But they weren't sneaky enough, and in 1684, the British government revoked the Massachusetts Bay charter.

BACON'S REBELLION

Sir William Berkeley was appointed governor of the colony of Virginia in 1641. Loyal to the king, Berkeley's policies favored the large planters and he clearly came down on their side. This was at the expense of backwoods farmers on Virginia's western frontier. Berkeley repeatedly refused to protect their settlements from Indian attacks. This, of course, made him very unpopular.

Enter Nathaniel Bacon in 1676, a poor gentleman farmer from England. He resented the economic and political control that Berkeley had, in essence, given only to a few large planters in the Chesapeake area.

- Bacon and the unhappy backwoods farmers rebelled against Berkeley's government.

- Bacon's army of volunteers raided and massacred Indian villages on the Virginia frontier.

- Berkeley's government in Jamestown accused Bacon of rebelling against royal authority.

- Bacon's army defeated the governor's forces and even burned the Jamestown settlement.

- Bacon died suddenly of dysentery. (This was an unexpected turn of events.)

- Without a leader, the rebel army quickly broke up and fled.

- Governor Berkeley brutally treated any of the rebels he could find.

Implications

Bacon's Rebellion brought up two problems that would eventually lead to two wars in America's history: 1) colonists showed their resistance to royal control, and 2) poor farmers in Virginia felt the huge class differences between them and wealthy planters.

NEW HAMPSHIRE,
THE LAST NEW ENGLAND COLONY

New Hampshire was the last colony to be founded in New England. Let's make a long story short: the New Hampshire territory was originally part of Massachusetts Bay. To increase his control over the colonies, King Charles II separated New Hampshire from the Massachusetts Bay Colony and made it a royal colony.

The longer version explains the controversy around the survey lines:

1622 — John Mason and Ferdinando Gorges receive a grant for land between the Merrimack and Kennebec rivers.

1623 — David Thomson settles present-day Rye. Thomson sets up a trading post, and the settlers begin farming and fishing. Thomson later leaves; colonists relocate to Portsmouth.

1623 — Edward Hilton settles Dover.

1629 — Gorges and Mason divide their land at the Piscataqua River. Gorges called his part, to the east/northeast, *Maine.* Mason receives the part to the west/southwest.

1635 — Mason dies. His heirs in England neglect his holdings, allowing others to occupy his land.

1638 — John Wheelwright settles Exeter. Stephen Bachiler settles Hampton.

1660 — Mason's grandson, Robert, finally claims his territory, leading to a dispute over land titles which is not resolved until 1746.

1679 — A new charter provides for a president and a council, selected by the king, and for an assembly chosen by the province's voters.

1689–1692 — Rivalry builds between New Hampshire and Massachusetts over land. Massachusetts grants land in parts of New Hampshire. Naturally, these grants conflict with ones made by New Hampshire.

1741 — New Hampshire wins a favorable decision from the king on its east and south boundaries with Massachusetts. New Hampshire gains more territory and a royal governor, independent of Massachusetts.

SETTLING THE CAROLINAS

To reward them for helping him gain the throne, England's King Charles II granted eight nobles vast territory between Virginia and Spanish Florida. Rounding out the mutual admiration society, they, in turn, called the land *Carolina*, after the Latin form of Charles, *Carolus*.

These eight men became the lord proprietors of Carolina. Some of them were colonists from England. Others were already familiar with growing sugar in Barbados and were ready to add to their wealth in America.

In 1670, the lord proprietors established a settlement in southern Carolina at Albemarle Point. Still perfecting the art of brown-nosing, they named it Charles Town. (We know it as Charleston, now across the Ashley River from the original site.)

At first, they traded furs to support the colony. Eventually, a plantation society based on growing rice emerged around Charles Town, and it looked a lot like the Barbados sugar plantations (except for the crop). Just like in Virginia, finding enough labor to keep the plantations running was a problem. By now, the supply of white indentured servants had greatly diminished. Soon African slaves made up most of the labor force.

Meanwhile, a different development plan was shaping up in the northern part of Carolina, also known as Albemarle. (The Albemarle of northern and southern Carolina were both named in honor of George, Duke of Albemarle.) For some time, unhappy Virginians, including criminals and runaway slaves, had settled the land around Albemarle Sound. Unlike the shore in the southern part of Carolina, the coast here was not suited for shipping. So, rather than the large plantations to the south, northern Carolina was home to more small farms that did not need the support of slave labor.

The northern region was eventually called North Carolina. In 1729, the British officially divided "the Carolinas" into two separate colonies, as North Carolina and South Carolina.

New Netherland Suddenly Becomes New York

Peter Stuyvesant took over the colony of New Netherland in 1647 and ruled it for the next seventeen years. In 1655, Stuyvesant seized Fort Christina, which is now Wilmington, Delaware, from the Swedish holding of New Sweden.

England's King Charles II wanted to round out his land holdings along the Atlantic Coast and close the gap between New England and Virginia. This meant he would have to get the Dutch to give up their New Amsterdam colony on Manhattan Island and in the Hudson River Valley.

In 1664 King Charles II gave the land located between the Connecticut and Delaware Rivers to his brother, the Duke of York (who would later become King James II). Backed by the English navy, James had a strong force at his disposal to take control of New Amsterdam from the Dutch. It wasn't much of a struggle, as the Dutch were not at all equipped to fight. Governor Peter Stuyvesant surrendered immediately, and James easily took control of the colony. New Netherland just as easily became New York.

James did some good things for the Dutch. He told his agents in the renamed colony to treat the Dutch settlers well. They were allowed to keep the freedom to worship that they were known for, and they were allowed to continue living as they pleased and speaking their own language.

James also did some not-so-good things for the Dutch. He ordered new taxes, duties, and rents without consulting the colony's representative assembly. In fact, he did not allow the colony to form a representative assembly at all. New York's English-speaking settlers did not agree one bit with James' strategy of "taxation without representation."

In 1683, James agreed to let New York's residents have civil and political rights, including a representative assembly.

THE PERFECT GIFT FOR YOUR FRIENDS? NEW JERSEY

As we've learned from cable TV and popular movies, being friends with the royal family can be dangerous, but it comes with its perks. This is what two friends of James II discovered. In 1664, Lord John Berkeley and Sir George Carteret became the lucky recipients of a section of the New York territory when James decided to break the area into manageable pieces.

Berkeley and Carteret found themselves holding the land between the Hudson and Delaware Rivers, then known as Nova Caesaria. Berkeley received the West New Jersey area, and Carteret got East New Jersey. To attract settlers, both proprietors made generous land offers and allowed religious freedom, trial by jury, and a representative assembly.

West New Jersey

Berkeley sold his share of the colony to two Quakers. When one of them went bankrupt in 1676, his creditors (including William Penn), took control. The creditors formed a joint-stock company, and shareholders became the proprietors. In 1677 Penn wrote a separate charter for West Jersey, which still guaranteed freedom of religion and personal liberty. It also provided for yearly election by secret ballot of a representative assembly with limited powers of taxation.

East New Jersey

Carteret kept control of the eastern half, where settlers turned toward New York City for trade. Carteret's heirs also formed a joint-stock company in 1682, and its shareholders became the board of proprietors for that area.

Because land titles in the Jerseys changed so often, property lines were drawn inaccurately. To settle matters, in 1702 the two Jerseys were combined into a single royal colony, New Jersey. By this time, a tradition of self-government had been firmly established.

WILLIAM PENN SHARES HIS INHERITANCE WITH THE SOCIETY OF FRIENDS

If you've ever dreamed of inheriting unexpected money or land, William Penn will be an inspiration, because he did both. Not only did his father leave him a nice sum of money, but the royal family also owed the father a large debt, which they paid to Penn in the form of a land grant in the Americas.

In 1681, Penn received the southeastern territory along the Delaware River, which he called Pennsylvania, or "Penn's Woods." As a new convert to the Quaker faith, Penn was excited to give the Society of Friends a new homeland. He got the king on board with his plan by promising that this would rid England of the troublesome Quakers.

Penn founded the new town of Philadelphia on the Delaware River. It was unique, employing his plan for a grid pattern of streets, which was later imitated by other American cities. With his Pennsylvania colony, Penn wanted to achieve three purposes:

- Provide a religious refuge for Quakers and other persecuted people
- Enact liberal ideas in government for political freedom
- Generate income and profits for himself

A forward-thinking man, Penn drafted a Frame of Government for the colony, guaranteeing a representative assembly elected by landowners, as well as a written constitution, guaranteeing freedom of worship and unrestricted immigration.

Advertising for Settlers

Penn mounted a real estate marketing campaign to attract settlers to Pennsylvania. He paid agents throughout Europe to distribute pamphlets in four languages. In exchange for paying their way and a small rent, each settler would get free land. The low fare of six pounds for a husband and wife (five pounds per servant), included shipping for one chest of their belongings.

SALEM WITCH TRIALS

In Salem, Massachusetts, during the years of 1692 and 1693, a form of mass hysteria spread as colonists accused each other of being witches. As bizarre as it sounds, they were serious: fourteen women and five men were hanged, one man was crushed to death under stones when he refused to participate in his trial, four people died in jail, and nearly two hundred were arrested.

What brought about this witchcraft craze? Well, in the big picture, the colonists brought their cultural background from the Old World, including a belief that the Devil could reward people who were loyal to him, i.e. *witches*, with the power to harm others. Then, in early 1692, two powerful Salem families, the Putnams and the Porters, were on either side of a village argument over whether to fire minister Samuel Parris. The Putnams wanted to keep Parris, while the Porters secretly wanted him out.

Some villagers said the Devil was behind all this unhappiness. And that's when things started to get out of hand:

- Parris's nine-year-old daughter, Betty, and eleven-year-old niece, Abigail Williams, with other neighborhood girls, started having fits, falling down suddenly, crying out in pain, and becoming mute.
- A local doctor suggested a supernatural cause.
- Panic struck Salem over the suggestion.
- Eleven-year-old Ann Putnam became afflicted. The Putnams asked local judges to examine the girls.
- As their parents, the court, and ministers urged the girls to explain themselves, they suddenly blamed three local women for afflicting them, saying they appeared to the girls as ghosts.
- The examiners assumed that the accused were witches.
- One accused, a slave named Tituba confessed, naming seven other witches in the neighborhood.
- Two accused elderly local farmwives denied being witches but agreed that witches might live nearby.
- A public hunt for more suspects, whom the young girls immediately labeled witches, heated up.

The girls did a good job of physically confirming their accusations: they rolled in agony, screamed in pain, and claimed to see ghosts harming each other. Pinch marks and bruises seemed to confirm their claims.

Within three months, nearly 150 accused witches, all of them respected church members, crowded the jails. The trials, fair or not, took place quickly—defendants were brought in groups to court, and juries took only a few hours to reach their conviction verdicts.

Then a new level of hysteria was reached. Some men and women realized that confession saved them from immediate conviction and death sentence. They began to confess to being witches and accused their neighbors of secret meetings with the Devil.

Finally, after nineteen villagers had been tried, convicted of witchcraft, and executed, people began to question the trial procedures. Were the quick verdicts fair? Was it valid to allow spectral evidence (basically, letting the girls tell about ghosts only they could see)?

Spectral evidence was not allowed in further trials. Without it, all but three women were acquitted. They were pardoned, as was everyone else. The colony's legislature even admitted that the trials had been a mistake.

Today, the trials, with their mass hysteria, panic, and superstition, are still regarded as a serious miscarriage of justice. In fact, a *Salem Witch Trial* means a hasty indictment or panic-stricken accusation.

Possessed or Just Tripping?

Many modern researchers have attempted to explain the strange symptoms exhibited by those who claimed to be possessed by the devil. Some believe the convulsions and hallucinations may be attributed to the consumption of rye bread containmated with the fungus *claviceps purpurea* (the same substance LSD is made from).

CRASH COURSE

DELAWARE

1610 — Sir Samuel Argall names a cape he sights in honor of Virginia's first colonial governor Thomas West, baron De La Warr.

1667 — Delaware is annexed by the Duke of York as part of his New York colony.

1682 — William Penn, the Pennsylvania colony founder, petitions for a direct outlet to the ocean. The Duke of York deeds all the land within a twelve-mile radius of New Castle and south to Cape Henlopen. The area includes what is now Delaware.

1682 — Charles Calvert, Lord Baltimore, opposes this transfer of land. Although an English court upholds it, the Maryland-Delaware boundary dispute continues.

1702 — Penn grants the lower three counties of Pennsylvania their own assembly. This creates Delaware as a separate colony, even though it has the same governor as Pennsylvania.

1704 — The first Delaware assembly meeting is held in New Castle.

The people of Delaware resented being controlled by the Quakers. They also wanted protection against Lord Baltimore's raids and pirates on the shore. To give the lower counties the representation they requested, Penn established a separate assembly. Thus, the people of Delaware provided for the development of their colony.

Delaware Indians

When Europeans first came to the area, they met a peaceful group of natives who referred to themselves as the *Lenni Lenape*, meaning "original people." The Europeans called them *Delaware*, after the region, which, in turn, was named after Thomas West, baron De La Warr. The Delaware were primarily farmers, growing corn, squash, and beans, and gathering fish, wild game, berries, nuts, herbs, and roots. Later, different groups of Delaware moved westward, eventually settling in southern Ontario, Canada, and Oklahoma.

GO TO GEORGIA TO GET OUT OF DEBT

Sure, you've heard that Georgia was originally a colony for prisoners. While that's true, they weren't hard-core. When Georgia was settled, England jailed people who owed money, and left them in jail until their debt was paid. You might wonder how to earn money to pay a debt when you're cooling your heels in jail, and your conclusion would be just about right.

So, in 1732, a group of English philanthropists figured out a way to give a "hand up" to otherwise law-abiding men who were in debtor's prison. King George II chartered a colony to be called Georgia on the land between the Savannah and Altamaha Rivers.

Of all the British colonies, it was the only one that the London government supported financially. Why did King George care so much about a new southern colony?

- It would create a buffer between the profitable South Carolina plantations and invasions from Spanish Florida.

- Overcrowded jails could be thinned out. Many of the colony's early settlers were shipped to America directly from English jails.

James Oglethorpe founded Georgia's first settlement, Savannah, in 1733. In 1736, he established Augusta and then built Fort Frederica on Saint Simons Island to defend against the Spanish.

Oglethorpe instituted strict regulations to make Georgia thrive: an absolute ban on drinking rum, a limit on land to fifty acres, and the prohibition of slavery. In fact, they grew silk—less profitable than rice or tobacco—specifically because it did not require slave labor.

The colony was not profitable under this plan, and by 1752, the King had lifted the rum and slavery restrictions. Georgia adopted South Carolina's plantation system and grew slowly. But by the American Revolution, it was still the smallest and poorest of the thirteen colonies.

ANSWERING THE QUESTION
OF LABOR

There are no words that can excuse the establishment and tolerance of slavery that is a part of our nation's history. Similarly, the most horrific images you read about cannot begin to truly describe the treatment early African Americans received here.

By the end of the seventeenth century, slavery was already an institution in American society. From only a few thousand slaves in the late seventeenth century, the numbers grew to tens of thousands in the early eighteen century. By 1750, half of the Virginia population and two-thirds of the South Carolina population were slaves.

What led to the increased demand for slaves?

- Fewer people migrating. Wages had increased in England, which meant not as many people were desperate to seek their fortune in America.
- Need for a dependable work force. Indentured servants asked too much from the owners of large plantations, who wanted a stable labor force over which they would have total control.
- Profit. Rice and indigo—and later, cotton—were the most profitable crops, but growing these crops required a large land area and a lot of cheap labor.

With the slave population growing, the white colonists adopted laws regarding bondage and slave status:

- 1641 — Massachusetts became the first colony to recognize the slavery of "lawful" captives.
- 1661 — Virginia enacted legislation stating that children automatically inherited their mother's slave status for life.
- 1664 — Maryland declared that baptism did not affect the slave's status, and white women could not marry African American men.

THE TRIANGULAR TRADE

The merchant ships that brought slaves to America followed a triangular trade route across the Atlantic. There were several different routes that served to benefit each of the ports.

- A ship loaded with barrels of rum, which would be used to trade for slaves, started out from New England and headed to Africa.

- The ship left Africa on the Middle Passage to the West Indies. Those Africans who survived the horrendous voyage would be traded as slaves for sugarcane.

- The ship returned to New England to sell the sugar for making rum.

Another route ran the opposite direction:

- A ship loaded with tobacco, furs, indigo, and timber left the North Atlantic Coast for England. The raw materials were traded for manufactured goods.

- The manufactured goods were shipped to West Africa and sold at port there. In West Africa, captive Africans would be loaded for the long trip back to Boston.

- In New England, the Africans were traded for more raw materials.

The Middle Passage

The Middle Passage is a term for the voyage that captured Africans made from their homeland to a life of slavery and horror.

The mortality rate during the Middle Passage has been estimated at 15 to 20 percent. Africans were packed into the ship's hold (an area only four to five feet high), forced to lie side-by-side so that as many as possible could fit into the space, and chained together.

The captives were fed only enough gruel to keep them alive, so they suffered from malnutrition. This led to many illnesses and the close quarters meant that when one person got sick, it soon spread to all. Many attempted suicide by jumping overboard or by refusing to eat.

THE PURITANS

Popular culture is always quick to seize on a cliché, since spouting clichés is always easier than thinking, and the Puritans have long been a ready-made target of anyone decrying anyone who decries fun. The blame for this can largely be traced to Nathaniel Hawthorne's *The Scarlet Letter*, in which self-righteous Puritans gang up on poor, adulterous Hester Prynne. Legions of schoolchildren tasked with reading the book took away only this image from it.

But the Puritans were of course more textured than Hawthorne's caricatures indicated. They even had fun. Granted, their fun might have been limited, but this was a rough era. It's hard to make time for fun when you're more concerned with getting a good value for your bloodletting dollar, or literally keeping the wolf (and badger, and flea, and rut-crazed moose) away from your door.

In *Puritans At Play: Leisure and Recreation in Colonial New England*, Bruce C. Daniels debunks many of the Puritan stereotypes. "New England's Puritans were not strict Calvinists; the fire-and-brimstone sermons that earlier historians cited as examples of a terrifying religion were the product more of the mid-eighteenth than of the seventeenth century ... and the Puritans did not prohibit alcohol as many people thought, but instead maintained taverns in almost every town."

Why Were They Called Puritans?

This gets into all that complicated stuff about the Church of England, established by Henry VIII to get rid of his first wife so he could marry--and later behead--Anne Boleyn. But, that was years before the Puritans reached America.

Basically, the Puritans wanted to "purify" the Church of England of any leftover Catholic rituals. They weren't particularly tolerant of any other religious beliefs. (King James I was threatened by the Puritans, which was not a good thing.)

CRASH COURSE
QUAKERS

Although its most famous icon is the smiling gentleman hawking milled oats, the religious sect known as the Quakers actually has a history that predates the breakfast food market by a few centuries, and has no tie to Quaker Oats (other than the occasional happenstance of a Quaker eating Quaker Oats; regularity and low cholesterol are attractive concepts to everyone).

Quakers are actually members of what is now the Religious Society of Friends, a group founded in seventeenth-century England as the "Friends of Truth." (The "Quaker" nickname comes from commentators who claimed that the Friends "quaked" with zeal.)

George Fox, generally acknowledged as the founder of the Friends, believed and taught that it was possible for everyone to directly experience God through an innate "Inner Light," without any intermediary factors such as clergy or sacraments. The Quakers further believed in the equality of all men and women, nonviolence, and resistance to military service.

The sect soon spread to the colonies, although there as in England, the Quakers faced persecution and jail for their beliefs. Quakers William Robinson, Marmaduke Stephenson, William Leddra and Mary Dyer, known as the Boston Martyrs, were hanged for their religious beliefs. A statue of Dyer is located outside the Massachusetts state capitol in Boston.

The persecution failed to quell the Quakers' influence, and, unlike the similarly named Shakers, Quakers remain a thriving religious group today, with about 350,000 members worldwide. Some of the group's most famous members are Susan B. Anthony, James Dean, Daniel Boone, Herbert Hoover, and Richard Nixon.

HIGHER EDUCATION IN AMERICA

Even in the days of colonization, education was important. The Massachusetts Bay Colony founded the oldest American university in 1636: Harvard University in Cambridge.

In 1693, a charter from King William III and Queen Mary II established the College of William and Mary in Williamsburg, Virginia. Yale University, the third oldest American college was founded in 1701 as the Collegiate School in Branford, Connecticut.

Higher learning (for men) continued to grow. Between 1785 and 1871, states established colleges in Georgia, North Carolina, Tennessee, South Carolina, Virginia, Indiana, Alabama, Wisconsin, Maine, Illinois, California, and Arkansas. From 1831 to 1850, the number of American colleges increased from forty-six to 119.

Nevertheless, in the early nineteenth century, most American men preferred to get their education from lyceums, local auditoriums offering readings, discussion groups, and lectures from prominent American intellectuals such as Ralph Waldo Emerson and Daniel Webster.

In 1862, the Morrill Act granted each public lands for state-maintained agricultural and mechanical (A&M) colleges. The Morrill Act of 1890 funded all-black A&M colleges.

EXTRA CREDIT: The College of William and Mary went co-ed in 1918; Columbia University not until 1983.

Higher Education for Women

Women's opportunities for higher education were almost nonexistent. Mary Lyon founded the female seminary Mt. Holyoke College in Massachusetts in 1837. It was the first of a few women's colleges: Vassar (1865), Wellesley (1875), Smith (1875), Bryn Mawr (1884), and Barnard College (1889).

AMERICAN CRIMINAL SETTLERS

Like all world centers of power, eighteenth-century England functioned as a miscreant magnet. Add in the standard amount of ale-stoked, uneducated smelly peasants who populated (and committed criminal acts) the world over, and it was only natural that England did a steady business in criminal-handling. Then as now, dealing with those miscreants was an expensive, unpleasant job, and hey, wouldn't it be nice to just ship these guys to that new country? Then we could just forget about them for a while.

This is exactly what England did. In Peter Okun's *Crime and the Nation: Prison and Popular Fiction in Philadelphia*, he writes,

> That the New World provided Europe with a repository for criminals and other undesirables is, of course, a commonplace of colonial history. As early as 1580, Richard Hakluyt had proposed that Britain transport 'condemned Englise [sic] men and women' to the colonies...The Act of James I mandated banishment of condemned felons to America in 1615, and the Transportation Act of 1718 instutionalized that policy. Until the Revolution, in fact, criminals flowed from British prisons to American ports in a steady stream.

Okun goes on to state that your average felon would receive a seven-year American vacation, but the really nasty received at least fourteen years.

> Because the most intractable were exiled forever, America was assured a disproportionate number of incorrigibles among its permanent population. By 1776, Britain had transported at least fifty thousand convicted criminals to her colonies in the New World. Shipping records from 1746-1775 indicate that nearly 40 percent of all persons to enter through Maryland ports were convicts; and though incomplete, Virginia records suggest similar percentages.

BEAVER TRADE

Ben Franklin famously wanted the turkey, not the bald eagle, to be the symbol of America, but a more accurate choice may have been one with large teeth, luxurious fur, and an innate talent for construction. The beaver is America's forgotten animal hero.

Beaver pelts have been turned into warm, sturdy hats and clothes items for centuries, and castoreum, a substance secreted in the beaver's scent gland, was used for medicinal purposes. The European appetite for beaver fur had resulted in the near-extinction of the European beaver by 1600.

The colonization of North America by Europeans meant the discovery of a new source of beaver pelts, the North American beaver. (Not the giant beaver of North America, which lived during the Pleistocene epoch, measured more than eight feet, and weighed as much as 220 pounds.) Colonists worked with Native Americans to provide Europe with a steady beaver supply, and the urge to trap more beavers helped drive settlement of new trapping grounds. The search for new beaver sources was one of the major reasons for Lewis and Clark's expedition. Trade and territory were thus increased by the humble beaver.

Like Americans, the beaver is industrious, sometimes building dams hundreds of feet in length. John Jacob Astor lived out the American "poor-immigrant-becomes-filthy-rich" dream by becoming a beaver fur merchant, then a New York real estate mogul and the wealthiest man in America. Because of Astor, the American beaver trade reached China, helping establish the new country's global economic influence. The New York City flag and seal both contain an image of a beaver. The beaver is, quite simply, an All-American.

CRASH COURSE
BEN FRANKLIN

If America hadn't given birth to Benjamin Franklin, it would have had to invent him. Few figures are so thoroughly American as this portly polymath.

Franklin was a child of the colonies, fittingly born in Boston on January 17, 1706, the tenth of seventeen children. He began an apprenticeship in his brother James' printing shop when he was only twelve, then ran away to Philadelphia when he was seventeen. A year later, he sailed to London, continuing to train as a printer. He returned to Philadelphia in 1726, opening his own printing office and becoming the owner and publisher of the *Pennsylvania Gazette*.

After his return to the Colonies young Franklin truly began to bloom. He founded the first circulating library, began publishing *Poor Richard: An Almanack*, proposed the idea for the University of Pennslvania, was appointed postmaster of Philadelphia, organized the first colonial militia. and dodged death with his kite-flying electrical experiment in June 1752.

Franklin began his career as a statesman in 1757, when he was fifty-one years old. He went to England to represent Pennsylvania; he would eventually represent Georgia, Massachusetts, and New Jersey as well.

In 1775, Franklin returned to Philadelphia, where he actively worked for the colonies' independence. He signed the Declaration of Independence, presided at Pennsylvania's Constitutional Convention, negotiated the Treaty of Alliance with France, helped negotiate the Treaty of Peace with England, and was elected president of the Pennsylvania Society for Promoting the Abolition of Slavery.

In addition to his political accomplishments, Franklin was a prodigious inventor and scientist. His fertile mind invented bifocal glasses, the lightning rod, a flexible urinary catheter, and the Franklin stove. He also conducted studies of electricity, chartered the Gulf Stream, and experimented with evaporation.

Franklin died in 1790, at the age of eighty-four. Some twenty thousand people attended his funeral.

POOR RICHARD'S ALMANACK

Popular statesman and author Benjamin Franklin was also an experienced printer. In his writings, he subscribed to the ideas of the age of Enlightenment, including faith in the intellect of human reason.

Beginning in 1732, Franklin published annual additions of an almanac, a mega-calendar that included useful and interesting facts ranging from the times of sunrise and sunset and phases of the moon to schedules of the tides and important days.

In his almanac, Franklin invented "Poor" Richard Saunders, through whose voice Franklin offered a version of homespun humor and wit mixed in with the weather forecasts. *Poor Richard's Almanack,* was published annually from 1733 to 1758, was very popular, selling as many as ten thousand issues each year.

Franklin was quick to admit that the sayings in the almanac were not necessarily his inventions. He borrowed ideas from age-old proverbs, Bible teachings, and ancient literature. But, he definitely put a spin on the words to make them matter to the people of the time.

Many of "Poor Richard's" thoughts are still repeated today. You'll probably recognize these:

- *He that lies down with dogs shall rise up with fleas.*

- *Fish and visitors stink in three days.*

- *Half the truth is often a great lie.*

- *Early to bed and early to rise, makes a man healthy, wealthy and wise.*

- *Keep your eyes wide open before marriage, half shut afterwards.*

- *A little neglect may breed mischief.*

1733 Edition

The cover of the 1733 edition of *Poor Richard's Almanack* quite clearly listed what you would find inside: "Wherein is contained The Lunations, Eclipses, Judgment of the Weather, Spring Tides, Planets Motions & mutual Aspects, Sun & Moon's Rising and Setting, Length of Days, Time of High Water, Fairs, Courts, and observable Days."

JOHN PETER ZENGER ESTABLISHES FREEDOM OF THE PRESS

When the Bill of Rights to the U.S. Constitution was drafted in 1789, the very first amendment guaranteed freedom of the press. This right was of utmost importance to the colonists, and it wasn't thought up on the spot in 1789.

We owe the cornerstone of freedom of the press to a German-born American newspaper publisher and printer named John Peter Zenger. After apprenticing with the royal printer for the colony of New York, Zenger opened his own printing company. In 1733 he founded the *New York Weekly Journal,* a newspaper backed by a group of prominent merchants and lawyers, including former New York attorney general James Alexander.

Zenger's sponsors wrote articles criticizing New York's colonial governor, William Cosby, and Zenger printed the articles. Although he did not write them, as publisher Zenger was legally responsible for the content. It was Zenger that William Cosby chose to punish. On November 17, 1734, Cosby arrested Zenger on charges of seditious libel and put him in jail.

A Scottish-American lawyer, Andrew Hamilton, defended Zenger during the 1735 trial. Hamilton established truth as a defense in cases of libel. While today we really can't imagine any other option, at the time, this was a new approach to a libel case. Hamilton eloquently argued that the allegations printed in the *Journal* were true and therefore not libelous.

Even thought the royal judge disagreed with Hamilton's arguments, the jury accepted them and declared Zenger not guilty. This verdict is considered the first milestone in the history of American freedom of the press.

EXTRA CREDIT: Zenger was appointed public printer for the New York colony in 1737 and the New Jersey colony in 1738.

Economics 101

Cash Crops of the Colonies

The colonies' goal was economic prosperity, and having an export crop went a long way toward earning hard cash. Plantations in Virginia and the Carolinas grew staples for world markets: tobacco in the Chesapeake area and North Carolina; rice and indigo in the coastal regions of South Carolina and Georgia. Tobacco, rice, and indigo were all crops that needed huge tracts of land and equally big labor forces.

Rice

Rice was an ideal crop for the wet coastal lowlands of Georgia and South Carolina. Two kinds of rice were grown there. *Oryza sativa*, know as "Carolina gold," was imported from Madagascar. *Oryza glaberrima*, a red rice, was probably imported from West Africa, along with the captives who knew how to grow it.

The most important factor in the success of rice plantations was the knowledge that African slaves brought with them from their homeland. Slaves introduced the plantation owners to irrigation techniques to dyke the marshes and flood the fields.

Indigo

Dye from the indigo plant was needed in the British textile industry. In the mid-eighteenth century, indigo arrived in the Carolinas and Georgia from Antigua. Indigo yielded about 25 percent return on investment, so it was a very popular cash crop right up until the American Revolution.

Tobacco

John Rolfe, the husband of Pocahontas, gathered information from sailors to Barbados about curing tobacco. He obtained seeds of the *Nicotiana tabacum* tobacco strain from Barbados, and prepared it to sell to Europeans. So in 1612, the Jamestown colony got started farming what turned out to be their lifeline to manufactured English goods. From that time onward, tobacco flourished in the rich soil and mild climate of the Virginia and Maryland tidewaters.

POPULATION GROWTH IN THE 1700S

	1701	1775
Atlantic Coast English Colony Population*	250,000	2,500,000
African-American Population*	28,000	500,000

*approximate values

From 1701 to 1775, the English colony population experienced a ten-time increase. This rapid population growth was the result of two main factors: immigration and a high birth rate in the colonies.

In addressing the high birth rate, it's hard to resist making a witty comment about cold nights or lack of cable TV. Actually, though, the motivation was almost as simple: the colonists were learning how to subsist and prosper on the land. Healthy parents who could expect to survive the winter therefore produced healthy babies with a good chance of surviving infancy. And, it didn't hurt to have a big family to help run the house and farm.

Immigrants came from Europe voluntarily and from Africa against their will. Some Europeans came in hopes of sharing in the wealth of the fertile land, and others came for religious freedom. As the Puritans had the New England colonies pretty much sown up, most European immigrants headed to the middle and southern colonies. By 1775, the colonial population was made up of 6 percent Germans, 7 percent Scotch-Irish, and 5 percent French Protestants/Dutch/Swede combined.

Germans settled west of Philadelphia in an area called Pennsylvania Dutch country. Scotch-Irish come to the "western" frontier (and this is not the west we think of now) in Pennsylvania, Virginia, the Carolinas, and Georgia.

Unfortunately, the largest single group of immigrants was Africans who had been taken captive and forced aboard slave ships. By 1775, African Americans made up twenty percent of the colonies' population. Ninety percent of these lived in the southern colonies of South Carolina, Georgia, North Carolina, Virginia, and Maryland.

THE GREAT AWAKENING

A religious movement swept through the colonies in the 1740s. Its greatest impact came from the realization that ministers were not the final authority. The colonists were united in a common experience that underlined their democratic tendencies and sense of American nationality before the American Revolution.

Preachers roamed the countryside, offering salvation to anyone who would listen. Their fiery sermons, which drew participants by the thousands and often had to be held outdoors to accommodate the large crowds, made Protestants repent their sins and seek salvation. Many small local revivals led to a general "Great Awakening."

Traveling revivalists were welcomed because they converted sinners, increased church membership, and inspired religious participation. The Great Awakening brought religion to groups such as blacks and the poor, who were not comfortable worshiping with the elitist Puritans.

As the Great Awakening spread from town to town, evangelical fervor coupled with church rivalry spread, too. Nevertheless, the revival's supporters came together with a sense of unity regardless of denominational or political affiliation.

Great Awakening Evangelists

Jonathan Edwards quoted Old Testament scriptures to support his argument that God was angry with human sinfulness. He preached good old-fashioned sermons about eternal damnation for those who disobeyed God's commandments. Jonathan Edwards visited primarily New England congregations.

George Whitefield toured all along the Atlantic seaboard, preaching the necessity for sinners to be converted. Whitefield reminded churchgoers in no uncertain terms, and with vivid descriptions, that those who did not profess belief in Jesus Christ would be cast into hell. Whitefield taught that ordinary people could accept the salvation of Christ without the authority of the ministers and church leaders.

SINNERS IN THE HANDS OF AN ANGRY GOD

Yes, the title is supposed to disturb you. That was Jonathan Edwards' intent when he wrote and delivered his sermon in 1741. Today, "Sinners in the Hands of an Angry God" is still used in American high school and college English courses as an example of Puritan literature. Just to give you the feeling of being back in tenth grade, we've included a little bit of the introduction here (the whole sermon is about eighteen pages long).

Deuteronomy 32:35. *Their foot shall slide in due time.*

In this verse is threatened the vengeance of God on the wicked unbelieving Israelites. ...There is nothing that keeps wicked men, at any one moment, out of hell, but the mere pleasure of God.. ...He is not only able to cast wicked men into hell, but he can most *easily* do it. ...We find it easy to tread on and crush a worm that we see crawling on the earth; ...thus easy is it for God when he pleases to cast his enemies down to hell.

GREAT BRITAIN, FRANCE, AND SPAIN AT WAR

Unlike a trip to Vegas—in many more ways than one, really—what happened in England didn't necessarily stay in England. During the early eighteenth century, Britain found itself struggling with domestic political issues. Constant conflict with France and Spain did eventually spill over into the English colonies.

During a span of seventy-five years, the British and French fought four wars that carried over to North America. Between 1689 and 1763, Great Britain and France struggled mightily to become the main ruling force, both in Europe and in North America. The rivalry that had continued for ages in the Old World now included colonies in the New World.

King William's War (1689–1697)

The "War of the Grand Alliance" started in Europe between England and its longtime enemy France. When the conflict spread to North America, the French Canadians allied with the Huron Indians; their opponents were the American colonists and the Iroquois Indians. Warfare between the two groups continued. Both the French and English colonists—along with their respective Native American allies—raided each other's settlements. The Treaty of Ryswick in 1697 stopped the fighting, but didn't resolve anything.

Queen Anne's War (1702–1713)

The next round of bloodshed in Europe was called the War of the Spanish Succession. It was waged between Great Britain, the Netherlands, and the Holy Roman Empire on one side against France and Spain fighting together on the other. Meanwhile, across the Atlantic Ocean, the conflict called Queen Anne's War was marked by Spanish attacks on the English colonists, and vice versa, to claim (and counter-claim) the Florida frontier. Again, not much was settled by this second war. The Peace Treaty of Utrecht transferred to British America a great deal of New France, including Nova Scotia, Newfoundland, and the Hudson Bay region.

King George's War (1744–1748)

By the time of the third war, Britain and France had reached the point of "irreconcilable differences" in their separate quests for control of North America.

Something happened in Austria that had consequences all the way across the globe in Nova Scotia. First, look at what was going on in Austria: Austrian Emperor Charles VI died. Of course, a War of the Austrian Succession broke out to determine who would be the next Emperor. To support their best interests (which, specifically, were to gain control of the Netherlands, which Austria then controlled), France sided with Prussia against Austria. Britain didn't want France to get the Netherlands, so the English king supported Austria.

Now, switch to Nova Scotia, in North America. French troops destroyed a British fort at Canso. The French carried their English colonial prisoners to their supposedly indestructible fortress, Louisbourg, on Cape Breton Island. After seven weeks of attack, colonial militiamen and British troops captured the fort at Louisbourg. The fighting ended with the Treaty of Aix-la-Chapelle, in which Louisbourg was returned to the French, and Britain was awarded control of Madras, India. (Yep, sometimes, the *colonies* that Britain worried about controlling were *colonies* in other lands besides North America.)

At this point, you're probably thinking that we're insulting your intelligence by telling you there were four wars, then only describing three. Smooth out your feathers: we wouldn't do that. The last war was the one that finally resolved the question of control of the colonies. This fourth and final war was the French and Indian War (1754-63), and it was so important to American history that it gets a page of its own.

THE FRENCH AND INDIAN WAR

The last of four North American wars over territory control was waged between the British and the French from 1754 to 1763. Unlike the first three, in this war the fighting actually began in the colonies and then expanded into Europe as the Seven Years' War.

The British will tell you that the French started it by building a series of forts in the Ohio River Valley. The French will tell you that they had to, to keep the British colonies from creeping west.

Either way, a young colonel named George Washington was there when the French and Indian War started. Washington led a small group of men to the Ohio River Valley with plans to stop the French from building another fort. After a brief victory, Washington's troops in 1754 suffered a tremendous loss (one-third of his men) at the hands of the Frenchmen. He surrendered the entire region to France. As we would say today, "It was on."

To begin with, it looked like the British might not win:

- In 1755, General Edward Braddock led an expedition from Virginia, with disastrous results. Near Fort Duquesne (present-day Pittsburgh), a small force of French and Indians defeated the more than two thousand British troops and colonial militia.
- The Algonquian Indians, allies of the French, terrorized frontier colonists from western Pennsylvania to North Carolina.
- British invasions of French Canada in 1756 and 1757 were repelled.

Finally, Britain's new prime minister, William Pitt, regrouped their war support in 1756, and things began to change.

- British and colonial troops recaptured the French fort of Louisbourg in Nova Scotia in 1758.
- British general James Wolfe defeated the Marquis de Montcalm, and the French surrendered Québec in 1759.
- In 1760, Jeffrey Amherst captured Montreal. The rest of the French army surrendered there, bringing all of Canada under British control.

The Treaty of Paris in 1763 ended the wars for control of North American lands. France gave to Britain: French Canada, Spanish Florida, and lands east of the Mississippi River. To make up for losing Florida, France also gave to Spain: the Louisiana Territory and lands west of the Mississippi River.

The French and Indian War not only stripped France of its North American holdings, it also changed Britain's relationship with its colonies. Britain thought little of the colonists' military efforts, while the colonists themselves gained confidence in their military abilities. It was a change that would eventually lead to the American Revolution.

Armed Forces

The three earlier wars were manned by small regular units of the European armies, while local colonial militiamen pitched in. In the French and Indian War, England and France recognized the full importance of their colonies. Therefore, rather than relying on the colonists' "amateur" forces, England and France this time shipped large numbers of troops overseas to support their efforts.

British Prime Minister William Pitt did make a bit of a misstep when he authorized the British troops to confiscate any supplies they needed from the colonial civilians and to impress any civilians if the troops needed to be refreshed. This outraged the colonists, and Pitt later changed his policy.

To help coordinate colonial defense, the British government called for a group of representatives to meet and discuss a plan for recruiting and funding troops. Their arrangement, called the Albany Plan of Union, provided for an inter-colonial government and taxation to go toward their common defense. While it was not successful at the time, the Albany Plan of Union did set the groundwork for more revolutionary congresses before the end of the century.

CASUALTIES OF THE FRENCH AND INDIAN WAR

General Edward Braddock

In 1755, at the age of sixty, Braddock led an expedition to take the French-held Fort Duquesne. With a force of 1,200 troops, he reached the Monongahela River, about seven miles from the fort. Braddock and his men were ambushed and roundly defeated. More than nine hundred men were killed or wounded. George Washington led the survivors led to safety because Braddock had been mortally wounded.

General James Wolfe

In 1759, James Wolfe moved about five thousand of his men about two miles southwest of Québec. The troops scaled a steep cliff to the Plains of Abraham above the town, surprising the French. The French commander, the Marquis de Montcalm, had not prepared for an assault on this side because he thought no one would be able to climb the cliffs.

The British troops decisively defeated the French. Wolfe, however, was shot, He reportedly heard cries of "They run," and then died at the age of thirty-two, knowing that his British troops were victorious.

Both military commanders on each side were killed at the Battle of the Plains of Abraham: Montcalm died the next day.

Tales from the Battlefield

Before he died, Braddock gave a special farewell to Washington: his ceremonial sash worn with his battle uniform. According to the legend, from then on, Washington never went anywhere without this sash. He even had it with him during his service as the Commander of the Colonial Army and later as the first president.

Pontiac's Rebellion

After you read about the real Pontiac, you'll understand how automakers could imagine giving the same name to a make of car that includes a screaming red '67 Firebird convertible and a shiny black '70 GTO.

Chief Pontiac was an Ottawa leader who planned a major attack against British settlements on the western frontier. After the French and Indian War, the Native Americans found themselves now dealing with the British instead of the French, whom they had accepted and given their trust.

British colonists didn't help the situation when they kept doing things to anger the natives more and more.

- European settlers moved westward onto Indian lands.
- British traders cheated the Indians.
- The British did not hide their contempt and disregard for the Indians.
- The British refused to offer gifts to the Indians.

This last one really irritated the Indians, who regarded gifts as payment for the land where the British had built their forts. Basically, now that the Indians weren't getting French backing, the British were no longer afraid of them. So, the British figured to save some money by cutting off their gifts of arms, ammunition, and clothing.

This withdrawal of arms, especially, signaled to the Indians that the British were planning to get rid of them by force. The Indians decided to do something before the British wiped them out.

Chief Pontiac formed an alliance from the following tribes: Ottawa, Potawatomie, Huron, Chippewa, Shawnee, Delaware, Miami, and other smaller groups. They destroyed forts and settlements in the Ohio Valley from New York to Virginia. When the "smoke had cleared," Pontiac's forces had killed about two thousand settlers and four hundred British troops and driven away thousands more.

Extra Credit: The Creek Indians called the colonists *ecunnaunuxulgee*, which means "people greedy for land."

CRASH COURSE
PROCLAMATION OF 1763

Why Was It Made? Britain decided that, rather then trying to defend the colonists against Indian attacks, it would be easier to give the Indians a place of their own to live.

What Was It? A royal proclamation was a measure to shut down white settlement of the west.

Where Did It Apply? The proclamation drew a line on the crest of the Appalachian Mountains, prohibiting colonists from settling or speculating west of there. Even further, the British government ordered squatters off Indian lands.

How Was It to Be Followed? Settlers were required to leave the newly established Indian territory. Traders were not allowed to enter the region until they had a license from one of the colonies' governors. Land purchases in the Indian territory were heavily restricted.

Who Reacted to It? The colonists immediately reacted with heated anger. After the French and Indian War, Americans expected to move westward and settle new lands. They were infuriated by Britain's denial of these lands.

What Did Colonists Do? Colonists ignored the proclamation, and thousands went ahead and migrated westward beyond the boundary line.

How Did Britain Feel? Britain's view was that the colonists had not done a lot to help the motherland, but they had certainly cost a whole lot for protection.

How Did Colonists Feel? The colonists resented Britain's interference. They thought that, after they had applied their own daring, labor, and money to settle the land, Britain was now conveniently meddling with increasingly restrictive measures. Colonists felt that this denial of their rights to the land was unforgivable.

Did It Succeed? The proclamation failed to protect the Indian territory it had created.

TOWNSHEND ACTS

Background

After the French and Indian War, Britain sat back and took a long look at the total price tag for gaining control of the North American lands. This included what had already been spent during the four wars and what would have to be spent to maintain a military force that would guard the American frontier. King George III decided that it would only be fitting to pass along the cost to the colonists.

In 1767, the newly appointed British treasurer Charles Townsend proposed and Parliament adopted new taxes to be collected on colonial imports of tea, glass, and paper. Called the Townshend Acts, these laws:

- required that the revenues raised be used to pay crown officials in the colonies.
- provided for searching private homes for smuggled goods without a specific warrant.
- suspended New York's assembly for that defying the Quartering Act.

As with almost everything else Parliament had handed down lately, it wasn't long before the colonists expressed their displeasure. Arguing that these taxes could not be passed without the consent of the colonies' representative assemblies, colonists claimed they were a form of taxation without representation. The colonists agreed to boycott British goods, and they stepped up their smuggling activities to compensate.

Britain's prime minister wisely saw that the Townshend Acts were not accomplishing what was intended. Instead, trade in the colonies had decreased with the boycott, and the amount of revenue from the new taxes was disappointing. Parliament repealed the Townshend Acts in 1770, and the colonists ended their boycott. (But, just to remind the colonists who was still in charge, Parliament did keep a small tax on tea.)

MINUTE MEN

Even the most slovenly students learned a few things in American history. As early as elementary school, the role of the Minute Men in the American Revolution is one of those easily digestable and remembered facts that lodges in the brain. Students who are slightly less slovenly might remember that the name of these fighting men came from their being ready to fight at a minute's warning. That's usually where the learning, or at least the remembering, stops.

There was more to the story. According to the National Park Service, Massachusetts colonial law required "all able-bodied men between the ages of 16 and 60 to keep a serviceable firearm and serve in a part-time citizen army." The British understood both the value and the vulnerability of their outlying colony.

But those forces weren't Minute Men. That group was created in October 1774, when the Massachusetts Provincial Congress asked Massachusetts towns to create a new group of fighting men. Whereas the militia defended Great Britain's assets, these men were to eventually fight for American freedom.

Unlike the militia's forced service, Minute Men were volunteers. And while the militia trained just a few times a year, the Minute Men trained several times a week.

Many Minute Men simply wore their own farm or work clothes. Others wore buckskin hunting outfits with special Indian touches added to intimidate the enemy, especially warpaint. Most Minute Men used their hunting rifles, which did not have bayonets but were accurate at long range. Their experience with frontier hunting was invaluable in helping practice their marksmanship. Minute Men sharpshooters quickly earned a reputation for their deadly accuracy.

STAMP ACT

At the end of the French and Indian War, the British found themselves the possessors of huge tracts of land in the colonies. But having land and keeping land are two different affairs, so they went from being tasked with acquisition to being tasked with defense. To pay for the defense of their newly acquired territory, the British enacted the Stamp Act of 1765. Though it might have seemed prudent at the time, the move would prove to be pence wise and colony foolish.

The act levied taxes on all manner of printed material—newspapers, wills, pamphlets, permits, even playing cards. The amounts varied from three pence to six pounds.

The act of taxation was nothing new to the colonists. Patriot Samuel Adams had even once served as a tax collector. But those taxes were levied by colonial governments to support themselves. What chafed the colonists, who could turn a phrase with the best of them, was of course "taxation without representation." England was like a landlord that kept the door hinges oiled and the privy stocked with corn husks, but refused to listen to suggestions about new wallpaper.

Colonial grumbling turned tangible through means like the Virginia Resolves, written by the Virginia House of Burgesses in 1765, which protested the tax. Patrick Henry, always good with a turn of phrase, said, "Caesar had his Brutus, Charles I his Cromwell and George III may profit from their example." With the anti-Stamp Act fire sufficiently kindled, it wasn't long before Britain had many more problems than revenue generation.

Daughters of Liberty

It wasn't just the men who opposed the British. The American women did their part, too. To support colonial boycotts of British goods, the Americans began to "make do" with the resources they had. The women made cloth themselves, spinning it out of yarn. Groups of "Daughters of Liberty" organized spinning matches and bees. They happily digested their homemade food and drink substitutions, such as rye coffee and bear venison.

SUGAR ACT

The Stamp Act of 1765 gets the lion's share of history-book mentions of Revolutionary War causes, but it was actually the successor to another onerous act, the Sugar Act of 1764. The Sugar Act irritated, and the Stamp Act aggravated.

The roots of the Sugar Act date back to March 1733, when Parliament passed the Sugar and Molasses Act, a protectionist bit of legislation aimed at pacifying plantation owners in the British West Indies. The plantation owners were facing competition from the French West Indies, and successfully pressured Parliament to impose a tax of sixpence per gallon on non-British molasses bound for the North American colonies.

Molasses was a key ingredient in rum, so the tax would have impacted the colonies greatly, if it had been successfully imposed. It wasn't. Smuggling and bribery allowed the colonists to keep the cheap rum flowing freely.

That changed when England was faced with finding a way to pay off the debts incurred during the French and Indian War. In the Sugar Act of 1764, the colonists' bosses decided to halve the sixpence-per-gallon molasses tax, but to also strictly enforce it. In addition, the list of taxable items would now include things like certain wines and coffee, and American exports would be more closely regulated.

Quartering Act

Another unpopular British act that signaled King George III's attempts to weaken colonial liberties was the Quartering Act of 1765. Simply stated, this act required colonists to feed and provide shelter for British soldiers stationed in the colonies.

Crash Course
The Sons of Liberty

An alliance of patriot groups throughout the colonies, the Sons of Liberty shared a dislike of British rule. In the beginning they remained loyal to the King, while disagreeing with the King's limits on their rights. Later, they were full-out agitators for colonial freedom.

The Sons of Liberty were instrumental in moving America further along the path to Revolutionary War:

Stamp Act of 1765

As soon as the act was announced, Sons of Liberty groups attacked royal stamp agents in their homes in Boston, New York City, and Wilmington, intimidating them into resigning their posts. By the time the law went into effect, there were no agents on duty to sell the stamps.

Tea Act of 1773

You'll recall that Parliament granted the East India Company a monopoly on the tea trade in the colonies. In response, Sons of Liberty dressed as Indians dumped the company's tea cargo into the Boston Harbor. (i.e. The Boston Tea Party)

Midnight Ride of Paul Revere

In 1775, the Sons of Liberty spurred the famous messenger ride. They spied on British troops in Boston, learning that the soldiers were moving toward Lexington. Leader John Warren sent Paul Revere off to warn Sam Adams and John Hancock.

PAUL REVERE

Listen my children and you shall hear
Of the midnight ride of Paul Revere,
Who of course was joined by William Dawes and Dr. Samuel Prescott.

Nope. Just doesn't scan. No wonder Henry Wadsworth Longfellow left Revere's compatriots out of *The Midnight Ride of Paul Revere.* But Revere wasn't alone on his ride. At least, not all the way.

Revere was born in Boston, into a French Huguenot family with the original surname "Rivoire." Revere apprenticed under his father, a gold and silversmith, then became involved in many different enterprises as an adult, including dentistry, goldsmithing, hardware sales, foundry operation, and copper milling.

He was an advocate of freedom for the colonies, taking part in the Boston Tea Party and other endeavors. On April 18, 1775, when Boston-based British forces began to cross the Charles River to Lexington, Revere compatriot Dr. Joseph Warren dispatched him to Lexington to warn Samuel Adams and John Hancock that they were in danger of capture.

Revere was ferried across the Charles River to Charlestown, then borrowed a horse and rode to Lexington, warning of the British move on the way and arriving at Adams' and Hancock's location at midnight.

But Revere wasn't the only emissary sent out that night by Warren. William Dawes was sent by the land route to Lexington, and made it there after Revere. Dawes and Revere then opted to continue to Concord. On the way, they were joined by Dr. Samuel Prescott, who had been spending the evening with his fiance Lydia Mulliken. All three were captured by British patrolmen. Prescott escaped first, and Dawes followed. Revere was held and then released. He returned, on foot, to Lexington.

EXTRA CREDIT: Colonial lawyer John Adams defended the British soldiers at their trial for murder, and they were acquitted.

CRISPUS ATTUCKS

The American Revolution might have been a battle between European settlers and their European rulers, but Crispus Attucks, the first casualty of the revolution, was actually the son of an African father and a Natick Indian mother.

As author Michael Lee Lanning wrote in his book *The African-American Soldier: From Crispus Attucks to Colin Powell*, Attucks was "a runaway slave who had eluded capture for twenty years," who "knew firsthand about the unfair treatment of which the colonists spoke and the acts of rebellion about which they dreamed. At forty-seven, he was a veteran of both, a man who had escaped bondage to find his freedom on the hazardous and arduous high seas."

Attucks, who had evidently sailed on whaling ships, was in Boston on the afternoon of March 5, 1770. Tensions between England and the colonists were high. The British were determined to maintain control of their upstart colony, and the colonists were just as determined to rebel against that control.

When a group of Bostonians including Attucks began jeering and throwing snowballs at a group of British soldiers, the soldiers fired on the crowd, killing Attucks and four others and beginning the conflagration known as the American Revolution.

The Boston Massacre

Samuel Adams angrily called the shooting a "massacre," and the incident came to be know as The Boston Massacre. It would be held up later as an example of the crown's brutality to agitate anti-British sentiment.

Hands-On History
Hutchinson Letters

Centuries before many an intemperate e-mailer learned that incendiary private correspondence becomes even more incendiary when exposed to the oxidizing forces of public knowledge, Thomas Hutchinson learned that principle firsthand. But that's a good thing for Americans, as Hutchinson's correspondence helped promote the cause of American independence.

The Hutchinson Letters were the culmination of a seemingly promising public career gone bad. Hutchinson was elected to the Massachusetts legislature in 1737, became Massachusetts' lieutenant governor in 1758, and then became governor in 1771. But while his fellow colonists were catching freedom fever, Hutchinson was remaining loyal to the crown. He began writing private letters to certain individuals who advocated extra British troops to fight American rebels. Benjamin Franklin, who was living in England at the time, received a packet of Hutchinson's letters. Franklin circulated the letters among his friends back in Boston, with the condition that they not reach the public. Predictably, that's exactly what happened.

The Boston Gazette published the content of the letters in June 1773, enraging both the Bostonians, who forced Hutchinson to flee to England, and the British, who wanted to know who had leaked the letters. Although three innocent men were initially accused, Franklin admitted his own complicity. He was publicly reprimanded by the British in 1774, and returned to the colonies later that year.

Franklin, of course, went on to become a Founding Father. Hutchinson, a native Bostonian, wasn't as lucky. He lived out his days in England, where he died in exile in 1780.

THE BOSTON TEA PARTY

Sometimes, it's just impossible to ignore a cliché. Such is the case with the Boston Tea Party. It's been done to death, but you leave it out of a history book at your peril. However, the one good thing about a cliché is that everybody is already familiar with the main details, so it's okay to just deal with some particulars.

When: The party took place December 16, 1773, in the middle of the night.

Where: Boston Harbor.

Who: A group of some fifty revolutionaries calling themselves the Sons of Liberty, some of whom disguised themselves as Mohawk Indians.

Why: British taxes. (What else?) Parliament's Tea Act of May 1773 effectively cut out the tea trade for American middlemen. Americans feared they would do the same to other trade.

What happened: The Sons of Liberty boarded three tea ships and dumped 342 casks, or about 90,000 pounds, of tea into the harbor.

What kind of tea: Darjeeling.

Who owned the tea: East India Company.

The reviews: Two thumbs up from the American critics. As historian Pauline Maier wrote for the PBS program "Liberty! The Chronicle of the Revolution:"

> The Boston Tea Party was one of the most effective pieces of political theater ever staged. John Adams, no fan of mob action, wrote of the dumping of the tea: "There is a dignity, a majesty, a sublimity, in this last effort of the patriots that I greatly admire."

Upshot: A severely miffed England passed the Intolerable Acts in retribution, which directly spurred the onset of the American Revolution.

JOHN DICKINSON

Pennsylvania writer, lawyer, and statesman John Dickinson was an active participant in shaping American government. He sat on the assemblies of Delaware and Pennsylvania, served in both Continental Congresses, represented Delaware at the Constitutional Convention, helped frame the U.S. Constitution, and wrote the first draft of the Articles of Confederation.

Dickinson originally favored reconciliation with Great Britain, and he opposed violent uprising. He declined to sign the Declaration of Independence. As events proceeded toward war, Dickinson wrote the "Declaration of the Causes of Taking Up Arms," concluding that Americans were resolved to die free men rather than live slaves.

Dickinson wrote many essays on colonists' rights and protested taxes imposed with the Townshend Acts. He warned against allowing Britain to get away with acts that would open the door for future abuse.

Letters from a Farmer in Pennsylvania

Dickinson's *Letters from a Farmer in Pennsylvania* became one of the most widely read books of the eighteenth century, reprinted in almost every newspaper.

While Dickinson agreed that Parliament could regulate commerce, his *Letters* stated that Britain's policies deprived colonies of their lawful rights. Dickinson argued that Britain's new duties were taxation without representation. He urged the colonists to unite in action. The essay begins as an appeal to those who love liberty: "Benevolence towards mankind excites wishes for their welfare, and such wishes endear the means of fulfilling them. Those can be found in liberty alone, and therefore her sacred cause ought to be espoused by every man, on every occasion, to the utmost of his power. As a charitable but poor person does not withhold his mite [sic], because he cannot relieve all the distresses of the miserable, so let not any honest man suppress his sentiments concerning freedom, however small their influence is likely to be."

INTOLERABLE ACTS

Parliament retaliated against the Boston Tea Party with a string of laws designed to punish Boston and tighten its hold on the American colonies in general. The point of the new laws was to underline Parliament's absolute authority over the entire British Empire. Colonists referred to them as a whole as Intolerable Acts.

Coercive Acts

- Boston Port Act — closed Boston Harbor to all commercial trade until all the spoiled tea was paid for.
- Administration of Justice Act — authorized royal officials charged with capital crimes to be tried in Great Britain (so defendants wouldn't have to face hostile colonial juries).
- Massachusetts Government Act — made most high elective offices subject to royal appointment, ending self-rule in the colony.
- Amended Quartering Act — required civilians to open their homes to British soldiers when existing barracks proved inadequate and applied to all of the American colonies.
- Quebec Act — extended the Canadian border south into the Ohio River Valley and gave Canada land previously claimed by Massachusetts, Connecticut, and Virginia.

Colonists' Reaction to the Intolerable Acts

On September 5, 1774, fifty-six delegates from twelve colonies (all but Georgia) met in Philadelphia to discuss what response they could put forth to answer the Intolerable Acts. The delegates' consolidated thoughts became the Declaration of Rights, drafted by John Adams.

The Declaration of Rights said that the colonies were not obligated to honor England's Parliament's decisions made about domestic colonial affairs. This document only allowed Parliament the authority to govern imperial trade. In addition, the delegates agreed to boycott British goods by avoiding importing and consuming them until the Intolerable Acts were repealed.

JOHN LOCKE

The writings of seventeenth-century English philosopher and political theorist John Locke had a strong influence on U.S. policy and freedom. Many of his political ideas, such as natural rights, property rights, the duty of the government to protect these rights, and the rule of the majority, provided a rationale for the American Revolution.

Along with his call for a series of governmental checks and balances, Locke's ideas were later considered in drafting both the Declaration of Independence and the Constitution of the United States.

In his *Two Treatises of Government*, Locke wrote that while the government is supreme, it only holds that position if it follows "natural laws" based on the rights that people have simply because they are human. He argued that citizens had a right and an obligation to revolt against any and whatever government failed to protect their rights.

Locke's Two-Step Government Growth Process

While Americans gathered assorted political truths from Locke's writings, the idea that had the most influence on Americans was Locke's theory that government grows out of a two-step process:

People contract among themselves to create a community. In reality, the people in Massachusetts already had this one covered. When the pilgrims landed at Plymouth Rock, they drafted the Mayflower Compact which created a society from the "state of nature."

A "contract" is formed between the sovereign and the society. In reality, the British Bill of Rights was essentially a contract about the terms on which William and Mary gained the throne.

WHO SAID WHAT, COLONIAL ERA

Sometimes, the roster of historical characters and their historic sayings can become a little jumbled. It's hard to tell your patriots without a program, in other words. So here's a little help with who said what, as well as a little lagniappe in the form of when and why.

- *"Give me liberty, or give me death!"*
  Patrick Henry, in a speech to the Virginia House of Burgesses on March 23, 1775. Henry wanted to encourage armed resistance to the British.

- *"I regret that I have but one life to lose for my country."*
  Nathan Hale, September 22, 1776, as he was about to be hanged in New York for spying on British troops.

- *"We must all hang together, or assuredly we shall all hang separately."*
  Benjamin Franklin, July 4, 1776, at the signing of the Declaration of Independence in Philadelphia.

- *"The tree of liberty must be refreshed from time to time with the blood of patriots and tyrants."*
  Thomas Jefferson, November 13, 1787, in a letter to William Stephens Smith, a soldier and statesman.

- *"I have not yet begun to fight."*
  John Paul Jones, Battle of Flamborough Head, September 23, 1779, in response to being asked "Have you struck [your colors]? Do you call for Quarter?" by the captain of the British ship *Serapis*.

- *"These are the times that try men's souls."*
  Thomas Paine, December 4, 1776, in *The Crisis*, a series of articles written to support the cause of the American Patriots.

- *"The distinctions between Virginians, Pennsylvanians, New Yorkers, and New Englanders are no more. I am not a Virginian, but an American!"*
  Patrick Henry in 1774 after the Boston Tea Party.

SAMUEL ADAMS

A superb political negotiator, Samuel Adams has since been described as the Lenin of the American Revolution. Some historians saw him as violent and manipulative, willing to do anything that would move the country closer toward his one goal of American independence. Others saw a different man who looked to other, more peaceable, responses to Britian's rules before resorting to force.

Whatever his personality and strategies were, Adams unquestionably lived for politics, and surely fit Thomas Jefferson's description of him as "truly the Man of the Revolution." It does seem that Samuel Adams was present for every defining incident that led to revolution:

1764 – In response to the Sugar and Molasses Act, Adams' vocal expression against its enforcement brought him to the forefront of the colonial politics arena.

1765 – In answer to the Stamp Act, Adams urged independence, arguing that colonists had the right to overthrow a government that continued to overstep its authority and limit or curtail their rights.

1770 – After Crispus Attucks became the first casualty of the revolution in the Boston Massacre, Adams demanded that all British troops be removed from Boston.

1772 – Adams persuaded the Boston town meeting to create another Committee of Correspondence to verbalize and broadcast patriotic complaints against the British.

1773 – In response to Parliament's Tea Act, Adams participated in the Boston Tea Party.

1774 – Adams was elected to the First Continental Congress, which instigated a boycott of British goods.

1775 – Adams was a delegate to the Second Continental Congress in Philadelphia

1776 – Adams was a signer of the Declaration of Independence.

Adams left the Continental Congress in 1780 to serve in the Massachusetts legislature. From there, he advanced to lieutenant governor, and became the governor of Massachusetts in 1794.

Supposedly...

We're not given to repeating gossip, so listen closely the first time: After being warned in the middle of the night by Paul Revere that the British were moving toward Lexington, John Hancock and Samuel Adams rode away at dawn the next morning.

Reports say that they heard the first shots of the Revolutionary War ("the shot heard 'round the world"), and Adams allegedly said, "What a glorious morning for America!"

Samuel Adams Beer

We couldn't let this one go, could we? Well, after mismanaging a newspaper that he founded straight out of college, Sam Adams took over the family brewery when his father died in 1748. (He "mismanaged" it, too.)

First, to settle the question we know you're asking: No, the adult beverage brewed by today's Boston Beer Company is not the same recipe from Sam Adams' eighteenth-century brewery.

In 1984, Jim Koch dusted off an old family beer recipe handed down to his father, a retired fifth-generation brewer. Koch brewed up a drink that he called Samuel Adams Boston Lager® because Samuel Adams was a Boston man of action. Moreover, Samuel Adams was a brewer, too, who had inherited a brewing tradition and a brewery from his own father.

FLINTLOCKS

The firearms of the soldiers in the American Revolution had a few things in common with modern-day firearms. They had metal barrels, and you pointed them at the bad guys then pulled the trigger. Other than that, the self-contained, clean-burning, efficient, and accurate guns of today are as far removed from Revolution-era guns as Formula 1 race cars are from Model Ts.

American foot soldiers usually fought with flintlocks, which were positively Rube Goldberg-ian in their complexity. Shooters would pour gunpowder down their weapon's barrel then ram a paper- or cloth-covered bullet down on top of the gunpowder. Then the shooter would pour some more gunpowder in the flintlock's pan, and he was ready to fire.

When the trigger was pulled, the hammer, which held a piece of flint clamped in a vise, swung down and struck the steel frizzen. (Yes, it was really called a frizzen.) The flint-frizzen collision produced sparks, which ignited the powder in the pan. The fire in the pan traveled from pan to barrel via an opening called a touch hole, and, finally, the bullet was forcibly ejected from the barrel.

The whole process was involved, lengthy and very hard to pull off while conducting a battle and remaining unshot. And, as complicated as the procedure was, flintlocks were actually an improvement on the matchlock method of firing a gun, which required the shooter to light a fuse that was attached to a lever, then move the lever into position to light the gunpowder.

Flintlocks began to be phased out in the 1800s, but they gave us at least one lasting expression. The term "flash in the pan" first referred to a fire that ignited in the pan but failed to enter the touch hole and thus required the shooter to reload.

CRASH COURSE
THE AGE OF ENLIGHTENMENT

Europe

A new movement in literature and philosophy known as the Age of Enlightenment celebrated an intellectual shift from centuries of darkness and ignorance into a new age enlightened by reason, science, and a respect for humanity. (The period was also called the Age of Reason.)

The most important tenet of the Age of Enlightenment was faith in the power of human reason. Enlightenment philosophers preferred discovering truths through observation instead of discovering truths through studying (such as the Bible). What this meant was, if we could change our long-time beliefs about discovering truths of the physical world, couldn't we also change our long-time beliefs about truths of government? Following that line of thought, then, couldn't we change our long-time beliefs about the basic rights guaranteed by government?

America

Educated Americans adopted this political philosophy, supported by the writings of John Locke and Jean-Jacques Rousseau. The future leaders of the American Revolution (Washington, Jefferson, Franklin, and Adams) subscribed to these theories and trusted human reason to solve the many problems of life, society, and politics.

If the purpose of human society was to guarantee the basic rights of men—and women—aren't we obligated to convert these ideas into action? To claim these basic rights of personal security, free enjoyment of property, equality before the law, and the participation of every citizen in government, the American colonies contemplated thoughts and actions that finally culminated in the American Revolution.

Meanwhile, back in Europe, the Enlightenment philosophers excitedly watched the American Revolution develop, watching their enlightened ideas be put into action.

POP QUIZ #2

1) True or False: corporate colonies were operated by joint-stock companies; royal colonies were under the direct rule of the king; and proprietary colonies were under the authority of individuals granted charters of ownership by the king

2) When the Jamestown colonists almost starved to death because they did not want to do the work necessary to grow or gather food, two things helped them survive: the stern leadership of Captain John Smith, and the establishment of the _____ crop.

3) Who was Jamestown's first governor, the baron De La Warre?
   a) Thomas West
   b) Thomas Gates
   c) Thomas Dale
   d) Thomas Haden Church

4) Did Anne Hutchinson preach that salvation was through obeying the laws of the church leaders and not by God's grace?

5) New Hampshire territory was originally part of what larger colony?

6) What present-day state was a gift from The Duke of York to his friends Lord John Berkeley and Sir George Carteret? (BONUS: Who got which part?)

7) True or False: William Penn settled Pennsylvania to give the Society of Friends a place to live.

8) What was the first colony to recognize the slavery of "lawful" captives?

9) Who, writing as Richard Saunders, shared his great wit and intellect in Poor Richard's Almanack?

10) True or False: King William's War did not resolve anything.

1) True
2) Tobacco
3) a
4) No. According to her, it was the other way around.
5) Massachusetts Bay
6) New Jersey; Berkeley received the West New Jersey area, and Carteret got East New Jersey.
7) True
8) Massachusetts
9) Benjamin Franklin
10) TruE (That's why there were three more wars right after that.)

ANSWERS:

THE FIRST CONTINENTAL CONGRESS

The Continental Congress was an inter-colonial assembly of fifty-six delegates from twelve colonies (Georgia did not attend). It was originally convened to discuss what response they could put forth to answer the Intolerable Acts, which the British Parliament had earlier enacted in retaliation for the Boston Tea Party.

- Met on September 5, 1774, in Carpenter's Hall in Philadelphia.

- Unanimously elected Virginia delegate Peyton Randolph as assembly president.

- Issued a petition to King George III, the Declaration of Rights and Grievances, requesting to restore harmony between Britain and the colonies.

- Called for the colonies to boycott trade with Britain per the Continental Association agreement.

- Evolved into the actual government that directed the revolutionary war for independence from Great Britain.

- Deliberated for almost two months.

- Debated an unstable situation in Massachusetts, concluding that they would not deny the people of Massachusetts the right to defend themselves, and agreeing that other colonists would come to their aid, if necessary.

- Agreed to meet again in May 1775 for further discussion and to review King George's response to the petition.

Continental Congress Participants

The delegates who came to the Continental Congress in 1774 were part of the most remarkable assembly that had ever taken place in America. Highly recognizable participants such as John Adams, George Washington, Patrick Henry, Richard Henry Lee, John Jay, John Dickinson, Joseph Galloway, John Hancock, Samuel Adams, and many others shared their measured opinions and intelligence to begin to form our country.

DRAFTING THE DECLARATION OF INDEPENDENCE

After meeting for more than a year, the Continental Congress began to see that they were moving away from reconciliation with Britain and toward independence. The Virginia delegates, especially, were ready to create a new inter-colonial federation.

On June 7, 1776, Richard Henry Lee of Virginia offered a resolution declaring the colonies to be independent. It was composed of three parts—a declaration of independence, a call to form foreign alliances, and a plan for confederation.

The Continental Congress asked a committee to write a statement supporting the Lee Resolution for independence. Although Thomas Jefferson wrote the bulk of this statement, other committee members were John Adams, Benjamin Franklin, Robert Livingston of New York, and Roger Sherman of Connecticut.

On July 2, 1776, the Congress voted to adopt Lee's earlier resolution, saying, "these united colonies are, and of right ought to be, free and independent states." The text of Jefferson's work, the Declaration of Independence, was adopted on July 4, 1776.

What Did the Declaration of Independence Say?

The Declaration of Independence intended to tell the world exactly why the colonists had decided to separate from Great Britain. Jefferson eloquently explained that the root of all governments' control is having "the consent of the governed." Therefore, a government without this consent has no authority to rule.

The declaration itemized many specific accusations against George III's government and also listed the basic principles that the delegates felt justified a revolution:

We hold these truths to be self-evident: That all men are created equal; that they are endowed by their Creator with certain unalienable rights; that among these are life, liberty, and the pursuit of happiness.

THE PURFUIT OF HAPPINEFF?

The Declaration of Independence is a stirring bit of country-shaping genius, as poetic as it is practical. What American soul is not moved to patriotic fervor upon reading Thomas Jefferson's words, "We hold these truths to be self-evident, that all men are created equal, that they are endowed by their Creator with certain unalienable Rights, that among these are Life, Liberty and the purfuit of Happineff"?

The declaration doesn't, of course, claim the right of purfuing happineff. It's *pursuit of happiness*, but anyone who's ever looked at a copy of the original document could be excused for thinking the former.

The fault for this confusion lies with the fact that eighteenth-century printers and calligraphers had three choices for printing the nineteenth letter of the alphabet. One was the big, uppercase "S" we're still using. The other was the small, lowercase "s" that we're also still using. But there was a third choice that looked a lot like a lowercase "f." It's those little devils that have caused countless schoolchildren to become so confufed.

They Were Serious About Pursuing Happiness

The Virginia Bill of Rights drafted by statesman George Mason in June of 1776 also addressed the pursuit of happiness:

That all men are by nature equally free and independent, and have certain inherent rights, of which, when they enter into a state of society, they cannot by any compact deprive or divest their posterity; namely, the enjoyment of life and liberty, with the means of acquiring and possessing property, and pursuing and obtaining happiness and safety.

THE LIBERTY BELL

The Liberty Bell that was (supposedly) rung after the first public reading of the Declaration of Independence on July 8, 1776, was the third bell to hang in the Independence Hall tower. (We say supposedly, because some historians say the steeple was in disrepair at the time, and it was unlikely that it could have supported a bell.)

The Liberty Bell was not always called that. Originally called the State House Bell, it was ordered to commemorate the fiftieth anniversary of Pennsylvania's 1701 original constitution, which was William Penn's charter for the colony. Made in London, the first bell arrived in Philadelphia in 1752 and cracked while it was being tested. The second bell was cast in Philadelphia in April 1753 but was also defective. The third bell, made in Philadelphia, too, was hung in June of 1753.

The bell weighs 2,080 pounds. The inscription, a verse from the Bible, reads, "Proclaim Liberty Throughout All the Land unto All the Inhabitants Thereof. Leviticus xxv:x."

When British troops captured Philadelphia in 1777, patriots moved the bell to Allentown, Pennsylvania, to save it from being melted down for cannons. It was returned to Independence Hall in 1778, where it was rung every July 4 in celebration of Independence Day and on every state occasion until 1835.

According to legend, the Liberty Bell was cracked in 1835 when it was being tolled at the funeral of U.S. Supreme Court Chief Justice John Marshall. It continued to crack until, in 1846, while being tolled on Washington's birthday, the crack expanded so much that the bell will no longer ring.

Today, it is located in the Liberty Bell Center of Independence National Historical Park.

When was it first called the Liberty Bell? In the 1830s, the New York Anti-Slavery Society adopted the bell as a symbol for their cause.

CRASH COURSE
THE DECLARATION OF INDEPENDENCE

Here are a few things you didn't learn about the Declaration of Independence in high school:

Youngest signer: Edward Rutledge (26)

Oldest signer: Benjamin Franklin (70)

First signer: President of the Congress John Hancock. He was also the only signer to attach his name on July 4, 1776.

Last signer: Alleged to be Thomas McKean of Delaware, who may have signed as late as 1781.

Signing order: After Hancock, the others signed by state delegation, from upper right in one column to five other columns, from the northernmost state of New Hampshire to the southernmost state of Georgia.

Total number of signers: 56

Famous descendant: Actress Reese Witherspoon is a direct descendant of signer John Witherspoon, and considerably better-looking.

Odd Facts About the Signers

Benjamin Rush became one of America's most famous physicians. His contribution to the Lewis and Clark expedition included "Rush's Thunderbolts," which were weapons-grade laxative pills that contained mercury.

George Wythe became the first professor of law in America, then was poisoned by a grandnephew.

Robert Morris founded The Bank of North America and was fabulously wealthy, but lost his fortune to land speculation and died in poverty.

Robert Treat Paine was so contrary that while serving in the Continental Congress, he became known as the "Objection Maker."

LEE RESOLUTION

If accuracy, and not popular belief, were the order of the day, America would celebrate its independence from England on July 2. No less an authority than John Adams once wrote,

> The second day of July, 1776, will be the most memorable epoch in the history of America. I am apt to believe that it will be celebrated by succeeding generations as the great anniversary festival. It ought to be commemorated as the day of deliverance, by solemn acts of devotion to God Almighty. It ought to be solemnized with pomp and parade, with shows, games, sports, guns, bells, bonfires, and illuminations, from one end of this continent to the other, from this time forward forever more.

Adams was many things, but he was no prophet, as the date of the adoption of the Lee Resolution has long since paled in comparison to July 4.

The story of the Lee Resolution begins on June 7, 1776, when Virginian Richard Henry Lee introduced a resolution to the Second Continental Congress that proposed independence for the colonies. Lee's resolution was composed of three parts—a declaration of independence, a call to form foreign alliances and a plan for confederation.

After a standard amount of government inertia was overcome, the Congress adopted Lee's declaration on July 2. Delaware's Caesar Rodney cast the deciding vote after riding eighty miles on horseback through a thunderstorm to Philadelphia.

He didn't know it at the time, but Rodney's action would eventually be commemorated by having his—and his horse's—image cast on the Delaware state quarter in 1999. Sadly, the names of Rodney's horse —he used two—are lost to history.

PATRICK HENRY: A RADICAL PATRIOT

Virginia lawyer Patrick Henry was a hothead and a radical, albeit an eloquent one. Through his participation in founding the new country of the United States of America, Patrick Henry left us with some memorable —and still quite quotable—declarations of his own.

Protesting the Stamp Act. In 1765, lawyer Henry said out loud what many were thinking when he presented seven resolutions to the Virginia House of Burgesses condemning the act. Standing up in front of the assembly, he demanded that the king recognize the rights of all citizens.

Arguing against taxation without representation, Henry's resolutions declared that only the colonial legislatures could enact taxes on the colonies, and he said, "Caesar had his Brutus, Charles the First his Cromwell, and George the Third ... may profit by their example."

The more conservative members of the House of Burgesses warned that Henry's statements could be misunderstood as treason. Henry replied, "If this be treason, make the most of it." (Later, when his remarks were printed in Boston and New York newspapers, readers were shocked by his radical statements).

The Committee of Correspondence. In 1773, Patrick Henry was instrumental in forming Virginia's Committee of Correspondence, which communicated with similar committees throughout the colonies to exchange information and opinions about complaints against the British.

The First Continental Congress. Henry was a Virginia delegate in 1774, when he urged the colonists to work together as a collective. Henry and his radical cronies at The First Continental Congress demanded the most compromise from Britain.

The Virginia Convention in 1775. Here, he gained support for armed resistance to the British. It was at this assembly in Richmond where Henry gave his speech that concluded with the now-historic words, "I know not what course others may take, but as for me, give me liberty, or give me death!"

Second Continental Congress of 1775. Henry was on his way to the Congress assembly when he found out that Virginia's governor seized the colony's supply of gunpowder and ammunition. (Remember, by the time the Second Continental Congress met in May 1775, the first shots of the Revolutionary War had already been fired in Lexington and Concord.) Henry mustered the militia, marched on Williamsburg, forced the governor to return the supplies, then headed to Philadelphia.

Governor of Virginia. In 1776 Henry was elected governor of Virginia for one year. He was reelected from 1784 to 1786. While in office, Henry helped draft the Virginia constitution.

The Constitution. At first, Henry was against approving the new federal Constitution, because he felt like it took away rights from the states and individuals. As you already know, the Constitution was ratified anyway. Adding the Bill of Rights to the Constitution helped him accept the role of the federal government after that.

The Rest of the Story. In 1790, Henry retired from public life and focused on his law practice. But, in 1799, President George Washington convinced him to run for the Virginia legislature. Henry campaigned and won the election as a Federalist—the party supporting a strong federal government—on a platform urging national unity. However, he died at home, before he could take his seat in the legislature.

The Quotable Patrick Henry

Although "give me liberty, or give me death" may be one of the best quotes of American history, Henry said many other things worth repeating. Take this catchy quote for example:

"I have but one lamp by which my feet are guided; and that is the lamp of experience. I know of no way of judging the future but by the past."

1776

It's doubtful any of America's founders anticipated just how blazingly apt an Independence Day celebrated on July 4 would be, but the summer date is perfect for all-American activities like barbecues, overeating, and taking off from work. But America's July 4, 1776, announcement that it was now its own country was little more than a piece of paper. The freedom that paper proclaimed still had to be won on the battlefield.

Great Britain was far less enthusiastic about freeing one of its trans-Atlantic cash cows than the cow was, and the battle for America's independence lasted far beyond that hot day in Philadelphia.

Here are a few events that took place after the founders signed that paper:

- In the Battle of Trenton, New Jersey (December 26, 1776), George Washington defeated a Hessian Brigade after crossing the Delaware River.

- Washington and his Continental Army wintered at Valley Forge, Pennsylvania, in the winter of 1777-78.

- France and the Continental Congress signed a treaty that sent French troops and supplies to America.

- Lord Charles Cornwallis became commander of British forces in the South on June 5, 1780.

- Cornwallis surrendered his forces on October 19, 1781.

- The Treaty of Paris, in which Great Britain recognized U.S. independence, was drawn up on September 3, 1783.

And even that date wasn't the official end of the war. The treaty still had to be ratified by the upstart country. Communication and transportation being considerably slower then than now, the U.S. ratification didn't take place until January 14, 1784. But who'd want to celebrate an Independence Day on January 14?

HENRY KNOX, FIRST SECRETARY OF WAR

Henry Knox, an American bookseller-turned-military leader, played a key part in forcing the British out of Boston in 1776 and was rewarded with a position in George Washington's first Cabinet.

Earlier, in May 1775, Ethan Allen had captured Fort Ticonderoga in New York from the British. This was important because, with the fort, he captured the British's bronze and cast-iron cannons.

When George Washington heard about the artillery, he knew he needed it to get British troops out of Boston. In February 1776, Washington sent Henry Knox, who had military experience from Bunker Hill to get the cannons.

Knox's mission was easier said than done: transporting the cannons by oxen teams over the Berkshire Mountains during winter's coldest month. But, Knox did haul the artillery more than two hundred miles from Ticonderoga to Dorchester Heights, overlooking Boston. Soon, the British in Boston realized they were within range of some powerful weapons and were forced to evacuate in March of 1776.

In 1790, Knox organized a scouting expedition of the Missouri River territory in order to gain reliable data on the Missouri River system for strategic planning. He sent out a small party, who, upon reaching the Mississippi River, realized they had drastically underestimated the trip's scope. They turned back before they even crossed the river.

Knox's Political Achievements

- *1776:* Named brigadier general by George Washington and placed in charge of the American army's artillery.
- *1781:* Promoted to major general.
- *1782–1784:* Commanded the West Point fortress.
- *1785:* Named secretary of war under the Articles of Confederation.
- *1789:* Named first secretary of war under the U.S. Constitution.

CRASH COURSE
DEFINING BATTLES OF
THE REVOLUTIONARY WAR

In the first years of the war, Washington's troops performed true to their hurried training and home-made equipment. Early skirmishes all seemed to end in defeat. A victory at Saratoga at the close of 1777 proved the turning point of the Revolutionary War.

- **1776, Battle for New York City.** Washington's forces were forced to retreat by the British, who chased them across New Jersey. The American forces settled safely on the Pennsylvania side of the Delaware River, and British troops occupied New York.

- **1777, Battle of Brandywine Creek, Pennsylvania.** In September, the British again routed Washington's forces, this time outside Philadelphia. British troops had occupied the city by the end of the year.

- **1777, Battle of Saratoga, New York.** In October, the British planned to cut off New England from the other colonies. But American forces under Horatio Gates and Benedict Arnold attacked the British troops, who surrendered.

- **1777-1778, Valley Forge, Pennsylvania.** After defeat in Philadelphia, Washington's demoralized troops suffered through a severe winter camped at Valley Forge. Washington chose the site because it was close enough to head off any British attacks on the Congress, meeting at nearby York, Pennsylvania, and because the landscape was easy to defend from attack. Bare countryside and a lack of supplies meant the men did not have enough shelter, food, or clothing, and many died.

- **1778, Alliance with France.** After the Battle of Saratoga, France began to see how it could really get under the skin of its rival, Britain, by siding with the colonists. France partnered with the Americans, and British troops withdrew from Philadelphia.

- **1778-1779, Illinois.** George Rogers Clark led the Patriots in capturing British forts throughout Illinois country to gain control of the Ohio Territory.

- **1780, Charleston, South Carolina.** A British fleet landed on the coast to besiege Charleston. After three months of bombardment, American forces surrendered the city.

- **1781, Guilford Courthouse, North Carolina.** British forces caused the American militia to retreat, but only after losing more than one-fourth of their troops.

- **1781, Yorktown, Virginia.** The last major battle of the Revolutionary War was fought on the shores of the Chesapeake Bay. With French support, Washington forced the surrender of General Charles Cornwallis's large British army.

- **1783, Treaty of Paris.** Seeing that the war was going to continue to drag on and cost even more money, British Parliament was ready to give up after the defeat at Yorktown.

BATTLE OF QUEBEC, VERSION 2.0

Canada is more than just the home of William Shatner, or that country with the beavers on its currency, or even that country where they bowl on ice—using brooms—and call it curling. It's also the site of a major battle in the American Revolution. It might not be as famous as Yorktown or Bunker Hill, but what it lacks in notoriety it makes up for in quirkiness.

The fact that a battle in the American Revolution was fought in Canada is strange, of course. But even stranger is that the battle in question shares a name with another battle in another American war. There's the Battle of Quebec of 1759, which took place during the French and Indian War. Then there's the Battle of Quebec, 1775 model, which took place during the Revolution.

The second Battle of Quebec began on the last day of the year in 1775. American soldiers attempted to capture Quebec and get French Canadian support for the Revolutionary War. (Exactly how capturing a Canadian city was supposed to make the Canadians sympathetic is a question lost to the ages.) Under Richard Montgomery and Benedict Arnold's command, and during a fierce blizzard, American forces attacked the city. Montgomery was killed, and the attackers were repelled. The British and Canadian casualties were around twenty. American casualties topped four hundred, including deaths and those captured.

Arnold withdrew his forces and besieged the city, although his siege had little effect. While ineffective, Arnold was tenacious. He didn't leave Canada until June 18, 1776.

Washington Crossing the Delaware

We've seen the paintings, we've seen the cartoon, so what's the real story? After being chased out of New York City on Christmas night 1776, Washington secretly re-crossed the Delaware River and surprised the sleeping, hung-over British troops at Trenton, New Jersey. While he did win the skirmish and that did help raise morale with the American army, the victory did not have any strategic significance.

BENEDICT ARNOLD

Timing, in comedy as in life, is everything. Benedict Arnold was at one time a hero of the American Revolution. But Arnold had the misfortune of outliving his valor, so what was a life meant for enshrinement instead became synonymous with treachery.

Arnold was born Benedict Arnold IV in Norwich, Connecticut, in 1741. His great-grandfather, Benedict Arnold I, had served as governor of Rhode Island. Young Arnold had success as a druggist and merchant, but it was in the military that he became famous, and then infamous.

In 1775, Ethan Allen and Arnold took the British installation at Fort Ticonderoga, New York, located on Lake Champlain. Arnold was a militia captain then, and his success there led to his being placed in charge of American forces in the area. Arnold was shot in the left leg at Saratoga, New York, in 1777, and a monument to Arnold's leg is now located at the Saratoga National Historic Park. Arnold would walk with a limp the rest of his life as a result of the wound.

Exactly what turned Arnold from patriot to traitor is still being debated, but it's theorized that he was bitter from his wound, in financial difficulty, in legal difficulty (he was court-martialed over misdemeanors in 1779), and generally disenchanted with the direction the war had taken. Whatever the reason, he offered to turn West Point over to the British in return for a commission and money. But when spy John André was captured, the plot was discovered and Arnold fled West Point to England. Arnold would return to lead British raids on American forces in 1781.

Arnold spent the rest of his days in exile in Canada and Great Britain. He died in England in 1801.

WOMEN IN WAR

During the Revolutionary War, soldiers depended on their women's support. Their most important contribution was maintaining life at home. As in other wars, while the men were away fighting, women ran the family farms and businesses. They also provided most of the food and clothing to the war effort.

Some soldiers' wives followed their men to the war camps and worked as cooks, washed their laundry, and nursed wounded soldiers. In a few instances, women actually fought in battle. They had watched the men do their drills enough times that they undoubtedly learned the drills, too.

Mary McCauley carried pitchers of water to her husband and other thirsty soldiers during the Battle of Monmouth and so was called "Molly Pitcher." Some legends also say that when her husband was overcome by heat, she fought in his place.

Margaret Corbin took charge of loading and firing a cannon by herself when her husband was killed at Fort Washington, New York. She was seriously wounded there herself when her arm was almost severed and her chest and jaw were lacerated by grapeshot.

Deborah Sampson enlisted in a Massachusetts regiment as a man named Robert Shurtleff. At 5 foot 7 inches with a slender frame, she could pass for a "boy" too young to grow facial hair. Reports show that "Robert Shurtleff" performed as well as any other man. Sampson was wounded in a battle near Tarrytown, New York, but treated herself so that her secret would remain hidden.

Abigail Adams wrote letters to her husband John as he traveled in his patriotic duties. In these letters, she asked him to include women's rights in the declarations being made for human rights: "I desire you would remember the ladies and be more generous and favorable to them than your ancestors."

REDCOATS

Given that one of the main goals of war isn't, as George C. Scott put it in the opening speech of "Patton," to die for one's country but to make the other man die for his (language slightly cleaned up for family-friendliness), it might seem strange that British Revolutionary War forces are so often depicted as wearing red coats. The eye-catching color red isn't generally considered the first choice in battlefield clothing. Exactly why and to what extent the British wore "Redcoats" is a combination of fact, fiction, and laziness.

The first Redcoat perception, that the color was chosen because it didn't show the blood from a wound, makes for a good story but doesn't pass muster. Blood might not show up as clearly on red as it does white, but it does show up, as any mother who's washed a football-scarred red jersey can attest.

In addition, the Redcoats of modern pop culture probably didn't resemble the actual historical Redcoats. Cloth-dying and clothes-washing technology weren't very advanced in the 1700s, so bright colors faded much quicker. Hardly any Revolutionary War-era battlefields had a decent laundromat, so clothes were quickly dirtied and rarely washed.

Finally, for the British government, perhaps the most attractive aspect of the red uniforms was the fact that, as Stephen Brumwell put it in his *Paths of Glory: The Life and Death of General James Wolfe*, "The redcoats were a mixture of volunteers, motivated by economic hardship or a craving for change and adventure, and conscripts swept up by Britain's emergency wartime Press Acts." Given the sometimes fleeting valor of volunteers and conscripts, the red coats provided an eye-catching means of identifying deserters.

HESSIANS

In the 1950 Warner Brothers® cartoon "Bunker Hill Bunny," Yosemite Sam squares off against Bugs Bunny in a Revolutionary War-era battle. (Yes, this is a history book that refers to cartoons. You're reading it in the bathroom. Consider us even.) Bugs is of course Bugs, but Sam isn't Yosemite Sam, he's Sam von Schmamm the Hessian, attacking Bugs' fort in the Battle of Bagel Heights.

And Hessians are referenced elsewhere, including Washington Irving's "The Legend of Sleepy Hollow." The Headless Horseman who torments Ichabod Crane is the ghost of a Hessian trooper. Christopher Walken played the Hessian trooper in Tim Burton's 1999 film "Sleepy Hollow," albeit without a cowbell.

But just what was a Hessian? Sam's nom de cartoon is one clue. The "von" in his name is indicative of German origin, as in Wernher von Braun. Hessians derived their name from the west-central German state of Hesse (although what we now call Germany didn't exist until 1871, but that's a story for another book). Not all Hessians were actually from Hesse, but some 12,000 of the 30,000 total were, and the name stuck.

These particular Hessians ended up in America because some German rulers saw the money in hiring out conscripted soldiers to warring countries, and Great Britain just happened to be fighting a bunch of upstarts calling themselves the United States. King George III sent money to the German rulers, the rulers sent conscripts to fight for the British, and eventually, Warner Brothers got to make their cartoon.

The Headless Hessian

In Washington Irving's story "The Legend of Sleepy Hollow," the spectral figure who terrorizes the townfolk is described as "the ghost of a Hessian trooper, whose head had been carried away by a cannonball, in some nameless battle during the Revolutionary War."

EFFECTS OF THE REVOLUTIONARY WAR ON SOCIETY

The ideas of the Revolution slowly became reflected in the thoughts and attitudes of the common people.

- **Aristocratic Titles:** State constitutions and laws did not provide for titles of nobility. No legislature was given the power to grant titles, and no court recognized the long-time right of the first-born son to inherit his parents' property (called *primogeniture*). Also, Loyalists, who would have been most likely to hold onto their Old World traditions, had their large estates confiscated by patriots during the war, so they couldn't even hand down land to their children if they had wanted to.

   (You'll recall that the Treaty of Paris provided for the return of Loyalists' lands. But, the Articles of Confederation had no power to enforce those terms. To make it even harder to return the property, many confiscated estates had been subdivided and sold to raise money for the war.)

- **Church and State:** After the Revolutionary War, there was a general movement toward religious freedom. Most states agreed on separation of church and state; that means they refused to financially support any religious group. The Anglican Church of Great Britain all but disappeared in the South when it lost states' financial support.

- **Economy:** During the war, American manufacturing suffered disruption, and British subsidies on certain American goods were lost. After the Treaty of Paris, Americans found themselves digging out of a commercial recession. Low-priced British goods flooded the markets. To help local artisans, New England states implemented a tax on imported manufactured goods.

- **Women:** Women supported the war effort in various ways, from traveling with the troops to cook for and nurse them, to running the farms and businesses left behind when the men went to war. Even so, they were not granted individual rights and remained a second-class status.

CRASH COURSE

THE ARTICLES OF CONFEDERATION

Having declared independence in 1776, the Continental Congress delegates realized they needed a more formal union of the states. In November 1777 Congress adopted the Articles of Confederation establishing the United States of America. All the states of the Continental Congress ratified them by March 1781.

The Articles allowed the Patriots to win the war and set up policies for surveying western lands and creating new states. They gave Congress the power to wage war, make treaties, send diplomatic representatives, and borrow money.

However, they protected individual states' powers instead of supporting a central government. From the beginning, it was clear that the central government created under the Articles was too weak:

- Congress was a single legislative body, with neither executive nor judiciary.

- Each state had a single vote.

- There was no way to enforce national laws.

- Congress couldn't collect taxes, but requested funds from the states.

- Congress had no authority over individual American citizens.

- Article amendments required unanimous approval; laws required nine votes out of thirteen.

Because the central government was limited from raising funds, a problem resulted in paying war debts. This affected foreign policy, because other countries could not respect a country that couldn't pay its debts.

DRAFTING THE CONSTITUTION

In May 1787, Congress called a convention of all thirteen states to revise the Articles of Confederation. Rhode Island did not send any delegates. The delegates from the other states voted to hold the meetings in secret, then publicize their conclusions. George Washington was unanimously elected chairperson.

After settling the question of whether to "fix" the Articles of Confederation or draft an entirely new document, James Madison, Alexander Hamilton, Gouverneur Morris, and John Dickinson were selected to write the specifics of the Constitution.

Popular opinion distrusted the government's potential for abusing power, so the drafters wanted to ensure that the new document was based on a system of checks and balances. (Refresher from government class: this means one branch of government has the power to check the other branches.)

In September 1787, convention delegates completed a draft to send to each state to ratify, or approve, requiring authorization from nine of the thirteen states to adopt the new Constitution.

Delaware was the first state to approve the Constitution on December 7, 1787. Six months later, New Hampshire was the ninth state to ratify it, officially establishing the new government. Rhode Island was the thirteenth, and last, state to adopt the Constitution on May 29, 1790.

What Took So Long?

Did you catch the part where the Articles were adopted in 1777 but weren't ratified until 1781? The holdup centered around the Mississippi River Valley territories. At that time, based on the colonies' original charters, seven states claimed their territories extended all the way west. Six states which did not border free land called "foul." Maryland refused to ratify the Articles until the seven states transferred their western claims to the new government. In 1777, Virginia (with the largest land claim) agreed, followed by New York and Connecticut in 1778.

ISSUES AND RESOLUTIONS IN DRAFTING THE CONSTITUTION

Issue: Representation

Larger states argued for a proportional number of representatives by size, while smaller states argued for an equal number per state.

Resolutions 1 & 2 (Rejected): The Virginia Plan and The New Jersey Plan

The Virginia Plan of three government branches favored the large states by recommending basing legislative representation on population. William Paterson offered the New Jersey Plan supporting three branches without one single executive, and favoring small states, giving each state one equal vote.

Resolution 3 (Accepted): The Connecticut Plan

Delegates agreed on the Great Compromise, which suggested a two-house Congress. In the Senate, each state was given equal representation; in the House of Representatives, each state was represented according to population size.

Issue: Slavery

Northern and southern states disagreed on allowing slavery and how to count slaves in the state populations.

Resolution: Three-Fifths Compromise

Delegates arrived at a Three-Fifths Compromise, counting each slave as three-fifths of a person to determine state population. They also agreed that the Constitution would guarantee that slaves could continue to be imported until 1808, when Congress could vote to abolish slavery.

Issue: Commerce

Northern and southern states disagreed on the central government regulating interstate commerce and foreign trade taxes.

Resolution: Commercial Compromise
Congress could regulate interstate and foreign commerce and tax foreign imports, but could not tax exports (such as tobacco and rice produced in the south).

Issue: The President
Delegates disagreed on the president's term and how to elect him.

Resolution: Limited Term
The delegates limited the presidential term to four years in office, and gave him power to veto Congress's acts. They established an electoral college giving each state a number of votes equal to their representatives plus senators.

Order of State Ratification of the Constitution

Delaware – December 7, 1787
Pennsylvania – December 12, 1787
New Jersey – December 18, 1787
Georgia – January 2, 1788
Connecticut – January 9, 1788
Massachusetts – February 6, 1788
Maryland – April 28, 1788
South Carolina – May 23, 1788
New Hampshire – June 21, 1788
Virginia – June 25, 1788
New York – July 26, 1788
North Carolina – November 21, 1789
Rhode Island – May 29, 1790

MARTHA WASHINGTON

Her husband might have been the "Father of His Country," but Martha Washington was a troubled spouse of that father. Of her service as wife of America's first president, Martha once wrote to a niece, saying, "I think I am more like a state prisoner than anything else, there is certain bounds set for me which I must not depart from."

Martha was born Martha Dandridge near Williamsburg, Virginia, on June 2, 1731. She married wealthy Virginia planter Daniel Parke Custis on May 15, 1750, then moved to Custis' 17,000-acre plantation. Prophetically, the plantation was known as White House Plantation.

The couple would have four children, but only two, John (Jacky) Parke Custis and Martha (Patsy) Parke Custis, would survive childhood. Custis died in 1757, possibly of a fever, and Martha became a very rich young widow.

A chance meeting with a young colonel named George Washington at a Williamsburg cotillion led to a marriage between the two on January 6, 1759.

George's success on the battlefield and in politics led him to the White House, and Martha followed, although she wasn't all that happy about the situation, as her remark to her niece shows. Still, she kept her spirits up, writing to writer and playwright Mercy Otis Warren, "I am still determined to be cheerful and happy, in whatever situation I may be; for I have also learned from experience that the greater part of our happiness or misery depends upon our dispositions, and not upon our circumstances."

After George's term as president ended in 1797, he and Martha returned to Mount Vernon. Two years later, George died. Three years later, Martha followed him in death. Both are buried at Mount Vernon, Virginia.

EDMUND JENNINGS RANDOLPH AND THE VIRGINIA PLAN

American founding father and Virginia governor Edmund Jennings Randolph played a leading role in the federal Constitutional Convention. As the head of the Virginia delegation to the Constitutional Convention in 1787, he submitted the famous Virginia Plan. Some called it the Randolph Resolutions, but the ideas were based on Alexander Hamilton's research, works, and writings.

The Virginia Plan proposed a government of three branches: executive, judicial, and legislative. The Plan provided for a legislature with two houses: a House of Representatives elected by the people and a Senate elected by a House of Representatives. The number of seats in each would be determined by state population. The Plan proposed a three-member executive council (instead of the one president we have today).

When this plan was rejected, Randolph was first against the final draft of the Constitution. But, by 1788, he urged his state to ratify the Constitution for national unity.

Edmund Jennings Randolph's Political Career

- *1775:* Aide-de-camp (or *confidential assistant*) to Continental Army commander-in-chief George Washington
- *1776:* Member of the Virginia Constitutional Convention
- *1776-1786:* Virginia state attorney general
- *1779-1782:* Member of the Continental Congress
- *1786-1788:* Governor of Virginia
- *1789-1794:* U.S. attorney general
- *1794:* Succeeded Thomas Jefferson as Secretary of State
- *1807:* Chief Counsel for Aaron Burr during his trial for treason

CRASH COURSE
THE FEDERALIST PAPERS

What You Need to Know Before Reading This: Once a Constitution was drafted in 1787, it was delivered to the delegates from each state to be approved. This was not simply a matter of formality; the delegates were split between those who favored a strong central government (called Federalists) and those who were afraid that a strong central government would take away each individual state's rights that had been so hard fought for during the Revolution (called Anti-Federalists).

Newspaper and pamphlet readers in New York and Virginia began to see essays supporting a strong central government that would be created when the U.S. Constitution was ratified (or *approved*). Clearly written by an anonymous source, at first the series of essays was signed "A Citizen of New York." Later, the pen name changed to "Publius."

A total of eighty-five essays were written promoting ratification of the Constitution. In 1788, the essays were collected into a two-volume set of books called *The Federalist*. The editor of the book, statesman Alexander Hamilton, turned out to be one of three authors writing under the "Publius" pseudonym. The other two contributors were James Madison and John Jay.

The Federalist is considered a brilliant set of essays on political theory and a contemporary account of the intentions of those who wrote and ratified the U.S. Constitution. In controversial cases, federal judges including those of the U.S. Supreme Court often refer to them for incisive and authoritative interpretations of the Constitution.

Why Did They Choose Publius?

Statesman Publius Valerius Publicola was one of the founders of the Roman Republic in 509 BC. His name Publicola meant friend of the people.

ANTI-FEDERALISTS AND
THEIR PAPERS

It's not politics if there's not two disputations of every theory, tenet, and law, and the Federalist Papers generated their own share of controversy as well as an ensuing series of papers against them. No credit for guessing that these were called the Anti-Federalist Papers. They're not as well-known as the Federalist Papers, but they did play a part in shaping the new country.

Simply put, the Anti-Federalist Papers argued against ratification of the Constitution. The Anti-federalists feared a strong central government, and didn't feel that the Constitution would protect them from such a government taking power. But that may be putting it too simply. As Herbert Storing wrote in his *What the Anti-Federalists Were for: The Political Thought of the Opponents of the Constitution*, the positions of the Anti-Federalists were complex.

> It would be difficult to find a single point about which *all* of the Anti-Federalists agreed. They did not, finally, even agree unanimously in opposing the adoption of the Constitution. Many favored adoption if amendments could be secured; and others finally accepted the Constitution, even without a guarantee of amendment, as the best of the available choices. There is in fact no hard and fast way of even identifying 'Anti-Federalists.'

So the Anti-Federalists clashed with the Federalists, except when they didn't. No wonder they're not that well-known.

EXTRA CREDIT: Most of the authors of the Anti-Federalist Papers wrote under pseudonyms. Major contributors included Cato (probably George Clinton), Brutus (Robert Yates), Centinel (Samuel Bryan), and the Federal Farmer (either Melancton Smith, Richard Henry Lee, or Mercy Otis Warren). The Anti-Federalist Papers also included speeches by Patrick Henry and Melancton Smith.

DOCTOR'S MOB RIOT

You'd think grave-robbers would be surreptitious about their activities, but you'd be wrong. A ghoulish and spectacularly ill-timed remark from a grave-robbing medical student led to America's first riot and the death of several.

Medical science wasn't as antiseptic or discreet then as it is now, particularly when it came to securing cadavers for medical research. Would-be physicians, ironically known as "resurrectionists," sometimes appropriated freshly dead subjects from their graves. A young boy peeked into a dissecting room at New York Hospital April. 13, 1788 and saw some resurrectionists at work. Supposedly, John Hicks Jr., one of the dissectors, spied the boy, waved a severed arm at him and said, "It's your mother's! Go away or I'll hit you with it!"

The medical student probably didn't know it, but the young boy's mother had in fact recently died. The boy ran home and began telling of his experience. Soon, a mob had formed and made its way to Trinity Church Yard, where they found the mother's grave opened and empty. Inflamed by the ghoulish discovery, the mob began rampaging through town, looking for Hicks, ransacking doctors' houses looking for the woman's body and destroyed the anatomy lab at the hospital.

Many of the town's doctors sought safety in the city jail, which was surrounded by rioters. Governor George Clinton ordered militia men to fire on the mob, and from five to eight men were killed, depending on the account.

Firing on the Doctor's Mob

According to stories, American Revolution leader Baron Friedrich von Steuben begged Governor Clinton not to order fire, hoping to calm the mob with words, not bullets. Just then angry rioters threw bricks, one of which hit Steuben's head.

The baron's tune immediately changed. "Fire, Clinton, fire!" he shouted, and so the order went out.

ALEXANDER HAMILTON

Alexander Hamilton is best known for his insistence on a strong central government to develop a powerful American nation. In fact, he delivered a six-hour speech during the Constitutional Convention arguing his point, campaigning for a single chief executive who would serve for life, as well as life terms for members of the Senate.

A brilliant New York lawyer, Alexander Hamilton was one of the three contributing authors to *The Federalist* Papers and was key in establishing the first National Bank.

Hamilton advocated interpreting the "implied powers" of the Constitution with a broad stroke to include whatever was "necessary and proper" to carry out the government's purposes. This theory of implied powers is still used today—and often—to justify occasionally extending federal authority. It has also been cited in many U.S. Supreme Court decisions.

Alexander Hamilton's Political Career

- *1777:* Personal secretary to General George Washington during the Revolutionary War
- *1781:* Commanded a New York light infantry regiment at the Battle of Yorktown
- *1782-1783:* Served in the Continental Congress
- *1787-1788:* Contributed to *The Federalist* in support of ratifying the Constitution
- *1789:* Appointed first secretary of the treasury under George Washington. In this position, Hamilton set about reorganizing the U.S. financial system. He wanted to strengthen the new government's powers by consolidating American debt, then creating a national bank to manage the debt and enacting federal taxes to pay for it
- *1793:* Persuaded Washington to adopt a neutrality policy after the outbreak of war in Europe
- *1795:* Returned to practicing law, to become a prominent lawyer in New York City
- *1798:* Appointed inspector general of the army by John Adams

THE DUEL WITH AARON BURR

In the presidential election of 1800, Thomas Jefferson and Aaron Burr tied for votes from the electoral college. The vote went to the House of Representatives to decide, and Hamilton—believing Burr to be a loose cannon—campaigned enthusiastically for Jefferson, who won.

Then, by 1804, Aaron Burr had formed a secret plot to unite the northern states and secede from the United States. A major point in his plot was to be elected governor of New York. However, Alexander Hamilton again campaigned strongly against Burr in the election, and he did not win.

Burr then overheard an insulting remark that Hamilton made about him, and they got into a heated discussion. This further led to Burr's challenging Hamilton to a duel. Hamilton accepted. On July 11, 1804, they met near Weehawken, New Jersey, where Hamilton was mortally wounded and died the next day.

A National Bank

"The Bank of the United States" sounds awfully close to today's "Bank of America,®" but they're not quite the same thing.

Alexander Hamilton used his "implied powers" argument to create a National Bank, which was chartered by Congress and President Washington in 1791. The Bank of the United States was privately owned. A major shareholder, the government owned 20 percent of the stock and appointed one-fifth of the directors. The First Bank could print paper currency and use federal deposits to stimulate business.

Hamilton's economic policy moved the United States toward becoming a commercial rather than an agricultural nation.

AARON BURR'S PRIDE
AND DOWNFALL

Like Benedict Arnold, Aaron Burr was a Revolutionary War hero who ended up besmirching his reputation. In Arnold's case, the thoughts of British money and a British military commission were too much, and he offered to turn over West Point to the British. Greed did him in. Burr's downfall was pride, both his own and that of Alexander Hamilton, whom he faced in a duel. Neither Hamilton nor Burr's political career survived the meeting.

To modern sensibilities, Burr and Hamilton were hardly candidates to become violent enemies. Both fought with distinction in the Revolutionary War, Burr at the Battle of Quebec and Hamilton at Yorktown. Both served high political positions in Washington. Burr was vice president under Thomas Jefferson (1801-05), while Hamilton was the first secretary of the treasury (1789-95). And the two even worked at the same law practice in New York.

But the seeds for the violent clash were planted in 1800. In the presidential election, Burr tied with Jefferson. Both won seventy-three Electoral College votes. The responsibility of choosing a president then fell to the House of Representatives, where Burr met opposition from Hamilton, among others. After thirty-six ballots, Jefferson was elected president. Burr later lost the 1804 election for New York governor. He blamed Hamilton for this loss, as well as his loss for president.

Burr was driven to violence when comments critical of him, made by Hamilton at a political dinner, were published in a New York newspaper. Burr demanded Hamilton recant those and other statements critical of Burr. Hamilton refused, and Burr challenged him to a duel. The two met in Weehawken, New Jersey, on July 11, 1804. Hamilton was mortally wounded and died the next day. Burr was unharmed, although his political career was over. After his term as vice president was over, he never again held public office.

CRASH COURSE
JOHN JAY OF NEW YORK

- Elected as one of the fifty-five delegates to the First Continental Congress in 1774 and again in 1775.
- Chaired the convention which drafted the first constitution of New York.
- Appointed New York State Chief Justice in 1777.
- Chosen president of the Continental Congress in 1778.
- Negotiated the Treaty of Paris of 1783 with Great Britain that ended the American Revolution.
- Wrote a series of papers, along with James Madison and Alexander Hamilton, under the anonymous pseudonym Publius in support of a strong national government and urging adoption of the Constitution. These essays were published as the *Federalist Papers*.
- Appointed first Chief Justice of the U.S. Supreme Court by President George Washington in 1789. He served until 1795.
- From 1794 to 1795, he negotiated an agreement with Britain known as Jay's Treaty.

Jay's Treaty (1794)

In 1794, George Washington sent Supreme Court Chief Justice John Jay on a mission to Britain to discuss their nasty practice of searching and seizing American ships and impressing (or kidnapping) American sailors into the British navy. At the time, the United States had no navy to speak of, so Jay didn't have much in the way of bargaining tools. After spending almost a year in negotiation, Jay brought back a treaty in which Britain agreed to give up its posts in the Northwest Territory. But the treaty didn't mention anything about seizures of American merchant ships. Understandably, Britain's failure to address the problem angered the Senate, and the Jay Treaty was very unpopular.

THE FIRST BATTLES OF THE REVOLUTIONARY WAR

Battle of Lexington and Concord

- The first serious engagement of the American Revolution was fought in Concord, Massachusetts, on April 19, 1775.
- After Paul Revere's famous "midnight ride," 300 to 400 minutemen were prepared to meet the British.
- About 700 British soldiers marched to Concord with orders to capture and destroy the colonists' arms and ammunition.
- The minutemen positioned themselves on the farther side of the North Bridge over the Concord River and held the British advance.
- The British troops fell back and retreated, being harassed by the colonial militia through Lexington and all the way to Charlestown.
- Casualties were small: not more than 270 British and fewer than a a hundred Americans.
- The battle was significant in demonstrating the Americans' grit and fighting power.

Battle of Bunker Hill

- The first large-scale engagement was fought in Charlestown, Massachusetts, on June 17, 1775.
- The British sought possession of Bunker Hill and Breed's Hill overlooking Boston Harbor. About 1,500 American troops faced about 2,200 British redcoats.
- The American commander allegedly ordered: "Don't fire until you see the whites of their eyes."
- The Americans did just that, waiting until the British had advanced almost to the base of the hill, and then opened fire.
- The British suffered severe losses and retreated.
- On a second British charge, they suffered more losses.
- The American troops ran out of ammunition and had to withdraw during the third British charge. The British captured both hills.
- Casualties were disproportionate: 1,000 British and 400 American losses.

The Second Continental Congress

By the time the Second Continental Congress met in May 1775, the first shots of the Revolutionary War had already been fired. Faced with the reality of war, the delegates debated what to do. Some favored reconciliation with Britain by reaffirming Parliament's rights to regulate trade; these delegates worried that a few hot-headed radicals were forcing their actions on the whole.

The congress adopted John Dickinson's "Olive Branch Petition" urging the British to compromise. King George refused to accept the petition, and the possibility of reconciliation was over. As fighting had already begun, the delegates realized that the time for compromise had passed and what they urgently needed was a military defense plan.

- The Congress had no basis in law and its delegates were uncertain about their functions.
- Under crisis, delegates formed committees and assumed governmental duties.
- George Washington of Virginia was unanimously appointed commander-in-chief of the Continental Army. He was one of the few Americans with any genuine military leadership experience.
- The Congress established trade regulations and issued paper money.
- Agents were sent abroad to negotiate with foreign powers for financial, diplomatic, and military assistance.
- Colonies were instructed to form their own governments.
- The Congress began debating a resolution of independence, which was approved on July 2, 1776.
- The Declaration of Independence was adopted on July 4, 1776.
- Delegates finally agreed on the Articles of Confederation, a list of procedures and powers, on November 15, 1777.
- When the Articles of Confederation were fully ratified on March 1, 1781, the Continental Congress was replaced by the Congress of the Confederation.

ARTICLES OF CONFEDERATION

You might have trouble asking the average American to recite specific parts of the U.S. Constitution, but those noble-sounding words there at the beginning of the document are certainly well-known. Just begin reciting "The Stile of this Confederacy shall be 'The United States of America'" and see if you don't incite a spontaneous sing-along of The National Anthem. And if you thought that the *first* words of the *first* Constitution were "We the People, of the United States..." then you weren't paying close attention in Mrs. Williams' history class.

That "We the People" part is the Preamble to the United States Constitution, true. And given the right score, it is undoubtedly sing-able, as the generation raised on "Schoolhouse Rock" can attest. But that was the *second* U.S. Constitution. The *first* U.S. Constitution was the Articles of Confederation, and it begins "The Stile [sic] of this Confederacy..."

The full title of that first document is "The Articles of Confederation and Perpetual Union Between The States of New Hampshire, Massachusetts-bay Rhode Island and Providence Plantations, Connecticut, New York, New Jersey, Pennsylvania, Delaware, Maryland, Virginia, North Carolina, South Carolina and Georgia." And it is indeed the first real U.S. Constitution.

The articles were drafted in 1777 by the Continental Congress, adopted on November 15 of that year, and became the law of the land on March 1, 1781, when Maryland ratified the document.

The drafters of the Articles were wary of a strong central government, and thus concentrated the majority of power with the individual states, including the power to collect taxes. Not surprisingly, that fact came to chafe Congress, and eventually the Constitution—the second one, with the Preamble—was adopted on September 17, 1787, and ratified on June 21, 1788.

THOMAS PAINE SHOWS SOME COMMON SENSE

English immigrant and republican Thomas Paine favored colonial independence in his writings, which had a big influence in moving America toward a declaration for freedom from Britain.

In January 1776, Paine anonymously published a fifty-page pamphlet arguing for the colonies to break political ties with the British monarchy and become independent states. He said that it was not common sense for a large continent (i.e, America) to be ruled by a small, distant island (i.e., Britain). The pamphlet was titled *Common Sense*, Paine's most famous work.

Furthermore, Paine said that it was not right for people to pledge allegiance to a king's corrupt and unreasonable government (like, ahem, the one in Britain ruling the American colonies). He emphasized that there was no advantage to the American colonies for remaining under Great Britain's rule and a monarchy exploiting them.

When *Common Sense* was published, Paine's ideas were radical for the time, but it quickly became a popular "best-seller." With statements like "The birthday of a new world is at hand," it led to changes in public opinion about establishing a republican government and paved the way for the Declaration of Independence in July of that same year.

Paine also wrote a pamphlet series between 1776 and 1783 entitled *The American Crisis*. George Washington had the tracts read to his troops for inspiration. Even from the first words, the soldiers drew encouragement:

> These are the times that try men's souls. The summer soldier and the sunshine patriot will, in this crisis, shrink from the service of their country; but he that stands it now, deserves the love and thanks of man and woman. Tyranny, like hell, is not easily conquered; yet we have this consolation with us, that the harder the conflict, the more glorious the triumph. . . .

THE FRENCH REVOLUTION AFFECTS AMERICAN POLITICS

In Europe

By 1789, a revolution was forming in France that would affect American politics. The lower classes in France rebelled against taxes and the monarchy's power, which had a big role in shaping George Washington's foreign policy during his first presidential term.

The Revolution in France soon spilled over to other European countries. By February 1793, Britain, with its ally Spain, was again at war with France. The British began capturing American ships trading in French ports.

In America

The American people and Thomas Jefferson supported the French people in their rebellion. Alexander Hamilton sided with the British for trade reasons.

George Washington thought there was a good chance that America's earlier alliance with France would mean siding with them now. Thomas Jefferson strongly agreed. Alexander Hamilton disagreed, saying because the 1778 alliance was made with a king who had since been ousted, America was no longer obligated to honor it.

However, Washington knew that the United States was just too young to go to war again. Jefferson agreed on the need to avoid war, though he wanted to support France. Washington carefully declared America's neutral position without actually using that specific word.

Potential Effects

By not offending either the French or the British, Washington wanted to:

- Get British troops out of the Northwest Territory
- Develop better trade in the Spanish West Indies
- Establish free navigation of the Spanish-held Mississippi River

PUC-PUGGY, THE GREAT AMERICAN NATURALIST

William Bartram may not be a household name, but he explored more of America than any other educated man of his time. His published notes from travels throughout the southeastern interior lands from 1773 to 1776 are the best descriptions we have of the unexplored land and the native people.

Early Life: A well-educated Philadelphia Quaker, as a young man, Bartram showed artistic talent, leading family friend Benjamin Franklin to suggest he become an engraver. Instead, he dabbled in several unsuccessful business ventures. He also accompanied his father on Florida exploratory trips. Bartram even served in North Carolina's colonial legislature.

Travels: Bartram's journey across the South began in 1773 from the Appalachian Mountains, to Florida, then across to the Mississippi River. His diaries describe the natural almost-unspoiled lands that are now North and South Carolina, Georgia, Florida, Alabama, Mississippi, Louisiana, and Tennessee.

Bartram attended an important Indian congress in Augusta. The Cherokee favored surrendering land to the Georgia colony in exchange for forgiveness of debts owed to traders. The Creek, who did not owe anything, thought, "Not so much." But, the Cherokee persuaded the Creek to agree to the deal. The tribes allowed Bartram to accompany the party surveying the land boundaries, which was beneficial to his travel research. (The Indians called him "Puc-puggy," meaning *the Flower Hunter*.) In 1791, Bartram published his travel notes. It became a classic, even if the title was somewhat long: *Travels Through North & South Carolina, Georgia, East & West Florida, the Cherokee Country, the Extensive Territories of the Muscogulges, or Creek Confederacy, and the Country of the Chactaws; Containing An Account of the Soil and Natural Productions of Those Regions, Together with Observations on the Manners of the Indians. Embellished with Copper-Plates.*

SHAYS' REBELLION

The peaceful image of farmers is a common enough fiction, but in actuality, farmers don't so much *make* their living from the land as they *wrench* their living from the land. Such year-long wrenching makes for the creation of mighty tough folk, as the leaders of America found out when a farmer named Daniel Shays led what is now known as Shays' Rebellion.

Shays was no stranger to violence, having served as a captain in the Revolutionary War. He saw action at Bunker Hill, Ticonderoga, and Saratoga, then retired from the military in 1780 and became a farmer in Pelham, Massachusetts. Shays and many of his fellow farmers were being squeezed by high taxes, and general economic hardship (i.e., lack of paper money), and the threat of debtor's prison after the American Revolution, and unrest fomented among them.

In August 1786, the former captain and an armed mob of some 1,200 fellow farmers prevented several Massachusetts courts from sitting. They also disrupted a session of the Massachusetts Supreme Court in Springfield. Shays' forces also planned to seize the federal arsenal in Springfield, but were turned back in January 1787 by militia.

Although Shays was originally condemned to death and forced to flee to Vermont, he was pardoned a year later. The rebellion that bears his name inspired Thomas Jefferson to write,

A little rebellion now and then is a good thing. It is a medicine necessary for the sound health of government. God forbid we should ever be twenty years without such a rebellion. The people cannot be all, and always, well informed. The part which is wrong will be discontented, in proportion to the importance of the facts they misconceive. If they remain quiet under such misconceptions, it is lethargy, the forerunner of death to the public liberty ... and what country can preserve its liberties, if its rulers are not warned, from time to time, that this people preserve the spirit of resistance? Let them take arms. The remedy is to set them right as to the facts, pardon and pacify them. What signify a few lives lost in a century or two? The tree of liberty must be refreshed, from time to time, with the blood of patriots and tyrants.

THE NORTHWEST ORDINANCE

The Confederation Congress set about the business of forming a new country, but its main legacy was policies on the lands in the west. In addition to setting precedents on statehood, the Confederation Congress passed the first national legislation to limit the expansion of slavery.

The Northwest Ordinance of 1787 addressed the Northwest Territory, the land bordered by the Appalachian Mountains to the east, the Mississippi River to the west, the Great Lakes on the north, and the Ohio River to the south. This law enacted the process for adding states to the Union and gave the new states the same powers and rights as the original thirteen states.

But, let's back up a few years to get some background. With the adoption of the Articles of Confederation in 1781, the question handling the Northwest Territory had been put forth and settled by transferring the western claims to the new government. Then, with the Land Ordinance of 1785, a congressional committee submitted a plan for dividing the territory into townships. Each township would be six miles square, with thirty-six sections of one square mile, which was 640 acres. The plots would sell for one dollar per acre, and five of the sections would be set aside for government and education.

The Northwest Ordinance of 1787 allowed between three and five states to be formed out of the Northwest Territory. It defined the boundaries of these states, and set the criteria for statehood as when the population reached 60,000 free males. In addition, it forbade slavery in all new states in the territory.

Districts Formed From the Northwest Territory

July 1800 – District of Indiana
March 1803 – Ohio state
January 1805 – Michigan Territory
February 1809 – Illinois Territory
April 1836 – Wisconsin Territory

CRASH COURSE
THE BILL OF RIGHTS

The Bill of Rights is an addition to the Constitution, which, as it name implies, lists specifically the rights guaranteed to the people under the Constitution. We're so used to claiming our "First Amendment Rights" or "Fifth Amendment Rights," that it's hard to imagine that there was a question as to whether to include a Bill of Rights. But, there was.

In fact, adding a Bill of Rights was a topic for heated debate between the Federalist and Anti-Federalist parties. Anti-Federalists wanted a Bill of Rights to protect the citizens from too strong of a central government. Federalists felt like it was better to assume that all the citizens' rights were protected, instead of limiting what was protected to what was specifically stated.

In the end, to convince the hold-out states to ratify the Constitution, the Federalists agreed to add a Bill of Rights. In September 1789, delegates delivered twelve Constitutional amendments to the states for approval. As you know, ten were ratified (the other two addressed the number of representatives and congressmen's pay) and became known as the Bill of Rights. The ninth and tenth amendments eventually satisfied the Federalists' arguments.

Today, there are a total of twenty-seven amendments to the Constitution. The last, restricting raises for congressmen (one of the twelve original amendments, and one of the two not immediately ratified) was finally approved in 1992. The twenty-sixth, regarding changing the voting age to eighteen, was proposed in 1971 and ratified within a hundred days.

EXTRA CREDIT: On the 150th anniversary of the ratification of the Bill of Rights in 1941, President Franklin D. Roosevelt declared December 15 to be Bill of Rights Day.

THE FIRST TEN AMENDMENTS

First Amendment: Freedom of Religion, Press, Expression
This amendment is often cited by protestors for their "freedom of speech" and newspapers for their "freedom of the press" in publishing material. It guarantees different religious groups the freedom to worship as they please.

Second Amendment: Right to Bear Arms
Interpretation of this amendment varies from allowing people to keep guns in their homes to allowing only armies to own guns. It does give Congress the right to limit gun ownership, such as prohibiting felons from owning firearms.

Third Amendment: Quartering of Soldiers
Before the Revolutionary War, the British government forced colonists to house and feed British soldiers. It was obviously a big sticking point, because avoiding the practice was ensured by the Bill of Rights. Today, we don't see many people invoking their Third Amendment Right to keep from housing armies.

Fourth Amendment: Search and Seizure
This amendment protects you against illegal searches without cause. It is why police have to get a search warrant before entering your home.

Fifth Amendment: Trial and Punishment, Compensation for Takings
You cannot be: prosecuted for a crime without being formally accused; prosecuted more than once for each crime (known as *double-jeopardy*); forced to testify against yourself (*self-incrimination*). Government cannot: take your property unless it's for public use and you get a fair price; randomly deprive you of life, liberty, or property (*due process*).

Sixth Amendment: Right to Speedy Trial, Confrontation of Witnesses

You have the right to a lawyer, to a trial by impartial jury, and to call witnesses for your case.

Seventh Amendment: Trial by Jury in Civil Cases

You have a right to a jury trial in federal civil cases.

Eighth Amendment: Cruel and Unusual Punishment

You can post reasonable bail and are protected against punishment that doesn't fit the crime.

Ninth Amendment: Construction of Constitution

Just because certain rights aren't listed in the Constitution doesn't mean you don't have those rights.

Tenth Amendment: Powers of the States and People

All the powers not specifically assigned to the federal government are reserved for the states.

The Original Bill of Rights

Only fourteen copies of of the Bill of Rights were originally made—one for the federal government and one for each of the thirteen states. Of those original documents, only three have survived. One is kept in the Library of Congress and another one can be viewed at the New York Public Library. North Carolina's copy, the only other original document still in existence, was stolen by a Union soldier during the Civil War. Miraculously, it was returned to the state in 2005.

A NEW GOVERNMENT

The delegates who signed the Constitution were pleased with the stronger—and actually workable—government they had created. This new national government had the power to collect taxes, print (or coin) and borrow money, make treaties with foreign countries, and regulate trade both among the states and with other nations.

The new government was based on three branches, each empowered to check the others. This was so that no one branch would have too much power over the others. The three branches were the executive, legislative, and judicial.

The Executive Branch: There was one single executive, a president, who was elected through an electoral college system. Each member of the electoral college was to vote for the two people they felt would serve the country best as president. In the beginning, the presidency went to the person with the highest number of votes. The person with the second highest votes was named vice president.

The Constitution authorized the president to appoint department chiefs, to be confirmed by the Senate. President Washington appointed four department heads who, with the vice president, formed a cabinet that met daily to discuss policies and issues. This set a precedent still followed today of calling cabinet meetings for opinion and discussion.

The Legislative Branch: The Constitution created a two-house Congress, with a Senate and a House of Representatives, both elected by the people.

The Judicial Branch: The Constitution established a Supreme Court and gave Congress the power to create other lesser federal courts. The Judiciary Act of 1789 established the number of Supreme Court judges (one chief justice and five associate justices) and gave the justices the power to rule on the constitutionality of state court decisions. The Judiciary Act also established thirteen district courts and three circuit courts of appeals.

Whigs and Tories and Such

Modern-day Americans might be familiar with one or two political parties, but the country has a long history of multiple parties and groups. Here are a few of the more memorable ones.

Whigs: What the American revolutionaries called themselves. The term "Whig" is short for Whiggamores, a group of upstart Scottish Presbyterians who had marched on Edinburgh in 1648 protesting royal power.

Whig Party: Not to be confused with the American Revolution-era Whigs, these latter Whigs were a political party formed in the early 1830s that opposed the Jacksonian Democrats. These Whigs would eventually become the Republican Party.

Tories: A Tory was the opposite of an American Revolution Whig. Whereas Whigs wanted independence from England, Tories remained loyal to the king.

Know-Nothings: An American nativist party of the 1850s that particularly despised Catholic immigrants. The party got its start in secret societies. When members were questioned about their efforts, they replied, "I know nothing."

Fire-Eaters: Pro-slavery nineteenth-century Southerners who urged Southern secession.

Free Soil Party: Antislavery ninetenth-century politicians from the Democratic, Whig, and Liberty parties who opposed the expansion of slavery into the Western Territories. They wanted "Free Soil, Free Speech, Free Labor, and Free Men."

Barnburners: Strongly anti-slavery nineteenth-century Democratic Party members. Their name comes from a farmer who would burn down his barn in order to destroy a rat infestation. A Barnburner would destroy his own party over the issue of slavery.

Democratic-Republican Party: This oxymoronically named group was founded by Thomas Jefferson and James Madison in 1792. Eventually, this party became the Democratic Party.

SIR ALEXANDER MACKENZIE

Scottish-born explorer Sir Alexander Mackenzie was the first man to explore the North American continent north of Mexico. He was the first man to reach the Pacific Ocean by land.

Still on the quest for the elusive Northwest Passage, Mackenzie first set out in 1789 to explore Canada's present-day Northwest Territories. From Great Slave Lake (due north of Montana) he canoed up what turned out to be the longest river in Canada all the way to the Arctic Ocean. He named it the River of Disappointment for his disappointment in not reaching the Pacific Ocean. It was later renamed the Mackenzie River. (During winter months, the frozen Mackenzie is used as an ice road, which we've seen recently on reality television about truckers in the Northwest Territories.)

In 1792 Mackenzie set out again to find a route to the Pacific. This time he followed the Peace River across present-day Alberta and British Columbia, crossing the Rocky Mountains and the Continental Divide. Heeding local native warnings to avoid hostile tribes, he followed the West Road River, crossed the Coast Mountains, and descended the Bella Coola River.

On July 20, 1793, Mackenzie first reached saltwater at South Bentinck Arm, an inlet of the Pacific Ocean north of present-day Vancouver. He published his travel journals in 1801 and was knighted the next year.

Sir Alexander Mackenzie Provincial Park

On July 22, 1793, Mackenzie found himself blocked by war-minded natives and could not proceed further west. He painted "Alex MacKenzie from Canada by land 22nd July 1793" on a rock using a red mixture of vermilion and bear grease. Then he headed back east.

Surveyors later permanently etched the words into the rock, which is today still located in Dean Channel at the Sir Alexander Mackenzie Provincial Park in British Columbia.

ELI WHITNEY

American inventor Eli Whitney developed the automated cotton gin that made cotton production profitable. For the southern states, it was a defining moment that meant slavery was there to stay.

Inventing the Cotton Gin

In 1792, while tutoring at the Savannah, Georgia, plantation of Nathanael Greene's widow, Whitney was encouraged to use his creativity to help the local cotton planters.

Whitney observed the hand process of separating cotton seed from raw cotton fibers. In 1793, he designed and built a machine—the first cotton gin—that automatically separated the seeds from the cotton fibers.

Before Whitney developed the automated cotton gin, farming cotton required hundreds of man-hours. With the cotton gin, almost fifty pounds of cotton could be cleaned or "ginned" each day. This invention revolutionized the cotton industry and economic development in the southern United States. Cotton farming became profitable, and cotton became the most important crop in the South.

Patenting the Cotton Gin

Whitney partnered with Mrs. Greene's plantation manager and second husband, Phineas Miller. They applied for a patent on the cotton gin in 1794, but a wording loophole in the patent law made it easy for other manufacturers to copy the invention. Soon, many different "brands" of gins were available, and ultimately, Whitney earned very little money from the invention that literally changed the economic and social landscape of the South.

Interchangeable Parts

In 1798 Whitney focused on manufacturing firearms. To satisfy a government contract for 10,000 military muskets, he experimented with a system of interchangeable parts. By standardizing the parts to be interchangeable, he used a method now common for mass production. Whitney made his fortune from muskets with interchangeable parts, not from the cotton gin.

POLITICAL PARTIES

By 1792, George Washington realized that political groups would become a part American politics. He saw that his two chief advisors, Thomas Jefferson and Alexander Hamilton, were becoming rival leaders with diametrically opposed political viewpoints.

Federalist Party
- Evolved from Hamilton's followers
- Supported war with France
- Supported Britain in foreign policy
- Favored growth of federal power and a strong central government
- Favored a loose interpretation of the Constitution
- Favored an active Treasury Department that participated in national economics
- Prevalent in the northeastern states with businessmen and large landowners
- Accused the Democratic-Republicans of attempting to bring down government by limiting its powers

Democratic-Republican Party
- Evolved from Jefferson's followers
- Opposed war with France
- Supported France against England in foreign policy
- Favored states' rights and a weak central government
- Favored a strict interpretation of the Constitution
- Frowned on government interference in economic affairs
- Prevalent in the southern states and on the western frontier with skilled workers, small farmers, plantation owners, and immigrants
- Accused the Federalists of elitism and threatening to American liberties

1796 Election
In the 1796 election, Thomas Jefferson ran as a Democratic-Republican (the first candidate from that party to run for president); John Adams ran as a Federalist. Adams was elected president and

Jefferson vice-president, creating an administration with a president and a vice-president from different parties.

Democratic-Republican Presidents
- 1801-1809 Thomas Jefferson
- 1809-1817 James Madison
- 1817-1825 James Monroe

Evolution of Parties
- The Federalist Party no longer held power of any kind by 1820.
- Around 1820, the Democratic-Republican Party started to split.
- Andrew Jackson's followers became the Democratic Party.
- John Quincy Adams' followers became the National Republican Party.

The Smithsonian Institution

Although having never visited the United States, British chemist James Smithson felt the country embodied his beliefs in individualism and democratic politics much better than England. Smithson left about $500,000--a lot of money back then--to the United States of America, to found the Smithsonian Institution in Washington.

Congress accepted the inheritance, and in 1838, eleven boxes of gold coins arrived from England. John Quincy Adams, then a U.S. representative, headed the organizing committee to found the institution.

WHISKEY REBELLION OF 1794

Yes, we've all seen someone stage a personal whiskey rebellion on Friday night at the local line dancing club. But, the Whiskey Rebellion of 1794 was for higher stakes than your average run-of-the-mill barroom brawl.

What started the Whiskey Rebellion was a new tax that Alexander Hamilton proposed on distilled liquor. He thought the tax could help pay off the federal war debt, and the legislature approved it.

This liquor tax was especially unpopular with western Pennsylvania frontier farmers. Already struggling to make ends meet, farmers had found they could save money by distilling extra crops into liquor, which was cheaper than hauling their grain or corn surplus to the east for trade. The new tax wiped out any little profit they might get from selling their distilled whiskey.

The farmers' solution: Don't pay the tax. However, revenue collectors came around to enforce the tax. In July 1794, farmers attacked federal marshals in Pennsylvania to defend their "liberties." They burned the excise inspector's house and began holding threatening armed meetings.

Pennsylvania Governor Thomas Mifflin reported to the federal government that his state could not muster enough militia to suppress the rebellion. Hamilton and Washington saw the episode as defiance of national authority and responded by mobilizing almost fifteen thousand militiamen from New Jersey, Maryland, and Virginia.

Alexander Hamilton himself led the army across the Appalachian Mountains and dismantled the Whiskey Rebellion without bloodshed. The farmers' resistance immediately ended.

Hamilton's army arrested more than 150 men. Twenty-five of those had their cases actually come to trial, and only two were convicted—sentenced to death. Washington later pardoned them.

The farmers of western Pennsylvania thought the Whiskey Rebellion was an unnecessary use of force against the common people. The incident left many of them agreeing strongly with anti-Federalists.

Science 101
Mather and Franklin

History justifiably credits Edward Jenner for introducing the process of vaccination against smallpox. But long before Jenner found out that cowpox could provide immunity from smallpox in 1796, a member of a famous New England family and the brother of one of New England's most famous minds fought over smallpox treatment.

Cotton Mather was a prominent Puritan minister, son of minister Increase Mather. In 1721, Cotton was living in Boston when a smallpox epidemic hit the city. A slave of Mather's named Onesimus told him how he had been inoculated against smallpox as a child in Africa. Material from an infected person's pustule was extracted and then scratched into the skin of the unaffected subject. (The practice was obviously not without dangers. Inoculated subjects could contract the disease, as well as pass it on to others.) Mather espoused the theory, and attempted to convince Boston doctors to employ it.

Understandably, Mather met with little enthusiasm, but one doctor, the spectacularly named Zabdiel Boylston, decided to try the technique. Boylston inoculated his son and two of his slaves. The procedure worked, but popular opinion wasn't swayed by Boylston's results. The public believed inoculation actually spread the disease. *The New England Courant*, published by Ben Franklin's older brother James, was foursquare against the procedure, and published letters from anti-inoculation writers.

For his part in the experiment, Boylston was rewarded by being forbidden to repeat the procedure, having his life threatened and a public outcry wanting him to be tried for murder. His inspiration, Mather, had his house grenaded. Mather had the last laugh, however. After publishing his results in London in 1724, he was elected to the prestigious Royal Society in 1726.

WASHINGTON'S PRESIDENCY
1789-1797

As you already know and are reminded each February on President's Day, George Washington was the first president of the newly formed United States of America. He was the unanimous choice of the electoral college and accepted the position in 1789.

Washington was chosen because of his immense popularity for engineering victory over Great Britain for independence in his role as commander-in-chief of the Continental army. Americans trusted him not to abuse his powers to lessen their liberties, although he was a staunch supporter of a strong central government for the survival of the United States.

He selected a diverse cabinet of officers from different regions and ideals. During his service as the first president of the United States, Washington sealed his place in American history, and is now known simply as the "father of our country."

A National Bank
During Washington's first term, Secretary of the Treasury Alexander Hamilton founded the first national bank, the Bank of the United States. Before he signed the bank bill, the president debated with his cabinet the Constitution's "implied power" to establish a bank until he was satisfied on the subject.

Foreign Policy
Washington wanted the government to remain neutral in relations to other countries. He sought to build a government that treated all nations evenly, especially in trade, while distancing the United States from foreign disputes, which the country was still too young to get involved in. This got tricky in the late years of the eighteenth century, with the French Revolution in Europe. Washington and his cabinet discussed the pros and cons of alliance versus neutrality and eventually carefully settled on a decision to remain neutral.

Location of the Capital
While Washington was in office, a proposal for permanently locating the capital passed in July 1790. The capital would be in Philadelphia until 1800, then moved to a federal district on the Potomac River.

Number of Representatives
Questioning its constitutionality, Washington vetoed a plan to reassign seats in the House of Representatives that favored northern states over the southern.

Pinckney Treaty with Spain
In the 1795 Treaty of San Lorenzo, the Spanish government gave the United States unrestricted use of the entire Mississippi River Valley with tax-free exporting through the port of New Orleans. Spain also agreed on West Florida's northern boundary.

Treaty with Algiers
To protect U.S. merchant ships in the Mediterranean from being seized by Barbary pirates, and to release captive American sailors, Washington agreed to pay an annual security payment of $24,000.

Northwestern Treaty
The Shawnee, Miami, and other northwest Native American tribes gave up their claim to the Ohio River and the river valley and southern Indiana to settlement.

Additions to the United States
Vermont became the first new state in 1791, followed by Kentucky in 1792 and Tennessee in 1796.

Washington's Cabinet

	1789-1793	1793-1797
Vice President	John Adams	John Adams
Secretary of State	Thomas Jefferson	Edmund Randolph
Attorney General	Edmund Randolph	William Bradford
Secretary of the Treasury	Alexander Hamilton	Oliver Wolcott, Jr.
Secretary of War	Henry Knox	Timothy Pickering

Two-Term Tenure and Washington's Farewell Address

By the time George Washington's second term came to a close in 1796, he was determined that he would not serve any longer as the nation's president. After eight years, he was tired and ready to relax at his home. He felt it was time for someone else to take over.

In his decision to leave office after two terms, Washington set an example that later presidents would follow. There was no text in the Constitution limiting a president's tenure in office. But, after George Washington, all presidents elected to two terms voluntarily retired after eight years. It wasn't until 1940 that Franklin Roosevelt broke the two-term tradition when he sought re-election to a third—and then a fourth—term.

In his famous farewell address, Washington explained his reasons for deciding to step down and included advice to his fellow citizens. While reports confirm that Hamilton and Madison helped Washington write parts of the address, it certainly clearly expresses Washington's own thoughts and character.

Because he was such a well-loved public figure, Washington's message was well-received by the public, who took his advice to heart. His farewell address warned Americans about policies and practices that he did not approve of. Among other topics, Washington cautioned:

- Do not get involved in European affairs
- Do not make permanent alliances in foreign affairs
- Do not form political parties
- Avoid sectionalism (getting wrapped up in advancing local interests)

Future presidents would take Washington's warning against permanent alliances as gospel. But regarding not forming political parties, Washington was already behind the times. By the time he left office, political parties were already well on the way to becoming an integral part of American politics.

PRESIDENTIAL BIOS 1

America has had forty-three presidents; therefore, it's kind of a tall order to learn all the interesting facts and trivia about them at once. So we're breaking down the list into manageable chunks, just because we're helpful and friendly and want you to like us. Here's the first batch.

George Washington, 1789–1797

First, about that incident where young Washington copped to the crime of cherry-tree chopping (history's first recorded incidence of cherry-tree chopping copping). Any Washington commitment to truth-telling notwithstanding, the cherry tree incident never happened. Washington biographer Mason Weems invented the story for an 1809 book. And the official quote from that account isn't, "I cannot tell a lie, Father," but, "I can't tell a lie, Pa; you know I can't tell a lie."

One thing Washington did in fact do, but isn't lauded enough for, is give the shortest inauguration speech ever. For his second inauguration on March 4, 1793, Washington orated for just 135 words. That's the kind of brevity more politicians should embrace.

John Adams, 1797–1801

Adams had the misfortune of following a legend, which is always a tough proposition, and which probably limits the attention Adams has received, even though Adams was a quite interesting character. He was the only Founding Father who never owned slaves, the first vice president (he was Washington's only vice president), and the first president to live in the White House. Adams was also unseated from the presidency by his own vice president, Thomas Jefferson. Jefferson's act caused lasting friction between the two. When Adams died on July 4, 1826, his last words were, "Thomas Jefferson survives." He was wrong. Jefferson had in fact died a few hours earlier.

Thomas Jefferson, 1801–1809

Jefferson was (among other things) an architect who began his estate at Monticello when he was only twenty-six. He's regarded as the author of the Declaration of Independence. His epitaph, which he wrote, doesn't mention that he was president. The first president to be inaugurated in Washington (Washington and Adams had been inaugurated in Philadelphia), Jefferson authorized the Lewis and Clark Expedition.

Jefferson didn't have much use for slackers. One of his quotes reads, "Of all the cankers of human happiness, none corrodes it with so silent, yet so baneful a tooth, as indolence. . . Idleness begets ennui, ennui the hypochondria, and that a diseased body."

James Madison, 1809–1817

Madison was the smallest president, measuring 5-foot-4-inches tall and weighing about one hundred pounds (Washington Irving said he was "but a withered little apple-john"), but he casts a historical shadow of far greater proportions. He's known as the Father of the Constitution for his efforts in support of the document. Madison, John Jay, and Alexander Hamilton co-wrote the *Federalist Papers*, which urged ratification of the Constitution. Madison was second cousin to Zachary Taylor, and was the first president to abandon knee breeches for trousers, an act every politician should venerate him for.

James Monroe 1817–1825

Before he took office as president, Monroe had fought in the Continental Army, attended the Virginia Convention that ratified the new Constitution, served as minister to France, and helped negotiate the Louisiana Purchase.

James Monroe is remembered for the Era of Good Feelings and the forceful Monroe Doctrine. Not a bad legacy, but there really couldn't be any other for a man of whom Thomas Jefferson said, "Monroe was so honest that if you turned his soul inside out, there would not be a spot on it."

The Era of Good Feelings was a time of celebrating nationalism, optimism, and goodwill. The Monroe Doctrine was his declaration that other countries could no longer expect to establish colonies in the Americas.

John Quincy Adams, 1825–1829

Until the election of George W. Bush in 2000, John Quincy Adams was the only son of a president who became a president. Born to the second president, John Adams, John Q. ironically took office under controversy, just as Bush would. In 1824, the Republican Party (the only party at the time) was splintered by sectionalism, and each section nominated its own candidate. Adams, William H. Crawford, Andrew Jackson, and Henry Clay all ran for president. No candidate won a majority of electoral votes, so the election went to the House of Representatives. Clay then sided with Adams, giving him the presidency.

Professor Adams

John Adams was the first president to become a teacher when he graduated from Harvard University in 1755 and became Latin master at a grammar school in Worcester, Massachusetts. It didn't take long before Adams was describing his students as "little runtlings, just capable of lisping A, B, C and troubling the master." After only two years of teaching, he fled education and became a lawyer.

THE NEW CAPITAL IN WASHINGTON, D.C.

While Congress had earlier met at the Pennsylvania State House in Philadelphia, Nassau Hall at Princeton University in New Jersey, and the Maryland State House in Annapolis by the time George Washington was inaugurated, the capital was located at Federal Hall in New York City. This was not the permanent location, and many debates centered around locating the capital. In fact, before the question was settled, sixteen different sites had been proposed.

The deciding factor was a compromise between Thomas Jefferson and Alexander Hamilton. Jefferson lent support to Hamilton's financial proposals, and Hamilton in turn supported Jefferson's efforts to locate the seat of government on the Potomac River.

Pennsylvania delegates agreed to support the plan in exchange for designating Pennsylvania as interim capital until the permanent one was built. (They hoped that once the capital was moved from New York, it would never be moved again. But they were wrong.)

A federal territory was established in 1790 as the site of the new nation's permanent capital. It was created from land donated by the states of Virginia and Maryland and named Washington, District of Columbia, for the first U.S. president, George Washington, and the first explorer to reach the Americas, Christopher Columbus.

Originally ten miles square, the central town was laid out by French architect Pierre Charles L'Enfant. L'Enfant named the broad diagonal avenues to feature the states arranged by geography and their role in the nation-building process. (Think 1600 Pennsylvania Avenue—the White House address.)

Benjamin Banneker

Benjamin Banneker was a free African-American farmer and self-taught mathematician. In 1789, George Washington appointed Banneker to the commission planning Washington, D.C.'s construction. He helped Major Andrew Ellicott survey the site of the national capital between 1791 and 1793.

JOHN ADAMS' PRESIDENCY (1797-1801)

In the election for the second president, John Adams barely beat Thomas Jefferson in the electoral college, seventy-one to sixty-eight. Jefferson became Adams' vice president.

John Adams may have been the highest-ranked Federalist in the party, but he never gained the same loyalty from that party that Alexander Hamilton enjoyed. Throughout his presidency, Adams worked at a disadvantage against Hamilton's power in his own party and Jefferson's opposing party views.

The main issue of the Adams administration was a quasi-war with France as a result of the XYZ Affair. The upshot of the quasi-war was that Adams established a standing army and armed merchant ships.

Hamilton showed clear disdain for Adams, thinking him weak and too moderate. While Adams preferred to avoid war, Hamilton thought a war with France would be to his own personal advantage in his rivalry with Thomas Jefferson. While Adams at first appeared to be following Hamilton's lead toward war, he finally stood his ground and negotiated an agreement with France that avoided armed conflict. This incensed Hamilton. The lasting consequence was a split in the Federalist Party, which affected him personally when he lost the election of 1800.

One of Adams' last official acts as president was to appoint quite a few Federalists to lifetime judgeship positions. This caught Thomas Jefferson off-guard, as Adams named the appointments after the election and before he stepped down. They were called "midnight judges," and Adams' appointments included naming Secretary of State John Marshall as chief justice of the United States, where he served for thirty-four years.

John Adams died on July 4, 1826, the fiftieth anniversary of the Declaration of Independence, only a few hours after Thomas Jefferson did. He had lived to see his son John Quincy Adams elected president of the United States in 1824.

ABIGAIL ADAMS LOBBIES FOR WOMEN'S RIGHTS

Until the election of George W. Bush as president in 2000, Abigail Smith Adams was the only member of a select club: first ladies who gave birth to a future president. Adams served as first lady from 1797 to 1801, when her husband John Adams was president. Twenty-four years later, her son John Quincy Adams became president, making Abigail a historical anomaly until Barbara Bush accomplished the first lady/first mother double.

Born Abigail Smith in 1744, she received no formal education as a child, but poor health often kept her housebound, where she educated herself in her father's large library.

Abigail married John Adams when she was nineteen and he was twenty-nine. John was a lawyer and farmer who would go on to represent Massachusetts as a delegate to the first Continental Congress. In 1775, Adams and two other women were appointed to question other Massachusettes Colony women charged with being British loyalists.

When the Second Continental Congress began drawing up the Declaration of Independence, Abigail wrote to her husband that this nascent government could make women the legal equals of men. Her arguments failed, but her letters would become known as some of the earliest women's rights efforts.

Abigail Adams on HBO

Laura Linney had this to say about portraying Abigail Adams in the HBO series *John Adams:* "We are spoiled, spoiled, spoiled. We would not survive. I wouldn't survive. I admire her fortitude. And I admire her strength. And that Yankee-fresh kind of 'get to it' attitude."

CRASH COURSE
XYZ AFFAIR

Would Abraham Lincoln have been as revered, or even elected, if he'd been born Elmer Harcourt Fechtenberger? Would the Battle of the Bulge have been as memorable if it had been called Operation Epizootic? Would the Watergate scandal have become part of the American lexicon if the break-in and spying had been at the Hayes Arms Hotel? No, no, and no are the most likely answers. Historical events need some sizzle to lodge in the public's mind, and something called "The XYZ Affair" that led to an undeclared and short-lived war just won't be remembered.

"The XYZ Affair" began in 1797 when President John Adams sent John Marshall and Elbridge Gerry to Paris as diplomats. Marshall and Gerry joined C. C. Pinckney, already in Paris. The mission of the three was to lessen the level of tension between America and France. France had taken to seizing American ships, a practice that the Americans took umbrage at.

But French foreign minister Charles Maurice de Talleyrand made the three Americans cool their heels for weeks, refusing to meet with them. In the meantime, intimations were made that the proper bribes—$250,000 to Talleyrand and a $12 million loan to France—would sufficiently grease the wheels of diplomacy. The insinuations were conveyed to the Americans by Jean Conrad Hottinguer, Mr. Bellamy, and Lucien Hauteval, who became Agents X, Y and Z, respectively, in a presidential report.

The diplomatic kerfuffle morphed into a quasi-war between the United States and France in 1798. Naval battles between the two sides occurred, although anti-France tensions ran high enough in the United States that George Washington was summoned out of retirement to head the American Army. A full-bore shooting war was avoided when the two countries adopted the Treaty of Mortefontaine in 1800, in which everybody promised to play nice.

POP QUIZ #3

1) On what date did the Second Continental Congress adopt the Declaration of Independence?

2) When the Articles of Confederation were ratified, what governmental body replaced the Continental Congress?

3) What radical future Virginia governor said, "If this be treason, make the most of it," and "Give me liberty, or give me death!"

4) Who was responsible for delivering the cannons that forced the British out of Boston in 1776?

5) Name two ways that women contributed to the Revolutionary War effort.

6) Regarding the social impact of the Revolutionary War, select the area that was not changed by the patriots' thoughts and attitudes.
   a) Aristocratic titles
   b) Separation of church and state
   c) Economic commercial recession
   d) Women's individual rights

7) True or False: The Articles of Confederation were weak because they gave most powers to the individual states and severely limited the powers of the national government.

8) Did the 1787 convention called by Congress decide to fix the Articles of Confederation or draft an entire new Constitution?

9) Who, as governor of Virginia, submitted the famous Virginia Plan to the Constitutional Convention?

10) Who is not recognized as one of the three authors of The Federalist Papers?
    a) Alexander Hamilton
    b) John Jay
    c) James Madison
    d) Benjamin Franklin

1) July 4, 1776
2) The Congress of the Confederation
3) Patrick Henry
4) Henry Knox
5) Any two of the following will be correct: ran the family farms and businesses; provided food and clothing; worked as cooks, washed their laundry, and nursed wounded soldiers in the war camps; fought in battle
6) d
7) True
8) Draft an entire new Constitution
9) Edmund Jennings Randolph
10) d

ANSWERS:

THE WHITE HOUSE

Since President John Adams and his wife, Abigail, moved into the executive residence more than 200 years ago (in 1800), the White House has been an enduring symbol for the people.

Although he never lived there, George Washington planned and managed the construction of a presidential residence, begun in 1792. John Adams was the first executive to live there, and Thomas Jefferson was the first to open the house—at 1600 Pennsylvania Avenue—to the public.

The White House has 132 rooms, thirty-five bathrooms, twenty-eight fireplaces, and three elevators. Presidential families have plenty of entertainment choices: tennis court, jogging track, swimming pool, movie theater, and bowling lane. As technology advanced, the White House was right there: running water flowed in 1833; central heating warmed the place in 1837; gas lamps lit rooms in 1849; the telephone rang in 1879 (the telephone number was "1"); electricity was wired in 1891; an electric refrigerator cooled food in 1926.

Construction and Renovation Timeline

- 1815 to 1817 – After being torched by the British during the War of 1812, it was reconstructed and ready for James Monroe's occupancy.
- 1824 – South Portico was built.
- 1830 – North Portico was completed.
- 1901 – Theodore Roosevelt officially named the residence *The White House*.
- 1902 – Roosevelt initiated a renovation that added the West Wing for offices and covered the parlor walls with cloth, renaming them the *Green Room, Blue Room*, and *Red Room*.
- 1934 – West Wing was rebuilt after a 1929 fire.
- 1942 – East Wing was built for more offices.
- 1948-1952 – Interior was gutted and rebuilt under Harry S Truman, because the house was not structurally sound. Original exterior stone walls were preserved.

ALIEN AND SEDITION ACTS OF 1798

In 1798, Congress enacted the Alien and Sedition Acts, seriously limiting the rights of free speech. The laws were introduced in Congress by the Federalist legislators, who had a majority in Congress. Their purpose was to control critical articles published by Democratic-Republicans and to ensure Federalists would have success in future elections.

A Federalist, President Adams signed the laws. Therefore, they really did not help Adams' approval ratings with Democratic-Republicans.

- *Naturalization Act* — Increased the residency requirement for citizenship from five to fourteen years. (This favored the Federalists because most immigrants voted Democratic-Republican.)
- *Alien Friends Act* — Authorized the president to deport aliens (or *foreigners*) whom he considered dangerous. (Again, most immigrants were Democratic-Republican, so this favored the Federalists.)
- *Alien Enemies Act* — During wartime, permitted arresting and kicking out any citizens from an enemy country.
- *Sedition Act* — Outlawed antigovernment activity, including criticisms of the president or Congress published in newspapers (especially newspapers owned by Democratic-Republican printers).

Long-Term Effects of the Sedition Act

An immediate effect of the Sedition Act was the arrest and conviction of Vermont congressman Matthew Lyon for opposing policies of Adams' administration.

The Federalists continued to abuse the Sedition Act, and Thomas Jefferson and James Madison led the Democratic-Republican Party's opposition of the act. The Kentucky and Virginia state legislatures went even further, passing resolutions to allow the states to review federal laws and invalidate any they considered unconstitutional.

This precedent would later figure prominently in the political scheming that led up to the Civil War.

CRASH COURSE
REVOLUTION OF 1800

The third Presidential tenure got off to a rocky start. Two Democratic-Republicans, Thomas Jefferson and Aaron Burr, both received the same number of votes in the electoral college. So, according to provisions set forth in the Constitution, a special election was held in the House of Representatives to break the tie.

Federalists, who still held a majority in the House (at least until the newly elected legislators were sworn in), debated for days. They finally gave a majority to Jefferson. Burr, therefore, was named vice president.

With the election of Jefferson and Burr, the executive branch moved to Democratic-Republican control. The election of 1800 saw more Democratic-Republicans elected for majorities in both the House and Senate when the new Congress first met in March 1801. The Federalists quietly accepted their defeat and peacefully turned over control of the federal government to the Democratic-Republicans.

The passing of power in 1801 from Federalist control to Democratic-Republican control is known as the Revolution of 1800. As far as revolutions go, it wasn't much of one: no violence, no bloodshed, no fighting, not even any pamphlet-writing.

It was a peaceful revolution, and it was important in showing that the instructions in the U.S. constitution had been well thought out and would last.

Jefferson recognized the need for a smooth and peaceful transition of power from the Federalists to the Democratic-Republicans. In his inaugural address of 1801, he stressed the necessity of accepting the main beliefs of the government created by the Constitution when he said, "We are all Republicans; we are all Federalists."

THOMAS JEFFERSON'S PRESIDENCY (1801-1809)

During his first term, Thomas Jefferson knew it was wise to court Federalist approval by keeping Alexander Hamilton's national bank and debt-repayment plan. In foreign policy, he maintained his predecessors' neutrality policy. But, he remained true to the Democratic-Republican principle of limited central government: he reduced the military's size, eliminated many federal jobs, repealed excise taxes, and lowered the national debt.

Jefferson commissioned Meriwether Lewis and William Clark to find a water route to the Pacific. Their trip confirmed the possibility of American fur trade in western territories, and, more importantly, planted ideas of a country spanning coast to coast.

The most important achievement of Jefferson's first term was the acquisition of extensive western lands in the Louisiana Purchase, which more than doubled the United States' size.

Under Jefferson, the Supreme Court decided a case stemming from John Adams' midnight judge appointments. Chief Justice John Marshall ruled that the Judiciary Act of 1789 was unconstitutional because it gave the court greater power than constitutionally allowed. This ruling established judicial review, in which the Supreme Court rules on the constitutionality of congressional or presidential acts.

In 1804, Jefferson was reelected president by an overwhelming landslide, receiving 162 of 176 electoral votes. His second term was marked by increasing difficulty remaining neutral in foreign politics.

Earlier, George Washington negotiated a treaty with Barbary pirates to protect American sailors. Now the pirates were demanding more money. Jefferson instead sent the American navy to the Mediterranean. Tripoli responded by declaring war, and fighting lasted for four years.

France and Britain continued fighting in Europe. The "innocent bystander" America sometimes landed in their crosshairs, especially with each country seizing U.S. ships and impressing sailors. The 1807 Embargo Act halted American sailing to any foreign port; it was intended to protect American ships, but only hurt American trade. So Jefferson repealed it shortly before leaving office.

SALLY HEMINGS

The unsubstantiated rumor that Thomas Jefferson fathered children with his slave Sally Hemings has been circulating publicly since his first presidential term. Jefferson's Federalist opponents published the rumor in newspapers throughout his tenure, presumably to hurt his credibility.

As with any personal attacks, Jefferson remained tight-lipped. He didn't stand up at a podium, wife by his side, and declare innocence (nor did he confirm the rumor's truth). No records indicate that he ever commented publicly or privately about it.

Sally Hemings became Thomas Jefferson's property as inheritance from his father-in-law. Records show that she was a "nurse" or companion to Jefferson's daughter, Mary, who was six years younger.

At Jefferson's estate, Monticello, her assigned household status was a lady's maid, looking after the children and doing light work such as sewing. Hemings's son Madison related that her duties included taking care of "[Jefferson's] chamber and wardrobe." Coupled with the fact that written descriptions say she was very attractive with long, stunning hair, it seems that Jefferson had the motive and the means, for what that's worth.

Jefferson's household records show Hemings had two daughters and two sons. Both sons broadcast widely their personal belief that Thomas Jefferson was their father. Based on DNA testing, review of historical documents, and lore handed down through generations, researchers disagree on whether or not the evidence supports that Thomas Jefferson was the father of any or all of Sally Hemings's children.

ROBERT FULTON AND THE EFFICIENT CLERMONT

American inventor, engineer, and mechanical genius Robert Fulton is known as the man who developed the first American steamboat. But, he actually was the man who designed the first efficient American steamboat.

As a young man, Fulton worked as a professional artist of some renown, but he turned his interests to engineering and inventing. He designed canal systems with inclined planes to replace locks, and he worked at making underwater torpedoes and submarines. Many of his devices were ignored.

But, in the early 1800s, his work finally reached the right audience. U.S. minister to France Robert Livingston had negotiated a statewide steamboat monopoly in New York that required his steamboats to travel 4 miles per hour. Fulton set about designing a fast steamboat, and drew up plans for the *Clermont*, a 150-foot vessel with an English engine.

On August 18, 1807, the *Clermont* made a successful run of 150 miles from New York City up the Hudson River to Albany in thirty-two hours. This meant that, at about 4.7 mph, he had developed a faster steamboat that shortened a four-day trip to a little over one day. Fulton received a patent for his design. More importantly, the *Clermont's* famous trial ushered in a new era of power-driven transportation.

The Inventor of the Steamboat

Robert Fulton is considered the inventor of the steamboat. We know that other men built steamboats before Fulton, but his steamship was the first to be commercially successful in American waters. So, that's what it takes to be famous--not simply an invention, but a successful invention.

American inventor John Fitch probably developed the first American steamboat. Records show for sure that he conducted a successful trial of a 45-foot steam-powered vessel on the Delaware River in 1787, twenty years before the *Clermont's* first run.

THE LEWIS AND CLARK EXPEDITION

In 1802, Thomas Jefferson excitedly read the notes of Alexander Mackenzie's trip overland to the Pacific Ocean. Together with his friend and private secretary Meriwether Lewis, Jefferson began planning an expedition to 1) explore the lands all the way to the Pacific, 2) take advantage of the fur trade opportunity in America's westernmost parts, and 3) promote peace among the various Indian tribes.

With Congress's financial backing, they formed the Corps of Discovery. Lewis signed on as commander and William Clark, an experienced surveyor and cartographer, accepted a second officer position. They started out with a party of twelve men.

In the end, Lewis and Clark did reach the Pacific Ocean, twenty-five months after they began. They endured hardship, but their notes and journals from the expedition were valuable in understanding the western lands. However, they did not find a water route across the continent, and their difficult trek proved that no trade route already existed.

From what he had witnessed and experienced, Lewis was able to envision an American trading empire: a series of forts along the Missouri River for trading furs, which could be shipped from the Columbia River across the Pacific Ocean to China.

The Route of the Lewis and Clark Expedition
- October 26, 1803: Started out from Clarksville in Indiana Territory
- Traveled down the Ohio River
- November 13, 1803: Reached the Mississippi River at the site of present-day Cairo, Illinois
- November 20, 1803: Paddled up the Mississippi to St. Louis
- December 8, 1803: Reached St. Louis; added another dozen men to the party
- Spent the winter at an encampment on the U.S. side of the Mississippi river across from the mouth of the Missouri River
- Mid-May 1804: Began trip up the Missouri River, expecting to be gone at least two years

- Mid-July 1804: Had covered seven hundred miles by this time
- Early August 1804: Encountered Otos Indians near the Platte River; Lewis assured them he was there from the country's "new father" to give them "good advice;" Otos chief asked for gun powder and whiskey, which Lewis provided; the party went on their way unharmed
- Late October 1804: Reached the Mandan Indian villages at the Great Bend of the Missouri, south of present-day Bismarck, North Dakota
- Began building Fort Mandan across the river from the Mandan villages for winter quarters; established good rapport both with the natives and with the British fur traders who had already been trading with them
- While at Fort Mandan: Lewis and Clark met French Canadian Toussaint Charbonneau, who offered interpreting services by virtue of his Shoshone wife, Sacagawea
- April 1805: Left Fort Mandan, continuing up the Missouri River
- Early June 1805: Camped at a fork of the Missouri; further scouting determined which branch was actually the Missouri; Lewis named the north branch Maria's River.
- Followed the Missouri River southward to the Great Falls; portaged over the falls
- Paddled to Three Forks, which Lewis named Madison, Gallatin, and Jefferson
- Chose to travel up the Jefferson fork
- August 13, 1805: Encountered Shoshone Indians; their chief, Cameahwait, turned out to be Sacagawea's brother
- Cameahwait's Shoshone tribe provided horses to the party, helped them transport their equipment, and loaned them another guide
- Proceeded to cross the Continental Divide
- September 3, 1805: Began descent from the Continental Divide toward the Pacific Ocean, trekking through snow
- Moving into the valley of the Bitterroot River, also moved into the valley of their trip (snow made it difficult to follow their guide, made it difficult to hunt food, made it difficult to progress, and disoriented the horses)

- Finally reached the Columbia River
- October 7, 1805: Headed downstream on the Columbia toward the Pacific Ocean
- Encountered dangerous rapids, but knowing they were so close to their destination, instead of portaging, they chose to save time and shoot the rapids
- November 7, 1805: Found themselves stalled by bad weather at the Columbia estuary
- November 15, 1805: Finally reached the Pacific Ocean; Lewis carved his name on a tree at the end of Cape Disappointment
- Upon his return from the Pacific Ocean, Lewis was appointed governor of the new Louisiana Territory

Sacagawea

During Lewis and Clark's expedition, Sacagawea's presence was invaluable. While some history books will say she was a guide, today's historians now believe she served as more of a goodwill ambassador, albeit one that could help interpret in communications with other tribes. Her mere presence as a woman in a party of men helped show other tribes that the explorers were peaceful, or, as Clark wrote in his journal, had "friendly intentions."

Surely she was a good sport, and the men did note that she was remarkable for her perseverance and resourcefulness. When one of the boats nearly capsized, Sacagawea was responsible for saving the irreplaceable journals that Lewis and Clark kept throughout the expedition. She saved other valuable possessions too, including navigational instruments and goods for trading with the Native Americans.

When Sacagawea was reunited with her brother, Cameahwait, in a group of Shoshone, it meant extra help for the party of explorers. The tribe treated them with hospitality and gave them food, horses, and guides.

The United States Mint issued a gold dollar coin in 2000 featuring Sacagawea's image.

Geography 101
The Louisiana Purchase

France originally owned the Louisiana Territory, then Spain took control, and in 1800, the French forced Spain to return it. The Louisiana Territory was a large and largely unexplored section that included the Mississippi and Missouri rivers. Its most valuable location was the Port of New Orleans.

In 1802, Spanish officials (who retained administration even though France officially owned the land then) closed the port to Americans, blatantly reversing an earlier treaty that opened the port to Americans. This was bad news for Indiana Territory settlers who shipped goods on the Mississippi River to sell at market. They cried "foul" to the government.

President Jefferson was upset because closing the port 1) affected American economics and 2) set a bad precedent for foreign relations. In April 1803, he sent ambassadors to offer France $10 million for New Orleans and the land eastward to Florida. (He also told the ambassadors that if they didn't get anywhere in negotiations with France, to go to Britain and work on arranging a U.S.-British alliance. But things never got that far.)

By then, France was preoccupied with other issues closer to home and was in debt from war costs. The French offered to sell New Orleans plus the entire Louisiana Territory for $15 million. Good bargain shoppers that they were, the ambassadors snapped it right up. This would more than double the size of the United States.

In a poor showing of party politics, the Federalists initially disapproved of the great opportunity, on the grounds that the deal was invalid because the president does not have the constitutional power to purchase foreign land. Fortunately, Republicans held the majority in the Senate, and arguing that the president's power to make treaties included adding lands to the country, they quickly approved the purchase.

ZEBULON PIKE

In 1805, when America found itself in the possession of 828,000 square miles in Louisiana Purchase territory it had purchased on the cheap from France (roughly three cents per square mile), young Zebulon Pike was sent on an expedition to explore those newly acquired miles.

Pike was first tasked by James Wilkinson, commander of the United States Army, to find the source of the Mississippi River. Pike and twenty men embarked from St. Louis in August 1805, eventually reaching the Falls of St. Anthony in what is now Minneapolis, Minnesota. The men continued on to Cass Lake, which they thought was the Mississippi's source, but they were wrong. (There is no truth to the rumor that this enraged Pike, and that his rage was known among his men as Pike's Pique.)

In 1806, Wilkinson sent Pike on a new expedition, ostensibly to explore the headwaters of the Arkansas and Red Rivers and accomplish some diplomacy with the Indians. In actuality, Wilkinson was sending Pike to spy on the Spanish and their possessions in the West. After some horrifying exploits that included desertions and frostbite, Pike and his remaining men were captured by Spanish authorities. Pike and company were taken to Mexico, then released back to the United States in July 1807. (There is no truth to the rumor that Pike attempted to communicate with the Spanish in a pidgin English known as Pike-speak.)

Today, Pike is best known for a 14,115-foot-high geographical formation in Colorado. Although Pike never climbed the formation, it is indeed known as Pike's Peak.

GERRYMANDERING

All politicians long to leave their mark on history, to have their name bandied about in the halls of government long after they are gone. But historical mention isn't always a good thing. Norwegian politician Vidkun Quisling collaborated with the Nazis during World War II, and was eventually convicted of treason and executed. To this day, collaborators and traitors are referred to as Quislings, which is most likely not what Quisling first had in mind when he entered public office.

Elbridge Gerry probably had no intention of his surname becoming part of the American political lexicon when he first ran for office, either. But almost 200 years after his death, "gerrymandering" is still used to describe the practice of drawing political boundaries to benefit one party or faction.

Gerry was governor of Massachusetts in 1812, when he signed a bill that created election districts that favored his Democratic-Republican Party over the opposition Federalist Party. One district in Essex County was so elongated and contorted that a Federalist politician compared it to a salamander. Another Federalist replied that it would be better termed a "gerrymander." When a cartoon by artist Gilbert Stuart that illustrated this "gerrymander" appeared in a Boston newspaper in 1812, one of the enduring expressions of American politics was born.

Congress attempted to render the gerrymander extinct by passing the Reapportionment Act of 1842, which ruled that congressional districts had to be "contiguous and compact," but the act merely made gerrymandering more difficult, not impossible. Politicians still indulge in "packing," or jamming voters into one district to minimize their effect on other districts, and "cracking," spreading out voters in order to prevent the creation of a successful voting bloc.

BETSY ROSS AND MARY PICKERSGILL

One is famous for something she most likely didn't do, the other isn't famous for something she really did. The differing fame of Betsy Ross and Mary Pickersgill shows just how fickle history can be.

Popular history has Ross creating the first flag in 1776, after a visit by George Washington and two other Continental Congress members. While that makes for a neat story, and while Ross did indeed create flags (she was actually an upholsterer, not a seamstress), the idea of Betsy creating the first flag is suspect on several grounds. The story didn't surface until 1870, when one of Ross's grandsons, William J. Canby, told it to the Historical Society of Pennsylvania. He based his tale on relatives' accounts, hardly a good source when almost one hundred years have passed since an event's occurrence and when a family's readiness to canonize one of its own is factored into the equation. Most historians consider Canby's tale as apocryphal at best, downright wrong at worst.

Mary Young Pickersgill, on the other hand, really did sew the flag that inspired Francis Scott Key to write what would become the national anthem. Fittingly born in Philadelphia in 1776, Pickersgill established a flagmaking business in Baltimore in 1807. In 1813, Major George Armistead, commander of the American forces at Fort McHenry, commissioned her to sew a flag "so large that the British will have no difficulty seeing it from a distance." Pickersgill's company sewed up a 30-foot by 42-foot monster, with stars and stripes each measuring two feet across. It was this flag that Francis Scott saw "by the dawn's early light."

Pickersgill's flag is currently being restored at the Smithsonian Institution in Washington. Pickersgill's fame, however, still plays a distant second to that of Ross.

THE ADAMS-ON'S TREATY OF 1819

First of all, because *Adams-On's Treaty* probably doesn't mean very much to you, we'll play nice and tell you that this is about acquiring Florida.

What we know today as the Florida Panhandle at one time extended all the way to New Orleans. Before the War of 1812, the Spanish (Britain's ally) controlled the Panhandle. During the War, American troops occupied the area.

After the War of 1812, Spain was concentrating on rebellion in its South American colonies and had to send most of its armed forces there. This meant Spain had difficulty controlling the Florida peninsula. Unsavory characters from the peninsula began raiding U.S. territories north of Florida. This gave President Monroe the argument he needed to send troops down to Spanish Florida.

General Andrew Jackson headed down to west Florida in 1818, and he really "put his foot down" while he was there. Some Congressmen thought he went too far: destroyed Seminole villages, hanged Seminole chiefs and British traders working with the Seminoles, captured Pensacola, and drove out the Spanish governor.

One result from Jackson's strong-arm tactics was to get Spain worried about American troops staging an all-out forcible seizure of Florida. (Remember, Spain was preoccupied with controlling unrest in South America. They dreaded taking on an American attack in Florida, too.) They figured that their best defense would be offense, namely, handing over Florida according to the terms of a peaceful treaty.

The Adams-On's Treaty of 1819 provisions:

* Spain turned over Florida to the United States.
* Spain turned over its claims in the Oregon Territory to the United States.
* The United States assumed $5 million in claims of damages against Spain.
* The United States gave up any territorial claims to Spanish Texas.

CRASH COURSE
MISSOURI COMPROMISE

The Missouri Compromise was all about keeping balance in the government. By the time Missouri applied for statehood in 1819, it was becoming clear that a seam was ripping between the North and the South. We could go ahead and say that, in hindsight, it's obvious that the nation was heading down the path to Civil War, but that would spoil it for later.

To understand the significance of the Missouri Compromise, we first have to understand why it was necessary. It all related to representation in Congress. Flip back to the pages on the Constitution, and you'll remember that representation in the House was based on population. Population in the North grew faster than in the South. So, by 1818, the northern free states held a majority over the southern slave states of 105 to eighty-one in the House of Representatives. The northern states, therefore, controlled the House.

You'll also remember that in the Senate, representation was divided evenly. So the eleven free states shared power evenly with the eleven slave states. This is where the problem came in.

In 1819, Missouri—a slave state—applied for statehood. The northern states worried that admitting a slave state would upset the political balance in the Senate to the South's favor. Even more disturbing was that Missouri was the first section from the Louisiana Purchase to apply for statehood. What would happen when other areas applied for statehood?

Various congressmen introduced suggested solutions, but all were rejected. Missouri's statehood stalled until, finally, Maine applied for statehood in 1820.

This is where the compromise came into play: The South agreed to admit Maine, a free state, in exchange for admitting Missouri; also, slavery was banned in all Louisiana Purchase lands above 36°30' North.

The Missouri Compromise sufficed for more than thirty-four years.

OREGON TERRITORY

The Oregon Territory included all the land west of the Rockies (the present states of Oregon, Washington, Idaho, and parts of Montana and Wyoming), and extended north to the Alaskan border.

At one time, four different nations claimed this land: Spain, Russia, Great Britain, and the United States. In an 1819 treaty, the United States absorbed Spain's claim to the territory. By 1825, Russia had withdrawn its claim as well.

This left the United States and Britain to sort it out between them. Britain based its claim on British fur trade in the Pacific Northwest; but fur traders weren't settlers, and the British population out there was quite low. The United States felt they had the more legitimate claim in light of Lewis and Clark's exploratory expedition coupled with the American missionaries and settlers who were flocking to the region.

In 1846, the two countries signed a treaty recognizing American claims to the Oregon country south of the 49th parallel, the border that separated the United States from Canada to the east of the Rockies. In 1848 President Polk signed a bill creating the Oregon Territory.

The Oregon Trail

Early missionary reports promised fertile soil and healthy climate in the Oregon country. Beginning in the 1840s through the late 1860s, the expectation of health and wealth encouraged more than 300,000 people to make the 2,000-mile journey.

Settlers traveled from Independence, Missouri, sticking to overland trails across the Great Plains of Kansas, then following the Platte and North Platte Rivers through southwestern Wyoming. After they crossed the Continental Divide in the Rockies, the trail split. Settlers then either headed toward California, or took the Oregon Trail northwest over the Blue Mountains. At Fort Walla Walla, they turned west to follow the Columbia River to Fort Vancouver.

PRESIDENTIAL BIOS 2

Andrew Jackson, 1829–1837

Jackson overcame a poor background, meager education and the killing of a rival in a feud (in defense of Jackson, the cad had insulted Jackson's wife, Rachel) to serve two terms as president. Jackson fought in the American Revolution when he was only thirteen. He achieved national acclaim when he defeated the British in the Battle of New Orleans, even if the War of 1812 was already over when the battle took place.

Jackson truly was the people's president. Rather then consulting with his official Cabinet, he often relied on the opinions of a group of close friends who came to be known as the Kitchen Cabinet.

Martin Van Buren, 1837–1841

The first president to be born a United States citizen, Van Buren spent a tumultuous four years in office. During his administration, "Sweet Sandy Whiskers" faced a national depression (the Panic of 1837), conflict with other countries, the issue of Texas' annexation and the expansion of slavery.

Van Buren was born in Kinderhook, New York, and was sometimes called "Old Kinderhook." The term "OK" or "Okay" has numerous stories about its derivation, including Van Buren's nickname.

William Henry Harrison, 1841

Harrison's presidency is noted for both length and brevity. The length came during his inauguration, when he delivered a speech that lasted an hour and forty-five minutes. Outside. In a snowstorm. Including references to classical literature, the speech was the longest inauguration speech of any president. Harrison's presidency, on the other hand, was the shortest. He died from pneumonia one month into his term, the first president to die in office. (Some say he caught pneumonia from standing outside for almost two hours in a snowstorm... .)

William Henry Harrison's grandson, Benjamin Harrison, became the twenty-third president in 1889.

John Tyler, 1841–1845

Tyler's administration wasn't exactly marked by sweetness and light. He was given the unfortunate nickname of "The Accidency," due to the way he became president after Harrison's death: instead of taking a role of "acting president" and holding a new election, Tyler had himself sworn in as president.

Tyler was also known as "The Veto President" because of his penchant for the practice. He was called the president without a party, since both the Whigs and the Democrats threatened to impeach him.

Tyler fancied himself such a political outlaw that when he retired from office, he lived in an estate he named "Sherwood Forest."

James K. Polk, 1845–1849

In poor health as a child, Polk focused on cultivating his mind and developed a fierce determination. His strong character was solidified when, at the age of seventeen, he underwent surgery for gallstones without the luxury of anesthetics.

The first dark horse, or little-known, candidate to win a presidential nomination, Polk's campaigning strategies (and his small stature) led his supporters to call him the "Napoleon of the stump."

Although we don't get a postal holiday in his honor, Polk was one of the nation's most successful presidents. Upon taking office, he stated the four objectives of his administration: reduce tariffs, reestablish an independent treasury; settle the Oregon boundary dispute with Britain, and acquire California from Mexico. He achieved all four goals. Having reached them all in one term, President Polk did not run again for reelection.

Manifest Destiny

Manifest Destiny was the Americans' belief that they were entitled to all unsettled land, without regard for Native Americans or other countries' claims. Pursuing "Manifest Destiny" involved the issue of admitting slave or free states to the Union. Therefore, the push to expand westward pushed closer toward Civil War.

215

TREATY OF GUADALUPE HIDALGO (MEXICAN CESSION)

In 1845, President Polk asked Mexico to sell the California and New Mexico territories to the United States. But Mexico refused, so Polk sent a platoon into Mexican territory, where they were attacked.

America declared war on Mexico, and soundly defeated Mexican forces in virtually every battle. One example: In 1846, John C. Frémont's small patrol captured northern California and declared California an independent republic, called the Bear Flag Republic because—well, you can probably guess this one yourself—the rebelling militia had a bear on their homemade flag.

Other skirmishes netted Palo Alto, Santa Fe, the New Mexico territory, southern California, Buena Vista, Monterrey, and Veracruz. General Winfield Scott captured Mexico City in September 1847, and the Mexican government was finally ready to agree to a treaty.

The Treaty of Guadalupe Hidalgo, signed in February 1848, provisions:

- Mexico recognized the Rio Grande as the southern border of Texas.
- Mexico gave up 525,000 square miles of land. This is known as the *Mexican Cession*.
- The United States paid $15 million to Mexico.
- The United States assumed all private claims of damages against Mexico.

The Mexican Cession land became the states of California, Nevada, Utah, and parts of Colorado, Arizona, New Mexico, and Wyoming.

In a recurring theme, Congress debated whether states from this new territory should be slave or free. Pennsylvania congressman David Wilmot proposed a bill forbidding slavery in any of the former Mexican territories. Called the Wilmot Proviso, it was passed in the House—twice—but overruled both times in the Senate. Even though it did not get enacted, the Wilmot Proviso was yet another step in the direction of war between the North and South.

EXTRA CREDIT: Now called Gustavo A. Madero, Guadalupe Hidalgo was a city near Mexico City.

JAMES MADISON'S PRESIDENCY (1809-1817)

James Madison had been Thomas Jefferson's Secretary of State and close friend. One of the founding fathers who had been involved in the country's government since the days of the Continental Congress and the Constitutional Convention, he was known by the American people to be a brilliant thinker and statesman. In the eight years of Madison's presidency, he focused his attentions on the growing strain between the United States and both France and Britain.

In the election of 1808, as one of three Republican candidates, Madison won the majority of electoral votes with Jefferson's support. George Clinton of New York became Madison's vice president.

When he took office in 1809, Madison inherited the same foreign relations problems with Britain and France that Jefferson had faced. From his inaugural address, Madison made clear that he wanted to continue the United States' policy of neutrality, but that he drew the line in the sand at foreign interference. This philosophy eventually led to the War of 1812.

In the election of 1812, that war was the primary campaign issue. Although with less support than in 1808, Madison was reelected. Elbridge Gerry of Massachusetts served as Madison's vice president in his second term.

The final two years of Madison's presidency saw growing national prosperity and a move toward expansion of the United States. He approved a bill creating a national bank and a tariff act to protect American industries from foreign competition.

Quids

A rebellious group called Quids opposed Madison as they did Jefferson before him. "Quids" were Federalists and "Old" Republicans. They disapproved of the War of 1812, saying it violated the classic Republican commitment to a government with limited power.

DOLLEY MADISON

The name is Dolley Madison, not Dolly Madison. The former was the wife of James Madison, *de facto* first lady of the United States during the administration of Thomas Jefferson (Jefferson was a widower, and Madison served as co-host at certain events that needed a feminine touch) and the actual first lady from 1809 to 1817, when her husband was president.

The latter is the manufacturer of snack foods that will forever be linked with the *Peanuts* animated holiday specials it sponsored. (Roy Nafziger, International Bakeries Corporation founder, wanted to create "Cakes and pastries fine enough to serve at the White House," although he dropped the "e" from Dolley.)

Madison was described by Washington Irving as "a fine, portly, buxom dame," back when such a description wasn't grounds for a vigorous face-slapping. Surprisingly for such a well-known hostess, Madison was born a Quaker in Piedmont, North Carolina, in 1768. She married lawyer John Todd Jr. in 1790, only to lose him to yellow fever just three years later. The next year, she married James Madison, a representative from Virginia who was seventeen years older and an Episcopalian to boot. It was after this marriage that she stopped wearing the low-key attire of the Quakers.

During her term as official first lady, Madison was a spectacular host of social events, popularized the dessert of ice cream in America and saved the Gilbert Stuart portrait of George Washington from being burned by the British during the War of 1812 (the *Landsdowne* portrait, not the unfinished one).

Political Party Girl

Political socialites were shocked when shy, taciturn James Madison announced his engagement to the vibrant and animated political party girl Dolley Payne Todd, who had occasionally hosted parties for the Jefferson administration. She was often criticized for gambling, wearing excessive makeup, and using tobacco.

Non-Intercourse Act

Don't look so horrified. It doesn't mean what you think it means. (Thank goodness!)

While he was still in office, Thomas Jefferson passed the Embargo Act of 1807 halting American sailing to any foreign port. He intended to protect American ships, but the actual result was to severely limit American imports and exports. Just before he left office, Jefferson replaced the Embargo Act.

So, when James Madison took office, the Embargo Act had been replaced by the Non-Intercourse Act of 1809. It reopened trade with all countries—except France and Britain. Madison supported his friend Jefferson's action and hoped it would end economic hardship while maintaining the country's right to be a neutral nation.

By 1810 it was apparent to Madison that America's boycott of trade with France and Britain was altogether ineffectual. Even worse, both countries continued to seize American ships, maybe even more than ever.

In May 1810, Madison repealed the Non-Intercourse Act. This meant that the United States could again trade with both France and Britain. However, by then, France and Britain had put their own restrictions on trading with America. Congressman Nathaniel Macon proposed a bill to go with the repeal (called Macon's Bill No. 2). It said that if either France or Britain dropped restrictions on American shipping and agreed to respect U.S. neutral rights at sea, then the United States would again prohibit trade with the other country.

Learning of this latest development, Napoléon thought that he would use it to his advantage. He declared that France would respect American neutrality in return for America's embargo on trade with Britain; he didn't really mean it. But, Madison did not know that, and he prohibited trade with Britain in 1810. The French continued to seize American ships anyway.

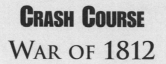

CRASH COURSE
WAR OF 1812

If nineteenth-century Americans thought that conflict with the British ended with the Revolutionary War, the War of 1812 showed that was far from the case. A French-British conflict led to a series of battles between America and British colonies, lasted three years, and cost 4,000 lives.

The Napoleonic Wars (1803-1815) were fought because France wanted to conquer Europe, while Britain didn't quite agree with that idea. The British instigated a blockade of Europe, but questioning the blockade's legality, the Americans continued exporting to Europe.

Miffed by American blockade-snubbing, Britain seized American merchant ships and sold the cargoes, then seized American sailors and pressed them into naval service. This aggression led to an American declaration of war against Britain on June 18, 1812.

- American forces battled British forces in the Atlantic Ocean, in Canada, and in the Southern states, spawning many famous American historical facts.
- On August 19, 1812, off Nova Scotia's coast, the *USS Constitution* earned the nickname "Old Ironsides" when British shots bounced off her hull.
- During the Battle of Lake Erie in 1813, Oliver Hazard Perry wrote, "We have met the enemy and they are ours" on an envelope sent to William Henry Harrison, commander of the Army of the Northwest.
- In 1814, American lawyer Francis Scott Key watching the bombardment of Fort McHenry during the Battle of Baltimore was inspired to write "The Defense of Fort McHenry," which got much greater buzz as "The Star-Spangled Banner."
- General Andrew Jackson defeated British forces in the Battle of New Orleans on January 8, 1815, fourteen days after the Treaty of Ghent was signed ending the war.

Under the treaty, Great Britain relinquished claims on the Northwest Territory, and both Great Britain and America pledged to work toward abolishing the slave trade.

JAMES WILKINSON

The title of "the most finished scoundrel that ever lived" applies not to Benedict Arnold, but to James Wilkinson, an utter ne'er-do-well. Congressman John Randolph, who put the "finished scoundrel" tag on Wilkinson, also said that Wilkinson was "a mammoth of iniquity...the only man I ever saw who was from the bark to the core a villain."

The budding scoundrel was commissioned a brigadier-general during the American Revolution, but had to resign his commission in 1778 when his role in what became known as the Conway Cabal surfaced. (Cabal members criticized Washington's war decisions and called for his replacement.) Wilkinson would later re-enter the service, serving as "clothier-general" from July 1779 to March 1781.

In 1784, Wilkinson moved to what is now Kentucky, where he founded Frankfort and also worked for the territory's statehood. City-founding and statehood-encouraging are perfectly honorable pursuits, of course. Conspiring with foreign governments, which Wilkinson also began to do, is not so honorable. Wilkinson pledged allegiance to Spain in 1787, and also became co-conspirator with Aaron Burr in a plot to split the western territories from the Union and bring them under Louisiana control.

Burr, banking on support from Great Britain, even began to train an army. But the British support failed to materialize, and Wilkinson sold out his co-conspirator to Thomas Jefferson. Later, Wilkinson would sell out Zebulon Pike to the Spanish, even though Wilkinson himself had sent Pike to spy on the Spanish.

Despite his chicanery, Wilkinson was never convicted of any wrongdoing, and even returned to military service, making it to the rank of major general during the War of 1812. After a disastrous defeat at Montreal, he resigned in disgrace.

MR. MADISON'S WAR

By April 1811 the United States was in negotiation with Britain over a number of issues. The most important was Britain's restrictions on American shipping. But, another issue that helped push America into war with Britain was an ambition to expand U.S. territory into British-held lands in the West and Canada, and into Spanish Florida.

Americans believed that Britain goaded the Native Americans to attack American frontiersmen. In November 1811, Shawnee Indians attacked American troops at the Battle of Tippecanoe. Madison used the incident to gain support for war with Britain.

President Madison set a June 1, 1812, deadline for Britain to remove restrictions on American shipping. He did not hear anything from Britain by June 1, so on June 18, Madison signed a declaration of war passed by both houses of Congress. Later, he learned (too late) that Britain had complied with the ultimatum two days earlier, on June 16.

Jefferson's presidency had done a good job of downsizing the military, which left Madison with the immediate problem of deploying forces for this war he had declared. Militias in states opposing war were reluctant to participate, so he couldn't count on them for help.

Madison also did not have unanimous Congressional support of the war: 1) The Federalists were against war with Britain from the start. 2) Northerners didn't care very much about taking over Spanish Florida. 3) Southerners didn't care very much about taking over Canada. 4) The New England states resented contributing their financial and military share. Federalists from this last group bitterly called the War of 1812, "Mr. Madison's War."

During the war, the British blockaded major ports in Chesapeake Bay, New York, Long Island Sound, and Boston. The blockade caused severe economic suffering for American merchants, and "Mr. Madison's War" became increasingly unpopular.

EXTRA CREDIT: *Moby Dick* author Herman Melville served as a seaman on the *United States* from 1843 to 1844.

OLD IRONSIDES AND NAVAL VICTORIES

The naval successes of the American frigates *United States* and *Constitution* (also called "Old Ironsides") in battle provided much-needed morale boosters among early disasters in the War of 1812:

*   From July into August of 1812, American Brigadier General William Hull was forced to surrender Detroit to a combined British-Indian expedition.
*   In October of 1812, the Americans made a second attempt to invade Canada, this time on the Niagara frontier. A small force crossed the Niagara River and stormed the British near the city of Queenston Heights. But they were outnumbered and also forced to surrender.

Both the *Constitution* and the *United States* were heavy frigates carrying at least forty-four guns. The thirty-eight-gun British vessels they encountered could not match their superior firepower: the American ships had a decisive advantage in the accuracy and rate of fire of their guns. Three naval victories in the last half of 1812 showed off the American ships' capabilities in successful fights.

*   In August of 1812, Captain Isaac Hull commanded the *Constitution* in capturing the British frigate *Guerrière* — all in less than thirty minutes!
*   In October Captain Stephen Decatur commanded the *United States* to seize the British frigate *Macedonian.*
*   Then in December, Captain William Bainbridge commanded the *Constitution* in taking the British frigate *Java* off the coast of Brazil.

Another Demoralizing Loss

In 1814, the British captured the capital city of Washington. They burned the Capitol, the White House, and the navy yard, including all the ships anchored there. Madison's humiliating flight from the city was soon mocked in political cartoons.

OLIVER HAZARD PERRY AND HIS BROTHER MATTHEW

Immediately after war was declared, the American government realized that all operations in the Northwest Territory depended on the Great Lakes waterways for transportation. In late 1812, the U.S. naval department started building warships on Lakes Ontario and Erie.

Battle of Lake Erie

Probably the most important naval battle of the war was fought in 1813 on Lake Erie. On September 10, a six-ship British squadron met American naval commander Oliver Hazard Perry's newly completed ten-ship fleet near Put-in-Bay, Ohio. The two sides were matched fairly evenly in vessels and men, but the Americans had "bigger guns." At the end of an unrelenting and murderous three-hour engagement, Perry defeated the British depriving them of free navigation on Lake Erie. The British recalled their advance forces, evacuating Detroit.

Facilitated Victory in the Battle of the Thames

Control of Lake Erie helped General William Henry Harrison in the Battle of the Thames (near Detroit). When Britain's General Proctor received news of the American victory on Lake Erie, he knew his supply chain by water was cut off. He immediately retreated to the Niagara frontier. On October 5, the Americans under Harrison overtook Proctor's troops at the Thames River and defeated the British.

Matthew Perry

American naval officer Matthew Perry commanded the expedition that established American relations with Japan, which had been closed to outside trade since the seventeenth century.

In 1853 Perry left on a mission to Japan. In Tokyo, he proposed a commercial and friendship treaty to the emperor. The treaty, signed on March 31, 1854, provided humane treatment for shipwrecked sailors and opened ports to U.S. commerce.

Tecumseh

Tecumseh, a Shawnee Indian chief originally from Ohio, opposed U.S. expansion into the Midwest and was known for his beliefs on transferring Native American lands to the "white" Americans, saying that if any one tribe handed over land without consulting and getting agreement from the other tribes, the deal was illegal.

- In 1808, Americans forced the Shawnee out of Ohio to Indiana.
- After this mandatory relocation, Tecumseh began organizing an alliance of tribes along the Mississippi River Valley to resist white encroachment onto Indian land.
- Tecumseh became the chief spokesman for the Native Americans in the lands west of the Appalachian Mountains.
- Tecumseh was not subtle, and his actions alarmed white settlers of those lands. They contacted the Indiana Territory governor, General William Henry Harrison, for help.
- Harrison took aggressive action. In November 1811, while Tecumseh was away, Harrison fought and defeated the Shawnees at the battle of Tippecanoe Creek.
- After Tippecanoe, Harrison marched on Prophetstown, burning it to the ground.
- Tecumseh was, understandably, upset, and formed an alliance with the British in Canada.
- By the War of 1812, Tecumseh helped the British capture Detroit.
- While fighting in the British ranks during the Battle of the Thames, on October 5, 1813, Tecumseh was killed.

Tenskwatawa

Tecumseh had a twin brother, Tenskwatawa, a religious mystic known as the Prophet. Tecumseh and his brother preached against Native American adoption of white customs, especially the use of liquor. Because Tenskwatawa's magic did not defeat the whites in the Battle of Tippecanoe Creek, he lost all credibility with his tribe.

ENDING THE WAR OF 1812

Campaigns of 1814

The Battle of Horseshoe Bend in present-day Alabama was important because it took out one of Britain's Native American allies. In March of 1814, General Andrew Jackson defeated the Creek nation, opening new lands to white settlers.

The Battle of Lake Champlain was even more significant: It persuaded Britain that it was time to seek peace. On September 11, 1814, Captain Thomas Macdonough defeated the British on Lake Champlain, which preempted a British march from Canada to take New York and New England.

Treaty of Ghent

Meanwhile, in mid-1814, President Madison sent ambassadors to Ghent, Belgium, to discuss peace with the British. The Americans demanded that the British end impressment, pay compensation for the ships they had seized, and follow international rules on the use of blockades.

The British put forth their own demands but dilly-dallied in negotiations. Then, they received news of the Battle of Lake Champlain, and suddenly the American ambassadors had the better bargaining tool.

The Americans and British signed the Treaty of Ghent on December 24, 1814. Provisions of the Treaty of Ghent:

- Britain pledged against impressments and surrendered its forts along the northwest frontier.
- A boundary commission was established to fix the U.S.-Canadian border.
- Britain surrendered American territory captured during the war.

"Mr. Madison's War" did not accomplish its purposes. But fighting the war gave Americans national pride and recognition of their country as a national entity. Madison had showed the world that the United States could declare war and negotiate peace with another nation, and that American soldiers and ships could hold their own.

BATTLE OF NEW ORLEANS

You may be wondering why we've listed the Battle of New Orleans after the Treaty of Ghent that ended the War of 1812. That would be because the battle took place after the war was over. News of the Treaty of Ghent did not reach the United States for nearly two months.

In the meantime General Andrew Jackson accomplished an impressive—but hollow—victory thwarting the British from taking control of the Mississippi River.

It looked like the Americans had no chance. In December 1814, the British fleet arrived, freshly re-fortified with 12,000 soldiers from some of the best regiments in the British army. Their purpose: to capture the American port of New Orleans. The British made their way through the bayous, and landed an advance party.

On January 8, 1815, more than 8,000 British soldiers attacked Jackson's troops camped at present-day Chalmette, about two miles east of New Orleans. Jackson had 5,000 soldiers, mostly Tennessee and Kentucky militiamen.

The British marched over open ground toward Jackson's improvised fortifications under cover. In less than a half hour, the British suffered 2,000 casualties, chiefly from American artillery fire. Jackson's force suffered only seventy-one casualties. The British broke off the attack, and on January 18 they withdrew.

The Battle of New Orleans, According to Johnny Horton

In the late 1950s, country singer Johnny Horton recorded a popular narrative of the Battle of New Orleans. All of the pertinent information was included: the year (1814), the American commander (Colonel Jackson) and his nickname (Old Hickory), the location (the "mighty" Mississippi at New Orleans), the American strategy (don't fire until you look them in the eye), and what happened ("we fired once more, and they began to runnin'"). It's worth another listen if you want to hear the super-condensed version.

After-Effects of War

Although President Madison felt that the War of 1812 did not accomplish any of his original goals, it did have lasting effects in the United States.

Politics

The War of 1812 marked the end of the Federalists' influence. They had openly opposed the war from the beginning, and when the blockades of the New England coast began to really hurt them in 1814, they organized secret meetings to discuss secession and other options including defeating certain bills in Congress. With the end of the war, their actions looked a lot like treason. The popular opinion of the day rated the Federalist Party two thumbs down, while the Democratic-Republican Party gained in popularity.

The war also gave the nation a new generation of leaders in war heroes such as Andrew Jackson and William Henry Harrison.

Industry

The embargo and the blockades both meant that Americans had to be more resourceful about getting the goods they needed instead of importing them. And, Americans were nothing if not resourceful. More U.S. factories were built, and American manufacturing and industry boomed.

Nationalism

Having now survived two wars with Britain, the United States gained the respect of other nations. The country was stronger and more close-knit. Even frontiersmen had showed they were eager to defend their country against foreign attack.

Westward Expansion

There was a growing belief that the future of the United States lay to the west, away from Europe. Native Americans, by virtue of their ill-fated association with Britain, were forced to surrender huge tracts of their land to white settlers.

SLAVERY CONTINUES

The supporters and leaders of the Revolution were vocal in their insistence that "all men are created equal." They fought an entire war based on that self-evident truth. They recognized that the institution of slavery conflicted with this idea. One thing that they did to correct this was vote in the Continental Congress to set a deadline of 1808 to abolish importing slaves.

Most states went along with the ban, either completely ending slavery, or voluntarily freeing slaves. Many people thought that slavery would gradually disappear, especially as soil in the coastal lands of Virginia and the Carolinas became depleted and crops became less profitable.

Hopes for slavery's disappearance, though, ended with the rapid growth of the cotton industry after Eli Whitney's invention of the automated cotton gin. Southern slave owners believed that they couldn't afford not to have slave labor; that it was necessary for their economy.

Slaves could be bought and sold according to their owner's needs, with no regard for their family units. They were not allowed to be educated, and they lawfully could be cruelly treated.

Phillis Wheatley, American Poet

Phillis Wheatley was an African-born slave owned by the Wheatley family in Boston, Massachusetts. While teaching her own children, Susanna Wheatley included Phillis, who enjoyed studying Alexander Pope and Thomas Gray. Susanna recognized the girl's intelligence and encouraged her poetry. For her work, Phillis Wheatley is considered the first important black writer in the United States. Her best-known poems are "To the University of Cambridge in New England," and "To the King's Most Excellent Majesty." In 1773, Phillis traveled with the Wheatley family to England, where *Poems on Various Subjects, Religious and Moral* was published. After returning to Boston, she was granted freedom.

POP QUIZ #4

1) Select the statement below that is NOT true about Alexander Hamilton.
   a) Served as personal secretary to General Washington
   b) Commanded a New York light infantry regiment at the Battle of Yorktown
   c) Served in the Continental Congress
   d) Contributed to *The Federalist* in support of ratifying the Constitution
   e) Served as secretary of the treasury
   f) Served as inspector general of the army
   g) Killed Aaron Burr in a duel

2) What was the name of the pamphlet written by Thomas Paine arguing that it was just common sense for the colonies to declare independence from Great Britain?

3) Which of the following statements is true about the Northwest Ordinance of 1787?
   a) It defined the boundaries of states in the Northwest Territory.
   b) It set the criteria for statehood for when the population reached 60,000 free males.
   c) It forbade slavery in all new states in the territory.
   d) all of the above

4) What document includes a section on "Freedom of Religion, Press, Expression?"

5) Of the words listed below, choose the three that are the three branches of government created by the new Constitution of the United States.
   a) Executive
   b) Congressional
   c) Judicial
   d) Electoral
   e) Legislative
   f) Military

6) Which of the following did Alexander Mackenzie travel on or across during his quests to reach the Pacific Ocean?
   a) The Mackenzie River (formerly called River of Disappointment)
   b) The Peace River
   c) The Rocky Mountains
   d) The Continental Divide
   e) The West Road River
   f) The Coast Mountains
   g) The Bella Coola River
   h) South Bentinck Arm
   i) All of the above

7) What invention by Eli Whitney revolutionized the southern cotton industry?

8) What party did Thomas Jefferson belong to?

9) What party did Alexander Hamilton belong to?

10) Fill in the word that correctly completes the sentence. The Whiskey Rebellion was highly unpopular in western Pennsylvania because it imposed a _____ on distilled liquor.

ANSWERS:

10) tax
9) Federalist
8) Democratic-Republican
7) The cotton gin
6) i
5) a, c, e
4) The Bill of Rights
3) d
2) Common Sense
1) g

IMMIGATATION AND MIGRATION IN THE EARLY 1800S

- By the 1830s, almost one-third of the population lived west of Pennsylvania's Allegheny River.
- From 1800 to 1825, the U.S. population doubled.
- From 1825 to 1850, the U.S. population doubled again.
- Population increases were due to both high American birth rate and European immigration.
- The African-American and Native American populations grew, even though there was a ban on importing slaves after 1808.
- The percentage of the U.S. population that was African-American or Native American actually declined about 5 percent to 15 percent by the 1850s.
- The slavery population in the South increased from one million in 1800 to four million in 1860.
- In some Southern states, slaves made up as much as 75 percent of the total population.
- Improved roads and canals, as well as the arrival of steamboats and railroads, made migration westward easier and more attractive.

The Cumberland Road

The next time you're breezing down the interstate, consider the Cumberland Road. Construction began on it in 1811, and it was not completed until 1852.

Even though roads that crossed state lines were unusual at that time—because enough Congressmen viewed roads as state improvements, and therefore voted against spending federal money to build them—the Cumberland Road did get approved. Also known as the National Road, it covered almost a thousand miles from Maryland to Illinois, and it became a major route to the lands in the west. It was paid for with federal and state money, and the states it passed through each were granted ownership of their highway segments.

ECONOMICS 101
THE SOUTH'S KING COTTON

At the end of the 1800s, slavery became much more profitable. Eli Whitney's cotton gin allowed one slave to do the same amount of work that it took fifty slaves to do by hand. (Yes, we keep bringing up Eli Whitney, but that's because we can't stress enough what an impact the gin had on the cotton industry and, therefore, on slavery.)

With cotton's new commerciality in the years after the cotton gin was developed in 1793, slavery boomed in the South.

- By 1860, the United States exported more than 5,000,000 bales of cotton.
- For perspective, compare that to 3,000 bales in 1790 and 800,000 bales in 1831.
- Cotton accounted for almost two-thirds of all U.S. foreign trade.
- The U.S. South became the world's leading cotton producer.

In addition to Georgia and South Carolina, which had been growing cotton and other plantation crops since colonial days, new states in the Deep South took advantage of the cotton potential: Alabama, Mississippi, Louisiana, Texas, and Arkansas.

Cotton also affected the social structure of the South. Southern whites placed wealthy planters at the top of a social hierarchy made up of the "aristocracy" of large plantation owners, followed by farmers with small holdings owning few slaves, then poor white subsistence farmers and mountain people who had no slaves.

"Cotton is King"

As the top Southern export, cotton was, indeed, king. British mills relied on American cotton to supply their industry, and American cotton plantations relied on slave labor to maintain their business. In debating the institution of slavery upon which the entire economy depended, South Carolina Senator James Hammond is reported to have said in an 1858 speech to Congress, "You dare not make war on cotton.... Cotton is king."

NATCHEZ TRACE

In 1801, the U.S. Army created a post road based on original Native American trails through Chickasaw and Choctaw tribal lands. The Natchez Trace was used by Native Americans and early settlers traveling between Nashville, Tennessee, and Natchez, Mississippi.

The paths of the Natchez Trace were used by animals, Native Americans, explorers, and soldiers. The trail was also used extensively in the 1800s by farmers and sailors who floated their goods down the Mississippi River to port markets in Natchez and New Orleans, Louisiana. After they sold their crops, coal, and livestock, they would take their boats apart to sell the lumber at port, and begin walking home.

These boatmen, from Tennessee, Kentucky, Ohio, and the Midwest, were all known as Kaintucks. They were such regulars along the Natchez Trace that in one year—1810—more than 10,000 Kaintucks traveled the route (according to the National Park Service). At 500 miles, it would take about thirty-five days to walk from Natchez to Nashville, where they would connect with other roads for the rest of their journey. If they were lucky enough to have a horse, Kaintucks could expect to reach Nashville about ten or fifteen days sooner.

Travelers along the Trace could expect hospitality from the Choctaw tribes whose lands they crossed. That is, until the Choctaw were forced to move to Indian Territory in Oklahoma in 1830. The fierce Chickasaw were relocated two years later.

The Natchez Trace Parkway

The Natchez Trace Parkway was officially established in 1938. It is administered by the National Park Service to commemorate this historic route, and granite markers identify the site of the old highway. Traveling the Trace today gives you glimpses of the land as it was two hundred years ago, as well as the people who traveled that land.

SLAVE RESISTANCE

Plantation owners could treat their slaves any way they wanted, without legal repercussions. Southern politicians argued that slaves were actually treated no worse than the free common laborers working in Northeast factories. (The Southern politicians probably only won that argument among themselves.)

Slaves knew how to challenge their owners, from intentional work slowdowns and sabotage, to escape and revolt. While escape was attempted far more often than revolt, a few major slave uprisings served to highlight the difficulties of the slaves to Northern states.

Contrary to their purpose of achieving slaves' freedom, revolts instead served to increase the severity of slave codes and dampen any Southern thoughts toward abolishing slavery.

Gabriel Prosser — 1800 — Richmond, Virginia

- Slave Gabriel Prosser envisioned creating a free black state in Virginia.
- Jack Bowler plotted with Prosser to seize the Richmond arsenal and kill whites with the firearms.
- Prosser wanted to burn down Richmond and capture Governor James Monroe.
- Those who opposed slavery, including Quakers and Methodists, would not be harmed.
- Almost 1,100 slaves agreed to participate in the revolt.
- Slave revolutionaries gathered near Richmond on August 30 for final preparation.
- House servants concerned about their master leaked Prosser's plan to Monroe.
- A heavy downpour and thunderstorm washed away a bridge vital to the rebels' march.
- Monroe sent the state militia to break up the revolt.
- Prosser and thirty-five of his followers were captured and hanged.

Denmark Vesey — 1822 — Charleston, South Carolina

- Freed black carpenter Denmark Vesey introduced his plans at religious meetings under pretense of worship.

- Vesey planned to seize arsenals in Charleston.
- He would use the captured firearms to kill the whites and burn the city to the ground.
- More than nine thousand blacks, slave and free, were lined up to join the raid.
- Vesey set the date for June 16, 1822.
- A frightened house slave revealed the plot to authorities.
- Vesey and dozens of his followers were arrested, tried, and convicted.
- Vesey was hanged, as were many others, while some were exiled.

Nat Turner — 1831 — Southampton County, Virginia

- Nat Turner's 1831 uprising has been called the bloodiest slave revolt in the history of the United States.
- An educated slave, Nat Turner was convinced that God had chosen him to lead his people to freedom.
- Turner saw a solar eclipse as a sign from God of his divine appointment.
- Like Vesey, Turner spread his message at praise meetings for local slaves.
- On August 22, 1831, Turner and seven other slaves killed their master and his family.
- About sixty blacks from neighboring plantations joined Turner in a revolt.
- By August 24, white militiamen and volunteers subdued the rebellion.
- Turner, however, remained on the lam for another six weeks.
- More than fifty whites were killed.
- White mobs lynched countless blacks in retaliation.
- Turner and fifteen of his companions were tried, convicted, and hanged.

As you can see, slaves themselves often turned in other slaves, either out of fear or loyalty to their masters. Slave informants leaked information to authorities in both the Prosser and Vesey revolts.

Sectionalism: A Forerunner to Civil War

In our world of job transfers and cross-country relocations, it's hard to understand the fierce loyalty residents held for their own region. Sectional differences ultimately led to the Union's worst crisis.

The Northeast

Industrial development led European immigrants and independent farmers to the cities to earn a living. But, factory owners only provided low wages, long hours, and unsafe conditions. Unhappy, workers formed unions and political parties in their interests. They established large working-class neighborhoods with crowded housing that bred poor sanitation, infectious diseases, and crime.

The Old Northwest

Except for forts, the Northwest remained unsettled until canals and railroads provided easy transportation to the Great Lakes. Many German immigrant farmers settled here, where corn and wheat became very profitable crops. (*The Old Northwest* meant Ohio, Indiana, Illinois, Michigan, Wisconsin, and Minnesota.)

The South

Southern economics were all but entirely based on farming and selling cotton; a need for many, many field workers perpetuated slavery. The cotton society contributed to a class system ranging from plantation owners at the upper end to poor farmers at the lower.

The West

The West implied unsettled, frontier territory promising new opportunities. By the 1800s, *West* meant land beyond the Mississippi River to the Pacific Ocean. Early whites were fur trappers known as "mountain men," who shared their knowledge of the land as guides. Settlers in the West lived the same primitive lives that the earlier generations of colonists had—in make-shift housing with homemade supplies and few luxuries.

THE EIGHTH WORLD WONDER: THE ERIE CANAL

An engineering feat of its time, the Erie Canal was called the Eighth Wonder of the World. So, we've listed eight notes on the canal, one for each World Wonder.

Location: In New York, from Lake Erie at Buffalo to the Hudson River near Albany.

Significance: Main route between the Northeast and the "West" (now the Mid-West).

Planning: A water route between the Great Lakes and the East Coast was discussed in 1783, but debates on paying for the project continued for years.

Construction Timeline:

- July 4, 1817 — work begins in Rome, New York.
- October 1819 — Rome-to-Utica section opens to navigation
- April 1820 — Utica-to-Montezuma section opens
- October 26, 1825 — first canal boat sails from Buffalo
- November 4, 1825 — first canal boat reaches New York City

Details:

- Original length: 340 miles
- Original surface width: forty feet (increased to seventy feet in 1862)
- Bottom width: twenty-eight feet
- Original depth: four feet (increased to seven feet in 1862)
- Construction cost: $7,144,000

Completion: When the first boat reached New York City, the governor celebrated by pouring a barrel of Lake Erie water into the Atlantic Ocean. The canal brought new growth to New York City, Buffalo, and New York State.

Operation: To navigate the canal, horse teams pulled boats from the ten-foot-wide towpath along the canal's bank.

Later: By the mid-1800s, although still used in commerce, the canal was surpassed by the railroads. Today, commercial traffic from the Great Lakes to the Atlantic uses the St. Lawrence Seaway, and almost all vessels on the Erie Canal are pleasure boats.

American Literature
James Fenimore Cooper

Novelist James Fenimore Cooper is regarded as the first great American fiction writer. His work featured action-packed plots and vivid descriptions of American frontier life.

While a young boy, Cooper gained firsthand knowledge of the wilderness and Native Americans near his home town. Later, Cooper was expelled from Yale University for his practical jokes.

Cooper's *Leather-Stocking Tales* introduced one of the most famous fictional characters in American literature, Natty Bumppo. In this wildly-popular series, Cooper described American frontier life complete with settlers and their interactions with Native Americans in the wilderness.

Natty Bumppo

The *Leather-Stocking Tales* relate the story of a frontiersman trying to reconcile his ties to white settlers with his life among the Native Americans. The five books—*The Pioneers, The Last of the Mohicans, The Prairie, The Pathfinder,* and *The Deerslayer*—published from 1823 through 1841, were a hit with both American and European readers.

Other James Fenimore Cooper Works

- *Precaution*, an unsuccessful novel of English manners. His first book, Cooper wrote it to support boasts to his wife that he could write a better book than the one she was reading.
- *The Spy*, about the American Revolution in New York State.
- *The Pilot*, one of his many sea tales written during the 1820s and 1830s.
- A 1830s trilogy on medieval Europe feudalism: *The Bravo, The Heidenmauer,* and *The Headsman*.

JAMES MONROE'S PRESIDENCY (1817-1825)

Jefferson — Like Thomas Jefferson, Monroe was a seasoned American Revolution veteran and statesman from Virginia.

American voters — In 1816, American voters elected Monroe in a resounding victory of 183 electoral votes over his opponent Rufus King's 34 votes.

Missouri Compromise — This bargain reached during Monroe's tenure helped settle the question of balance between the North and the South in the Senate.

Era of Good Feelings — The early part of Monroe's first term was a time of celebrating nationalism, optimism, and goodwill.

Spanish Florida — Monroe presided over the 1819 treaty in which Spain handed over Florida's western panhandle and eastern peninsula.

Monroe Doctrine — In 1823, Monroe declared to Congress that the Americas were no longer up for consideration when European powers decided to go a-colonizing.

Optimism — During Monroe's presidency, national optimism and patriotic themes influenced American society, culture, and economics.

Nationalism — Young voters elected Monroe with the expectation of expanding the country westward.

Republicans — Monroe's Republican Party moved to the forefront in all regions of the country, as the Federalists quietly faded away.

Opponent — Monroe was so well-liked, and the country was so happy, that he ran for his second term unopposed. In the 1820 election, he received all but one of the electoral votes.

Economy — During Monroe's presidency, the nation focused on economic growth, by supporting the construction of roads and canals, and by buying American-made products over European imports.

THE ERA OF GOOD FEELINGS

The Era of Good Feelings—a time in James Monroe's presidency during which the American people felt a sense of nationalism and optimism—was so named because only one political party was in existence, resulting in political harmony and very few political battles.

Nationalism: National identity grew. Instead of people thinking of themselves as from a certain state (such as *Virginians* or *New Yorkers*) they thought of themselves as *Americans*.

Expansion: Americans heated up their interest moving westward toward the frontier's potential for new opportunities.

Transportation: The construction of roads and canals improved the flow of commerce throughout the nation.

Economics: The national economy grew due to country-wide support of taxes limiting European competition.

The Monroe Doctrine: In a December 1823 address to Congress, Monroe laid out what was called the Monroe Doctrine. It was in response to concerns about a Russian presence in Alaska and possible Spanish bids for power in South America.

The Monroe Doctrine declared that, in the Americas, the United States would not allow new colonies or any other interference by outside powers, namely European countries. It would become one of the most important foundations of U.S. foreign policy in future years.

Not-So-Good Feelings

Of course, everyone did not agree on everything. Political debate continued on questions ranging from the National Bank, to sectionalism and the future of slavery, to tariffs on imports. In addition, Monroe objected to using federal funds for "internal improvements" such as roads and canals, leaving it to the individual states to pay for their own improvements.

BY THE TIME MONROE TOOK OFFICE...

Two things happened in the last days of Madison's presidency:

- Tariff of 1816 — Congress raised taxes on certain imported goods. As the purpose of the tax was to protect U.S. manufacturers from European competition, it was called, quite logically, a protective tariff.
- The American System — To reduce U.S. dependence on Europe, Henry Clay developed the American System. He meant to 1) stimulate demand for American products by encouraging northeastern factory construction; 2) discourage competition from foreign imports with protective tariffs; 3) provide a national currency to funnel more money into the economy by chartering a second national bank; 4) encourage internal improvements in each state. (Only on this last one did Monroe disagree; he felt that federal funds should not be spent on roads and canals, and repeatedly vetoed acts that would have provided funds for such projects.)

The Panic of 1819

After the War of 1812 ended, 1) the country found itself again with war debts to be paid; 2) caught up in all the "good feelings," a number of people bought Western land on credit.

The Second Bank of the United States decided to take steps to control inflation and pay off the war debts. In January of 1819, The Second Bank of the United States suddenly tightened credit policies and called in loans for payment. A financial panic followed:

- State banks closed
- The value of paper money fell
- Unemployment increased
- People declared bankruptcy
- Western farmlands faced foreclosure

TIME MARCHES ON: FIFTY YEARS AFTER THE DECLARATION

A quick review of the country fifty years after declaring independence reveals a successful Constitution-based political system. With a central government based on healthy competition between political parties, the country had seen great territorial growth and industrial change. Specifically, America was a democratic civilization, both in society and politics. Without the rigid class system of European countries, everyone (or, specifically, every white male) was treated equally, in their job opportunities, their dress, their financial potential, and public interactions.

Changes in the political scene were just as democratic. New states wrote their constitutions to allow all free white males the power to vote and the original states revised their constitutions to match. Political parties began holding conventions to nominate their candidates. In presidential elections, states moved from allowing the legislature to choose the members of their electoral college to allowing the people to choose the members of their electoral college by popular election.

Now with two major political parties, third parties surfaced that could also influence political decision-making. Another change that influenced politicians was the way they achieved their office: More and more government officials on all levels, local, state, and national, were elected to office instead of being appointed.

Major Supreme Court decisions during this time include:

- *Marbury v. Madison* (1803): Established judicial review of the Supreme Court ruling on the constitutionality of laws and executive actions
- *Fletcher v. Peck* (1810): Set a precedent ruling state laws unconstitutional
- *Martin v. Hunter's Lease* (1816): Established Supreme Court jurisdiction over state courts
- *McCulloch v. Maryland* (1819): Gave the federal government implied powers and gave federal laws supremacy over state laws
- *Gibbons v. Ogden* (1824): Established federal government control of interstate commerce

JOHN QUINCY ADAMS' PRESIDENCY (1825-1829)

John Quincy Adams was the oldest son of John Adams, the second president of the United States. If anyone was born with American politics in his blood, John Quincy Adams would surely qualify.

Adams ran for president in 1824 against three opponents from his own party. Naturally, the electoral votes were split with no majority: Andrew Jackson got ninety-nine votes, Adams got eighty-four votes, William H. Crawford got forty-one, and Henry Clay got thirty-seven votes. Henry Clay aligned with Adams, and transferred his votes to Adams. Then, Adams chose Clay as his Secretary of State.

Jackson's supporters accused Adams of a "corrupt bargain" with Clay, and continued to dwell on the accusation throughout his presidency. The controversy contributed to Adams's loss in the 1828 campaign. Both sides spread nasty rumors about each other, and in 1828 Jackson defeated Adams 178 to eighty-three.

Throughout his long political career, John Quincy Adams believed in taking whatever measures benefited the country as a whole, even when that did not benefit his own region.

Adams believed in promoting arts and sciences, especially scientific research, and battled disapproval of government financing for such projects to benefit all the people in the nation.

During Adams' presidency, Congress passed the Tariff of 1828, also known as the Tariff Abominations. The high import duties on manufactured goods and raw materials were meant to protect Northern industry from foreign competition. While it did that, it also hurt the South, where cotton farmers depended on those imports for their production needs.

American Literature
Edgar Allan Poe

American poet and author Edgar Allan Poe is most famous for his morbid works and psychological horror tales, and for writing the original modern detective story. He was born in 1809. Considering that his father abandoned the family in 1810 and his mother died in 1811, Poe's obsession with death—reflected in his writings—is understandable.

Poe led a reckless life. While attending college, he spent his time drinking and gambling, and left in 1827 for a clerking job to pay off debts. Soon, he quit and began a two-year army tour. In 1830 he secured a position at West Point's military academy, which lasted about five years before he had himself deliberately expelled for neglect of duty. In 1835, he became editor of the *Southern Literary Messenger*, where he wrote for two years, but was fired in 1837 for drunkenness.

Poe's personal life was equally rough. At the age of twenty-seven, Poe married his thirteen-year-old cousin in 1836. She was unhealthy throughout their marriage and died of tuberculosis in 1847. Poe himself died two years later at the age of 40; many assume from alcoholism and drug abuse.

Famous Works of Edgar Allan Poe

- *Tamerlane and Other Poems* (1827)
- *Poems* (1831)
- "The Fall of the House of Usher" (1839), horror story
- "The Murders in the Rue Morgue" (1841), detective story
- "The Pit and the Pendulum" (1842), horror story
- "The Tell-Tale Heart" (1843), horror story
- "The Purloined Letter" (1844), detective story
- "The Cask of Amontillado" (1846), eerie revenge tale
- "The Bells" (1849), a poem manipulating rhythm and sound to echo bells chiming
- "Annabel Lee" (1849), about losing a lover

How Do You Spell N-o-a-h W-e-b-s-t-e-r?

The next time you drag out your trusty dog-eared dictionary to look up a word, thank journalist Noah Webster for collecting and documenting American usage of the English language.

Webster was a firm believer in the United States' independence, including cultural distinction. He believed in preserving the differences in American English from British in its spelling, grammar, pronunciation, idiom, and style.

In 1828, after more than twenty years studying the English language as it was used in America, Webster published the monumental *American Dictionary of the English Language*. With 70,000 entries, it introduced 12,000 more words (including *skunk* and *chowder*) and about 40,000 more definitions than Americans had ever seen in any earlier English dictionary.

To arrive at this historic contribution to the English language, Webster first relied on his experience from publishing two earlier books: a 1783 spelling book, *Webster's Elementary Spelling Book,* and the 1806 *A Compendious Dictionary of the English Language*. He traveled to both England and France in his research. Astonishingly, he learned twenty-six languages, including Anglo-Saxon and Sanskrit, for first-hand information on word origins.

Aside from his enduring gift to the American language, Noah Webster was a Yale-educated intellectual who served in the American Revolution, studied law, and taught school (in fact, he helped found Amherst College in Massachusetts). Among works he wrote on politics, economics, and physical science:

- *Sketches of American Policy,* 1785, urging adoption of the U.S. Constitution from his Federalist Party perspective.
- The New York City daily newspaper *The Minerva,* and a semiweekly, *The Herald,* both supporting the Federalists.
- The two-volume *A Brief History of Epidemic and Pestilential Diseases,* 1799.

THE ANDREW JACKSON TOP TEN LIST

Top Ten Things About Andrew Jackson's Presidency (*in no particular order*)

10. Symbol of the Common Man. Jackson chewed tobacco, fought duels, and had a bad temper. After his inauguration, Jackson had planned to host a public reception at the White House for everyone. His excited followers thronged the White House, crowding every room. Punch was spilled on the floors, glass and china were broken, and mud was tracked in onto the rugs. Finally, creative waiters carried the liquor out onto the lawn, and the crowds moved the party outside.

9. The Spoils System. Jackson was the first president to "clean house" when he took office, meaning he removed officials that had been appointed by previous presidents of other parties, and replaced them with his own people. This became known as "the Spoils System" after New York Senator William L. Marcy justified the practice, saying, "To the victor belong the spoils."

8. Indian Removal Act of 1830. In the ongoing struggle between pioneering settlers on the western frontier, and the Native Americans already occupying the lands, Jackson came down squarely on the side of the Americans. His solution was to relocate the Native Americans from their homelands to territory west of the Mississippi River. Thousands of Native Americans were forcibly resettled, and Jackson created the Bureau of Indian Affairs in 1836.

7. Nullification. Some states got the notion that states had the right to decide whether or not to obey a federal law or to nullify it (*nullify* means "to make invalid.") Subscribing to this nullification theory, South Carolina said the Tariff of Abominations of 1828 was unconstitutional. Arguments on both sides escalated, and in 1832 Jackson declared that nullification was treason. This effectively got all states onto the federal authority bandwagon.

6. The Second Bank. Jackson did not trust the Second Bank of the United States, feeling that it served the wealthy without providing for the common man. He determined to "kill" (his word) the bank, first by withdrawing all federal funds from the bank at a time when Congress wasn't in session to okay or deny the move. (He could do this because the bank was actually a privately-owned bank that held federal deposits and served the public.) He moved all the federal money to selected state banks, which his opponents called his "pet banks."

5. Specie Circular. In 1836, Jackson issued the "Specie Circular" stating that, going forward, western lands could only be purchased with actual silver or gold (or *specie*). It would no longer be possible to use paper money to buy land.

4. Panic of 1837. In response to Jackson's removal of federal funds from the national bank, Second Bank president Nicholas Biddle thought he knew how to get back at Jackson. He started calling in loans and not making new loans. Whether or not it affected Jackson on a personal level, the main impact of this action was an economic depression.

3. Texas. During Jackson's second term, the Texans fought for and won independence from Mexico. Jackson did not annex Texas, because he worried about the implications of bringing in another slave state. But, he did recognize the independent republic of Texas.

2. Chief Justice Roger Brook Taney. After U.S. Supreme Court Chief Justice John Marshall died in 1835, Jackson named Secretary of the Treasury Roger Brook Taney to succeed him. Along with five other associate justices whom Jackson appointed, Jackson imprinted his political beliefs on the Supreme Court for years to come.

1. Martin Van Buren. Jackson all but hand-picked Martin Van Buren to be his successor as president.

Rachel Jackson

When Andrew Jackson arrived in Nashville in 1788, he found room and board at the home of John Donelson's widow. He soon fell in love with her twenty-one-year-old daughter, Rachel. Rachel, however, was married to Lewis Robards, although by then they were already separated.

Believing that Robards had divorced Rachel in 1790, Andrew married her in 1791, and they began living as husband and wife. Two years later they found out that back in 1790, Robards had filed a petition for divorce, but the actual decree had just become final in 1793. They quietly held a second (legitimate) marriage ceremony in 1794.

However, gossips like nothing more than scandal, and political opponents know how to spin a good scandal. They weren't unprovoked. If you'll recall, before Jackson was elected president, John Quincy Adams served one term after an election that was so close it had to be decided by the House of Representatives.

At the time, Andrew Jackson felt that John Quincy Adams had achieved his win by corrupt means. Jackson and his followers took every chance they could get to hinder Adams in his executive duties.

In turn, Adams' followers dug up some dirt on Andrew Jackson—namely, adultery and bigamy—which just happened to disgrace his wife as well, even if it was more than thirty years after the fact.

Rachel quietly endured the slander and humiliation. Andrew, however, was more aggressive in defending his wife's honor. In fact, Jackson almost challenged Henry Clay to a duel over the accusations.

Less than three weeks after Andrew Jackson learned of his election victory, and before he was even able to take office, Rachel died.

What Did You Say About My Wife?

In 1806, Charles Dickinson made the mistake of muttering something crude about Rachel in the presence of her husband. During the subsequent argument, Dickinson shot Jackson in the chest, just a few inches from his heart. But Jackson was too enraged to collapse in pain. Instead, he shot and killed Dickinson and then walked away.

THE EATON AFFAIR

This little tidbit has all the classic components of scandal: a politician, a married woman, an unsuspecting husband, juicy rumors, snobby "society" ladies, and even a U.S. President.

The President: Andrew Jackson

The Politician: John Henry Eaton, Secretary of War under Jackson

The Married Woman: The beautiful Margaret O'Neill Eaton, better known as Peggy, the daughter of a Washington barkeeper

The Unsuspecting Husband: U.S. Navy purser John B. Timberlake, who died in 1828 while on duty in the Mediterranean

The Juicy Rumors: Peggy Timberlake, lonely while her husband was away at sea, may have already been intimately familiar with John Eaton before John Timberlake's untimely passing

The Hasty Ceremony: After John Timberlake's death, Peggy and John Eaton were quickly married in 1829, the same year he became Secretary of War

The Snobs: Wives of other cabinet members, especially Vice President John C. Calhoun's "better half," snubbed Mrs. Eaton publicly and led Washington society to do the same

The Only Supporter: Of Jackson's entire Cabinet, widower and Secretary of State Martin Van Buren was the only one who defended Peggy Eaton

The President's Reaction: Jackson, who knew firsthand the humiliation of gossip (and even blamed his beloved wife's death on grief over whispers of scandal), defended Peggy Eaton's reputation. He replaced certain men in his cabinet, not coincidentally the ones whose wives had been the nastiest to Peggy. He bonded with Van Buren, and assured Van Buren he would be nominated for president in 1836— instead of Vice President John C. Calhoun

EXTRA CREDIT: After John Eaton died, fifty-six-year-old Peggy married a nineteen-year-old Italian dancer. They were later divorced.

INVENTORS WHO GAVE US ADVANCES IN FARMING

Cyrus McCormick

Inventor Cyrus Hall McCormick developed the first successful reaping machine in 1831. Before 1830, it took sixty-one hours to cultivate one acre of land; after McCormick invented the reaper in 1831, the number was reduced to three.

McCormick's reaper was a major contributor to the change, which meant more acres could be farmed. His technically advanced reaper was truly the basis for developing modern agriculture; McCormick's industrial applications are still used today in reaping equipment.

In addition to his original invention, McCormick tinkered with the design, and added a self-rake and a twine binder. A shrewd businessman, McCormick himself took part in manufacturing and marketing his invention. He built a factory for large-scale reaper production then proceeded to sell the machines with field demonstrations and advertising testimonials coupled with product guarantees and deferred payment plans.

John Deere

Inventor John Deere began by inventing a plow blade to till the sticky prairie sod, and you know the rest.

Deere's early blacksmithing apprenticeship in Vermont proved to serve his later career quite well. You see, back then, blacksmiths did a lot more than shoe horses, including other ironwork like making and repairing farm tools.

Even Deere's early unsuccessful business ventures as a Vermont blacksmith served him well, as he racked up debt and then moved further west toward the land of opportunity. In 1836, he relocated his blacksmith trade to Grand Detour on the Rock River in Illinois.

Upon arriving in Illinois, Deere saw that the land was quite different from the soil back east. Farmers in Illinois did not have the same success with their "eastern" tools when trying to plow the thick, sticky sod. In 1837, he designed a polished, smooth steel blade that sliced through the mud and became known as a "self-scouring steel plow."

John C. Calhoun, Political Giant

South's Carolina's John C. Calhoun was indeed a political giant of his day. Throughout his career, he debated issues, offered his strong opinions favoring slavery, and affected change from the War of 1812 until the eve of the Civil War. In fact, Calhoun played a large role in South Carolina's first threat to secede from the Union, thirty years before the Civil War.

Nationalist Beliefs: Calhoun was part of a group of nationalists who disagreed with President Madison's peaceful solution to Britain's seizure of American ships. These "War Hawks" were instrumental in urging declaration of war on Britain in 1812. (Within two decades, Calhoun had reversed his beliefs from nationalism to states' rights.)

Territory Expansion: As Secretary of War, Calhoun sent General Andrew Jackson to take care of the Seminole War in Florida, in any way that Jackson thought best. Jackson thought it best to take Florida from the Spanish; he did, managing to upset Britain and thus anger Calhoun in the process.*

As a U.S. Senator, Calhoun supported annexation of Texas and opposed the Wilmot Proviso banning slavery in western territories.

Nullification Crisis: Calhoun led his native South Carolina in opposing taxes that benefitted the North but not the South. Calhoun wrote and published an anonymous essay emphasizing that a state could refuse to enforce (or *nullify*) any federal laws.

In 1832, the South Carolina legislature nullified the 1828 and 1832 federal tariffs, refused to collect the taxes in the state, and threatened to leave the Union if the federal government tried to enforce the taxes. To show they meant business, the state started training its own military forces.

Mere days later, President Jackson told the people of South Carolina that threatening disunion by armed force bordered on treason, insisted that all federal laws be obeyed, and got Congress's permission to use federal troops to enforce the taxes. In the meantime, secession was avoided that time with a compromise tariff.

Proslavery Debate: Shortly before his death, Calhoun debated with Massachusetts Senator Daniel Webster over slavery and states' rights.

On March 4, 1850, Calhoun began by demanding a specific constitutional amendment guaranteeing political balance between the North and South. He said Southern slaveholders had as much right to settle the West as any Americans. The clincher: If Northerners thought otherwise, it probably was time for the North and South to separate in peace.

Webster responded on March 7. Speaking in favor of preserving the Union, Webster criticized northern abolitionists and southern secessionists alike as extremists. He said that slavery in the west was a nonissue, because the land and economy were not suited to large plantations and slave labor. Webster concluded by saying that separation of the North and South could not be peaceful, but would be by war.

Calhoun's last statement on the Senate floor was in response to Webster, saying that the Union could, indeed, be broken. He died on March 31, 1850.

*The political relationship between Calhoun and Jackson remained rocky. Calhoun was elected vice president under Andrew Jackson. It was Calhoun's wife who led the other cabinet wives in snubbing Peggy Eaton. Partly over the Eaton affair, Calhoun in 1832 was the first U.S. vice president to resign the office.

John C. Calhoun's Political Offices

1811–1817: South Carolina Representative
1817–1825: James Monroe's Secretary of War
1825–1829: John Quincy Adams's Vice President
1829–1832: Andrew Jackson's Vice President
1832–1844: South Carolina Senator
1844–1845: John Tyler's Secretary of State
1845–1850: South Carolina Senator

CRASH COURSE
REMEMBER THE ALAMO

There's more to the Texas Revolution than the Alamo, but the famous cry sums up the grit and determination of the men who developed the Republic of Texas.

In 1820 Moses Austin got the Spanish government's permission to settle Americans in Texas. After he died, his son, Stephen Austin, continued the plan. Over the next fifteen years, Austin furthered the objectives of declaring independence.

In 1834, Mexican soldier Antonio López de Santa Anna took control of the Mexican government and decided to suppress talk of Texas independence. The first battle of the Texas Revolution in October 1835 ended in the Mexicans' forced retreat. Texans mustered an army that won several battles in the fall of 1835, including capturing San Antonio in December.

The Alamo: The Mexican army initiated the most historic battle in the war for Texas independence. On February 23, 1836, General Santa Anna led more than two thousand soldiers to San Antonio. The 155 Texas soldiers retreated to The Alamo, an old mission. Mexican troops surrounded the fort and attacked. Reinforcements of thirty-two men arrived for the Texans on March 1. They held the Mexican army until March 6. All 187 of the Texas soldiers, including American frontiersmen Davy Crockett and James Bowie and Colonel William Barrett Travis, were brutally killed, but they did take out about six hundred Mexican soldiers in the process. Only the civilians in the mission were spared.

In the meantime, a convention of Texans formally declared independence from Mexico on March 2, 1836, and named David G. Burnet as provisional president, and Sam Houston as commander in chief of Texas forces.

On April 21, 1836, the Texan army, sounding the battle cry of "Remember the Alamo!" defeated the Mexican troops, captured Santa Anna, and gained their independence at the Battle of San Jacinto.

MARTIN VAN BUREN'S PRESIDENCY
(1837-1841)

As Andrew Jackson's secretary of state (first term) and later vice president (second term), Martin Van Buren was a Jackson favorite. To support his friend, Jackson vocalized Van Buren as his handpicked successor. As such, Van Buren had little trouble winning the election.

Van Buren received 170 electoral votes, William Henry Harrison received seventy-three, Hugh Lawson White of Tennessee received twenty-six, Daniel Webster managed to get fourteen, and Willie P. Mangum of North Carolina eked out eleven.

Van Buren's son Abraham served as his private secretary. Because Van Buren's wife had died almost twenty years earlier, Abraham's wife Angelica (Dolley Madison's relative) fulfilled first lady duties for Van Buren.

During Van Buren's term of office:

- In taking over the country's leadership, Van Buren stepped into financial panic. Banks refused to accept paper money, bankruptcies were declared, and unemployment rates spiked.
- Van Buren inherited the Seminole war in Florida. At issue: the government's relocating all Native Americans west of the Mississippi River. Under their chief Osceola, the Seminole resisted until Osceola was seized in 1837; then they were forced westward.
- Van Buren introduced a bill establishing an independent treasury system to hold and distribute government funds. It did not get Congress's approval until 1840, when the country was beginning to come out of depression.
- Van Buren introduced an executive order limiting labor on federal public works to no more than ten hours daily.

By the end of Van Buren's first term, Jackson had returned home, leaving Van Buren without his strong Washington advocate. More damning, the Whig Party blamed Van Buren's Democratic Party for the recent depression (calling him "Martin Van Ruin"). William Henry Harrison defeated Van Buren, 234 electoral votes to sixty.

SHOT HEARD 'ROUND THE WORLD

The battle for America's independence began on April 19, 1775, when Minute Men and militia members clashed with British troops in and around Lexington and Concord, Massachusetts. "The shot heard 'round the world" was fired during the skirmish. Of course, the event wasn't immediately called that, as good catchphrases sometimes require a gestation period. Ralph Waldo Emerson coined the expression in the first stanza of *The Concord Hymn*, written in 1837 to commemorate the erection of a monument honoring the fighters of that day sixty-two years earlier.

The full stanza reads:

> *By the rude bridge that arched the flood,*
> *Their flag to April's breeze unfurled;*
> *Here once the embattled farmers stood;*
> *And fired the shot heard round the world.*

Emerson was fortunate to strike catchphrase gold with that line, as the rest of the hymn doesn't quite have that kind of oomph. The third stanza, for example, goes:

> *On this green bank, by this soft stream,*
> *We set today a votive stone,*
> *That memory may their deeds redeem,*
> *When, like our sires, our sons are gone.*

It's doubtful that "placed with joy a votive stone" would have ever stirred anybody's patriotic blood. But it's no matter. Like other verses of "The Star-Spangled Banner," the rest of "The Concord Hymn" are mostly forgotten, and Emerson's place in historic phraseology is secure. That first stanza is engraved on the Minute Man statue at Minute Man National Historic Park in Concord.

TIPPECANOE AND TYLER, TOO

It might not sing to our ears, but "Tippecanoe and Tyler, Too" once had serious marketing sizzle. Long before modern campaigns spent millions to convince voters that it was morning in America, or that they like Ike, a nineteenth-century pop song cost Martin Van Buren—and his Brobdingnagian sideburns—his re-election.

The story begins in 1811, when Indiana Territory governor William Henry Harrison led American forces against Indian forces at Prophetstown, Indiana. Harrison wanted to rout a nascent revolt known as Tecumseh's War, for Shawnee chief Tecumseh's Indian alliance. Harrison's forces triumphed, albeit with heavy losses. Of such things are popular legends born, and Harrison became known as "Old Tippecanoe," after the river Prophetstown was located on.

Fast-forward to 1840, when Democrat Martin Van Buren sought re-election to the presidency, running against Whig candidate Harrison and his vice president running mate, John Tyler. Newspaper publisher and politician Horace Greeley began publishing *Log Cabin*, a campaign paper supporting Harrison. The paper pitched Harrison as a downhome man of the people, as opposed to the high-falutin' Van Buren, and included the main hymn of the campaign, "Tippecanoe and Tyler, Too."

Written by Alexander Coffman Ross, an Ohio merchant, the song began:

What's the cause of this commotion, motion, motion,
Our country through?
It is the ball a-rolling on

For Tippecanoe and Tyler too.
For Tippecanoe and Tyler too.
And with them we'll beat little Van, Van, Van,
Van is a used up man.
And with them we'll beat little Van.

Maybe it sounded better back then. At any rate, Harrison-mania took off, and he defeated Van Buren. But Harrison's victory would be short-lived. Thirty days after he took office, he died of pneumonia.

LOG CABIN AND HARD CIDER CAMPAIGN

In the election of 1840, the Democrats again nominated current president Martin Van Buren. They didn't even nominate a vice president running mate for him, which makes you wonder exactly how badly they wanted Van Buren reelected (or not).

The Whig party nominated popular war hero William Henry Harrison as their candidate with Virginia's John Tyler as the vice-presidential running mate. Their campaign slogan was "Tippecanoe and Tyler, Too!"

The candidates running in the election of 1840 didn't have a whole lot to say on the issues of the day. This led to a lot of other, less substantial, things being said and done:

- Democrats said "old" Harrison would be just as happy drinking a jug of hard cider in front of his log cabin as serving president.
- Whigs spun this insult into their "Log Cabin and Hard Cider" campaign, to show that Harrison was a man of the people.
- Whigs even began serving hard cider at campaign stops.
- Whigs accused Van Buren of not being a man of the people, drinking wine instead.

Such comments led to political poems such as this lovely ditty, which was not so much accurate as it was iambic. (Of the two, Van Buren was the less wealthy, while Harrison led a more comfortable life.)

Let Van from his coolers of silver drink wine
And lounge on his cushioned settee
Our man on a buckeye bench can recline
Content with hard cider is he.

EXTRA CREDIT: Harrison's campaign was hardly contributing to the delinquency of the people. Hard cider is the fermented juice of apples, used both as a beverage and for making vinegar. It is 2 to 8 pecent alcohol. Cider brandy, on the other hand, is made by distilling fermented cider, and it is 40 to 50 percent alcohol.

GEORGIA GOLD RUSH

Today, Georgia is well-known for peaches, a peanut-growing president, the busiest airport, and traffic congestion. But twenty years before anyone found gold in California, the first American gold rush took place in Georgia.

According to the *New Georgia Encyclopedia*, the first reliable citation of finding gold in Georgia was on August 1, 1829. *The Georgia Journal*, a Milledgeville paper, wrote,

> A gentleman of the first respectability in Habersham county, writes us thus under date of 22d July: "Two gold mines have just been discovered in this county, and preparations are making to bring these hidden treasures of the earth to use."

Word of the gold strike circulated, and thousands of would-be Midases headed for Georgia. On just one stream, more than 4,000 miners attempted to pan up a fortune. By 1830, the state produced more than 300 ounces of gold a day. The area near Dahlonega became the nexus of gold production, and boomed as a result.

The fact that Cherokee Indians owned the land was little deterrent to the swarming gold seekers, who simply overwhelmed the Cherokee with sheer numbers. The Cherokee, understandably, dubbed the gold rush "the Great Intrusion." *The New Georgia Encyclopedia* quotes a *Cherokee Phoenix* report:

> Our neighbors who regard no law and pay no respects to the laws of humanity are now reaping a plentiful harvest.... We are an abused people.

The good gold times didn't last. Or, actually, the *great* times didn't last. Although the gold petered out in the 1840s, miners continue to remove gold from the state today, albeit in much smaller quantities. As a reminder of the Georgia gold rush, the state capitol dome in Atlanta is covered in native-mined gold.

Trail of Tears

While Americans continued to move westward as pioneers settling new frontier, Native Americans did not move voluntarily. As white settlers took over their homelands, Native Americans were forced to migrate.

Background:

- 1803 — President Jefferson set aside Louisiana Territory land for Native Americans agreeing to give up eastern lands.
- 1824 — Secretary of War John Calhoun created the Bureau of Indian Affairs to oversee treaty relations and remove natives.
- 1830 — Congress passed the Indian Removal Act to move eastern tribes west of the Mississippi River.

Meanwhile: The main Southeast tribes were the Cherokee, Choctaw, Chickasaw, Creek, and Seminole. To show acceptance of American ways, Cherokee leader Sequoyah developed an alphabet of eighty-five characters. The Cherokee could read and write in their language, and they published newspapers and books.

Assimilating with American culture was not enough. Gold was discovered in Cherokee territory in Georgia, and the American whites insisted they were entitled to it.

Removal: The government forced the southeastern Native Americans to Indian Territory in present-day Oklahoma. From 1838 to 1839, soldiers marched men, women, and children thousands of miles. The path from Georgia to Oklahoma was called the Trail of Tears because around 4,000 Native Americans died from starvation, disease, and exposure on the journey.

Legacy: By the late 1830s, the government had relocated more than thirty tribes westward. By 1850, most Native Americans were living west of the Mississippi River. Soon, settlers began demanding the fertile lands of the Indian Territory in Oklahoma, too.

HENRY CLAY, THE GREAT PACIFICATOR

Henry Clay's reputation as a peacemaker—he was called "The Great Pacificator"—was earned through compromises he engineered during his career. With his moderate views, Clay contributed to American history in the U.S. Senate and as Secretary of State.

Clay's policy also included proposing the "American System" after the War of 1812. It suggested a protective tariff, a strong national bank, and internal improvements.

Compromises of Henry Clay

Treaty of Ghent: Clay was one of the negotiators of the Treaty of Ghent, ending the War of 1812 with Britain. (Here's the whole story: Clay was also one of the "War Hawks" who pushed declaring war on England to begin with.)

Missouri Compromise: In 1820, Clay was the Missouri Compromise's main author, suggesting how to maintain balance between free and slave states.

Compromise Tariff: During the 1830s Nullification Crisis, South Carolina threatened secession over taxes; President Jackson whispered "treason" against South Carolina. Clay drew up a compromise tariff, allowing both sides to back down honorably.

Great Compromise of 1850: Clay drafted the terms of the compromise that again settled the slavery question in new territories, postponing civil war another decade.

Trail of Tears Motorcycle Ride

For about fifteen years now, each fall, hundreds of thousands of motorcycle riders have gathered in Chattanooga, Tennessee, to commemorate the removal of Native Americans to Oklahoma. In the largest organized motorcycle ride in the world, riders today follow along one path taken in 1838.

ANTEBELLUM SOCIAL REFORM

The early 1800s were a time of reform in society. In addition to women's rights and abolishing slavery, reformists turned their attention to education, welfare, and liquor.

Education

Fearful of the uneducated poor, middle-class reformers in the 1840s began creating free schools supported by government taxes. Horace Mann of Massachusetts advocated improved schools, attendance requirements, a longer school year, and teacher training. While Protestants emphasized hard work, punctuality, and sobriety in the state schools, Roman Catholics founded private schools to teach their religious beliefs. Private colleges also flourished in the 1830s and 1840s.

Public Institutions

Reformers took up the cause of those unable to care for themselves, namely criminals, the mentally ill, and the poor. They suggested new public institutions, such as state-supported prisons, mental hospitals, and poorhouses.

Newly built, clean prison buildings replaced crude jails. These *penitentiaries* were designed to allow prisoners to repent from their sins through disciplinary rules, moral instruction, and work programs.

Mental hospitals were transformed from unsanitary versions of prisons to refuges where the emotionally disturbed could receive treatment.

Special, separate institutions addressed the needs of the physically disabled. Thomas Gallaudet founded a school for the deaf, and Samuel Gridley Howe founded another for the blind.

Alcoholic Temperance

With a high rate of alcohol consumption in 1820 America (five gallons of hard liquor per person), reformers targeted alcohol as the cause of social problems. Various groups believed that excessive drinking led to crime, poverty, and decreased work output, and provided their own solutions for temperance.

The American Temperance Society, founded by Protestant ministers in 1826, urged everyone not just to drink moderately but to pledge against drinking alcohol at all.

The Washingtonians, founded by recovering alcoholics in 1840, approached alcoholism as a disease to be treated.

The state of Maine in 1851 passed a law completely prohibiting making and selling liquor.

By 1855, thirteen other states had enacted similar laws prohibiting alcohol.

The temperance cause was deferred during the Civil War but later validated by the eighteenth amendment, passed in 1919, prohibiting making, selling, or transporting intoxicating liquors. The time until the twenty-first amendment repealed the eighteenth amendment in 1933 was called *Prohibition*, because alcohol was prohibited.

Reaction to Social Reform

Most of the reformation was happening in the North, and to some extent, to the West. Southerners, on the other hand, loved their traditions and were not quick to accept change. They viewed all the social revolutions as a package deal with the antislavery movement, and developed a distrust for reform of any kind.

EXTRA CREDIT: The word *temperance* means "moderation in indulging a passion, especially the use of alcoholic liquors." The word *antebellum*, in Latin means "before the war," and now specifically means "before the Civil War." The word *penitentiary* literally means "showing penance or remorse."

WESTERN CHARACTERS

If the Wild West had truly been as wild as portrayed in movies and pulp novels, it's doubtful anyone would have ever survived long enough to settle the vast expanses. Still, the era did produce some notable characters, including these two judges.

Judge Roy Bean, 1825–March 16, 1903

Bean was an eccentric-to-crooked entrepreneur, swindler, self-styled law dispenser and all-around rake who gained fame as a bar owner and justice of the peace in Texas. Bean's reported exploits include ending every wedding ceremony he performed with "and may God have mercy on your souls." While living in San Antonio, Bean sold milk that he watered down. When a customer noticed a minnow in his milk bottle, Bean blamed the occurrence on his practice of watering his cows in the river. He fined a corpse for sleeping in his courtroom/bar. (The doubly unfortunate corpse had $40 in his pockets.) Bean is sometimes called a "hanging judge," although no evildoer was ever hanged as a result of Bean's rulings.

Judge Isaac Parker, October 15, 1838–November 17, 1896

Unlike Bean, Parker was really a hanging judge. Parker became judge of the federal court for the Western District of Arkansas in Fort Smith in 1875. During the first term of Parker's court, eight men found guilty of murder were sentenced to death. In his 21-year term on the Fort Smith bench, Parker sentenced 160 people to death. But Parker wasn't really the bloodthirsty judge of myth. For 14 years of his term, federal law required Parker to hand down a death sentence for guilty verdicts in rape and murder cases. In addition, Parker never ended his death sentences with the statement that the guilty party was to hang by his neck until "dead, dead, dead."

INDIAN CHARACTERS

Here are some thumbnail sketches of a few notable Native
Americans.

Sitting Bull, circa 1831-December 15, 1890

This Hunkpapa Sioux chief is most famous for leading the Native
American defeat of Gen. George Custer's troops at the Battle of Little
Bighorn on June 25, 1876. Some 3,000 warriors who had left their
government reservations to follow Sitting Bull defeated Custer's 7th
Cavalry, killing 263 of Custer's men as well as Custer himself. Sitting
Bull's victory was a Pyrrhic one, however, as public outcry over the
battle led the Army to pour thousands more troops into the area, and
Sitting Bull was forced across the U.S. border to Canada.

Geronimo, June 1829–February 17, 1909

Born Goyathlay (or "One who yawns"), this Apache leader refused
to move to a reservation and instead began raiding areas in New
Mexico, Arizona, and northern Mexico. Finally captured at Skeleton
Canyon, Arizona, in 1886, Geronimo was shipped by rail car to
Florida's Fort Pickens, while his family was sent to Fort Marion, also in
Florida. Geronimo and his family were reunited at Alabama's Mount
Vernon Barracks in 1887. Later, Geronimo became something of a
tourist attraction, appearing at the 1901 Pan-American Exposition, the
1904 Louisiana Purchase Exposition, and sometimes being presented as
the "Apache Terror."

Crazy Horse, circa 1845–September 5, 1877

A Lakota Sioux, Crazy Horse determinedly fought against changes
in his people's way of life. He refused to have any pictures taken of
him, fought against settlement of Indian lands by white settlers, battled
alongside Sitting Bull at the Battle of Little Bighorn and died while
resisting imprisonment by American forces. Crazy Horse's legacy lives
on in the Crazy Horse Memorial, which is being carved in the Black
Hills of South Dakota. When completed, the sculpture will be almost
600 feet high.

HOMESTEAD ACT OF 1862

Daniel Freeman's name isn't exactly up there with Wild Bill Hickock or Jesse James when it comes to Wild West fame, but it should be. Because of Freeman and a few million like-minded individuals, the American expansion that led to the Wild West took place.

Freeman's story began when President Abraham Lincoln signed the Homestead Act on May 20, 1862. Any U.S. citizen, or even an intended citizen, who had never taken up arms against the U.S. government could file an application to take possession of 160 acres of government-owned land. All the applicant had to do was live on the land for five years, build at least a twelve by fourteen foot dwelling, and grow crops. After that, he could file for a deed of title and make the land his own.

The Homestead Act was to go into effect on January 1, 1863. Coincidentally, Freeman, a Union Army scout who had his eye on some land in Gage County, Nebraska, was scheduled to leave Nebraska for St. Louis on January 1, 1863. On December 31, 1862, Freeman attended a New Year's Eve party. His co-partiers included some local land officials. Told of Freeman's plight, a land office clerk opened the office just past midnight, allowing Freeman to file his claim and become the first person to reap benefits from the Homestead Act.

Freeman and 417 other homesteaders filed claims that January 1. In the decades afterwards, more than 1.6 million would file claims, possessing more than 270 million acres of public lands. The Homestead Act wasn't repealed until the passage of the Federal Land Policy and Management Act of 1976, and even then, a special ten-year exemption on Alaskan land claims was included in the legislation. Today, Freeman's homestead near Beatrice, Nebraska is the site of the Homestead National Monument.

CRASH COURSE

WILLIAM LLOYD GARRISON

When we call William Lloyd Garrison an Abolitionist, we use a capital "A." That's because he was THE voice of human equality, once even burning the Constitution in protest of its permitting slavery and suggesting it might be necessary for the North to secede from any Union allowing slavery.

Early on, Garrison voiced his views on human rights in anonymous articles to incite Northerners to act against slavery. In 1829, he joined publisher Benjamin Lundy in producing a monthly magazine, *Genius of Universal Emancipation.* One article angered a slave trader who sued him for libel in 1830. Garrison spent seven weeks in jail when he could not pay the penalty fine.

Garrison's views on slavery became increasingly radical, and he eventually left Lundy. He believed that slavery was a moral issue too deep to solve by voting or compromise. From his perspective, slavery was, quite simply a sin, and sin was not open to compromise. He also did not condone violent slave uprisings, because violence was a sin, too. Garrison saw slavery as an equality issue, and pushed for its entire abolition.

On the very first day of the year in 1831, Garrison published the first issue of the *Liberator,* one of the most influential newspapers in the country. In the *Liberator,* Garrison argued for immediate and complete abolition of slavery. He continued to publish the paper, with its articles pushing complete abolition, until the Thirteenth Amendment ending slavery was ratified in 1865.

Garrison organized the New England Anti-Slavery Society and the American Anti-Slavery Society, and also crusaded for women's rights, alcohol prohibition, and the elimination of tobacco use.

EXTRA CREDIT: In 1831, Garrison so offended the State of Georgia that a $5,000 reward was offered for his arrest and conviction under Georgia law.

Dorothea Dix, Social Reformer

Not nearly as many accused criminals would be so quick to cop to an insanity plea these days if they knew that it would result in imprisonment under the dreadful conditions that Dorothea Dix observed of inmates in the 1840s: "confined in cages, closets, cellars, stalls, and pens, where they were chained naked, beaten with rods, and lashed into obedience."

Schoolteacher and headmaster Dorothea Dix developed her concern for the treatment of the mentally ill after she agreed to teach a Sunday School class in a local jail. In addition to convicted criminals, she learned that many mentally ill patients had been locked away in the same facilities—even the same cells—with felons. She was horrified.

Dix was just the kind of take-charge person to do something about it. She spent months traveling to institutions that claimed to treat the mentally ill, and found the same kind of abuse was prevalent almost everywhere. Then, she began reporting her findings, first to the Massachusetts state legislature in 1843, then to other states throughout the country.

Through the campaigning of Dorothea Dix, at least fifteen states began work to improve existing conditions and build new, humane institutions for treating mental patients at the state's expense.

Nursing During the Civil War

Not just involved in reforming the state of mental hospitals, Dix served during the Civil War as superintendent of female nurses. In April 1861, she volunteered with the Union army and two months later was given charge of all women nurses in military hospitals. By all accounts, she was a stern, efficient, and effective administrator (which we would have already guessed, based on her accomplishments for the treatment of the mentally ill).

Union Pacific Act

The Homestead Act of 1862 helped begin the exodus of settlers into the new lands of the west, but America still needed a way to supply the settlers and keep the wheels of industry ever rolling westward. A railroad was the obvious choice to achieve those dual goals, but railroads were expensive to build. Private industry wanted federal money to help defray the cost of building a railroad, but the federal government didn't want to just give away that money (it was in the middle of a war, after all), or the land that the railroad would cross. The rather ingenious solution to the problem came in the form of a checkerboard.

On July 1, 1862, President Lincoln signed into law "An Act to aid in the Construction of a Railroad and Telegraph Line from the Missouri River to the Pacific Ocean." The act, which came to be known as the Pacific Railway Act, threw in the added benefit of a telegraph line. The Union Pacific would build westward from Omaha, Nebraska. The Central Pacific would build eastward from Sacramento, California. The two railroad companies would receive thirty-year government bonds for every mile of track they laid. The companies received $16,000 for each mile of flatland track, twice that for foothill track and three times that for mountainous track.

The checkerboard came into play in the form of land grants. The rail companies received every other "section" of land (roughly one square mile, or 640 acres) for ten miles on each side of the track, as well as a 400-foot right-of-way. Congress further tweaked the process with the Pacific Railroad Act of 1864, which doubled the size of the land grants to twenty square miles and also allowed the two rail companies to issue their own bonds. The rail companies were able to fund their expansion, the government didn't have to completely play Santa Claus with its largesse and settlers were able to locate along the route of the new railroad.

From 1862 to 1871, when the land grants were stopped, the federal government had given about eighty railroads more than 123.5 million acres of federal land.

TRANSCONTINENTAL RAILROAD

With the Pacific Railway Acts of 1862 and 1864 providing the funding and incentives, and with the Civil War's end freeing up labor and ending wartime deprivations, the Central Pacific Railroad and Union Pacific Railroad were soon in a full-speed race to lay the most track. Glory, land, and money were all at stake.

The Central Pacific had to overcome the hardest obstacle, that of getting through the Sierra Nevada mountain range. In August 1866, the CP began work on Tunnel 6, which would present incredible challenges for the railroad. With the UP racing eastward, the CP needed to get through the granite of the tunnel as quickly as possible, so the CP attacked construction of the tunnel on four fronts. At the midpoint of the proposed tunnel route, workers dug a tunnel straight down to the depth of the planned tunnel. Once the vertical shaft was complete, crews worked on the tunnel in four directions—outward from the vertical shaft in both directions, and inward from both ends of the proposed route. The number of workers, most of whom were Chinese immigrants, sometimes reached 12,000. Using only manual labor, workers broke through the tunnel in August 1867, one year after beginning the vertical shaft.

The UP and CP continued racing toward each other, but with no agreed-upon meeting point, the two railroads actually began overlapping in their grade work in Utah. With political pressure for a common meeting point mounting, UP engineer Grenville Dodge and CP leader Collis P. Huntington met in January 1869 and agreed to meet at Promontory Summit, Utah. The two crews met at that point on May 10, 1869. Leland Stanford (one of the CP's "Big Four," along with Huntington, Mark Hopkins, and Charles Crocker) drove the Golden Spike that signified the completion of America's Transcontinental Railroad.

WILD WEST TRIVIA

One would expect a rollicking era like the Wild West to produce quite a couple interesting trivia facts, and one would be right. Here's a few the movies and history books might have skipped over.

- What do the Spanish expression "Quien es?" and a roadside urination stop have in common? The deaths of two noted Western characters. In 1881, Sheriff Pat Garrett shot and killed outlaw Billy the Kid when the Kid entered a dark room and didn't recognize Garrett. The outlaw asked "Quien es? Quien es?" Garrett answered with two shots from his revolver, killing the outlaw. In 1908, Garrett was involved in a land dispute with Jesse Wayne Brazel when the two met on a New Mexico road. Garrett and Brazel began arguing. When Garrett stepped to the roadside to urinate, Brazel shot him twice, killing him.

- Chain restaurants might not be the first thing associated with nineteenth-century living, but long before McDonald's put a restaurant on every corner, hundreds of Harvey Girls were serving up Harvey House meals to railroad travelers. Harvey Houses got their start in 1876, when Englishman Fred Harvey worked out a deal to manage the restaurants and hotels of the Santa Fe Railway. He hired Harvey Girls to serve as hostesses at his houses. His girls wore simple outfits of black dresses with a white apron, and were usually well-educated, sophisticated hostesses who lived in nearby dormitories. Eventually, more than a hundred Harvey Houses were built, with a total of some 100,000 ladies serving as Harvey Girls over the years.

WHO SAID WHAT, WILD WEST

An era as deeply mythic, as beloved, as flat-out American as the Wild West pretty much had no choice but to turn out memorable sayings. Here's a few well-turned phrases from that era.

- "Where the Indian killed one buffalo, the hide and tongue hunters killed fifty." Chief Red Cloud
  This pithy contrast between the Native American and white man approaches to ecology is credited to Chief Red Cloud, a Sioux leader.

- "I'll be in hell before you've finished breakfast, boys! Let her rip!" Black Jack Ketchum
  Ketchum was an outlaw in the New Mexico territory who was executed in 1901 for an attempted train robbery. Ketchum had the misfortune of being hanged by an inexperienced hangman who used too long a rope, so he was in fact decapitated. His tombstone reads, "And how his audit stands who knows save Heaven."

- "They say I killed six or seven men for snoring. Well, it ain't true. I only killed one man for snoring," John Wesley Hardin
  Texas gunman Hardin may have had his excesses (he reportedly killed more than forty men), but he wanted to set the record straight about his night-time killings when he made this statement.

- "I hate all white people. You are thieves and liars. You have taken away our land and made us outcasts." Sitting Bull
  The famous chief made his impolitic remarks at an 1883 dinner celebrating the completion of the Northern Pacific Railroad's transcontinental track. But Sitting Bull spoke only Sioux, and the audience spoke only English, so instead of actually translating his words, a quick-thinking Army officer serving as Sitting Bull's interpreter dispensed some pro-white platitudes. Sitting Bull, no doubt perplexed, received a standing ovation.

- "I am a great chief among my people. If you kill me, it will be like a spark on the prairie. It will make a big fire—a terrible fire!" Chief Satanta

  The Kiowa chief, who was arrested for his part in the 1871 Warren Wagon Train Raid, uttered this gem of self-defense at his trial for murder. Perhaps because of Satanta's statement, Governor Edmund Davis commuted Satanta's death sentence to life imprisonment. He served only two years before being released.

- "The more we can kill this year, the less will have to be killed the next war, for the more I see of these Indians, the more convinced I am that they all have to be killed or be maintained as a species of paupers." General William Tecumseh Sherman

  The general with the ironically Indian middle name made this comment in 1867. Sherman was also the originator of the infamous quote, "The only good Indian is a dead Indian."

- "Tombstone has two dance halls, a dozen gambling places and more than twenty saloons. Still, there is hope, for I know of two Bibles in town." Judge Wells Spicer

  Spicer was the justice of the peace in Tombstone, Arizona when the Gunfight at the O.K. Corral took place.

- "Gentlemen, I find the law very explicit on murdering your fellow man, but there's nothing here about killing a Chinaman. Case dismissed." Judge Roy Bean

  Bean, the famous bar owner/justice of the peace, allegedly rendered this verdict in the case of an Irishman charged with killing a Chinese worker.

GOODNIGHT-LOVING TRAIL

The next time you slice into a steak dinner, give a nod of thanks to Charles Goodnight, Oliver Loving, and Joseph McCoy. Without the foresight and business acumen of these three men, the Texas cattle industry might never have become such a part of American history, and the all-American meal might have been pork or chicken.

Goodnight was a former Texas Ranger who had established a Texas cattle ranch, then left it in 1861 to fight for the Confederacy in the Civil War. For the four years of the war, the few hundred head of cattle Goodnight owned roamed and bred, increasing in number. When he came back to his ranch, he found himself the owner of some 8,000 head. Goodnight partnered with fellow rancher Loving, who had made money selling beef to Confederate soldiers during the war. In 1866, the two drove some 2,000 head of cattle north from Texas to Fort Sumner, New Mexico, where they sold some cattle to the U.S. Army. Loving drove the rest of the cattle on to Denver, while Goodnight returned to Texas for more cattle. Goodnight and Loving had shown the economic sagacity of selling Texas beef, and had created the Goodnight-Loving Trail, the first great western cattle trail.

McCoy, a Chicago livestock trader, provided the missing link between Texas cattle and the vast, hungry populations of the east. Besides the logistical problem of driving cattle thousands of miles, Texas Longhorn cattle couldn't be driven through other states because they carried Texas fever, which longhorns survived but which killed other breeds. So McCoy established a cattle shipping point on the Kansas-Pacific Railroad in the Kansas town of Abilene, and Texas cattlemen began driving cattle by the thousands to Abilene. The cattle were bought in Abilene, then shipped to the Chicago stockyards. Texans had a ready outlet for their cattle, and Americans' love of beef was well established.

GROWTH AND ECONOMIC PROSPERITY IN THE EARLY 1800S

Before 1840, most factories had been located in New England, specifically textile mills. After that time, industrialization spread rapidly to the other states of the Northeast. In addition to iron products for railroads and other technologies, new American factories produced:

- shoes
- sewing machines
- ready-to-wear clothing
- firearms
- precision tools

Inventions that advanced American industry

- The sewing machine, 1846, (by Elias Howe) meant clothes were now being produced in factories instead of by hand at home.
- The electric telegraph, 1844, (by Samuel F. B. Morse) meant much faster communication across long distances.

Transportation Expands

Foreign trade expanded in the mid-1800s from shipping advances: utilization of departure schedules for ship voyages; design of first, the fast American clipper ship and then, the steamship; and a boom in the whaling industry due to demand for whale oil.

New rail lines opened up commerce from the Northeast to the Midwest.* It wasn't long before the railroad industry was America's largest industry. Railroads became complex business organizations because they needed capital and labor.

*Expanding rail lines in the Northeast and Midwest didn't do much for the South, which turned out to be a big factor in terms of strategic advantage in the Civil War.

MASON-DIXON LINE

The Englishmen charged with ending a land dispute between two famous families had no way of knowing it at the time, but their efforts would impact far more than which family got what land. Charles Mason and Jeremiah Dixon surveyed themselves right into history.

The story of the Mason-Dixon Line begins in 1632, when England's King Charles I gave George Calvert a charter for Maryland. (Actually, Charles gave Calvert's descendants the charter, since Calvert died five weeks before the charter was enacted.) In 1682, King Charles II gave William Penn a charter for Pennsylvania. The only problem was that the Calverts and Penns couldn't agree on where the dividing line between the two charters was, and a controversy ensued. Eventually, Cresap's War broke out over the boundary dispute.

The two families went to the British courts, which in 1750 decreed that the boundary line was to lie fifteen miles south of Philadelphia. Ten years later (family land squabbles can be like that), the Calverts and Penns agreed with the British decision, and decided to have the land surveyed.

Mason, an astronomer (stars were necessary to accurate surveying), and Dixon, a surveyor, began work on the task of surveying the line in November 1763. The two men placed stones weighing as much as 600 pounds along the line at one-mile intervals, placing a *P* on the stones' north-facing side and an *M* on the south-facing side.

The arduous work of surveying and placing the stones along a 233-mile line took the two men almost four years to complete. They ended their work a little short of their intended finishing point (conflicts with local Indians ended the effort early) on October 9, 1767.

In 1820, the boundary was called the Mason-Dixon Line in Congress during debates over the contentious Missouri Compromise.

Uh-Oh! Panic!

As the saying goes, "All good things must come to an end." And so it was with the economic boom that lasted through the 1850s. A financial panic in 1857 brought with it a drop in prices for goods and crops and unemployment.

Transcending Religion

In the late 1700s and early 1800s, Protestantism made a comeback in another Great Awakening. This time, though, the emphasis was less on hellfire and brimstone and more on love and harmony.

A new denomination—Unitarianism—emerged, embracing the belief that humans are naturally good and demoting the status of Jesus from divine to simply great. Out of Unitarianism grew Transcendentalism and thoughts that everyone has a personal spirituality found within the inner self.

Ralph Waldo Emerson was the best-known Transcendentalist and leader of transcendental philosophers, writers, and reformers. He supported self-reliance: finding your own inner god. Emerson's important writings and works:

- *Nature* (1836) argued against materialism and urged individual freedoms
- "The American Scholar" lecture (1837) to Harvard's Phi Beta Kappa Society urged intellectual independence
- "Address at Divinity College" (1838) to Cambridge divinity graduates argued for self-reliance and intuitive spirituality
- *Essays* (1841) emphasize the self (You probably read some of these in English class: "Self-Reliance," "Compensation," "Spiritual Laws," "Love," "Heroism," "Art")
- *Essays* (1844) recognize limitations of real life ("The Poet," "Manners," "Character")

Henry David Thoreau, a close friend of Emerson, put the transcendental belief of self-reliance to his own test by living in the woods alone for two years. His well-known account of that time, *Walden; or, Life in the Woods* (1854), includes his thoughts during the experiment. Even more importantly, his observations of interaction with nature gave us lasting ecological and conservational descriptions. Thoreau also wrote an essay, "On Civil Disobedience" (1849), advocating nonviolent protest.

TRANSCENDENTAL WRITERS

The Transcendentalist viewpoint influenced an entire generation of distinctly American writers. Their contributions to American literature reflect the thoughts and beliefs prevalent among intellectuals of their time.

Author Nathaniel Hawthorne: Hawthorne's works all revolved around sin, punishment, and individual responsibility. Even in college, Hawthorne had begun his prolific writing career. His contributions to literature include:

- *Grandfather's Chair: A History for Youth* (1841) — sketches of New England history for children
- *Mosses from an Old Manse* (1846) — short stories written while living in a house called the Old Manse, including "Rappaccini's Daughter" and "Young Goodman Brown"
- *The Scarlet Letter* (1850) — his masterpiece novel about Hester Prynne's adultery in a Puritan society, exploring themes of guilt and persecution
- *The House of the Seven Gables* (1851) — novel tracing the corruption of Puritanism in an old New England family
- *The Blithedale Romance* (1852) — a novel inspired by his life at Brook Farm

Author Herman Melville: A friend and neighbor of Nathaniel Hawthorne, Melville wrote about his adventures at sea, including vivid descriptions of nature, both romantic and harsh. *Moby-Dick,* his best-known work of 1851, on the surface was about a captain's search for a white whale; but it was an allegory for conflicts about faith and God's intelligence. Melville's other works include:

- *Omoo, a Narrative of Adventures in the South Seas* (1847) — a sequel based on life in the Polynesian Islands
- *Mardi* (1849) — an allegorical fantasy
- *Redburn, His First Voyage* (1849) — based on Melville's first trip to sea
- *White-Jacket, or the World in a Man-of-War* (1850) — a fictional account based on his U.S. Navy experience

Poet Emily Dickinson: Considered one of the most original nineteenth-century American poets, Dickinson was a deeply sensitive woman who questioned her Puritanical background and explored her spirituality through poetry.

During her lifetime, she published only seven of her almost 2,000 poems. The first volume of *Poems of Emily Dickinson* was published after her death. Dickinson's poetry covered subjects from the agony and ecstasy of love and humor, to death and religious belief. Some of her more famous works include:

- "After Great Pain, A Formal Feeling Comes"
- "Because I Could Not Stop for Death"
- "God Gave a Loaf to Every Bird"
- "I Felt a Funeral in My Brain"
- "Success is Counted Sweetest"

Poet Walt Whitman: Whitman's many influential poems were controversial for the time: some described nature and homosexual love with explicit descriptions of the human body; others shared his philosophy on democracy, war, politics, and slavery (which he strongly opposed).

First self-published in 1855, Whitman's *Leaves of Grass* collection was almost a "living" work; he revised and added to it over and over. The following poems were eventually included in Whitman's collection:

- "Song of Myself" asserts individual worth
- "I Sing the Body Electric" immodestly praises the human body
- "Crossing Brooklyn Ferry" entertains his fascination with ferries and ferry passengers
- "Drum-Taps" reflects his hope for reconciliation between the North and South
- "Oh Captain! My Captain!" was written upon hearing of Abraham Lincoln's death
- "When Lilacs Last in the Dooryard Bloom'd," is a heartfelt deeply mournful lament for the loss of President Lincoln

JOHN TYLER'S PRESIDENCY (1841-1845)

To discuss John Tyler's presidency, first we must address how he became president. Tyler was William Henry Harrison's vice president. During the campaign of 1840, Democrats accused Harrison of being too old for the presidency, calling him "Old Granny" and saying he did not have enough energy to get the job done.

Turns out, the Democrats might have been right. When he took office, Harrison was already sixty-eight years old. He served one month, then died. Tyler moved from the wings to center stage. (To continue the theater metaphor, we'll say that Tyler didn't wait for his cue before plunging into his part: Rather than consider other options for filling the vacated presidency, Tyler had himself immediately sworn in. This proved to be controversial at the time, although today it is the accepted practice.)

Formerly a Democrat, John Tyler was on Harrison's Whig ticket to attract Southern voters. Once he became president, the Democrats wouldn't claim him. He wouldn't allow the Whigs to steamroll him, and they dropped him, too. That didn't leave him a lot of clout in Congress. But, he did have some foreign policy power, and he was able to annex Texas into the United States a week before leaving office.

"His Accidency"

Tyler had himself sworn in as president, even though the Constitution does not specifically say whether a vice president should assume the office or simply act in the office until new elections can be held.

Tyler set a precedent that has been followed ever since, but he paid for it. Both Whigs and Democrats disagreed with this action. People mailed him letters addressed "Ex-Vice President Tyler" and "Vice President-Acting President Tyler." He refused to open mail addressed this way. Congress called him "His Accidency," and his Cabinet opposed his policies.

CRASH COURSE
SANTA ANNA'S LEG

The only way to ratchet up the weirdness of something called the Pastry War would be a famous general losing his leg when he stopped to eat roast chicken. Well, maybe if soldiers took the leg to Illinois where it is still exhibited today. Luckily for historical-oddity buffs, that's what happened to General Antonio Lopez de Santa Anna.

Mexican General Santa Anna, who defeated Davy Crockett, Jim Bowie, and others at the Alamo in 1836, helped lead Mexico in—and this is really what it's called—the Pastry War of 1838.

A French pastry cook claimed that Mexican soldiers had destroyed his shop. (That the alleged destruction took place in 1828, ten years before the Pastry War broke out, is just perfect for this tale.) One thing led to another, culminating in Mexican and French soldiers slugging it out. Mexico won, but Santa Anna was shot in his leg and lost the bottom half of it. He wore a cork prosthesis after that.

Time-travel nine years: Santa Anna was fighting in the Mexican-American War. During the Battle of Cerro Gordo, he stopped for a meal of roast chicken. While he was eating, the 4th Regiment Illinois Volunteers surprised him. He fled, leaving his chicken and his leg. (It's not certain why he removed the leg, but maybe it was more comfortable.) The Volunteers seized both poultry and prosthesis.

The poultry was consumed, and the leg was taken back to Illinois, where it is now in the Illinois State Military Museum. Its inscription reads, "General Santa Anna's cork leg, captured at the Battle of Cerro Gordo, Mexico, by Private A. Waldron, First Sergeant Sam Rhoades, Second Sergeant John M. Gill April 18, 1847, all of the Fourth Regiment, Illinois Volunteers of the Mexican War."

JAMES K. POLK'S PRESIDENCY (1845–1849)

In the 1844 election, James K. Polk was the dark horse nominee (meaning he was a lesser-known candidate). He can thank Martin Van Buren and John C. Calhoun—and their disagreement over annexation of Texas and the accompanying slavery debate—for his even getting on the ticket.

Polk won a close election that centered around annexing Texas (a region that allowed slavery) into the United States. As he made clear during the campaign, Polk favored the annexation. Lucky for him, his predecessor, John Tyler, did the dirty work the week before he left office. This left to Polk the task of dealing with an unhappy Mexico.

When Polk took office, he named his four objectives: reduce tariffs; reestablish an independent treasury; acquire California from Mexico; and settle the Oregon boundary dispute with Britain. He accomplished all four goals in his first term, and therefore did not feel the need to run again for a second term.

Reduce Tariffs. In the past, the debate for protective tariffs focused on the differences in the North and South: they benefited Northern manufacturers by protecting them from competition with Britain, but they were costly to Southern planters, who imported most of their ready-made goods.

Polk introduced a new tax plan with a main goal of revenue, providing protection only as an incidental benefit. The new plan taxed luxuries at a higher rate than essential items. In addition to lowering taxes, it allowed Western farmers to sell their grain in free trade with Britain.

Reestablish an Independent Treasury. By the time Polk took office, the national financial system had already seen its share of ups and downs, from Andrew Jackson's withdrawal of all funds from the national bank, to Van Buren's establishment of an Independent Treasury System in 1840, to Congress's abolition of the same system in 1841, and finally to Tyler's veto of another national bank charter.

Polk was fortunate to have a Democratic-led Congress in favor of reviving the Independent Treasury System in 1846. (It was a system of public depositories for storing and dispensing federal money.) The Independent Treasury was the one American financial institution until it was replaced by the Federal Reserve System in 1913.

Acquire California from Mexico. Keep in mind that Mexico was chapped about the annexation of Texas, and they were not in any way inclined to work with Polk on the California question.

After unsuccessfully trying to arrange talks with Mexico, at the first provocation, Polk declared war on the country to the south in May of 1846. American troops dominated Mexican forces over the next fifteen months, and the Mexican army surrendered in September 1847.

With the February 2, 1848, Treaty of Guadalupe Hidalgo, Mexico gave up the territories of New Mexico and California and recognized the earlier Texas annexation.

Settle the Oregon Boundary Dispute with Britain. One of Polk's campaign points, "Fifty-four Forty or Fight," promised to gain control of Britain's claims to the northern part of Oregon Territory. The slogan referred to the north latitude of 54°40', the southern border of Russian Alaska.

Polk intended to extend American claims to the Oregon Territory all the way up to Alaska, promising to fight for it, if necessary. But, once he got into office and saw that trouble was brewing in Mexico, Polk decided not to spread American troops too thin. Instead of going to war over the northern latitude, Polk agreed with Britain's boundary demand. The line was drawn at 49° to keep it straight with the border separating the United States from Canada on the east side of the Rocky Mountains.

EXTRA CREDIT: James K. Polk was a great-grandnephew of John Knox, the founder of the Scottish Presbyterian Church.

PAIUTE INDIANS AND MORMONS

This is a story of two very different kinds of religion.

First, the Paiute Indians: They were a tribe of the Great Basin area (encompassing the present-day states of Nevada and Utah, and parts of all the surrounding states), probably a branch of the Ute Indians. The Southern branch of Paiute Indians were peace-loving tribes, happy to hunt, fish, farm, and dig for roots. In fact, they were known for spending a lot of time digging for roots and insects to eat. In addition, they grew food crops of corn, squash, melons, gourds, sunflowers, and winter wheat.

Beginning in the mid-1800s, more and more white settlers encroached on the Paiute lands. Specifically, a religious group called the Mormons arrived in the 1850s, building their settlements right where the Paiutes usually camped and gathered food. The Paiutes suffered from starvation and disease brought by the white settlers. The Mormons, unfortunately, focused on saving the Indians' souls more than their bodies.

In 1889, a leader named Wovoka, from the Northern branch of Paiutes, founded a religion based on the Ghost Dance that would protect the tribes from the white settlements and restore the Natives' old ways. It spread across the different Indian tribes of the Great Basin area, who were desperate to get an edge over the American settlers and armies in their lands. The young Indian warriors fully believed that the Ghost Dance would protect them from the American soldiers' bullets.

The U.S. government recognized trouble brewing and sent reinforcements out west. The result was the famous December 29 massacre of Sioux warriors at Wounded Knee, South Dakota. The Indians settled down after that. Chief Sitting Bull was killed in his cabin on December 15 which was fourteen days before the battle.

Next the Mormons: About twenty years before they migrated west, Joseph Smith founded the Church of Jesus Christ of Latter-day Saints (called Mormons) in New York State. Smith's religion was based on restoring the church of Christ on earth, and he developed quite a following of "saints." But even more "unbelievers" lived in the area, and with their pressure, Smith decided to relocate his community westward.

The Mormons hopped from New York to Ohio to Missouri, finally settling in Nauvoo, Illinois, in 1839. Smith continued to share his visions from God, and coupled with the group's practice of polygamy, neighboring Protestants became worried about the Mormons in their area. An angry mob killed Smith in Illinois in 1844.

That's when the Mormons decided it was time to move on along. Brigham Young took over control of the group, leading them further west to the Great Salt Lake Valley in Utah, where they settled in 1847. In 1849, Young decided to preserve Mormon ways by creating a state, called Deseret (meaning "honeybee"), that included eight present-day states. Congress did not recognize the state of Deseret, but in 1850 created the smaller Utah Territory, appointed Young as governor and made Great Salt Lake City the capital.

The Mormons were very protective of their land and culture, to the point of hostility to federal troops and other settlers traveling through to California. (And, by "hostility," we mean burning wagons, killing cattle, destroying federal property, ambushing wagon trains both themselves and by inciting the Paiutes to attack.) A large American military presence in the area discouraged further bloodshed.

The Utah Territory size was decreased, and Utah became a state in 1896.

EXTRA CREDIT: In 1890, the Mormon Church officials denounced polygamy, although small splinter groups still practice it.

SAM HOUSTON

An imposing man, both in size (6-foot-3-inches) and appearance, Sam Houston is known for his roles in helping Texas gain independence from Mexico and in early Texas statehood.

Born in Virginia and then relocated to Tennessee, Samuel Houston ran away from home at the age of fifteen to live with a Cherokee tribe for three years; they called him Black Raven.

During the War of 1812 he fought as a private and later, third lieautenant, in the U.S. Army against the Creek under Andrew Jackson at the Battle of Horseshoe Bend in Alabama. He was wounded in the thigh by a Creek arrow.

In 1827, Houston was elected governor of Tennessee. Two years later, he resigned, returned to live with the Cherokee, and represented them in Washington, D.C., in cases of fraud against government Indian Bureau agents. His relationship with the Cherokees ultimately led him to Texas: Houston was selected by President Jackson to negotiate treaties with the Native Americans in that territory.

Houston traveled to Texas to fulfill his duties, and stayed there. He got involved in the Texas fight for independence from Mexico, and is famous for his role in that state's history.

- November 1835 — Appointed Major General of the Texas army
- 1836 — Captured Mexican General Santa Anna at San Jacinto to win Texas's independence from Mexico
- 1836–1838 — President of the Republic of Texas
- 1841–1845 — Reelected president of the Texas Republic
- 1846–1859 — Senator for the new state of Texas
- 1859–1861 — Elected governor of Texas; opposed secession from the Union
- 1861 — Removed from governorship for not swearing allegiance to The Confederate States of America
- July 26, 1863 — Died at Huntsville, Texas, which was renamed Houston in his honor

MIDTERM

1) Which of the following events took place after July 4, 1776?
   a) The Battle of Trenton, in which George Washington defeated the Hessians after crossing the Delaware River.
   b) The Continental Congress signed a treaty with France to get French troops and supplies.
   c) Charles Cornwallis surrendered the British forces.
   d) The Treaty of Paris recognized U.S. independence.
   e) All of the above

2) True or False: Aaron Burr challenged Alexander Hamilton to a duel after Hamilton made critical comments about Burr in public.

3) Barbara Bush joins what early women's rights champion in the very exclusive "My Husband and My Son Were Both United States Presidents" club?

4) What convenient solution with regard to America did Britain devise for dealing with criminals?

5) What is the name of the papers that were written to dispute the Federalist Papers?

6) What do we call the document that is officially titled "The Articles of Confederation and Perpetual Union Between The States of New Hampshire, Massachusetts-bay Rhode Island and Providence Plantations, Connecticut, New York, New Jersey, Pennsylvania, Delaware, Maryland, Virginia, North Carolina, South Carolina and Georgia?"

7) Did Benedict Arnold and Richard Montgomery take the city during the second Battle of Quebec?

8) Select the activity or event which cannot be credited to Benjamin Franklin.
   a) Published *Poor Richard: An Almanack*
   b) Served as postmaster of Philadelphia
   c) Signed the Declaration of Independence
   d) Conducted studies of electricity
   e) Died in the Battle of Quebec

9) True or False: Benedict Arnold was originally an American patriot who later betrayed his country.

10) What do we call the event of the Sons of Liberty dumping 90,000 pounds of tea into the Boston Harbor to protest British taxes?

11) Select the item below that is NOT an example of Colonial-era clothing.
   a) Banyan
   b) Mob cap
   c) Pannier
   d) Stomacher
   e) Tunic

12) Select the word that best completes the sentence. In early New England, burglary was considered a capital offense on the _____ (first or second) occurrence.

13) Select the words that best complete the sentence. The Colonists held _____ (positive or negative) feelings toward lawyers, whose abilities they _____ (trusted or doubted).

14) Who has the distinction of being the first casualty of the American Revolution?

15) Of the fifty-six men who signed the Declaration of Independence, match the name with his significance.
   1. Youngest signer   a. Benjamin Franklin
   2. Oldest signer   b. John Hancock
   3. First signer   c. Thomas McKean
   4. Last signer   d. Edward Rutledge

16) What was the incident called when a mob formed and rioted against New York City doctors suspected of robbing graves for anatomy-class cadavers?

17) Of Dolley Madison and Dolly Madison, which one was the wife of James Madison, and which one is a brand of snack cakes?

18) Fill in the blank. The Hessians were hired soldiers that Britain "rented" from _____ .

19) Who leaked Thomas Hutchinson's letters that supported British troops against American rebels?

20) John Adams predicted that July 2, 1776, would forever be celebrated with parades, bonfires, and fireworks because of what resolution?

ANSWERS:

20.) The Lee Resolution
19) Benjamin Franklin
18) Germany
17) Dolley Madison was James Madison's wife. Dolly Madison is a cupcake.
16) The Doctor's Mob Riot
15) 1-d; 2-a; 3-b; 4-c
14) Crispus Attucks
13) negative; doubled
12) second
11) e
10) The Boston Tea Party
9) True
8) e
7) No.
6) Articles of Confederation
5) The Anti-Federalist Papers
4) Ship them to America
3) Abigail Adams
2) True
1) e

COSMETICS THROUGH HISTORY

The use of cosmetics to change appearance has been around for thousands of years: Ancient Egyptians and Greeks painted their faces with minerals; the Romans added oil-based perfumes to their baths and fountains, and even polished their teeth.

Middle Eastern alcohol-based perfumes arrived in Europe by the thirteenth century. Perfumes were made from crushing natural plants such as flowers, roots, fruits, rinds, or barks.

Nineteenth-century women wanted to appear as fragile ladies. Everyone understood that tanned skin indicated working in the sun out of necessity, so they wanted to have pale skin to imply a higher rank in society, and to look like delicate flowers.

Before the nineteenth century, women whitened their faces with a mixture of carbonate, hydroxide, and lead oxide. At the time, they did not realize that these compounds soaked through their skin into their bloodstream, causing lead poisoning, with muscle paralysis and even death. More natural ways to remain pale included drinking vinegar, avoiding fresh air, and bleeding yourself with leeches.

By the nineteenth century, using cosmetics was frowned upon. Generally, everyone believed that cosmetics were used by prostitutes and actresses. Women who did wear makeup, however, started using the safer zinc oxide as a base facial powder, which is still used today. But they continued to use other poisonous dangerous chemicals on and around their faces:

- lead and antimony sulfide on eyelids
- belladonna (or "deadly nightshade") for dilating pupils
- mercuric sulfide, or geranium and poppy petals to redden lips
- burnt matchstick ash on eyelashes
- Ladies also used *papier poudre*, or books of powdered papers to "powder their noses" and cheeks.

The acceptance of using cosmetics really took off in the twentieth century with the rise of the movie industry.

WOMEN'S ANTEBELLUM FASHIONS

Women throughout the country eagerly read *Godey's Lady's Book*, first published in Philadelphia in 1830. It included sketches of French fashions, articles, illustrations, hairstyles, clothing patterns, and directions.

In 1850, the typical woman wore: a chemise (underslip), a corset, several petticoats, drawers (underpants), a two-piece dress (a matching skirt and bodice), stockings, shoes, gloves, a bonnet, and a shawl (when necessary). Hairstyles and hats varied widely, based on the shape of a woman's face and the skill of her hairdresser.

A note on corsets: Corsets were not nearly as tight as *Gone With The Wind* would lead you to believe. They were sold in waist sizes ranging from 18 to 30 inches, and could even be found up to 42 inches; the laces added at least another inch in back.

By the 1860s, steel hoops called crinolines replaced the layers of fabric petticoats. Carol Burnett's hilarious depiction of trying to gracefully sit without exposing herself notwithstanding, most women liked the crinolines better than their predecessors.

Men Cared About Fashion, Too

Just as at home today, when the women get so much more closet space, here we'll briefly discuss men's fashions.

Menswear of the 1800s was marked by a simple style with less embellishment but elegant tailoring: dark wool suits and a knee-length jacket called a frock coat.

For formal events, gentlemen wore a top hat, and a tail coat, a short jacket with tails at the back. Working class men wore the less formal soft cap.

By the 1860s, men's hairstyles began featuring sideburns, and facial hair began to come into style.

INVENTORS SHAPING THE 1800S

Charles Goodyear: Vulcanized Rubber

We'll resist the obvious joke about Star Trek humanoids, and just discuss the importance of discovering the rubber vulcanizing (weatherproofing) process.

When you consider that untreated rubber melts in summer's heat and breaks from brittleness in winter's cold, you'll understand weatherproofing's importance. American inventor Charles Goodyear experimented for years to make rubber useful in manufacturing.

In 1839, Goodyear accidentally dropped a piece of sulfur-treated rubber on a hot stove. When he peeled off the cooked rubber, he noticed a difference in its qualities. He set about working on the right combination of sulfur and rubber for optimum weatherproofing.

Unfortunately, Goodyear's patent was stolen, and he did not make money from his revolutionizing invention that is still used today. The word *vulcanization* was suggested by the patent "thief's" friend, after Vulcan, the god of fire.

Elisha Graves Otis: Safe Elevators

If not for Elisha Otis, we would all have a healthy—and valid—distrust of riding in elevators. While elevators and lifts have been around since about the third century, American manufacturer Otis pioneered steam-powered elevators and devices.

In 1854, at a New York City exposition, Otis unveiled his most important invention: an automatic safety device to stop an elevator in case the cable breaks. Three years later, he installed the first passenger elevators.

Otis's elevator advances led to the age of the skyscraper. Shortly before he died in 1861, Otis patented a steam-driven elevator. Today, when you step onto an elevator and see the Otis Elevator Company logo, you'll know you are riding on years and years of experience.

John Augustus Roebling: Suspension Bridges

German-born American civil engineer John Roebling was a pioneer in suspension bridge construction. After immigrating to Pennsylvania,

Roebling worked with the Pennsylvania Railroad Corporation, surveying and supervising construction on canals, locks, and dams.

In 1841, he introduced twisted steel wire-rope cables in bridge construction. This cable could support long spans and extremely heavy loads, so Roebling showed that it could be used for the decks of suspension bridges.

Roebling was known as an excellent bridge engineer and completed dozens of major bridges, including railroad suspension bridges over the Ohio and Niagara Rivers. He also completed plans for New York City's Brooklyn Bridge in 1869 shortly before his death.

Christopher Latham Sholes: Typewriter

The next time you type a report or even an e-mail, thank American printer Christopher Sholes for developing the first practical machine for typing faster than writing by hand.

By the time Sholes and his partners Carlos Glidden and Samuel Soule took on the task of creating a practical typewriter, at least seventy-five other versions had been designed for the public. Sholes himself produced three: a crude and cumbersome model in 1867; a more practical model in 1868; and an improved model in 1873. Sholes's 1873 model had features that are still part of modern machines: a keyboard; a carriage with a platen (large roller); and rollers to hold the paper in place.

The Typewriter Keyboard

We've all wondered why the letters on a keyboard are arranged in such a seemingly unorganized manner. When Sholes improved his 1873 typewriter, he arranged the keyboard letters alphabetically. It was easy to find the keys, but there was a problem: whenever two keys next to each other were hit one after the other, the bars jammed.

So, Sholes helped develop the keyboard layout we still use today, the "QWERTY" layout. It separates the letters that most often appear in combination in the English language, so that chances of hitting two next to each other in a row are much smaller.

CRASH COURSE
ANTISLAVERY MOVEMENT

The early 1800s were a time of reform in society, from education to welfare to personal rights. And the ongoing issue of slavery certainly involved personal rights. Northerners began to regard slavery as a sin, and they went about trying to remedy the problem, using several very different approaches.

American Colonization Society: Antislavery reformers decided to transport freed slaves to an African colony. In 1822, the Society founded an African-American colony in Monrovia, Liberia. Only about 12,000 blacks settled in Africa.

New England Anti-Slavery Society: New Englander William Lloyd Garrison formed this society in 1822 as the first immediatist society in the country.

American Anti-Slavery Society: Garrison published an abolition (or, *ending slavery*) newspaper, *The Liberator*, and formed this society in 1823. Their solution was the immediate abolition of slavery in every state and equal rights for blacks. They were a bit vigilante in their methods, though, and that served to turn off many people from their particular brand of abolition.

American and Foreign Anti-Slavery Society: This group, which split off from the American Anti-Slavery Society in 1840, encouraged abolitionism preached in the nation's churches.

Liberty Party: More conservative abolitionists sought to achieve their goals politically, nominating abolitionist candidates for public office. Even this party disagreed internally on their tactics: Northerners favored declaring slavery illegal everywhere, while Mid-Westerners favored ending slavery in the territories and the District of Columbia.

The Underground Railroad: Abolitionists and free blacks ran a network of secret "safe houses" to help slaves escape into the North and Canada. Former slave Harriet Tubman is probably the most famous "conductor" on the Underground Railroad, which assisted about 1,000 slaves each year.

As women joined the campaign for improved circumstances for blacks, both free and slave, they slowly began to realize that they, too, deserved better.... (Keep reading for more on women's rights.) At the same time, Southerners bristled at all the Northern action against slavery.... (Keep reading for more on causes of the Civil War.)

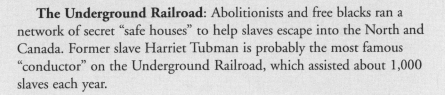

Sojourner Truth

Former slave Isabella (freed at the age of thirty when New York State abolished slavery in 1827) changed her name to Sojourner Truth in 1843. With a rich, powerful, engaging voice, she campaigned both for emancipation and women's rights. So profound were her words, that President Lincoln himself invited her to the White House in 1864.

In May 1851, Sojourner Truth spoke to a women's rights convention in Akron, giving her famous "Ain't I A Woman?" speech:

That man over there says that women need to be helped in carriages, and lifted over ditches, and to have the best place everywhere. Nobody helps me any best place! And ain't I a woman? Look at me! Look at my arm! (She flexed her muscles.) I have ploughed, I have planted and I have gathered into barns. And no man could head me. And ain't I a woman? I could work as much, and eat as much as a man—when I could get it—and bear the lash as well! And ain't I a woman? ...If the first woman God ever made was strong enough to turn the world upside down all alone, these women together ought to be able to turn it back and get it right-side up again. And now that they are asking to do it, the men better let them.

HARRIET BEECHER STOWE

"So you're the little woman who wrote the book that started this great war!"

— Abraham Lincoln, meeting Stowe at the White House, November 1862 (reportedly)

In 1852, Harriet Beecher Stowe published *Uncle Tom's Cabin*, one of the most powerful and popular novels in American literature. She wrote the book in disagreement with the Fugitive Slave Law of 1850, which declared helping slaves escape to be a crime.

A descriptive condemnation of slavery, the book played an important role in perpetuating Northern antislavery thoughts. Some historians even go so far as to claim, as Lincoln may actually have, that the book moved the country in the direction of Civil War.

(It might very well have done so. Northerners read Stowe's descriptions of slave cruelty with horror. Southerners vehemently denied the descriptions' truth, and suspected Stowe of prejudice against the region.)

To give her credit, while living in Ohio in her early twenties, Stowe had gained first-hand knowledge of slavery practices. She did know of what she wrote.

Uncle Tom's Cabin

The title character is a slave originally owned by a peaceful family that falls on hard times and is forced to sell their slaves. Tom is sold and shipped to New Orleans. On the boat, he saves little Eva's life; in turn, her father purchases him. Tom lives for two years with Eva's kind family, but they also meet with misfortune. He is sold again, to the cruel Simon Legree, who whips Tom to death. As Tom is dying, the son of his original master arrives and vows to devote himself to campaigning for abolition in Tom's memory.

THE ILLINOIS SENATE RACE

Main Players: 1. Lawyer Abraham Lincoln (Republican)

                          2. Incumbent Senator Stephen Douglas (Democrat)

Positions: 1. Lincoln was a moderate against expansion of slavery

                          2. Douglas supported popular sovereignty

Situation: Lincoln was running for Douglas's seat in the U.S. Senate. He challenged Douglas's indifference to slavery as a moral issue. He questioned Douglas on how to reconcile popular sovereignty (that territorial residents could decided the question of slavery on their own) with the *Dred Scott* decision (which said slavery was legal everywhere).

Reaction: Douglas declared that slavery would not exist in a community where the local residents did not pass slave codes to maintain it. Made in Freeport, Illinois, during the second Lincoln-Douglas debate, the statement became known as the Freeport Doctrine, and it angered Southerners who interpreted Douglas as saying that the *Dred Scott* decision could be ignored.

Implications: Lincoln lost the Illinois Senate seat election to Douglas. However, Douglas's campaign speeches were not popular with Southern Democrats, and he lost their support for future presidential campaigns. Lincoln's words were received favorably by Republicans, and he did get that party's nomination for president in the campaign of 1860.

JOHN BROWN

American abolitionist John Brown is known for a violent attempt to start a slave uprising. Brown dedicated most of his life to abolishing slavery, and his most spectacular abolitionist act ultimately caused his death. He believed that slavery could not be abolished peacefully, and planned a raid that he hoped would start a slave rebellion.

The Plan: Northern abolitionists channeled funds to Brown's project to use armed force to free slaves then establish a slave refuge in the Virginia mountains. He assembled Brown's Provisional Army: twenty-one soldiers, five blacks and sixteen whites.

The Attack: On October 16, 1859, three "soldiers" remained at their rented farm as rear guard. Eighteen men quietly approached Harpers Ferry in present-day West Virginia. They cut the telegraph lines, overtook two night watchmen, seized the United States armory, and took control of the town.

The Flaw: A devout Christian, Brown believed that God had appointed him to abolish slavery. He trusted God to take care of the details. He didn't have a strong plan beyond seizing and holding the arsenal.

The Capture: Colonel Robert E. Lee led U.S. marines and local militia in reclaiming Harpers Ferry. Ten of Brown's men, including two of his sons, were killed in the battle. Brown was wounded and surrendered.

The Conviction: Brown was arrested, tried, and convicted of treason and murder. He was executed by hanging in Charles Town, Virginia (now West Virginia), in December 1859. For many years after, abolitionists held up Brown as a martyr to the cause of banishing slavery.

The Consequences: John Brown's raid on Harpers Ferry increased tension between the North and the South before the Civil War. Northerners were more sympathetic to the abolitionist movement. Southerners began to doubt the strength of their slavery interests in the Union.

The Presidential Election
of 1860

Party Nominations

Democrats: The party would not support slavery, so Southern Democrats walked out. Northern Democrats nominated Stephen Douglas.

Southern Democrats: Southern Democrats nominated then-current vice president John C. Breckinridge of Kentucky to run for unrestricted expansion of slavery in the territories.

Republicans: The moderate Abraham Lincoln was nominated on a platform against the spread of slavery but not necessarily for abolition.

Constitutional Union Party: A new party of conservative Whigs, moderates, and Know-Nothings nominated Senator John Bell of Tennessee to preserve the Union and enforce the Constitution.

The Votes

Douglas and Breckenridge split the Democratic vote. Bell carried three border states. Lincoln did not get even one popular vote in nine Southern states, but victory in all Northern states meant an electoral majority. This greatly distrubed Southern Democrats—clearly, there was no way they could win any election over the populous North's many more electoral votes.

Secession

Even though Lincoln moderately opposed slavery, Southerners warned that if a Republican was elected, they would secede from the United States. Within days, before Lincoln even took office, Southern legislatures made good on the threat. South Carolina led the way, voting in state convention for secession from the Union.

They really believed that they were upholding the tradition of the American Revolutionary War—that they had a right to independence and the right to be protected from tyranny of the North.

In less than two months, six more Southern states had left the Union and formed their own country—the Confederate States of America.

THE CONFEDERATE STATES OF AMERICA

On February 4, 1861, delegates from South Carolina, Mississippi, Florida, Alabama, Georgia, and Louisiana met in Montgomery, Alabama. They formed a new nation—the Confederate States of America, which they also called the Confederacy.

They began drafting a constitution that was modeled after the U.S. Constitution. However, the Confederate States' constitution limited the government's powers to impose taxes and to restrict slavery. On February 9, Jefferson Davis of Mississippi was elected provisional president and Alexander Stephens of Georgia was elected vice president of the new nation. Their terms were to be temporary, but they were later reelected permanently.

Jefferson Davis selected a six-member cabinet with representatives from the different states at the meeting. Three members of the cabinet remained with Davis throughout the Confederacy's existence: Judah P. Benjamin was attorney general (and later secretary of war and state); Stephen R. Mallory was secretary of the navy, and John H. Reagan was postmaster general.

The Confederate Army was fortunate to gain former U.S. Army officers and enlisted men who had seceded with their states. (For example, Brigadier General P. G. T. Beauregard became commander of the Confederate forces in Charleston.)

The Confederates immediately began seizing U.S. government property in their states, and occupying the arsenals, navy yards, and federal forts, even those offshore. Only four forts remained under Union control: Fort Sumter at the mouth of the Charleston harbor; Fort Jefferson in the Dry Tortugas, Florida; Fort Pickens in Pensacola Bay, Florida; and Fort Taylor at Key West, Florida. Control of Fort Sumter was an immediate important issue.

Originally located in Montgomery, Alabama, the Confederate capital was relocated to Richmond, Virginia, on May 30, 1861.

ELEVENTH-HOUR EFFORTS FOR UNION

Congress made one last attempt to keep the Union together. Kentucky Senator John Crittenden proposed a constitutional amendment that would guarantee the right to own slaves in all territories south of 36'30° (the 1820 Missouri Compromise line) all the way across the country. But it was too late: Southerners were bent on secession, and Northerners were adamant on not extending slavery.

Then, on March 4, 52-year-old Abraham Lincoln delivered his first presidential inaugural address at the Capitol in Washington, D.C. He stated again his objective of containing slavery's growth. He also very clearly said he did not believe that slavery could be outlawed in states where it already existed.

Lincoln purposefully leveled his conclusion squarely at Southerners, to let them know that he would not be the one to start war:

In your hands, my dissatisfied fellow-countrymen, and not in mine, is the momentous issue of civil war. The government will not assail you. You can have no conflict without being yourselves the aggressors.

The Confederate States of America (listed in order of secession):

December 20, 1860: South Carolina
January 9, 1861: Mississippi
January 10, 1861: Florida
January 11, 1861: Alabama
January 19, 1861: Georgia
January 26, 1861: Louisiana
February 1, 1861: Texas
April 17, 1861: Virginia
May 6, 1861: Arkansas
May 20, 1861: North Carolina
June 8, 1861: Tennessee
Four slave-holding states remained in the Union: Delaware, Maryland, Missouri, and Kentucky.

FORT SUMTER: WHAT STARTED IT ALL

Of course, the conflict over Fort Sumter in South Carolina's Charleston Harbor started before Confederate soldiers fired on the Union fort on April 12, 1861.

As soon as South Carolina seceded in December 1860, Southerners began seizing federal property throughout the region: forts, arsenals, and shipyards. Fort Sumter remained under Union control, and President Buchanan refused to abandon the property to the South. This left the soldiers surrounded by hostile territory.

The fort's commanding officer, Major Robert Anderson, sent word to Washington that they were running low on supplies. Buchanan understood that sending a U.S. Navy warship into Charleston Harbor, even for the one peaceful purpose of delivering supplies, would be viewed by South Carolina as an act of hostility.

To try to avoid provoking the Southerners, on January 9, 1861, the War Department sent a merchant ship—an *unarmed, civilian* ship—with supplies for the federal fort. The *Star of the West* sailed toward Charleston Harbor, but was stopped before it arrived at Fort Sumter.

A group of cadets from the Citadel (a South Carolina military academy) stationed on Morris Island outside Charleston Harbor were determined to keep the supplies from reaching Fort Sumter. The soldiers fired on the *Star of the West*. They didn't damage the ship or harm the ship's crew, but it was enough to force the ship to turn back. The supplies were not received.

When Lincoln took office, the issue of delivering supplies to Fort Sumter still existed. He understood the importance of handling the problem carefully, especially after he had already declared that the Union expected to keep control of all federal property in the South. So, now he had to figure out how to get provisions to Fort Sumter (and all federal property in the South, for that matter) without provoking a war and making more states secede.

On April 6, 1861, Lincoln sent a message to South Carolina Governor F. W. Pickens that the federal government intended to send provisions to the troops holding Fort Sumter. Lincoln promised that he would not send any troop reinforcements as long as South Carolina allowed a peaceful mission to come in and resupply the fort.

Pickens forwarded the message to the Confederate War Department, which demanded that Fort Sumter surrender at once. Further, the War Department said if this did not happen, Confederate troops would be ordered to capture the fort in any way they could.

So, on April 11, three Confederate officers demanded the fort's surrender. Sumter's Union officer Anderson refused. Then, at 4:30 a.m. on April 12, 1861, General Beauregard's Confederate troops opened fire on the Union fort.

Anderson knew that, without fresh supplies, his command could not last long. For more than a day, Union soldiers at Fort Sumter fought back, but sustained heavy damage. On the second day, April 13, Anderson surrendered the fort.

President Lincoln saw the Confederates' action as revolution, and he knew that it was time to make a move. Congress was not in session, so, by virtue of his position as commander-in-chief with executive powers he acted:

- Called for 75,000 volunteer troops.
- Authorized spending for the war.
- Suspended the writ of habeas corpus (meaning he allowed taking prisoners of war).
- Declared a blockade of the Confederate coast.

A House Divided

Abraham Lincoln accepted the Republication nomination with his "House Divided" speech:

In my opinion, [slavery agitation] will not cease until a crisis shall have been reached and passed. "A house divided against itself cannot stand." I believe this government cannot endure, permanently, half slave and half free. I do not expect the Union to be dissolved; I do not expect the house to fall; but I do expect it will cease to be divided. It will become all one thing, or all the other....

The Howes, Samuel Gridley and Julia Ward

Known for advocating human and women's rights, and abolition, Samuel Gridley Howe and his wife, Julia, made American history in more ways than one.

Samuel Gridley Howe: Before marrying Julia Ward in 1843, Samuel Gridley Howe was already an accomplished reformist, participating in Greece's war for independence. He organized what is now the Perkins School for the Blind, which Helen Keller attended.

He firmly expected his wife to remain in the home. In contrast to personal beliefs, Samuel Gridley Howe advocated women's rights, saying that denying equal status to women was just as wrong as denying equal status to blacks.

A radical abolitionist, Howe wrote for and edited the antislavery *Boston Commonwealth*. He financially supported John Brown's raid on Harpers Ferry.

Julia Ward Howe: Julia Ward Howe is best known for writing the famous poem "Battle Hymn of the Republic" to inspire Union soldiers in fighting slavery.

An educated and independent woman, Julia Ward married Samuel Gridley Howe, who was eighteen years older and who suppressed her intellect and accomplishments. Julia was an unhappy wife; she anonymously published a poem collection, *Passion Flowers* (1854), about her domestic misery.

In later life, Julia Ward Howe founded the New England Woman's Club and the Association for the Advancement of Women and headed the American branch of the Woman's International Peace Association.

Battle Hymn of the Republic: In 1861, Julia Ward and Samuel Gridley visited a Union army camp outside Washington. That night, she wrote "The Battle Hymn" to the tune of the popular patriotic song, "John Brown's Body." *The Atlantic Monthly* paid five dollars to publish the poem in the February 1862 issue, and the song caught on.

HARRIET TUBMAN

Another "Harriet" had a profound impact on the American Civil War. Former slave Harriet Tubman is known for her prolific work with the Underground Railroad, a network of secret "safe houses" to help slaves escape.

Historians report that, at great danger to herself, Tubman made nineteen different trips to bring three hundred slaves to freedom in the North, and she never lost anyone. With each trip, Tubman risked her own freedom and life. Southerners offered rewards of $40,000 for her capture.

Tubman's Motivation: When she was about twenty-nine years old, slave Harriet Tubman heard rumors that she would be sold, and she fled north to freedom. She became an Underground Railroad "conductor," first rescuing her sister and her sister's children from slavery in Maryland. She also brought her brother and parents to freedom on subsequent trips.

Tubman's Methods:
- Wore disguises (a deranged old man or an old woman)
- Administered sleeping powder to crying babies
- Carried a pistol to persuade her charges against changing their minds
- Varied her routes and strategies
- Began treks on Saturday night to get more than a day's lead on trackers; slaves did not work on Sundays and wouldn't be missed until Monday

Tubman's Ministrations: During the Civil War, Tubman served as nurse, scout, spy, and cook for the Union Army. After the war, she worked to improve the lives of blacks, promoted women's suffrage, and supported particularly the rights of black women.

Tubman's Monikers: Freed slaves called her "Moses;" John Brown called her "General Tubman."

CIVIL WAR TRIVIA, PART 1

- Abraham and Nancy Todd Lincoln had four sons, but only the first, Robert Todd, lived into maturity. Edward Baker Lincoln died before his fourth birthday from what was thought to be diphtheria. William Wallace Lincoln died at eleven from an acute malarial infection. Thomas (Tad) Lincoln died at eighteen from pleurisy.

- Jefferson Davis, president of the Confederacy, also had his share of family tragedy. Davis married Sarah Knox Taylor on June 17, 1835. The couple left on a trip to see members of Davis' family, first brother Joseph E. Davis and then sister Anna Smith, of West Feliciana Parish, Lousiana. The newlyweds both came down with either malaria or yellow fever. Davis survived, but his bride died on September 15, two days from the couple's three month anniversary. Davis married Varina Banks Howell in 1826, and their first child, Samuel Emory, died before he was two from measles. Their fourth child, Joseph Evan, died at age five after falling from a porch on the White House of the Confederacy. Their fifth child, William Howell, died at eleven from diphtheria.

- Hire badges were metal badges worn by slaves who had been "rented out" for day labor. The badges served several purposes, from identifying the slaves to providing tax revenue to preventing slave labor from competing with white laborers. (Slave labor was cheaper than white labor, so badges for occupations more likely to be done by whites were limited.) Although several cities, including Mobile, Alabama, New Orleans, Louisiana, and Savannah, Georgia issued badges, only those from Charleston, South Carolina are known to exist today.

CSS ALABAMA

The most famous and successful Confederate ship was built in England, destroyed off France, and carried the name of a Deep South state. Before the *CSS Alabama* was sunk off the coast of Cherbourg, France in 1864, it had claimed some Union merchant ships.

The *Alabama* was built in Liverpool, England, by John Laird Sons and Company in 1862. Since the Civil War had already started, the Union understandably looked askance at England helping out the Confederacy, so the ship was known as simply *290* while in the shipyard.

The ship was launched as the *Enrica*, then commissioned the *Alabama* in August 1862. Under the command of Captain Raphael Semmes, the ship immediately began its attacks on Union ships, wreaking havoc in the Atlantic, then the West Indies. It sank the *USS Hatteras* off the coast of Texas, sailed to Cape Town, South Africa, visited Southeast Asia and then made port at Cherbourg, France, on June 11, 1864, for repairs.

The *USS Kearsarge*, under Captain John A. Winslow, had been pursuing the *Alabama*, and Winslow blockaded the harbor at Cherbourg on June 14, waiting for his quarry. Semmes then challenged Winslow to a duel between the two ships. Winslow accepted.

The *Alabama* steamed out of port and towards its doom on June 19. Semmes was an accomplished captain, but his ship's deteriorated condition, including its powder and shells, meant the *Alabama* was no match for the *Kearsarge*. The *Alabama* was sunk roughly an hour after the battle began.

The wreck of the *Alabama* was discovered in 1984, and a 2002 expedition retrieved many items from the wreck.

The U.S. government pursued the Alabama Claims against England for that country's part in the destruction the *Alabama* caused, eventually winning $15.5 million.

CSS SHENANDOAH

The Aleutian Islands are a chain of islands in the North Pacific Ocean that separate the Bering Sea from the Pacific Ocean. That's hardly the location one would associate with the Civil War, but the Aleutians were in fact where the last shot of the Civil War was fired. To make things even weirder, the ship that fired those shots surrendered in Liverpool, England, seven months after the Civil War ended.

The ship that would become the *CSS Shenandoah* began life as the *Sea King* in Scotland in 1863. She was put to sea in October 1864, then met up with another ship off the coast of Madeira, and was converted into a warship and took on Confederate Navy officers and crew members.

Captain James Iredell Waddell was given the task of using the *Shenandoah* to raid commerce ships. Waddell steered the ship, which was 230 feet long, thirty-two feet wide and had a 250-horsepower engine, for Melbourne, Australia, arriving there on January 25, 1865. Along the way, the *Shenandoah* burned some seven ships and ransomed two. (Accounts differ as to the exact numbers.)

Waddell spent three weeks in Melbourne, then set out back to sea, capturing four ships by the end of May. Robert E. Lee had surrendered in April, but Waddell had no way of knowing it, so he continued his raiding ways.

The *Shenandoah* reached the Bering Sea in June, and began disrupting the whaling trade there. Waddell and crew captured twenty-four ships before he learned of Lee's surrender on August 2. Believing he would be hanged for his actions, Waddell disarmed his ship and steered for Liverpool, 17,000 miles away. He reached his destination on November 5, then surrendered the *Shenandoah* to the British.

CIVIL WAR TRIVIA, PART 2

- Confederate officer Daniel Weisiger Adams must have been part cat, because he obviously had a stash of at least nine lives. In *Medical Histories of Confederate Generals,* author Jack D. Welsh wrote that Weisiger was hit in the head during the Battle of Shiloh in 1862. "The projectile penetrated the skull above the left eye and came out just behind the left ear, resulting in the loss of the eye." Adams was removed from combat and put in a wagon with other wounded soldiers, but the wagon driver thought Adams was dead and dumped his body along the side of the road. Other soldiers found Adams and nursed him back to health. Later that year, Adams was wounded in the left arm. In 1863, he was again injured in the left arm, but stayed in the field until he collapsed from exhaustion and was captured by Union forces. At a Union hospital, the ball that had fractured his left humerus, along with six bone fragments, was removed. But Adams wasn't done yet. He was turned over to Confederate troops, and after he recuperated, returned to command a cavalry brigade.

- Mary Virginia Wade had no intention of becoming part of history on July 3, 1863, but then, few historical figures ever do. All "Jennie" wanted to accomplish was the baking of some bread for Union soldiers near her sister Georgia McClellan's Baltimore Street house. But while Wade was kneading dough in McClellan's kitchen, a bullet penetrated two wooden doors, striking Wade in the back and killing her instantly. Wade had become the only civilian killed during the Battle of Gettysburg.

ELIZABETH KECKLEY

Elizabeth Keckley was born a slave, but she went on to buy her freedom, became a confidante in the Abraham Lincoln White House and worked to help black Americans of the time.

Keckley was born Elizabeth Hobbs in February 1818, the daughter of Agnes Hobbs, a slave, and Agnes's white owner, Armistead Burwell. She was taught to read and write, although such education was illegal for slaves at the time, and was also taught to be a seamstress by her mother.

As a result of her owners' moving, the young woman ended up in St. Louis, where her seamstress skills earned her a loyal roster of clients. One of those clients loaned her the $1,200 she needed to buy her freedom, a loan that she paid back in full. She also married James Keckley in 1852.

The debt repaid, Keckley left St. Louis for first Baltimore and then Washington, D.C., where she came to the attention of Jefferson Davis's wife, Varina, and other prominent women. Ironically, Keckley's work for Davis (whose husband would become the president of the Confederacy) ended up getting her the job as Mary Todd Lincoln's dressmaker and close confidante.

Lincoln and Keckley worked together to help freed slaves through the Black Contraband Relief Association, which Keckley founded. The two women had a falling-out after Keckley published *Behind the Scenes*, a book that detailed the inner workings of the Lincoln White House. Keckley would go on to serve as a sewing instructor at Ohio's Wilberforce University.

CIVIL WAR BATTLES

Exposition of all the Civil War battles is the work of an encyclopedia, not a bathroom reader, so here's a capsule look at some of the most famous battles.

1. Battle of Gettysburg, July 1-3, 1863, Gettysburg, Pennsylvania

Confederate General Robert E. Lee attacked Gen. George G. Meade's Army of the Potomac. Lee's forces numbered some 83,000, Meade's 75,000. The Confederates succeeded in driving the Union soldiers back the first day, but both sides sent in reinforcements that night. On July 2, Union forces began repelling the Confederate attack. Lee began withdrawing his men on July 4. The total number of casualties was estimated at 51,000, or 23,000 for the Union side and 28,000 for the Confederates. Gettysburg is generally accepted as the tipping point of the war.

2. Battle of Antietam, September 17, 1862, near Sharpsburg, Maryland

Lee had won the Second Battle of Manassas August 28-30, 1862, and intended to press his advantage northward. Lincoln tasked General George B. McClellan with responding to Lee's advances. The Battle of Antietam began at dawn on the seventeenth. General Joseph Hooker, General Joseph Mansfield, and General Edwin Sumner led Union assaults on Confederate forces. Twelve hours after the battle began, the single bloodiest day of battle in American history ended with 23,000 casualties. By comparison, in World War II, American casualties on D-Day would number 2,510.

3. Battle of Chickamauga, September 18-20, 1863, Catoosa and Walker County, Georgia

Union General William S. Rosecrans was seeking to capture the strategically important rail hub and river shipping city of Chattanooga, Tennessee. Rosecrans was convinced that Confederate General Braxton Bragg was continuing to retreat from the area, but Bragg had in fact begun to advance toward Chattanooga. Over the course of three days, Bragg's forces managed to repel Rosecrans' forces. Union casualties numbered 16,170, while the Confederates had 18,454 casualties.

JOHN ERICSSON

The man responsible for one of the most famous naval battles of the Civil War worked for the Union, but he was no Yankee. John Ericsson was a Swede who left his homeland and became one of America's greatest inventors.

Ericsson was born on July 31, 1803 in the Swedish province of Värmland. He began showing flashes of his future brilliance at an early age, designing a mechanism that pumped water out of iron mines when he was only ten.

The mine invention brought Ericsson to the attention of Baron von Platen, who headed the Gotha Ship Canal project that employed Ericsson's father. von Platen hired Ericsson, only fourteen, to work on the project.

Ericsson joined the Swedish army at seventeeen, then moved to England in 1826 to work on engineering projects. He and co-inventor John Braithwaite developed the steam locomotive *Novelty*, which lost a contest to George Stephenson's *Rocket* in 1829. In addition to the locomotive, Ericsson developed a steam fire engine, superheated steam engines, condensers for marine steam engines, and his most important invention, the screw propeller.

It was the propeller and other naval improvements that earned Ericsson Civil War acclaim. He designed and built the *Monitor* for the Union Navy. The *Monitor* featured a steam-powered screw propeller, it carried its engine below the waterline for better protection, had a revolving gun turret and was made of iron, not wood. The *Monitor* influenced warship design for years after its debut.

Ericsson was inducted into the National Inventors Hall of Fame in 1993. The John Ericsson National Memorial in Washington, D.C., honors this largely forgotten engineering hero. In addition, a U.S. Navy torpedo boat and two destroyers were named the *Ericsson* in his honor.

WHO SAID WHAT, CIVIL WAR

Continuing with the theme of giving background to some notable quotes begun in the Colonial era, here are a few from the Civil War era.

- "War is Hell." William Sherman
  One of the most famous U.S. military quotes of all time, this one is also fraught with uncertainty as to just what, where, when, and if Sherman said it. Depending on the account, Sherman either said those three words in battle, to the graduating class at the Michigan Military Academy in 1879, or to a group of Union veterans in 1880. And a *New York Times* article from 1922 quoted Thomas D. Collins, a Civil War survivor who was with Sherman, who said that the actual quote was delivered to the mayor and city officials from Fayetteville, North Carolina. Furthermore, Collins contended that Sherman actually said, "War is cruel."

- "If you don't want to use the army, I should like to borrow it for a while." Abraham Lincoln
  In 1862, the president was frustrated by General George B. McClellan's lack of activity against the outnumbered Confederate forces, so he sent McClellan this sarcastic quote in a letter.

- "It is well that war is so terrible, lest we grow too fond of it." Robert E. Lee
  Lee made this comment on the Battle of Fredericksburg, in which almost 1,300 Union soldiers were killed and some 9,600 wounded.

- "They couldn't hit an elephant at this distance." Union General John Sedgwick
  Sedgwick allegedly uttered this statement milliseconds before he was shot and killed by a Confederate sharpshooter on May 8, 1864.

- "Damn the torpedoes, full speed ahead!" Union Admiral David Farragut
  Farragut supposedly made his famous comment when he ordered his forces to press on in the face of Confederate torpedoes, or what would be called naval mines today.

Civil War Trivia, Part 3

Wartime songs have long been sung, setting down to vocal memory heroic deeds, fierce battles, and aching sentiment. Take this song from the Civil War, for instance.

> *There were companions on the march,*
> *as every soldier found,*
> *With ceaseless zeal in digging deep in every spot around,*
> *And though each hero killed a lot,*
> *still thousands more abound,*
> *The graybacks so tenderly clinging.*

Quite the moving bit of songcraft, isn't it? It's almost pretty enough to make you forget you're singing about lice. Yes, the "graybacks" in the song are body lice, hence the song's title, "The Graybacks So Tenderly Clinging." In his 1887 book *Hard Tack and Coffee*, author John D. Billings wrote of the ubiquitous graybacks, "Hot water was the sovereign remedy, for it penetrated every mesh and seam, and cooked the millions yet unborn, which Job himself could not have exterminated by the thumbnail process unaided. So tenacious of life were these creatures that some veterans affirm they have seen them still creeping on garments taken out of boiling water, and that only by putting salt in the water were they sure of accomplishing their destruction."

EXTRA CREDIT: The Old Testament book of Joel, chapter three, verse 10, says, "Beat your plowshares into swords and your pruning hooks into spears." During the Civil War, a Nashville company took the first part of that statement to heart. The Nashville Plow Works company left agriculture for warfare, turning out swords until Nashville fell on April 1, 1862.

MATTHEW BRADY

One of America's most famous photographers help turn photography from curiosity to indispensable record of history, then had history turn its back on him. Matthew Brady foresaw the utility of photographs as a record of current events, but couldn't foresee changes in the market for those records.

The future photography icon was born in Warren County, New York, in 1823. When he was fifteen, Brady met the American portraitist William Page, who instructed him in painting portraits. In 1841, Page also took Brady to New York City, where he studied under inventor Samuel F. B. Morse. Brady learned daguerreotypy, an early photographic process, from Morse, and opened his own photography studio in New York City in 1844. Brady opened a second studio in Washington, D.C. in 1849 and another New York City studio in 1854.

It was in 1845 that Brady began photographing notable Americans, including Daniel Webster, John James Audubon, and Millard Filmore. When the Civil War broke out in 1861, Brady hired a staff of photographers that he sent to the war zones. Brady mainly served as coordinator of the war-photography effort, and many of the images labeled "Photo by Brady" were actually taken by his staff photographers. Brady did take some notable photographs of battle scenes, as well as some of Abraham Lincoln and Robert E. Lee.

Brady brought the war to American citizens in 1862, when he exhibited pictures of the carnage at the Battle of Antietam at one of his New York galleries.

Unfortunately for Brady, interest in his war photographs ended when the war did. A war-weary America didn't care to be reminded of its bloody conflict, and Brady found himself in financial straits. The U.S. government bought many of Brady's photographic plates at auction for $2,840, then Congress paid $25,000 for all Brady's images in 1875. It wasn't enough. Brady died, broke, in a charity hospital in 1896.

WILMER MCLEAN

War witnesses never lack for stories, but few war witnesses can rival Wilmer McLean's stash of war stories.

McLean's unsought claim to fame began on July 18, 1861, a little more than three months after the Confederate shelling of Fort Sumter began the Civil War. McLean, the owner of a Prince William County, Virginia estate known as Yorkshire, had seen his home turned into the temporary headquarters of Confederate General Pierre Gustave Toutant Beauregard. Confederate forces had dug in along a nearby stream known as Bull Run, and when Union troops began firing at the Confederates, one of the Union shells wreaked some havoc on the McLean house. A shell pierced the walls of the house, landing in a kettle of stew. As Beauregard put it, "A comical effect of this artillery fight was the destruction of the dinner of myself and staff by a Federal shell that fell into the fire-place of my headquarters at the McLean House."

What started as a "comical" event soon grew into the First Battle of Bull Run, the first major land battle of the Civil War, with Union casualties reaching an estimated 3,000 and Confederate casualties numbering 2,000.

McLean, no fool, decided that battlefields made for poor homesteads, and eventually moved his family to another location in southern Virginia. The McLeans lived in relative peace in their new home, but history wasn't through with Wilmer.

On April 9, 1865, McLean was walking in the town near his house when he encountered an emissary who had been sent by Robert E. Lee to scout a location for Lee to meet with Ulysses Grant. McLean showed the emissary first the courthouse and then his house, and McLean's house was chosen as the meeting spot. Lee, Grant and other Union officers arrived at McLean's house later in the day, eventually signing the papers that ended the Civil War in McLean's parlor.

For McLean, as he once remarked, "The War began in my dining room and ended in my parlor."

WHO SAID WHAT,
CIVIL WAR PART 2

Just so you'll be able to drop a few pithy sentences into the next conversation around the watercooler, here's a few more notable Civil War-era quotes.

- "An honest politician is one who, when he is bought, stays bought." Simon Cameron.
  Cameron served under Lincoln as his secretary of war. Evidently, he carried a very utilitarian view towards politicians.

- "It's just like shooting squirrels, only these squirrels have guns." attributed to a Union musket instructor.
  It's probably apocryphal, but it's just too good a quote not to print.

- "Tonight we will water our horses in the Tennessee River." Confederate General Albert Sidney Johnston
  Johnston made the comment shortly before the Battle of Shiloh. He was esteemed as a brilliant military mind, but he was no prophet. He died early in the battle.

- "The rebel army is now the legitimate property of the Army of the Potomac." Union General Joseph Hooker
  Hooker was no prophet, either. He was thrashed by Robert E. Lee's forces at Chancellorsville.

- "Success and glory are in the advance, disaster and shame lurk in the rear." Union General John Pope
  Maybe the lesson is that generals shouldn't make cocky announcements. Pope made this statement before he was defeated at the Second Battle of Bull Run.

- "I am short a cheek-bone and one ear, but am able to whip all hell yet." Union General John M. Corse

  Give the man credit. He could turn a phrase, even after suffering a head wound. And he was as good as his word. Corse and his men held out until reinforcements arrived in the Battle of Allatoona.

JOHN WILKES BOOTH

Before John Wilkes Booth became infamous as the man who shot and killed Abraham Lincoln at Ford's Theater, he was a famous actor in a famous acting family.

Booth was the ninth of ten children born to Junius Brutus Booth and Mary Ann Holmes, Britain-born actors who moved to Maryland in 1821. John sought a lasting legacy at an early age. As Chris Ellis and Julie Ellis wrote in *The Mammoth Book of Celebrity Murder*, "Booth's desire for fame was not confined to the realms of acting—once in discussion with friends at school he pondered out loud the prospect of him knocking over the Colossus of Rhodes, one of the Seven Wonders of the World. He remarked that if he could achieve this task then he would live for a thousand years in print, each generation learning his name."

The dark-haired, trim and handsome John Wilkes Booth became a successful actor at a young age, appearing in Philadelphia, New York City, and Richmond. But the true fire in Booth's heart was one of politics, specifically the support of the Confederate cause. He devised two plans to kidnap Lincoln, both of which were thwarted by last-minute changes to Lincoln's schedule.

On Friday, April 14, 1865, with the Civil War over, it was announced that Lincoln would attend a performance of the comedy *Our American Cousin* at Ford's Theatre in Washington the next night. Booth saw his chance. During Act III, Scene 2 of the play, Booth slipped into the presidential box fired a single slug from a .44-caliber Derringer into the back of the president's head. Lincoln would die from his wound the next day.

After he shot Lincoln, Booth attempted to jump to the stage floor, but caught one of his spurs in a flag hanging from the presidential box. He landed awkwardly on the stage, breaking his left leg. Ever the actor, Booth then cried, "Sic semper tyrannis!" (Latin for "Thus always to tyrants"), limped off the stage and made his getaway on his horse.

He was discovered by Federal troops twelve days later, hiding in a tobacco barn near Bowling Green, Virginia. Like his victim, Booth died from a gunshot, either self-inflicted or from a Federal gun. His last words were, "Useless, useless."

ROBERT TODD LINCOLN

The life story of Robert Todd Lincoln, the first child of Abraham Lincoln and Mary Todd Lincoln, is a curious one of tragedy, success, and truly strange coincidences.

Robert was born on August 1, 1843 in Springfield, Illinois. Unlike his lanky father, Robert was of a shorter build, causing Lincoln to remark, "Bob is short and low, and, I expect, always will be." Described as a shy child, Robert nonetheless went on to graduate from Harvard College, and spent four months at Harvard Law School to enter the Army. He served on Ulysses Grant's staff, and was one of the Union officers present when Robert E. Lee surrendered to Grant at Appomattox Courthouse. The young Lincoln, the only one of the Lincoln's four children that survived to maturity, thus inadvertently began his lifelong pattern of being present at historic intersections.

Sadly for Robert, the next historic event he would witness was the death of his father. When Lincoln was shot in Ford's Theater, Robert was in his room at the White House. Told of his father's shooting, Robert rushed to the Petersen House, where his father died.

Robert went on to honor his father's wishes and become a lawyer, then served as secretary of war under President James A. Garfield. Lincoln was a witness when Garfield was fatally shot in a Washington railroad station in 1881.

In 1901, Lincoln was present when an anarchist shot President William McKinley at the Buffalo Pan-American Exposition.

Not everything in Robert's life was tragic. He was a successful lawyer and businessman, becoming president of the Pullman Car Company in 1897. He was also director of Commonwealth Edison Company and the Chicago Telephone Company.

CIVIL WAR MASCOTS

The comfort of an animal friend has gotten many a person through tough times, and animal companionship was particularly appreciated by Civil War soldiers, who made various and sundry animals their mascots. Some of the mascot's stories might have gotten inflated over the years, but that just makes for better storytelling.

- Sallie, a Staffordshire Bull Terrier, served as the mascot of the 11th Pennsylvania Volunteer Infantry. Brought into the regiment as a puppy, it was said that she knew each member of her regiment, and distrusted outsiders. She stayed with the 11th Pennsylvania through battles at Cedar Mountain, Antietam, Fredericksburg, Chancellorsville, and Gettysburg. She was wounded in the neck at Spotsylvania, then killed at Hatcher's Run, Virginia. A bronze likeness of Sallie "sleeps" on the monument to the regiment at Gettysburg.

- Old Abe the bald eagle was the mascot for Co. C, 8th Regiment Wisconsin Volunteers, which was known as the Eagle Regiment. Named—of course—in honor of Abraham Lincoln, Abe became the image of many fundraising efforts, including soldier relief. After the war, Abe went to live in the Wisconsin state capital. He died there seventeen years later from smoke inhalation when the capital caught fire. Officials had Abe stuffed, but a second fire later destroyed Abe's body. A replica of Abe is now on display in the capital.

- Other dog mascots included Jack, the 102nd Pennsylvania Infantry's bull terrier mascot, Old Harvey, mascot of the 104th Ohio and two Irish wolfhounds of the 69th New York.

- And there were stranger mascots, including a donkey (3rd Louisiana), a bear (12th Wisconsin Volunteers) and a sheep named Dick (2nd Rhode Island). But the strangest mascot may have been Old Douglas, the mascot of the 43rd Mississippi Infantry. Douglas was a camel owned by Lieutenant William H. Hargrove that carried the officer's mess on his back. Tragically for the 43rd Mississippi, also known as the Camel Regiment, Douglas was killed during the Siege of Vicksburg.

CIVIL WAR SONGS

The advent of the mp3 player was about 150 years off, but Civil War soldiers still transported their music with them, mainly in the form of popular songs they memorized and sang. Some of them don't exactly resound in catchiness to twenty-first-century ears, but in their day, they were quite the popular choices. Some were Union songs, some Confederate and some were sung by both sides.

"Marching through Georgia" was a popular Union song, and it made an appearance in "Gone With the Wind." It's sung by one of the occupants of a wagon that refuses to give a ride to an injured Confederate soldier.

> *(Chorus) Hurrah! Hurrah! We bring the jubilee!*
> *Hurrah! Hurrah! The flag that makes you free!*
> *So we sang the chorus from Atlanta to the sea,*
> *While we were marching through Georgia.*

Another Union song, "My Maryland," mocked the cleanliness of the Confederate troops.

> *Hark to our noses' dire appeal,*
> *Maryland, my Maryland!*
> *Oh unwashed Rebs to you we kneel!*
> *Maryland, my Maryland!*
> *If you can't purchase soap, oh steal*
> *That precious article—I feel*
> *Like scratching from the head to heel*
> *Maryland, my Maryland!*

The Confederates countered with songs like "The Bonnie Blue Flag," which also received a "Gone With the Wind" mention. Rhett Butler and Scarlett O'Hara's daughter was named Bonnie Blue Butler.

> *We are a band of brothers, and native to the soil,*
> *Fighting for the property we gained by honest toil;*

And when our rights were threatened, the cry rose near
and far:
"Hurrah for the Bonnie Blue Flag that bears a single star!"

George Lindsey might not have known it, but his most famous
character on "The Andy Griffith Show" owes his name to a
Confederate ditty, "Goober Peas."

Sittin' by the roadside on a summer's day,
Chattin' with my messmates, passing time away,
Lying in the shadow, underneath the trees,
Goodness, how delicious, eating goober peas!

(Chorus) Peas! Peas! Peas! Peas!
Eating goober peas!
Goodness, how delicious,
Eating goober peas!

When President Lincoln called for 300,000 volunteers to join the
Army in 1862, James Sloan, an abolitionist Quaker, was inspired to
write the song "We Are Coming, Father Abraham."

We are coming, Father Abraham, three hundred thousand
more,
From Mississippi's winding stream and from New
England's shore;
We leave our plows and workshops, our wives and children
dear,
With hearts too full for utterance, with but a silent tear;
We dare not look behind us, but steadfastly before,
We are coming, Father Abraham, three hundred thousand
more.

(Chorus) We are coming, coming our union to restore,
We are coming, Father Abraham, with three hundred
thousand more.

CIVIL WAR TRIVIA, PART 4

- Today, the Confederate prison at Andersonville is remembered for its horrible conditions and the death of some 13,000 Union soldiers there. But the prison also has an enduring legacy in language. The prison had two fences, one located roughly twenty feet inside the outer wall. Anyone caught between the two fences would be shot dead, so the line of the inner fence became known as the deadline.

- Four of the most famous battles of the Civil war are the First Battle of Bull Run, the Second Battle of Bull Run, the First Battle of Manassas and the Second Battle of Manassas. Only the four battles are really just two battles, with two different names. It was the practice of the Union forces to name battles after the nearest body of running water, while the Confederates named battles after the nearest town. So what the North called Bull Run, after a nearby stream, the South called Manassas, after the town of Manassas, Virginia.

- When the body of John Wilkes Booth was searched following his death, he was found to have been carrying photographs of five women. Four—Alice Grey, Effie Germon, Helen Western and Fanny Brown—were prominent actresses of the era. The fifth, Lucy Hale, was the daughter of John P. Hale, who served under Lincoln as minister to Spain. Hale and Booth were reported to have become engaged a month before Booth assassinated Lincoln, and Hale is also reported to have taken Booth to Lincoln's second inauguration.

CIVIL WAR TIMELINE

Dates can sometimes be hard to keep in perspective, especially when dealing as many notable events as the Civil War had. So here's a timeline of some of the most notable events.

1860

- November 6: Abraham Lincoln elected president.
- December 20: South Carolina secedes from the Union.

1861

- January 9: Other states begin seceding, starting with Mississippi. Florida (January 10), Alabama (January 11), Georgia (January 19), Louisiana (January 26), Texas (February 1), Virginia (April 17), Arkansas (May 6), North Carolina (May 20) and Tennessee (June 8) follow.
- February 4: Provisional Confederate Congress convenes in Montgomery, Alabama.
- February 9: Jefferson Davis is elected provisional president of the Confederacy.
- February 18: Jefferson Davis is inaugurated.
- March 4: Abraham Lincoln is inaugurated.
- April 12: Confederate forces begin bombardment of Fort Sumter, in the harbor of Charleston, South Carolina.
- April 13: Fort Sumter surrenders.
- July 12: First Battle of Bull Run.

1862

- March 9: The Union's *Monitor* and the Confederacy's *Virginia* fight the first naval battle between ironclad ships.
- Aug. 28: Second Battle of Bull Run.
- December 13: Battle of Fredericksburg, Virginia.

1863

- January 1: Emancipation Proclamation goes into effect.
- May 18: Union siege of Vicksburg, Mississippi begins.

- July 1-3: Battle of Gettysburg
- July 4: Vicksburg surrenders.
- Sept. 19-20: Battle of Chickamauga, Georgia.

1864
- May 7: Union begins the Atlanta Campaign.
- Sep. 2: Atlanta occupied by Union troops.
- November 16: General William Tecumseh begins his March to the Sea from Atlanta.
- December 21: Savannah, Georgia is occupied by Union forces.

1865
- April 9: General Robert E. Lee surrenders at Appomattox.
- April 14: Abraham Lincoln shot by John Wilkes Booth.
- April 15: Lincoln dies.

The Lincoln-Kennedy Coincidences

While some think the strange-but-true links between Abraham Lincoln and John F. Kennedy are incredible, others are skeptical. Freaky but historically accurate, is this a twilight-zone trick or simply a coincidence?

- Lincoln was elected to Congress in 1846; Kennedy was elected to Congress in 1946.
- Lincoln was elected president in 1860; Kennedy was elected president in 1960.
- Both were shot with one bullet, in the head, on a Friday.
- Lincoln was shot in the Ford Theatre. Kennedy was shot in a Ford Lincoln vehicle.
- Lincoln's secretary was named Kennedy. Kennedy's secretary was named Lincoln.
- Both men's succesors were named Johnson.
- John Wilkes Booth, who assasinated Lincoln, was born in 1839. Kennedy's assassin, Lee Harvey Oswald, was born in 1939.
- Both assassins were assassinated before their trials.

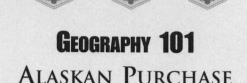

GEOGRAPHY 101
ALASKAN PURCHASE

It's hard for modern minds to even consider the concept of purchasing land—any land—for a little less than two cents per acre. But in 1867, when Secretary of State William Seward and Russian minister Edouard de Stoeckl haggled out a price of $7.2 million dollars as payment for almost 600,000 square miles of Alaskan territory, the move was derided as "Seward's Folly" or "Seward's Icebox."

Russia's role in Alaskan history began in 1741, when Vitus Jonassen Bering (of the eponymous Bering Sea and Bering Strait), a Danish navigator in the Russian Navy, led the first European expedition to the Alaskan coast. Russia later sparsely colonized the area, but it wasn't a profitable colonization, so Russia pitched a sale of the territory to America in 1859. Faced with first the threat and then the fact of a civil war, America was in no position to take over a farflung territory, and the deal lay dormant until the Civil War ended.

Negotiations resumed once the war was over, and on March 30, 1867, Seward and de Stoeckl agreed to the $7.2 million purchase price. Senate approval followed on April 9, but opposition by the House of Representatives stalled the appropriation of the required funds until July 14, 1868.

America now had a vast new frontier, but it was still dealing with its contiguous frontier, so development and governance of Alaska was mainly an afterthought for almost thirty years. That changed in August 1896, when Skookum Jim Mason, Dawson Charlie, and George Washington Carmack discovered gold in a tributary of the Klondike River, kicking off a major gold rush to the Alaskan Territory.

In 1967, one hundred years after Seward's Folly, the largest oil field in North America was discovered at Prudhoe Bay. More than ten billion barrels of oil have been produced from the field.

Benjamin Singleton and the Exodusters

The Civil War had set the slaves free, but it didn't erase all the former slaves' problems. Being set free was one thing, being accepted into society and making a new life for themselves was another. And when Federal military forces left the South in 1877, beginning a period known by some Southerners as Redemption, many black Americans found themselves free but with little hope for the future in the face of new laws prohibiting land ownership by blacks and postbellum racism.

While blacks in the South were continuing to experience hardship, lands were opening up out west. The Homestead Act of 1862 had made it easier for private individuals to get 160 acres of land to homestead, and since black Americans could now travel wherever they wanted, some began to consider a mass movement out of the South their best option.

A former slave, Benjamin "Pap" Singleton of Nashville, Tennessee, addressed the 1875 Tennessee State Convention of Colored Men to urge a migration out of the state, then urged the issue again at the next year's convention. Singleton also began to organize an exodus from the South to Kansas. A board of commissioners was created to urge relocation to Kansas, and men like Singleton became "conductors" for black families heading to Kansas.

The South wasn't the only home of anti-black racism. Senator William Windom, a Republican from Minnesota, introduced the William Resolution on January 16, 1879, encouraging blacks to leave the South. That year, what would become known as the Kansas Exodus exploded, with some 6,000 blacks known as "Exodusters" leaving the South for Kansas.

Nicodemus, Kansas, was an all-black town founded by Exodusters. Today, Nicodemus is a National Historic Site.

BUFFALO

The destruction of the staggeringly large American buffalo herds, and with them a major part of many Native Americans' lifestyles, is often cited as a classic example of American shortsightedness and wastefulness. But new research indicates that Europeans, not Americans, were the reason for the near-extinction of the buffalo.

Estimates of the American buffalo herd's size in 1800 vary from 30 to 60 million. By 1900, there were less than six hundred. According to author Wayne Gard's 1960 book *The Great Buffalo Hunt*, the great buffalo kill began in earnest in 1871, when a Kansas City trader named J. N. DuBois began sending out circulars to buffalo country, offering to buy any hide at any time, for a good price.

In a 2006 paper titled "Buffalo Hunt, International Trade and the Virtual Extinction of the North American Bison," M. Scott Taylor, a professor of economics at Canada's University of Calgary, explained his theory of European complicity in that decrease. Taylor believes that a new European innovation in tanning buffalo hides (something U.S. tanners couldn't yet do) led to DuBois' willingness to buy hides.

Taylor posits that Europeans used their tanning innovation to create leather for European Army forces and for industrial belting to drive European machinery.

Americans were obviously complicit in the destruction of the buffalo, but if Taylor is correct, the epic levels of buffalo predation would never have occurred without European demand.

EXTRA CREDIT: Although nowhere near their numbers in the early nineteenth century, the American buffalo, or bison as it is more properly called, has made a comeback. Currently, the population is estimated at around 350,000.

BUFFALO SOLDIERS

During the Civil War, more than 180,000 black soldiers fought for the Union, albeit in segregated regiments. In 1866, Congress organized two regiments of black cavalry, the Ninth and Tenth United States Cavalry, and six regiments of black infantry. The infantry regiments were consolidated into the Twenty-Fourth and Twenty-Fifth United States Infantry in 1869. These four regiments, especially the cavalry regiments, became known as the Buffalo Soldiers.

The four regiments were largely led by white officers (including Abner Doubleday), although Henry O. Flipper, the first black graduate of West Point, was assigned to the Tenth Cavalry. The soldiers received the nickname "Buffalo Soldiers" after fighting Plains Indian tribes like the Kiowa, Apache and Cheyenne. Out of admiration for the soldiers, the Cheyenne called the soldiers "wild buffalo," which gradually became Buffalo Soldiers.

The Buffalo Soldiers served with distinction during the Indian Wars, with thirteen enlisted men and six officers winning the Medal of Honor. In the Spanish-American War, all four regiments fought in Cuba, and five more enlisted men won the Medal of Honor.

In the Phillipine-American War of 1899–1902, the four regular regiments and two volunteer regiments served. The Tenth Cavalry helped John J. "Black Jack" Pershing pursue Pancho Villa.

No Buffalo Soldier regiments went to Europe in World War I, and the Ninth and Tenth cavalries were disbanded during World War II. The Twenty-Fifth Infantry fought in the Pacific, then was disbanded in 1949. The Twenty-Fourth Infantry, the last segregated black regiment, fought in the Pacific during World War II, and also fought in the Korean War.

ABNER DOUBLEDAY

Forget that bit about him inventing baseball. Most likely, Abner Doubleday was not the inventor of America's favorite pastime. But what he lacks in baseball cred, Mr. Doubleday more than makes up for in interesting trivia.

Doubleday's brushes with history started on April 12, 1861. He was second in command of Fort Sumter, in the harbor of Charleston, South Carolina. Confederate forces began shelling Fort Sumter in the pre-dawn hours of April 12, and Doubleday began the Union response by firing the first shell back at the Confederates.

That auspicious start was just the beginning of Doubleday's brushes with history. He fought at the Second Battle of Bull Run. At Antietam, he served with distinction and earned a promotion to lieutenant colonel. At Gettysburg, Doubleday took over corps command when his General John F. Reynolds, his commanding officer, was killed early in the first day of fighting. After the Civil War, Doubleday served in the Mexican-American War and the Seminole wars. But he wasn't finished carving out a niche in American history. In 1873, Doubleday left the Army for San Francisco, where he got a charter for the cable car line.

The legend of Doubleday inventing baseball, however, is probably puffery. But don't take our word for it. A 2004 article Major League Baseball's website quoted National Baseball Hall of Fame vice president and chief curator of the museum as saying, "The Doubleday thing is a total myth. We've got proof in writing. We've got all the papers here."

Here are a few arguments againts the Doubleday baseball myth:

• When Doubleday died in 1893, his *New York Times* obituary made no mention of his inventing baseball.

• The man who claimed to have seen Doubleday invent baseball, Abner Graves, was a sketchy character who killed his wife and lived the rest of his life in an asylum for the criminally insane.

• And although Doubleday was alleged to have invented the game in Cooperstown, New York in 1839, he was actually at West Point that year.

ANDERSONVILLE

Just twenty-two miles from Plains, Georgia, home of former president Jimmy Carter, sits the National Prisoner of War Museum. The museum, which serves as a memorial to all American prisoners of war, was located in Andersonville, Georgia, because Andersonville was the home of an American atrocity, and is the final resting place of 13,000 Civil War soldiers who died there.

The prison, originally given the name Camp Sumter, was designed to hold 10,000 prisoners, a number that it might have held were it not for an incident known as the Fort Pillow Massacre. On April 12, 1864, a number of black troops who had surrendered to Major General Nathan Bedford Forrest's forces were killed. The incident caused the Union to cease the exchange of prisoners it had been engaging in with the Confederacy, and Andersonville's population exploded. At its height of population, it held 33,000 prisoners of war.

Living conditions were execrable. Poor sanitary practices led to the death of many from dysentery. Food was often in short supply, water supplies were contaminated (prisoners bathed in and drank from the same stream), living space was scarce, and medical care largely nonexistent. Groups of prisoners calling themselves the Raiders preyed on their fellow inmates, stealing everything of value. Later, a group called the Regulators caught, punished and, in some instances, killed the Raiders.

Some 49,000 prisoners were sent to Andersonville, with more than 13,000 dying there. After the war ended, Henry Wirz, who had become camp commandant in 1864, was tried for conspiring with Jefferson Davis to "injure the health and destroy the lives of soldiers in the military service of the United States." He was convicted on all counts, then hanged on November 10, 1865.

CRASH COURSE
WOMEN'S RIGHTS

Mississippi's Married Women's Property Act of 1839 was the first to recognize a woman's right to own property separate from her husband. Probably founded on Native American inheritances through the female, it was unheard of in its time.

Women in the 1800s

Apart from in Mississippi, American women in 1840 had virtually no personal rights, political or civil. No married woman could own property (even property she inherited) separate from her husband, women could not attend college, almost all had to give up their careers when they got married, and speaking publicly branded them as prostitutes.

The only educational choices of the time: in 1837, Oberlin College in Ohio began admitting women, and the female seminary Mount Holyoke College opened in Massachusetts.

Nineteenth century middle-class women took a hard look at their role as the moral leaders in the home and the children's educators. They resented the way men "demoted" them to secondary positions in the home and denied them outside opportunities, especially in the antislavery movement. In fact, crusading for the rights of blacks made women acutely aware that they had none of those rights, either.

The Ladies Speak Up

- Sisters **Sarah** and **Angelina Grimké** spoke against the horrors of slavery, comparing the predicament of blacks to that of women. Criticized for speaking publicly, as a man would, Sarah wrote *Letter on the Condition of Women and the Equality of the Sexes* (1837), asserting that men and women were created equal.

- **Lucretia Mott** and **Elizabeth Cady Stanton** attended an antislavery convention in London in 1840. They were not permitted to sit in open public, watching from behind a curtain. That's when they decided to campaign for women's rights. In 1848, Stanton petitioned for the New York State Married Women's Property Act.

- Mott and Stanton, with **Jane Hunt**, **Martha Wright**, and **Mary Ann McClintock**, planned the first women's rights convention in American history for July 1848 in Seneca Falls, New York. More than 250 women and forty men attended. (Men who agreed with their stance included William Lloyd Garrison, Wendell Phillips, Gerrit Smith, and Samuel Gridley Howe.)

- After the convention, **Susan B. Anthony** joined Stanton in leading the campaign for equal rights and fair treatment for women.

The Seneca Falls Convention

The convention wrote a "Declaration of Sentiments," modeled after the Declaration of Independence, declaring that "all men and women are created equal." It listed objections to laws and customs discriminating against women and included resolutions for women to receive: equal treatment, equal public opportunities, property rights, and the right to vote. Sixty-eight women and thirty-two men signed the declaration.

The Declaration of Sentiments stirred up plenty of negative reaction. But, bad publicity is better than none at all. Angered publishers printed the Declaration in its entirety in well-read well-respected newspapers.

Legacy

The slavery crisis and the Civil War overshadowed women's rights issues in the 1850s. Seventy-two years later, the nineteenth amendment granted women the right to vote. An Equal Rights Amendment against sexual discrimination was introduced in 1923; it was reintroduced in 1972 and failed with only thirty-five of the thirty-eight needed votes.

Congress approved it in 1972 as the twenty-seventh amendment. Only thirty-five states approved it, instead of the thirty-eight needed for ratification. Although the deadline for ratification has passed, it has been reintroduced in every Congress since 1982.

HENRY WARD BEECHER

Harriet Beecher Stowe's book *Uncle Tom's Cabin* was a literary impetus for the Civil War, igniting anti-slavery passions across America. On the other hand, Stowe's brother, Henry Ward Beecher, became famous across America for supposed passions of his own.

In 1847, Beecher became pastor of Plymouth Church in Brooklyn, and his sermons regularly drew in thousands every Sunday. He became nationally known for his anti-slavery views, as well as his support of temperance and women's suffrage. After Beecher raised money to buy rifles for Kansas and Nebraska residents opposed to slavery, the rifles became known as "Beecher's Bibles."

Beecher's problems began in 1872, when Victoria Woodhull, a women's rights advocate, published an article accusing Beecher of adultery in *Woodhull and Claflin's Weekly*. In addition to being in favor of women's rights, Woodhull was in favor of free love, and alleged that Beecher had participated in just such a practice. Woodhull alleged that Beecher had had an affair with Elizabeth Tilton. Tilton and her husband Theodore were both members of Plymouth Church. (Woodhull's publishing of the alleged affair's details earned her an arrest for violating federal obscenity laws, courtesy of crusader Anthony Comstock. Comstock would go on to successfully lobby passage of the federal Comstock Law, which made it illegal to mail "obscene, lewd, or lascivious" material.)

Confessions, retractions, retractions of retractions, finger-pointing, and published charges flowed between the Tiltons, Beecher, and other parties until 1875, when Theodore sued Beecher alienation of affection. The ensuing trial lasted six months and captivated the nation. In the end, the jury could not reach a verdict, and Beecher was acquitted.

Being implicated in America's first national sex scandal didn't harm Beecher. He remained at Plymouth Church, and today, a statue of him stands in Brooklyn's Columbus Park.

SAMUEL MORSE AND THE TELEGRAPH

The biblical book of Numbers, the fourth book of the Torah, is credited to Moses and dates back to between 400 and 550 BC. But a sentence from that book started a communication revolution that would keep the far-flung and ever-expanding corners of America in contact with each other.

Samuel Finley Breese Morse was a Massachusetts-born Yale College grad who had already experienced success in the invention world (he and his brother Sidney patented a water pump for fire engines in 1817) and in the artistic world (he had painted portraits of Eli Whitney and Noah Webster). In 1829, Morse left America for Europe, where he painted for three years. On the ship back to America in 1832, Morse met Dr. Charles Thomas Jackson of Boston. Jackson told Morse of electromagnetism experiments that had been conducted in Europe.

His conversations with Jackson led Morse to draw up the plans for a telegraph ("tele" from the Greek word for "far" and "graph" for the Greek "write). Previous designs for telegraphs had required many strands of wire, but Morse planned to use only one wire, cutting down on complexity and cost. Morse began working on his project with partners Leonard Gale and Alfred Vail, and by 1837 the team had produced a single-wire system, although decoding messages sent with this system was complicated and difficult. By the next year, the team had created a simpler system, now known as Morse Code, that communicated with dots (short pulses) and dashes (longer pulses).

By 1844, Morse and his team were ready for their first public demonstration of their telegraph. He set up telegraph equipment in the Supreme Court and in the Mount Clair train depot in Baltimore, Maryland, and on May 24, 1844, he successfully transmitted a section of Numbers 23:23, "what hath God wrought" from Washington to Baltimore.

Use of the telegraph exploded. Western Union completed the first transcontinental telegraph line in October 1861, and America had its communication lifeline.

ELIZABETH BLACKWELL, PIONEER

The important thing to know is that Elizabeth Blackwell was the first female doctor in America. Blackwell wasn't the settler kind of pioneer who lived in a log cabin and spun wool. But, to American women, she definitely was a pioneer.

Blackwell overcame opposition in every step of her career. It sounds like a "That's Good/ That's Bad" game:

BAD: Numerous medical schools, including Harvard and Yale, rejected her applications.
GOOD: The administration of New York's Geneva College accepted Blackwell in 1847.

BAD: Geneva's all-male student body didn't accept her at all.
GOOD: Blackwell worked diligently to prove herself to her classmates and professors. She had the opportunity to practice medicine during an 1848 summer program at the Philadelphia Hospital in Pennsylvania.

BAD: Other doctors in the program did not accept a woman, and Blackwell was forced to practice self-reliance.
GOOD: She hung in there and graduated from Geneva College in 1849. Blackwell traveled abroad to continue her medical studies, taking a midwifery course at Paris' La Maternité.

BAD: Unfortunately, her dreams of becoming a surgeon ended when an infection blinded one eye.
GOOD: The midwifery course did lay the groundwork for later specialization.

BAD: In New York in 1851, Blackwell faced more rejection. No medical institution would hire her to practice.
GOOD: Quakers expressed confidence in Blackwell's abilities and began using her medical services.

BAD: Landlords in New York wouldn't rent space for a woman practicing medicine.
GOOD: Blackwell bought a house in a less-than-trendy neighborhood. She opened an office in 1853; by 1857, it became the New York Infirmary for Women and Children.

BAD: Blackwell's plans to open a women's medical school were shelved during the Civil War.
GOOD: Her Women's Medical College of the New York Infirmary opened in 1868.

In Memoriam

A memorial tablet to Elizabeth Blackwell can be found on the wall of Rock House in Hastings, England, where she lived for thirty years. The inscription reads:

Here lived and worked for thirty years
Dr. Elizabeth Blackwell
Born at Bristol 1821, Died at Hastings 1910
The first woman to graduate in Medicine in the United States at Geneva (Syracuse University) New York 1849
The first woman to be placed on the British Medical Register 1859.
"One who never turned her back but marched breast forward, never doubted clouds would break, never dreamed, though right were worsted, wrong would triumph, held we fall to rise, are baffled to fight better, sleep to wake."

ZACHARY TAYLOR'S PRESIDENCY (1849-1850)

During the campaign, Taylor promised to only use the presidential veto on proposals that he found unconstitutional. Some of his immediate predecessors had vetoed whatever they wanted to. This meant that for even an unpopular proposal, if it fell under the guidelines of the Constitution, its supporters could count on Taylor signing it into law.

When Taylor took office in March 1849, he was ready to grant statehood to New Mexico and California, especially with the discovery of gold out west. To skirt the slavery question that arose whenever land received territory status, Taylor decided to go straight to statehood. He accomplished this by secretly offering the areas statehood before Congress assembled in December, which was accepted. Taylor emphasized to Congress that he would veto any bill that linked California and New Mexico statehood to any fugitive slave bill.

Zachary Taylor died in office on July 9, 1850. He was succeeded by his vice president, Millard Fillmore.

Decisions Before, After, and During 1850

Prior to 1850

- *1787 — Northwest Ordinance:* Congress banned slavery in the Northwest Territory (present-day Ohio, Indiana, Illinois, Michigan, Wisconsin, and Minnesota)
- *1820 — Missouri Compromise:* Congress drew a northern slave territory limit at 36°30' north latitude
- *1836–1844 — Gag Rule:* The House of Representatives automatically tabled all petitions about slavery without discussion
- *1845 — Texas Annexation:* The question of allowing slavery in the new territories of Texas, California, and New Mexico widened division between the North and South
- *1846 — Wilmot Proviso:* A bill proposing forbidding slavery in the former Mexican territories never passed

The Compromise of 1850
- Settled $10 million in Texas debt
- Created the territories of New Mexico (now New Mexico and Arizona) and Utah (now Utah, Nevada, parts of Wyoming, and Colorado)
- Let the settlers in those regions decide the question of slavery by voting on it
- Abolished the slave trade in the District of Columbia
- Admitted California to the Union as a free state
- Provided for returning runaway slaves to their masters (the Fugitive Slave Law) and punishment for those who helped runaway slaves

Following the Compromise of 1850

The Kansas-Nebraska Act of 1854 divided Nebraska Territory into separate Kansas and Nebraska territories and allowed settlers there to vote on slavery. It was a huge Southern victory because all land was north of the Missouri Compromise line—it basically repealed the Missouri Compromise and opened up new territories that might take the Southern side of the slavery issue.

The highly-debated Kansas-Nebraska Act was a purely political move on the part of Illinois's Senator Stephen Douglas. His proposed act served his Illinois constituents—to get Southerners to approve federal funds for a railroad through his state, Douglas offered up this very appealing proposition to them.

The Taylor Girls

Zachary Taylor had five daughters and one son. Two daughters died as infants; two lived to distinguish themselves in adult life.

- Sarah, the oldest, married Jefferson Davis in 1835, but died three months later. Davis had served under Taylor in the U.S. Army, and later became president of the Confederate States of America.
- Mary Elizabeth, Taylor's favorite, served as her father's hostess in the White House while he was in office. Zachary's wife was ill and unable to handle those duties.

MILLARD FILLMORE'S PRESIDENCY (1850–1853)

Vice President Millard Fillmore succeeded Zachary Taylor after the President's sudden death. He was a New Yorker, and therefore from an antislavery region. But, when he took office, most people did not know his own feelings on slavery or the Compromise pending in Congress. Turns out, he was a strong supporter of the Compromise of 1850.

After taking office President Fillmore delivered a speech to Congress making clear his stand: He wanted to compromise on California. Taylor's Cabinet jumped ship, immediately resigning.

President Fillmore appointed Daniel Webster his secretary of state. Other new members of his Cabinet were Thomas Corwin, William Graham, Charles Conrad, Alexander H. Stuart II, John J. Crittenden, and Nathan Hall.

Fillmore signed the Compromise of 1850 after Congress passed it, admitting California as a free state but allowing settlers in all the other former Mexican territories to determine their own slaveholding status. The Compromise also included a stronger Fugitive Slave Law.

Fillmore was responsible for opening trade with Japan. It was Fillmore who sent Commodore Matthew Perry to Japan in 1853 to propose a commercial relationship to the emperor. A treaty signed on March 31, 1854, after Fillmore had left office, provided humane treatment for shipwrecked sailors and opened ports to U.S. commerce.

Fillmore did not receive his party's nomination in the 1852 presidential election. But, in 1856, he accepted the American Party's nomination, running against Democrat James Buchanan and Republican John C. Frémont. Fillmore received the electoral votes from only one state, Maryland.

EXTRA CREDIT: Fillmore and his wife Abigail installed the first bathtub and kitchen stove in the White House.

FRANKLIN PIERCE'S PRESIDENCY (1853–1857)

During the 1852 presidential campaign, both parties endorsed the Compromise of 1850, but Democrat Franklin Pierce of New Hampshire won on his platform of maintaining the status quo regarding slavery.

In 1853, Pierce's agent James Gadsden negotiated with Mexico to buy a strip of land south of the Gila River. Known as the Gadsden Purchase and including the areas of present-day Phoenix and Tucson, the land was purchased for $10 million, with plans to build a transcontinental railroad through it to the Pacific Ocean. However, Illinois Senator Stephen Douglas had his own plans to route the railroad through his state.

Pierce supported Douglas' Kansas-Nebraska Act of 1854, which let settlers in those territories vote on allowing slavery. Therefore, he was blamed for the fiasco after it was approved. Suddenly, strong supporters from each side flooded into Kansas with plans to stuff ballot boxes with votes favoring their position (some claimed that 6,000 votes were cast in a territory with only 1,500 eligible voters).

Pierce wanted to extend American claims into Cuba, which he tried to purchase from Spain, but they refused to sell. In 1854, his agents discussed the issue with Great Britain and France; both countries urged America to simply seize the land from Spain. But Northerners did not like the thought of acquiring the potential slave territory of Cuba, and that's as far as that plan went.

Last Call for Alcohol

Rumors of Franklin Pierce's excessive drinking darkened his reputation as a senator in the 1830s. His wittiest opponents called him "a hero of many a well-fought bottle." Pierce's years as president were plagued with loneliness and criticism. In 1869, he died of stomach inflammation, probably as a result of excessive alchohol consumption.

JAMES BUCHANAN'S PRESIDENCY (1857–1861)

James Buchanan viewed slavery as morally wrong, but believed it was Constitutional; therefore the federal government was obligated to preserve slavery in the states where it already existed.

In the 1856 presidential campaign, three parties supported candidates: Democrat James Buchanan, Republican John C. Frémont, and the American Party's Millard Fillmore. Buchanan won by a small margin.

Buchanan did try to pacify Southern states to keep them from leaving the Union. Even with his inaugural address on March 4, 1857, Buchanan tried to keep the peace, urging everyone to accept the Supreme Court's pending decision in the Dred Scott case, whatever it might be. (Actually, the Court had already told Buchanan that its decision would uphold the southern position on slavery.)

Then, in February 1858, he asked Congress to admit Kansas as a slave state under the Lecompton Constitution. Congress did not approve the proslavery document. (Kansas was admitted as a free state in January 1861)

In domestic policy, Buchanan was not successful, and the Civil War between the North and the South officially began shortly after he left office. In addition, during his administration the country faced a short but deep economic depression, the Panic of 1857, when banks and businesses failed, and unemployment soared.

Things got worse for Buchanan. In the election of 1860, Abraham Lincoln based his campaign on opposing slavery's expansion. As soon as Lincoln was elected, South Carolina and six other Southern states formally seceded from the Union—*while Buchanan was still in office.* Needless to say, Lincoln's inauguration on March 4 could not have come soon enough for Buchanan; he crossed his fingers, hoping Civil War would not officially begin until he was out of office. Nevertheless, historians have not been kind to Buchanan for his inability to halt secession.

After his first term, Pierce wanted to run again, but his party nominated James Buchanan instead.

American Literature
Stephen Crane

Novelist and poet Stephen Crane was one of the first American authors to introduce the Impressionism style of writing. His works are characterized by a naturalistic, pessimistic, yet sympathetic, view of human nature. The tragedy is that Crane died very early, at the age of twenty-eight.

Nevertheless, Crane left to American literature what has been called the first modern war novel. Still read today, it realistically described the Civil War from an ordinary soldier's point of view — all the more remarkable when you find out that Crane never experienced any military service.

After being shipwrecked on an expedition to Cuba in 1896, Crane developed tuberculosis. He settled in England in 1897 amid American rumors of extramarital affairs and drug addiction. He died in 1900.

The Red Badge of Courage (1895)

Set during the Civil War, the novel follows the development of a young Union soldier, Henry Fleming. Henry experiences a procession of emotions while under fire, starting with fear and cowardice, and ending with heroism.

Crane's descriptions of battle and personal thought were so accurate, that many believed the book to be about his own experiences.

Other Works of Stephen Crane

- *Maggie, a Girl of the Streets* (1893), based on his observations as a reporter covering New York City slums
- *The Black Riders and Other Lines* (1895), experimental free verse
- *The Open Boat and Other Stories* (1898), based on his shipwreck experience
- *War Is Kind and Other Poems* (1899), experimental free verse
- *The Monster and Other Stories* (1899)
- *Active Service* (1899)
- *Whilomville Stories* (1900)
- *Wounds in the Rain* (1900)

HENRY WADSWORTH LONGFELLOW

Popular American poet Henry Wadsworth Longfellow is best known for his 1855 *Song of Hiawatha*. It was a sympathetic tribute to North American Indians and their way of life, a romantic tale mingling fact and legend.

Longfellow knew in childhood that he wanted to be a poet, and his education and life experiences took him along that path. He taught college and traveled extensively, even once attending tea with Britain's Queen Victoria.

In 1831 Longfellow married Mary Storer Potter. Four years later, she suddenly died after a miscarriage. Longfellow wrote "Footsteps of Angels" about her. Then in 1843 he married Francis "Fanny" Appleton, with whom he had six children. In 1861, Longfellow witnessed Fanny's death in a household fire. His grief changed his life forever; twenty years later he wrote the sonnet "The Cross of Snow" describing feelings of loss.

Longfellow continued to write poetry until he died in 1882. In 1884 he was the first American citizen honored in the Poets' Corner of Westminster Abbey in London, England.

Longfellow's lengthy bibliography includes:

- *Outre-Mer: A Pilgrimage Beyond the Sea* (1835), inspired by his own Spanish travels
- *Voices of the Night: Ballads; and other Poems* (1839), containing "A Psalm of Life"
- *Hyperion, a Romance* (1839), autobiography
- *Ballads and Other Poems* (1841), including "The Wreck of the Hesperus," "The Village Blacksmith," "The Skeleton in Armor," and "Excelsior"
- *Poems on Slavery* (1842)
- *Evangeline* (1847), epic about lovers separated during the French and Indian War
  The Seaside and the Fireside (1849)
- *The Courtship of Miles Standish and Other Poems* (1858), a colonial New England love triangle
- *Divine Comedy* (1861), a translation of Dante's Italian original

- *Tales of a Wayside Inn* (1863), with "Paul Revere's Ride"
- *The Divine Tragedy* (1871)
- *Kéramos and Other Poems* (1878)
- *Ultima Thule* (1880)
- *In the Harbor* (1882)

Major Causes of Civil War

As a quick run-up to the Dred Scott case and the Supreme Court's ruling, let's review the problems quickly leading the nation toward Civil War:

- Slavery: A moral issue in the North; an economic issue in the South.
- Constitutional Disputes: Federal rights versus states' rights.
- Economics: Industrialization in the North versus agriculture in the South meant laws favoring one area (i.e., tariffs or internal improvements) were sure to bring disadvantage in the other.

Finally, political bungles and extremism did little to smooth feathers. And nothing was more bungled than the Dred Scott case outcome.

DRED SCOTT

Dred Scott — The Man: Virginia planter Peter Blow owned the slave Dred Scott. Blow moved to St. Louis in 1830, when Army surgeon John Emerson purchased Scott. Emerson moved Scott to Fort Snelling in Minnesota in 1836 (then a free territory under the Missouri Compromise). Scott married another slave, Harriet Robinson, and they had two children. Dred and Harriet stayed at Fort Snelling until 1838; Emerson took them back to St. Louis in 1840.

The Case: In 1846, Scott sued for his family's freedom arguing that living in Fort Snelling's free territory made them free, even after returning to Missouri.

It should have been easy to settle. Missouri law of the time said any slave living on free soil automatically became free. Naturally, in January 1850, the St. Louis Circuit Court said this was so for Scott, too.

But, in 1852 the Missouri Supreme Court reversed its own precedent, and said Scott was still a slave. They declared that times had changed since earlier decisions had been made.

In 1854, Scott escalated his case to the U.S. Circuit Court in Missouri. Federal Judge Robert Wells said free citizens could sue in federal court; however, Scott was still a slave according to the 1852 Missouri Supreme Court ruling.

Scott persisted, appealing to the U.S. Supreme Court in 1856. In March 1857, the Court ruled that Scott was still a slave. He was not a free citizen and therefore could not sue in court.

Supreme Court Ruling in Scott v. Sandford: U.S. Supreme Court Chief Justice Roger Taney used the case as his personal opportunity to settle the question of slavery once and for all. His opinion went far beyond the simple case of whether one man should be granted freedom. The Supreme Court final declaration said:

- African Americans, even when free, could never become United States citizens. Therefore, they did not have a right to sue in federal courts.

- Any law prohibiting a master from taking a slave into the territories violated the Fifth Amendment protecting the right to private property.
- Prohibiting slavery in federal territories was unconstitutional. Therefore, the Missouri Compromise of 1820 (banning slavery in the western territories) was invalid.

Implications of the Dred Scott Ruling: The decision added fuel to the ongoing fire that was the slavery debate and widened the chasm between the North and South.
- The anti-slavery Republican Party criticized the proslavery decision and the Supreme Court.
- Antislavery Democrats left the party, and proslavery politicians took control.
- Northerners viewed Chief Justice Taney's decision as a personal rant in favor of slavery.

Dred Scott's Final Days: No thanks to the Supreme Court, Dred Scott did become a free man. On May 26, 1857, his first owner's son purchased the Scott family and granted them freedom. Scott died less than a year later, on February 17, 1858.

EXTRA CREDIT: Dred Scott was buried in Calvary Cemetery in St. Louis. His wife, Harriet, was believed to have been buried beside him, but it was recently discovered that she was buried in Greenwood Cemetery in Hillsdale, Missouri. She died eighteen years after her husband.

POP QUIZ #5

1) What is another word for the Antislavery Movement?

2) What is the significance of Harriet Beecher Stowe's novel, *Uncle Tom's Cabin*?
   a) It played an important role in perpetuating Northern antislavery thoughts.
   b) It may have actually moved the country in the direction of Civil War.
   c) It provided horrific descriptions of slave cruelty to Northern readers.
   d) All of the above

3) What candidate (and future president) declared, "A house divided against itself cannot stand," upon accepting the Republican nomination in the Illinois Senate race of 1858?

4) What abolitionist led a raid on the U.S. arsenal in Harpers Ferry in 1859, hoping to incite slaves to rebellion?

5) Did John Brown succeed in his plans to seize weapons at Harpers Ferry to start a slave uprising?

6) Of the four presidential nominees in the election of 1860, who won the majority of the electoral votes, forcing Southern states to follow through on threats to secede from the Union?
   a) Stephen Douglas
   b) John C. Breckinridge
   c) Abraham Lincoln
   d) John Bell

7) What are the states that made up the Confederate States of America?

8) What is the significance of Fort Sumter in South Carolina's Charleston Harbor?
   a) Southern cadets fired on an unarmed supply ship
   b) It was the site of the first conflict in the Civil War, April 12-13, 1861
   c) The Union surrendered the fort to the Confederacy in less than two days
   d) The battle resulting from Confederate rebellion moved President Lincoln to action
   e) All of the above

9) Who wrote "Battle Hymn of the Republic?"

10) What former slave, known as "Moses" and "General Tubman," led at least 300 other slaves to freedom on the Underground Railroad?

11) Which state first granted a woman the right to own property separate from her husband?

12) Did Elizabeth Blackwell have an easy time in her pursuit of a medical degree to become the first female doctor in America?

13) What president died in office after introducing statehood to California and New Mexico?

14) What act passed in 1850 settled $10 million in Texas debt, created the territories of New Mexico and Utah, let the settlers in those regions decide the question of slavery by voting on it, abolished the slave trade in the District of Columbia, admitted California to the Union as a free state, and provided for returning runaway slaves to their masters?

ANSWERS

1) Abolition
2) d
3) Abraham Lincoln
4) John Brown
5) No.
6) c
7) South Carolina, Mississippi, Florida, Alabama, Georgia, Louisiana, Texas, Virginia, Arkansas, North Carolina, and Tennessee.
8) e
9) Julia Ward Howe
10) Harriet Tubman
11) Mississippi
12) No.
13) Zachary Taylor
14) The Compromise of 1850

PRESIDENTIAL HOMES

George Washington: Mount Vernon — Washington inherited Mount Vernon from his half-brother. He increased the plantation's size to 8,000 acres, divided into five separate self-subsisting farms. Located south of Washington, D.C., the three-story mansion atop a hill overlooks the Potomac River.

Thomas Jefferson: Monticello — Jefferson himself designed Monticello. Construction began in 1769, and after remodeling and enlarging, was completed in 1809. Monticello plantation consisted of 5,000 acres with slaves to run operations. When Jefferson died in debt, his daughter sold the plantation and all its contents.

Andrew Jackson: The Hermitage — Jackson purchased a 425-acre farm outside Nashville and added land until the Hermitage operations included more than 1,000 acres and 150 slaves.

William Henry Harrison: Grouseland — Harrison lived at Grouseland while he was Indiana Territory Governor.

James Monroe: Highland — Monroe's Highland in Virginia included 3,500 acres with about forty slaves. In 1826, Monroe relocated to Oak Hill, south of Leesburg.

John Tyler: Sherwood Forest — Tyler purchased this plantation east of Richmond in 1842. Originally 1,600 acres, the Tyler family has owned the land ever since. The grounds still have a gingko tree that Captain Matthew Perry brought back from Japan in the 1850s.

James K. Polk: Polk Place — Polk retired from office to his downtown Nashville mansion, where he was buried three months later. Demolished in 1901, a Polk Place fountain can be seen at the Polk Home in Columbia, Tennessee.

Zachary Taylor: Cypress Grove — Taylor owned a 2,000-acre plantation on the Mississippi River north of Natchez. More than one hundred slaves were involved in running the plantation.

Franklin Pierce: The Pierce Manse — The Pierce family home is now located in Concord, New Hampshire.

James Buchanan: Wheatland — After his term of office, Buchanan returned to the house and twenty-two acres in Lancaster, Pennsylvania, named for lovely views of surrounding wheat fields.

PRESIDENTIAL BIOS 3

Zachary Taylor, 1849–1850

War veteran and hero Zachary Taylor earned the nickname "Old Rough and Ready" among his troops for his bravery and leadership, and maybe a little bit for his disrespect for President Polk.

In the election of 1848, Taylor received the Whig party nomination. The Whigs banked on his promise not to veto any constitutional laws appealing to Northern voters. They hoped his position as a Louisiana plantation owner favoring slavery would appeal to Southern voters, too. Taylor was elected, even though he had never voted in his life.

Taylor left office quite unexpectedly on July 9, 1850. Five days earlier, he had celebrated Independence Day, spending hours under Washington D.C.'s broiling July sun. Overcome by heat, he returned to the White House to cool off with cold beverages and fruits. He died of stomach flu.

Millard Fillmore, 1850–1853

Millard Fillmore was born in a log cabin and self-educated by reading the only material available in the house: the Bible and a hymn book. He later attended school and fell in love with his schoolteacher (who was only two years older), eventually marrying her. As first lady, Abigail Powers Fillmore established the White House library.

Millard Fillmore was the second vice president to assume the role of president because of death. He supported the Compromise of 1850 that was pending when Taylor died and signed it into existence. He also was the president who opened up trade with Japan, which had been closed to foreign commerce for almost two hundred years.

Franklin Pierce, 1853–1857

A Mexican War veteran, Franklin Pierce was known as a "doughface," a northern Democrat sympathetic to South's position on slavery. He chose as his vice presidential running mate William R. King of Alabama, and, upon election, named his close personal friend Jefferson Davis as secretary of war.

His sympathies sprung from his devotion to the Union and upholding the Constitution as the final law of the land—Pierce truly believed that slavery was constitutional, and therefore should not be banned. Committed to maintaining the union of the whole United States, Pierce wanted to avoid civil war at all costs.

Pierce's critics accused him of alcoholism, and, in a play on words about his military victories, called him, "the hero of many well-fought bottles."

James Buchanan, 1857–1861

While in his twenties, James Buchanan got engaged to be married. However, the love of his life broke the engagement then died suddenly. Heartbroken, Buchanan never pursued marriage with anyone else.

Before he was elected president, Buchanan had already served his country as a diplomatic representative to Russia and to Great Britain, as a congressman, and as secretary of state.

Considered an aging, fussy bachelor, Buchanan was another doughface. He ran for office on a conservative platform, sharing his belief that Congress not interfere with slavery in the territories. For this, he is known as the president who was unable to stop the Southern states from seceding from the Union.

One bright moment in Buchanan's term: He accepted the first official transatlantic telegram message from Queen Victoria on August 16, 1858.

Presidential Penny Pincher

As a young man, President James Buchanan was a stickler for a tight budget. His account books included nearly every penny he gave and received throughout his entire life. Even when he was worth more than $200,000 while serving as American Minister to Great Britain, Buchanan kept a careful list of everything he purchased—down to the buttons on his suspenders. In fact, he once refused a $15,000 check from his friend Jeremiah Black because it was miswritten by ten cents.

TREATY OF MEDICINE LODGE, FORT LARAMIE TREATY

As America expanded west after the Civil War ended, the federal government sought to end conflicts between settlers from the east and the native tribes of the American plains. Congress created a Peace Commission to negotiate treaties with the tribes in July 1867. The commission was comprised of the Commissioner of Indian Affairs, three civilians, and three Army generals (one of which was General William Tecumseh Sherman), and was given a three-pronged goal: end conflicts between Indians and settlers, protect frontier settlements, and begin "civilizing" the natives.

In October of that year, the Peace Commission met with the representatives from the Kiowa, Comanche, Kiowa-Apache, Arapaho, and Southern Cheyenne tribes near Medicine Lodge, Kansas. The commission brought with it a caravan of some one hundred wagons loaded with supplies and gifts for the Indians. (Just to be on the safe side, five hundred 7th Cavalry troops also came along.) The total number of native Americans eventually reached 5,000.

The Treaty of Medicine Lodge that the two sides worked out was in fact three treaties, signed over the course of one week. On October 21, the Kiowa and Comanches signed one treaty, and the Kiowa-Apaches another. The Southern Cheyennes and Arapahos signed a treaty on October 28.

The treaties created two reservations in Indian Territory, one for the Kiowa, Kiowa-Apache and Comanche tribes and one for the Arapaho and Cheyenne. The U.S. government was to provide the reservations with food, "annuities" and educational, medical and agricultural facilities. The Indians were to cease attacking settlers and opposing construction of railroad or military facilities, and also ceded all lands outside the reservations.

Once those treaties were signed, the commission went on to Fort Laramie, in what is now Wyoming, to forge a treaty with the Sioux. Negotiations there didn't go as smoothly, as the Fort Laramie Treaty would not be signed until November 1868. That treaty set aside the Black Hills as exclusively belonging to the Sioux.

JAMES BUCHANAN EADS

St. Louis's Gateway Arch is a 630-foot monument to the Missouri city's role as a gateway to the West. But without the contributions of a self-taught engineer with a tremendous intellect and an equally tremendous curiousity, the city might have taken much longer to function as that gateway. James Buchanan Eads, showed the world that the Mississippi River could be safely bridged.

Eads was born on May 23, 1820, in Lawrenceburg, Indiana, near another major river, the Ohio. The Eads family wasn't well-off, and frequently moved around in search of a better life. When Eads was thirteen, his family was heading to St. Louis on the *Carrolton*, a ship that caught fire as it approached its landing. Eight people were killed, and the Eads family escaped with nothing but the clothes they wore.

Eads got a job as a clerk in a dry-goods store, and the owner allowed him to read from his personal library. It was in this library that Eads educated himself, honing his natural aptitude to an amazingly sharp edge.

The first confluence of Eads' great intellect with the Mississippi's great force came in 1842, when, while working on the steamboat *Knickerbocker*, the ship hit a snag and sank, carrying a cargo of lead to the bottom of the river. Realizing that there were hundreds of similar wrecks on the river's bottom, Eads developed plans for a salvage boat and went into the salvage business with two partners. Fifteen years later, Eads retired from the salvage business. The boy who had landed at St. Louis with nothing was now worth $500,000.

Eads' greatest victory would come after the Civil War. In 1867, St. Louis needed a bridge across the Mississippi, one strong enough to support rail travel. To ensure ships' smokestacks could pass underneath the bridge, it would also have to be built fifty feet above the river level. Conventional wisdom held that no such bridge could be built, but Eads' design called for the bridge to be arched, instead of using the usual truss design, and for it to be built of steel, rather than the usual building material, wrought iron.

On July 4, 1874, the Eads Bridge, which allowed St. Louis to truly become the gateway to the West, opened to the public. It is still in use today.

JOSEPH GLIDDEN AND BARBED WIRE

Henry Rose and Joseph Glidden don't exactly rank up there with Billy the Kid and Wyatt Earp in terms of Western fame, but that's just due to a hiccup of history. Without Rose and Glidden, the West would have taken a lot longer to settle.

Rose was an inventor who patented a design for a wooden strip with spikes that was to be attached to a wire fence. He was exhibiting his invention at the Dekalb (Illinois) County Fair in 1873 when Glidden visited the fair. Intrigued by Rose's invention, Glidden began to develop a wire with barbs located in it already. Although his was not the first barbed wire, Glidden's was the first to use two strands of wire wound together to hold the barbs in place. Glidden applied for a patent on his new wire on October 27, 1873, and received his patent on November 28, 1874.

The new wire was perfect for use on the vast expanses of the West, but persuading cattle ranchers to use the wire to confine their cattle was no mean feat. The success of barbed wire was secured in 1877, when a 21-year-old wire salesman named John W. Gates, who would later become known as "Bet-You-A-Million" Gates, erected a barbed-wire corral in San Antonio, then penned up twenty-five Texas Longhorn cattle in the corral. Not even the ornery, tough Longhorns could escape from the enclosure, earning the respect of the watching cattlemen and securing that Glidden would have a lasting legacy in the American West.

In addition to keeping cattle on ranches, the new invention was used to keep cattle off railroad tracks. Railroad companies began installing barbed-wire fences along their rights-of-way, in order to ensure that their trains didn't go slamming into errant cattle.

GOVERNMENT 101
YELLOWSTONE ACT

It wasn't that long ago that the great outdoors were just the outdoors. If an American wanted to experience nature, it was most likely snuffling right outside his door or trying to break into his root cellar and eat up all his turnips. But with the advent of the railroad, the Second Industrial Revolution and other advances, it became obvious to some far-thinking individuals that access to the outdoors might one day be in short supply, and took steps to ensure that future generations could experience what their ancestors took for granted.

On March 1, 1872, President Ulysses S. Grant signed the Yellowstone National Park Act, which created the world's first national park. The park, which covered more than two million acres in Wyoming, Montana and Idaho, was to be a "a public park or pleasuring-ground for the benefit and enjoyment of the people," under control of the Secretary of the Interior, who "shall provide against the wanton destruction of the fish and game found within said park, and against their capture or destruction for the purposes of merchandise or profit."

The setting-aside of so much land and natural resources was certainly a new development for a bustling, expanding country. But while the concept was a noble one, the execution of that concept was a little more problematic. Since Yellowstone was the first national park, the government had no experience to draw from, no handbook to instruct with. Nathaniel P. Langford was named the park's first superintendent, but he had no staff, no funding and no salary.

The park became more stable in 1886, when the U.S. Army began establishing what would become Fort Yellowstone. The park would be under the control of the Army until 1916, when the National Park Service took over.

Today, more than two million tourists visit Yellowstone annually. They take in the more than 10,000 hydrothermal features, including 300 geysers like the famous Old Faithful. Yellowstone is also home to an active volcano and sees between 1,000 and 3,000 earthquakes annually.

PRESIDENTIAL BIOS 4

Abraham Lincoln, 1861–1865

Standing 6-foot-4-inches tall, Lincoln was the tallest president, the first Republican president and the first to be assassinated. Born in Hardin County, Kentucky, on February 12, 1809, Lincoln was inaugurated president on March 4, 1863, a little more than one month before Confederate forces fired on Fort Sumter to begin the Civil War. He died from wounds inflicted by assassin John Wilkes Booth's gun on April 15, 1865, six days after General Robert E. Lee surrendered at Appomattox. Lincoln signed the Homestead Act of 1862, which encouraged private settlement of formerly government-owned lands. On January 1, 1863, Lincoln signed the Emancipation Proclamation, which abolished slavery in the secessionist states. The proclamation didn't in fact end slavery, since the states had seceded and therefore didn't recognize the federal government, but it did obligate the United States to end slavery. Lincoln's mother's maiden name was Hanks, and he is a distant relative of movie star Tom Hanks.

Andrew Johnson, 1865–1869

Like Lincoln, Johnson had no formal education, but the tailor born in Raleigh, North Carolina, became mayor of Greeneville, Tennessee, at the age of twenty-six, a member of the Tennessee Legislature at twenty-seven, a member of the U.S. House of Representatives at thirty-five, governor of Tennessee at forty-five and a U. S. Senator at forty-nine. When Tennessee seceded, Johnson remained in the Senate, earning him favor in the North and scorn in the South. Johnson, a Democrat, was nominated by the Republican party as its vice-presidential candidate in 1864, then became president upon Lincoln's assassination. In 1867, Johnson became the first president to be impeached, following his dismissal of Secretary of War Edwin M. Stanton. Johnson was tried in the Senate the next year, and won acquittal by one vote.

Ulysses S. Grant, 1869–1877

The man with the patriotic initials "U. S." actually had the more pedestrian initials "H.U." He was born Hiram Ulysses Grant, the son of a leather tanner, in Ohio, but when Ohio Congressman Thomas L. Hamer got the young man an admission to the U.S. Military Academy at West Point, he filled out the application "Ulysses Simpson Grant." Simpson was his mother's maiden name. Grant excelled as a general during the Civil War, most notably in the Battle of Vicksburg, capturing that key Southern stronghold. During his presidential administration, Grant permitted and supported the onerous Radical Reconstruction of the South.

Rutherford B. Hayes, 1877–1881

Long before "hanging chads" became a part of the American historical lexicon in the 2000 presidential election, Hayes suffered through a supremely frustrating and drawn-out election drama before finally winning the presidency by one vote. The Republican Hayes lost the 1876 popular election to Democrat Samuel J. Tilden, governor of New York, 4,300,000 to 4,036,000. But, as Al Gore can attest, it's Electoral College votes that detemine the presidency, and Electoral College votes in Louisiana, South Carolina and Florida were the subject of so much dispute that in January 1877, Congress established an Electoral Commission to determine the winner. The commission ruled that Hayes had won the election with 185 electoral votes to Tilden's 184. Because of the controversy, Hayes had to take his oath of office secretly, in the Red Room of the White House.

James A. Garfield, 1881

Garfield, an Ohio Republican, was a university professor who became a successful Union officer in the Civil War and then represented Ohio in the House for eighteen years. During the 1880 Republican presidential convention, Garfield nominated his friend John Sherman for election as the party's candidate, but thirty-four ballots later, the convention still hadn't picked a candidate. Delegates for Sherman and James G. Blaine then threw their support to Hayes, and he won nomination on the thiry-sixth ballot. He went on to narrowly defeat Democratic candidate General Winfield Scott Hancock. On July 2, 1881, only four months after taking office, Hayes was shot by Charles J. Guiteau, a mentally disturbed attorney, while at the Baltimore and Potomac Railroad Station, in Washington, D.C.

Hayes was taken first to the White House and then to Elberon, New Jersey, to be with his family. Alexander Graham Bell unsuccessfully attempted to find the bullet in Hayes' body with an electrical device he had designed, but Hayes passed away on September 19, 1881, the second president to be assassinated.

Chester A. Arthur, 1881–1885

Arthur was a Vermont native who was known as "Gentleman Boss" for his stately bearing and good taste in clothes. He was elected vice president in 1880, then became president upon Garfield's assassination. Once in the White House, the man who had been a comfortable cog in the New York City Republican machine turned into a reformer, becoming a supporter of the Pendleton Civil Service Act that mandated a merit system for jobs with the federal government. Although Arthur had suffered from Bright's disease (an inflammatory kidney disease) since 1881, he kept his affliction secret from the public. Arthur ran an unsuccessful campaign for president in 1884, but lost. He died from Bright's disease in 1886.

Grover Cleveland, 1885–1889 and 1893–1897

Cleveland became and remains today an anomaly, the only president to serve two non-sequential terms. For his first term, he was able to win election to the nation's highest office despite a sex scandal that linked him (possibly accurately) to the birth of an illegitimate child, the daughter of one Maria Halpin. He took office as a bachelor, then in 1886 married twenty-one-year-old Frances Folsom, becoming the only president to marry in the White House. Cleveland was forty-nine at the time. Although he won the popular vote in 1888, he lost to Benjamin Harrison on electoral votes. After his 1892 re-election, Cleveland was diagnosed with oral cancer, and had secret surgery on a private yacht to remove the cancer on his left upper jaw. Afterwards, he was fitted with a rubber plate that allowed him to resume speaking publicly.

Benjamin Harrison, 1889–1893

The grandson of William Henry Harrison, the ninth president, Harrison was hardly a charismatic figure. He was sometimes referred to as "the human iceberg" for his cool demeanor. The most notable aspect of Harrison's term was his 1890 signing of the trustbusting Sherman Antitrust Act, which would be used to break up the Standard Oil Company and American Tobacco Company monopolies. Harrison was also in favor of high tariffs on imports, and supported the McKinley Tariff of 1890, which was supposed to protect American interests but actually raised prices.

William McKinley, 1897–1901

This Ohio native served in the 23rd Ohio Volunteer Infantry during the Civil War, where his commanding officer was future president Rutherford B. Hayes. He earned the rank of major, then after the war ended, opened a law office. He won election to Congress as a representative, where he wrote the protectionist McKinley Tariff Act, which raised federal tariffs on imports to an average of 48.4 percent. McKinley served two terms as governor of Ohio before becoming president. His term in the White House included the 113-day Spanish-American War. He won re-election in 1900, but in September 1901, he was shot twice by Leon Czolgosz, an anarchist, while standing in a receiving line at the Buffalo Pan-American Exposition. He died from his wounds eight days later.

Theodore Roosevelt, 1901–1909

William McKinley's assassination put Roosevelt into the White House at the young age of forty-three, making him America's youngest president at the time. Roosevelt was a child of privilege, born into a wealthy and prominent New York City family. His first wife, Alice Lee Roosevelt, died on Valentine's Day 1884 from Bright's disease (the same disease that had killed President Chester A. Arthur), just two days after delivering Roosevelt's first child, also named Alice. The same day his wife died, his mother Martha died from typhoid. Roosevelt, who had discovered the American West in 1883, went back west to live the rugged life and recover from the shock of the two deaths. He returned to New York in 1886, and married his second wife, Edith Kermit Carow. He famously fought in the Spanish-American War, leading the First U.S. Volunteer Cavalry (the "Rough Riders"). Roosevelt won election as New York governor in 1898.

It was Roosevelt's term as governor that somewhat inadvertently landed him in the White House. Roosevelt's reforming efforts had made him the scourge of many in New York, including political boss Thomas Collier Platt. Platt pushed Roosevelt as McKinley's vice president, expecting him to disappear into the abyss of obscurity that the office of vice president often creates. McKinley's assassination scuttled Platt's plan, instead giving Roosevelt a national platform for his reforms.

Once president, Roosevelt became a reforming force. He wielded the Sherman Antitrust Act with skill and power, earning him a reputation as a trust-buster. He led the United States to a bigger role in world politics, famously quoting his saying, "Speak softly and carry a big stick." The nature-loving president set aside some 160 million acres as national forests, and created the 800,000-acre Grand Canyon National Monument in Arizona. He won the 1906 Nobel Peace Prize for his negotiation of an end to the Russo-Japanese War.

William Howard Taft, 1909–1913

The only man to serve as both chief justice of the Supreme Court and president, Taft was, figuratively and literally, a large figure in American politics. In addition to his high offices, Taft also weighed around 332 pounds, a sufficiently large amount of adipose tissue that he required the installation of a special Taft-sized bathtub in the White House. (The story that he once got stuck in a bathtub, however, is most likely just folderol.) Taft advanced in public service quickly. He was appointed to the Ohio Supreme Court when he was only thirty. Taft was appointed U.S. solicitor general two years later, and he later remarked that "like every well-trained Ohio man I had my plate the right side up when offices were falling." Taft won the White House when Theodore Roosevelt clashed with his own Republican Party, but in contrast to his predecessor's aggressive and successful reforming policies, Taft's administration largely swung from mediocrity to disappointment. He did manage to make progress in the areas of worker safety and labor standards, however. Taft served only one term, then lost the 1912 election to Woodrow Wilson. President Warren G. Harding appointed Taft chief justice of the U.S. Supreme Court in 1921.

YELLOW FEVER EPIDEMIC

Surrounded by high-tech devices, treatments and vaccines, it's easy to forget that what is today called medicine is mostly a recent development. Louis Pasteur, Joseph Lister, and Robert Koch were still hashing out germ theory in the mid-nineteenth century, so the ties between poor sanitation and disease were far from commonly understood by the average American of the time. And when 20,000 people died from an 1878 yellow fever epidemic in the Mississippi Valley, the world was three years away from even comprehending that the disease was transmitted by mosquitoes, much less being able to do anything about it.

Yellow fever is a viral disease that incubates in the human body for three to six days. Then its victims begin an "acute phase" of fever and chills, muscle pain, nausea, fatigue, shivers, headache and weakness. As bad as that phase is, it's just an opening act for the real things. About 15 percent of yellow fever victims enter a "toxic phase," which includes hematemesis (also known as "black vomit"), bleeding from the gums, nose, eyes and stomach, kidney function deterioration, confusion, seizures, coma, and death.

The last great American yellow fever epidemic occurred in 1878, beginning in late May when a sailor was removed from the *Emily B. Souder* and mistakenly diagnosed with malaria. The ship was fumigated before it was allowed to dock at its intended port of New Orleans, but a crew member died that night, followed by another crew member a few days later. By August 10, New Orleans had suffered 431 yellow fever cases, and 118 deaths.

The epidemic wasn't only a New Orleans tragedy. Its worst effects would take place farther up the Mississippi River. On August 13, a Memphis restaurant owner named Kate Bionda died from yellow fever. Memphis residents knew the dangers of a yellow fever epidemic, having endured them in 1855, 1867, and 1873. Within a week after Bionda's death, almost half the city's 50,000 residents had left town. Not all of them found refuge, as armed men kept yellow fever refugees out of their cities.

Of the ones who stayed in Memphis, some 17,000 caught the

disease, and more than five thousand died. Memphis took on the look of a medieval plague town. Body collectors went through the streets proclaiming, "Bring out your dead!" Residents kept their doors and windows shut to prevent infection, and victims' clothing and beds were burned for the same reason.

The epidemic ended with the coming of cold weather in October, but by then, the Southeast had lost twenty thousand lives to the disease. Another eighty thousand caught yellow fever but survived.

Kick the Bucket Bandwagon

During Benjamin Harrison's administration from 1889 to 1893, a whopping twenty of his friends, family members, and political associates kicked the bucket and left him to his lonesome. Former President Rutherford B. Hayes and Secretary of State James G. Blaine died. (Some physicians reported that the latter simply gave up on life because he "lacked the courage to live.") Harrison's wife also died, and his adorable granddaughter Marthena succumbed to scarlet fever. Despite his grief, Harrison moved on. In 1901, after remarrying and having another child in his early sixties, Harrison died of pneumonia like his grandfather William Henry Harrison, the ninth president of the United States.

PRESIDENTIAL CAMPAIGN SLOGANS

Americans have always loved a good turn of phrase, particularly when electing a president. Some real gusset-busting campaign slogans have been unleashed on the populace. Time hasn't been good to all of them, but you'll enjoy a few choice examples, as well as their meanings.

Tippecanoe and Tyler, Too: William Henry Harrison's 1840 campaign slogan. Harrison was the hero of the Battle of Tippecanoe. John Tyler was his running mate.

54-40 or Fight: From a time when geography was obviously a more popular subject, the slogan referred to latitude line of 54°40'. In James K. Polk's 1844 campaign, the line was part of the dispute over the Oregon Country territory.

Free Soil, Free Labor, Free Speech, Free Men, and Fremont: Cutesy (and ineffectual) slogan used in John C. Fremont's 1856 campaign. Fremont ran as the first Republican presidential candidate.

Vote Yourself a Farm: Abraham Lincoln came to power in 1860 with this one referring to Republican support for a law encouraging the Western frontier homesteading.

Blaine, Blaine, James G. Blaine, The Continental Liar from the State of Maine: It sounds like a lame schoolyard taunt, but it won Grover Cleveland the 1884 election. Blaine was rumored to have engaged in untoward business transactions.

Ma, Ma, Where's My Pa, Gone to the White House, Ha, Ha, Ha: This is so sophomoric it makes Cleveland's read like Shakespeare. Cleveland allegedly fathered an illegitimate child.

He Kept Us Out of War: Woodrow Wilson rode this masterpiece of low standards to the White House in 1916.

Cox and Cocktails: In 1920, Warren G. Harding supported Prohibition. His opponent James Cox didn't.

A Chicken in Every Pot and a Car in Every Garage: Herbert Hoover's 1928 promise of prosperity ironically was followed by the Great Depression's onset during his administration's first year.

DEPARTMENT STORES

Most of the ladies already know this, but a department store is a retail business which specializes in selling a wide range of products.

Early Department Stores

Hudson's Bay Company in Canada was the first store to include departments. By today's definition, we wouldn't view it as a department store because of the limited number and variety of items sold there, but it definitely was a forerunner.

The first true department store, Le Bon Marché, opened in Paris in 1838. In America, Alexander Turney Stewart opened the "Marble Palace" in New York City in 1848. He offered a variety of dry goods at fixed price. In 1862, Stewart built a "Cast Iron Palace" further uptown, with departments featuring dress goods and furnishing materials, carpets, glass and china, toys, and sports equipment.

A Boom of Stores with Departments

Other department stores soon followed in New York City: Macy's, Benjamin Altman, Lord & Taylor, McCreary's, and Abraham & Straus in Brooklyn (later to become A&S).

In Chicago, Marshall Field and Company, the second-largest department store in the world, sprang up along State Street in 1868. In Salt Lake City, Zion's Cooperative Mercantile Institution opened in 1869 as a new community store for Mormons. In Philadelphia, Wanamaker's opened in 1876 in the remodeled Pennsylvania Railroad terminal.

A New World of Retailing

By 1890, department stores had replaced general stores. Mass transit lines leading to downtown stores made shopping easy. Shopping was even easier with standardized store layouts and exotic customer services such as restaurants, restrooms, reading rooms, home delivery, wrapping services, store hours, and bridal registries. Department stores were building their reputations as universal providers.

MARK TWAIN

Born Samuel Langhorne Clemens, Southern writer Mark Twain's contributions to American literature were the first instances of truly American themes, settings, and language. His novels and stories featured vivid characters treated humorously.

Twain's childhood in 1840s Hannibal, Missouri, taught him about life along the Mississippi River. Twain's many career choices ranged from printer to steamboat pilot to volunteering in the Confederate cavalry during the Civil War.

Twain's early experiences provided the base for his two most popular books: *The Adventures of Tom Sawyer* and *The Adventures of Huckleberry Finn.*

Tom Sawyer (1876): Twain's novel about the excitement of boyhood on the Mississippi River, based on memories from life in Hannibal, established his reputation for wittily depicting real-life characters and settings.

Huckleberry Finn (1884): A companion to *Tom Sawyer* and a true American literature classic, this book details adventures on the river before the Civil War. Huck's travels with a runaway slave, Jim, highlight his internal struggle between the humanity of aiding slave escape versus the legality of it. (Huck decides in favor of humanity.)

Other Works

- "The Celebrated Jumping Frog of Calaveras County" (1865) — A "tall tale"
- *Roughing It* (1872) — His silver mining and journalism adventures
- *The Gilded Age* (1873) — Novel about greed, wealth, and corruption in 1870s politics
- *The Prince and the Pauper* (1882) — Children switch identities in English court
- *Life on the Mississippi* (1883) — Autobiographical riverboat experiences
- *A Connecticut Yankee in King Arthur's Court* (1889) — Satire on feudalism
- *Pudd'nhead Wilson* (1894) — Criticism of pre-Civil War South racism

MARY BAKER EDDY, CHRISTIAN SCIENCE FOUNDER

Influential American religious leader Mary Baker Eddy founded the Church of Christ, Scientist (or *Christian Science*). Eddy developed the religion, with its ideas about spirituality and health, based on a lifelong study of the Bible.

Mary Baker had been unhealthy all her life. Personal setbacks—early widowhood while pregnant and the infidelities of her second husband—did not help her physical condition.

Struggling to feel better, Mary Baker tried alternative medicine: diets, hydropathy (water cures), homeopathy, and hypnotism. Experimenting with placebo medications, she deduced the role of spiritual beliefs in the healing process.

Then, in 1866, Mary Baker slipped and fell on ice, apparently paralyzed. Doctors offered little hope for recovery. She resigned herself to a life in bed, and began reading her Bible. Miraculously, she soon got up and walked.

Mary Baker credited her recovery to her understanding of Jesus' miracles of healing. The doctrine of the Church of Christ, Scientist, which she founded, was based on her spiritual healing beliefs.

1875: Published *Science and Health with Key to the Scriptures.*

1879: Chartered the Church of Christ, Scientist.

1892: Reorganized as The First Church of Christ, Scientist (*The Mother Church*).

1908: Established, at age eighty-seven, international daily newspaper the *Christian Science Monitor.*

The Three Husbands of Mary Baker Eddy

* George Washington Glover. Shortly after their marriage in 1843, he died, leaving her a pregnant widow.
* Daniel Patterson. In 1853 she married a traveling dentist, for her son's sake. She divorced him twenty years later on grounds of adultery and desertion.
* Asa Gilbert Eddy. In 1877, she married a student of her new religion.

American Literature
Louisa May Alcott

Author Louisa May Alcott wrote children's and adult fiction alike. She is best known for *Little Women,* about the lives of four sisters in Civil War-era New England.

The daughter of a women's-suffrage-and-abolitionist-advocate mother and transcendentalist-philosopher-and-social-reformer father, Alcott was raised in the intellectual society of Ralph Waldo Emerson, Henry David Thoreau, Margaret Fuller, and Nathaniel Hawthorne as friends and professional contemporaries.

While her father was more of a thinker than an earner, fifteen-year-old Louisa began working to support her family, taking jobs such as teacher, seamstress, and household servant. Her writing talent, though, proved to be the breadwinner.

Herself an activist favoring abolition and women's rights, Alcott weaved themes of family, devotion, and love into her tales of strong women. When the Civil War began, thirty-year-old Alcott offered her nursing services for the Union Army. She contracted typhoid fever while there. Alcott suffered from mercury poisoning for the rest of her life, dying at the age of fifty-six.

Works of Louisa May Alcott

- *Hospital Sketches* (1863), experiences as a volunteer Union nurse
- *The Rose Family: A Fairy Tale* (1864)
- *Moods* (1865), women's struggles in marriage
- *A Long Fatal Love Chase* (1866), suspense story
- *Good Wives* (1869), sequel to *Little Women*
- *Little Men* (1871), sequel to *Little Women*
- *Work: A Story of Experience* (1873) a woman's quest for
- fulfillment in work
- *Eight Cousins* (1875)
- *Rose in Bloom* (1876)
- *Jo's Boys* (1886), sequel to *Little Women*

MAJOR AMERICAN ARCHITECTS

Daniel Hudson Burnham (1846–1912) Burnham designed Chicago's twenty-story Masonic Temple Building, the first important skeleton skyscraper. Among other works were the Flatiron Building and the Wanamaker store in New York City and Union Station in Washington, D.C.

William Le Baron Jenny (1832–1907) The father of the American skyscraper, Jenny designed the Home Insurance Building in Chicago, the first fully metal-frame building and considered the first American skyscraper. His designs used metal columns and beams, instead of stone and brick to support a building's upper levels.

Robert Mills (1781–1855) President Jackson appointed Mills architect of public buildings in Washington, responsible for design and construction of the Treasury building, the patent office, and the post office. He designed the Washington Monument as well.

Henry Hobson Richardson (1838–1886) Richardson was noted for his revival of Romanesque design. His first monumental work, Boston's Trinity Church, exemplified the "Richardson Romanesque" style. Among principal works are Boston's New Brattle Square Church; Harvard's Sever Hall and Austin Hall; and the Marshall Field store in Chicago.

William Strickland (1788–1854) Strickland combined ancient architecture with modern needs. In Philadelphia, he won a competition for the Second Bank of the United States. His most distinctive building is the Merchants' Exchange there. In 1828 he restored the steeple of Independence Hall.

Frank Lloyd Wright (1867 1959) The greatest American architect, Wright radically innovated both structure and aesthetics, achieving open planning and fluidity by eliminating interior walls. Wright designed New York City's dynamic Solomon R. Guggenheim Museum with dramatic spiral ramps. Among other notable works are The Larkin Office Building, Buffalo; Oak Park Unity Temple, Chicago; The Imperial Hotel, Tokyo, which withstood the effects of the 1923 earthquake; and Edgar Kaufmann's Pennsylvania house, "Fallingwater," which is built over a waterfall.

MARKETING 101
QUAKER OATS

While there is no direct tie between the religious group known as Quakers and Quaker Oats, the brand with the beatific, smiling Quaker icon is one of the most well-known in American history. Herein are some facts about the face that launched a billion breakfasts, courtesy of QuakerOatmeal.com:

- In 1877, Quaker Oats registered the first trademark for a "figure of a man in 'Quaker garb.'"
- In 1891, Quaker Oats introduced the first packaged premiums. The company shipped boxes of oats with chinaware items inside.
- In 1915, Quaker Oats introduced round containers.
- In 1921, Quaker offered a portable crystal radio set as a premium.
- In 1946, artist Jim Nash created the smiling portrait of the Quaker man.
- In 1957, artist Haddon Sundblom created the full-color image of the Quaker man.
- In 1972, John Mills produced the current Quaker man image.

William Penn and Humphrey Bogart share a common bond—both are falsely rumored to be famous advertising icons. Penn is supposedly the smiling face on the Quaker Oats box, but the company says,

> The "Quaker man" is not an actual person. His image is that of a man dressed in the Quaker garb, chosen because the Quaker faith projected the values of honesty, integrity, purity and strength.

Bogart was supposedly the inspiration for the Gerber Baby, although Gerber revealed that the actual inspiration for that image was Ann Turner Cook, who was sketched by artist Dorothy Hope Smith. The craggy-faced Bogart was born in 1899, so he would have been twenty-nine when the Gerber Baby was created in 1928.

AMERICAN PLAYWRIGHTS

Edward Albee (1928–) Best known for skillful dialogue, most of Albee's work features absurdist commentary on American life. He is best known for *Who's Afraid of Virginia Woolf?* (1962), *Tiny Alice* (1965) and the Tony Award-winning *The Goat, or Who Is Sylvia?* (2002).

Lillian Hellman (1905–1984) Hellman's plays, while melodramatic, exhibit her intelligence and craftsmanship. Her best-known works, often telling of injustice, include *The Children's Hour* (1934), *The Little Foxes* (1939), and *Watch on the Rhine* (1941). In 1931, she met writer Dashiell Hammett, who remained her companion until his death in 1961.

David Mamet (1947–) Mamet's works deal with success and failure of the American dream. His plays feature sharp, profane, and masculine dialogue. *Sexual Perversity in Chicago* (1974) and *American Buffalo* (1975) gained public attention, and he achieved more success with the Pulitzer Prize-winner *Glengarry Glen Ross* (1983) and *Oleanna* (1992).

Arthur Miller (1915–2005) Perhaps the finest realist of the twentieth-century stage, Miller wrote about morality reflected in the individual's response to family and society pressures. His masterpiece, *Death of a Salesman* (1949), won a Pulitzer Prize. Miller was married to Marilyn Monroe from 1956 to 1961.

Clifford Odets (1906–1963) Odets was regarded as the most gifted of 1930s social-protest dramatists. *Waiting for Lefty* (1935) and *Awake and Sing* (1935), considered his best, are two works of social and political protest. Other plays include *Golden Boy* (1937) and *The Big Knife* (1949).

Eugene O'Neill (1888–1953) A Nobel-prize winner, O'Neill introduced realism into American drama. His plays were the first to include talk in everyday language. Along with the outstanding plays *Mourning Becomes Electra* (1931) and *The Iceman Cometh* (1946), O'Neill won four Pulitzer Prizes: *Beyond the Horizon* (1920), *Anna Christie* (1922), *Strange Interlude* (1928), and *Long Day's Journey Into Night* (1957). His daughter Oona married Charlie Chaplin.

William Saroyan (1908–1981) Saroyan's works combined optimism, sentimentality, and love of country. These include *The Time of Your Life* (1939), for which he won the Pulitzer Prize but refused the award.

Sam Shepard (1943–) Growing up during the 1960s, Shepard presents a pop art version of America using wild humor, satire, myth, and haunting language. His surrealistic plays include *Operation Sidewinder* (1970), *Curse of the Starving Class* (1977), *Fool for Love* (1984), and *Buried Child* (1978), which won a Pulitzer Prize. Shepard has been Oscar-winning actress Jessica Lange's companion since 1983.

Wendy Wasserstein (1950–2006) Wasserstein brought contemporary women and their concerns to the American stage, exploring love, careers, relationships, and feminism. Her most celebrated play, *The Heidi Chronicles* (1989), won both the Pulitzer Prize and a Tony Award.

Thornton Wilder (1897–1975) Wilder often used nonrealistic techniques, such as scrambled time sequences, minimal stage sets, characters speaking to the audience, and a narrator. He first won a Pulitzer Prize for his novel *The Bridge of San Luis Rey* (1927) and did not receive recognition as a playwright until *Our Town* (1938), perhaps the most familiar and most frequently produced of all American plays, for which he won another Pulitzer. He rounded out Pulitzer's three-of-a-kind with his play *The Skin of Our Teeth* (1942).

Tennessee Williams (1911–1983) One of America's foremost 20th-century playwrights, Williams achieved early success with *The Glass Menagerie* (1945) and *A Streetcar Named Desire* (1947), winning a Pulitzer for the second. As in many of his works, they explore the intense passions and frustrations of a disturbed and brutal society. He went on to win another Pulitzer with *Cat on a Hot Tin Roof* (1955) and write the acclaimed *Night of the Iguana* (1961).

THE SECOND INDUSTRIAL REVOLUTION

The Industrial Revolution began in the eighteenth century in Great Britain, and transformed the machine from a curiosity into an integral part of life. But while Britain and other parts of the world were enjoying the fruits of that revolution, America was involved in a revolution of its own, one that presented more pressing challenges. In addition, Britain and other European countries had a few centuries' head start on infrastructure and overall development. America's participation in the Industrial Revolution would have to wait until the nineteenth century.

America's share of the Industrial Revolution was so successful and far-reaching that it's been called the Second Industrial Revolution. While the first revolution was centered around making machinery work for man, the second was centered around making machinery work better, faster, and more efficiently.

What came to be called the American system of production began in the northeast. Manufacturers like Connecticut gunmaker Samuel Colt used machinery to create many interchangeable parts, which were then assembled into finished products. Quality was the same from part to part, uniformity of the parts meant replacing them was easier and economies of scale increased profitability.

The second revolution also got a boost from a British source. In 1855, Henry Bessemer patented a means of removing impurities from pig iron in order to produce steel. The ability to produce large quantities of high-quality steel using Bessemer's process created fortunes for steelmakers like Andrew Carnegie, and allowed the booming American industrial sector to boom even more.

Henry Ford's moving auto assembly line was another leap forward in American manufacturing. Instead of one worker having to perform many tasks on a product, a worker only performed one or two tasks as the product moved by him. That specialization allowed Ford, and the manufacturers who saw his success and copied him, to dramatically increase production and lower costs.

THE GILDED AGE

If America became a country in 1776, it became *America*—wealthy, industrious, ingenious, and unique in character—during the Gilded Age. Taken from the title of a novel co-written by Mark Twain, the Gilded Age of the late 1800s had everything from rich captains of industry to high-minded reformers to corrupt politicians.

The Gilded Age spanned roughly coincided with the completion of the Transcontinental Railroad in 1869 and ended about 1901, when Theodore Roosevelt became president. The advent of cross-country train travel meant scattered settlers had to be supplied with necessities, and Montgomery Ward saw to it that they were. The company began selling items by mail in 1872. Alexander Graham Bell received a patent for his telephone in 1876, starting off a communications revolution. Thomas Edison received a patent on his electric light bulb in 1880.

Millions of immigrants flooded into America during the period, with Europeans landing on the East Coast and Asians on the West Coast. On January 1, 1892, a fourteen-year-old Irish immigrant named Annie Moore became the first person registered at the new immigration facility known as Ellis Island.

The age created vast riches for some. Scottish immigrant Andrew Carnegie went from a cotton factory bobbin boy making $1.20 a week to a steelmaking fortune estimated at $500 million in 1900. John Pierpont "J. P." Morgan became a banking, railroad, and manufacturing titan. His U.S. Steel Company became the world's first billion-dollar corporation in 1901.

Black Americans were free, but still held back by practices and laws. Women couldn't vote and wouldn't acquire that right until 1920. But conditions were getting better for the common person. Labor unions were formed and began working for better conditions and wages. The Sherman Antitrust Act of 1890 allowed the government to break up monopolies, and the Pendleton Civil Service Reform Act of 1883 began a merit system for government jobs, instead of the cronyism that had been such a part of American politics.

The Gilded Age had its excesses, but it also signified the presence of America as a major player on the world stage. The country, and the world, would never be the same.

THOMAS EDISON

Thomas Edison is the quintessential American inventor, with a determination to succeed so intense that he received 1,093 patents for inventions including the electric light bulb, the phonograph and the motion picture camera. His saying, "Genius is 1 percent inspiration, 99 percent perspiration" is the most all-American thing not uttered by people with a hand over their hearts, facing the flag.

Edison was born in 1847 in Milan, Ohio. Although he didn't speak until he was almost four years old, Edison more than made up for lost time once he did begin speaking, badgering his first teacher with so many questions that he only spent three months in school. The rest of his education came from his own reading.

The young inventor earned his first patent in 1868, for a telegraphic vote-recording machine that met with no commercial success. His first business success from one of his inventions came in 1869, when his design for an improved stock ticker earned him $40,000.

Edison founded an "invention factory" in New Jersey's Menlo Park in 1876, and it was at this location that he would earn the most fame, as well as the title "Wizard of Menlo Park." Here, he designed an incandescent light bulb as well as a system of creating and distributing electricity.

The young boy with the penchant for asking questions became the key figure in the electrification of America. The modern world owes much of its form to developments that sprang from his inquisitive mind, so much that 1954, Raritan Township, New Jersey, where Edison's Menlo Park laboratory was located, changed its name to Edison. The city refers to itself as "the Birthplace of the Technological Revolution."

ANDREW CARNEGIE

Andrew Carnegie became famous for amassing an epic fortune, then became more famous for giving large portions of that fortune away. Thanks to his philanthropy, the man who largely created the American steel industry also funded a vast number of institutions.

Carnegie was born in Dunfermline, Scotland, on November 25, 1835. Although he was born the son of a relatively well-off weaver, the advent of the industrial revolution cost the Carnegie family its fortune. The family sailed for America in 1848, settling in Allegheny, Pennsylvania, about sixty miles from Pittsburgh.

Andrew's first job in America was at the same cotton factory his father William worked in. The man who would become one of the richest figures in history earned $1.20 a week as a bobbin boy. Carnegie later became a messenger boy for a telegraph office, where he became self-taught in telegraphy and met Pennsylvania Railroad official Thomas Alexander Scott. Eventually, Scott would hire Carnegie as his secretary and telegrapher for what Carnegie considered the astounding sum of $35 a month. Carnegie eventually rose to become general superintendent of the Pennsylvania Railroad's Pittsburgh division.

Carnegie began investing, first in a railroad company, then in an oil company and an iron bridge company. But Carnegie created his fortune in the steel industry. Using Henry Bessemer's new method of purifying pig iron to make quality steel, Carnegie and his partners built a steel mill near Pittsburgh in 1873. By 1900, Carnegie's steelmaking interests produced more steel than Great Britain. When Carnegie sold his steelmaking interests in 1901, he was paid $480 million.

With several king's ransoms safely in his grasp, Carnegie began giving most of them away. He paid for some 2,500 Carnegie Libraries in Great Britain, the Unites States and Canada. He founded the Carnegie Institute of Technology (now known as Carnegie Mellon University), the Carnegie Endowment for International Peace, and other organizations. In all, Carnegie gave away about $250 million.

When *Forbes* listed the all-time richest Americans in 2007, it calculated the amount of riches each individual had at his or her peak of wealth, in 2006 dollars. Carnegie's total of $281.2 billion was second only to John D. Rockefeller's $305.3 billion.

J. P. MORGAN

One of America's business giants turned a garden variety fortune earned by his father into one of the all-time American fortunes. In addition, John Pierpont "J. P." Morgan's financial moves were so cunning that they led to the creation of the Federal Reserve system.

Morgan's father, Junius Spencer Morgan, rose from clerk in a Boston dry goods store to head the international banking firm of J. S. Morgan & Company. That entity was sufficiently well-heeled that in 1870 it loaned $50 million to the French government in order for the French to continue fighting in the Franco-Prussian War.

When Junius died in 1890, J. P. took over his father's firm. The younger Morgan had already shown himself to be a ferocious, canny businessman. He had already built a successful railroad empire, and was famous for his process of "Morganization," in which he took over faltering businesses and reorganized them.

After J. P. came to power, he formed U.S. Steel, the first billion-dollar corporation in the world. He also had success in mining and shipping, but he truly became an American financial icon when he rode to the rescue of the U.S. economy during the Panic of 1907.In October 1907, the Knickerbocker Trust had backed an attempt to corner the copper market. The effort failed, and soon, so had the Trust. In addition, the Westinghouse Electric Company had failed. The nation was on financial edge.

Morgan assembled a group of banking and financial leaders at his home on New York City's Madison Avenue. For the next three weeks, the group pooled resources, enacted strategy to keep the panic from blowing entirely out of control, and prevented an all-out economic catastrophe. While Morgan and his cabal had been successful, they had also drawn the attention of the federal government, who realized the power that financial institutions wielded. In 1913, the Owen-Glass Federal Reserve Act created what is today called "the Fed," in order to maintain stability in the financial markets, albeit not through the actions of bankers aiming to follow in Morgan's footsteps.

In a curious twist, 101 years later, the firm of JP Morgan Chase would receive money from the Fed in March 2008 to take over financial firm Bear Stearns and prevent a feared financial panic.

CRASH COURSE
IMMIGRANTS AND ELLIS ISLAND

A country as widespread and varied in makeup as America can't really have a central point, but if you were forced to pick such a point, the federal immigration station at New York City's Ellis Island would be the most logical choice. From the time it opened in 1892 to the time it ceased operations in 1954, Ellis Island processed more than 12 million immigrants, beginning the immigrants' process of transformation from steamship passenger to American.

In actuality, more than 12 million could trace part of their history to Ellis Island, as not all the passengers arriving there were required to go through inspection. First- and second-class passengers were believed to be less of a threat to become any kind of drain on the state, and were therefore allowed to pass through without an inspection.

Poorer passengers weren't as fortunate, instead undergoing a three- to five-hour inspection process that included a "six-second physical" by a medical doctor and also a legal inspection. However, these inspections were mainly cursory in nature, not serious obstacles to entry. Less than 2 percent of the immigrants who applied were rejected.

Ellis Island peaked in 1907, when it processed 1.25 million immigrants. Changes in immigration laws led to the facility becoming a detention center beginning in 1924. The station ceased operations in 1954, when Arne Peterssen, a Norwegian detainee, was released.

A $160 million restoration effort was begun in 1984 and completed in 1990, when the facility re-opened as the Ellis Island Immigration Museum.

SPANISH-AMERICAN WAR

Americans might remember the Alamo is in Texas, even if they don't remember exactly what about the Alamo is supposed to be memorable. But "Remember the Maine," in its time, was just as important a phrase, especially since it led to a war that is itself often forgotten.

In January 1898, the U.S. Navy battleship *Maine* was sent to Havana, Cuba. Many Cubans had wanted independence from Spanish rule for many years, and had in fact fought the Ten Years War against Spain from 1868 to 1878 and the War of '95 in an unsuccessful attempt to gain independence. The *Maine* was to protect American interests in Cuba.

On February 15, 1898, the forward gunpowder magazines on the *Maine* exploded, sinking the ship. Two-hundred and sixty-six men were killed, and another eight later died from injuries suffered as a result of the explosion. Exactly what caused the magazines to explode is still unknown, but whatever the reason, the incident led to the creation of the American phrase "Remember the *Maine*, and to Hell with Spain!"

Tensions between the United States and Spain escalated until Spain declared war on April 23. Two days later, Congress declared that a state of war had existed between the two countries since April 21.

The war largely consisted of two naval battles. Commodore George Dewey destroyed the Spanish fleet at Manila Bay in the Philippine Islands on May 1. Two months later, Admiral William Sampson completed the Spanish defeat off Santiago, Cuba.

When the war ended, America had emerged as a major naval power, and also had gotten ownership of Puerto Rico, the Philippines, and Guam, all of which were formerly Spanish colonies. Cuba had won its independence from Spain, but was now under U.S. control.

TEXAS OIL

The American oil industry began in northwestern Pennsylvania in 1859, when Edwin Drake began pumping oil from the ground, setting off an "oil rush" in the area. Pennsylvania would furnish one-half the total world oil production until it was unseated in 1901 by an oil rush that dwarfed the Pennsylvania one. That Texas oil rush owes a great debt to Patillo Higgins, a fighter-turned-visionary who saw riches where others saw wasteland. The fact that Higgins is largely forgotten today makes his story even more interesting.

Higgins was a Texas native, born in Sabine Pass on December 5, 1863, who scrapped more than a few times in his young life. He was wounded with a gunshot while seventeen, and his left arm had to be amputated below the elbow as a result. Higgins went on to work in logging camps, taking part in their rowdy lifestyle, until he became a Christian, left his dissolute ways behind him and moved to Beaumont to sell real estate and teach Sunday School.

The newly reconstructed Higgins became interested in Spindletop Hill, south of Beaumont. Spindletop was a salt-dome formation where oil seeped from the ground. Higgins believed he could extract that oil, but he still had to figure out how, and had to secure funding for his enterprise. He formed the Gladys City Oil, Gas and Manufacturing Company in 1892, but for several years afterward, the company produced only heartache for Higgins.

In desperation, Higgins ran an ad in a New York trade magazine. That ad produced only one response, but it was the only one Higgins needed. Anthony Lucas was the respondent, and Lucas was a mechanical engineer from what is now Croatia who had mined salt in Louisiana.

Higgins and Lucas resumed drilling at Spindletop, but were faced with the problem of drilling through several hundred feet of sand before they could reach the salt dome. Holes dug in sand easily collapsed, complicating the drilling procedure. A driller named Curt Hamill proposed flooding the hole with mud, thereby flushing out the cuttings made by the drill while simultaneously supporting the hole and preventing it from collapsing.

Using Hamill's technique (still the standard technique for oil drilling), the crew struck oil at 10:30 a.m. on January 10, 1901. Oil gushed from the hole to a height of two hundred feet, and Spindletop was soon producing 100,000 barrels of oil a day. This, from a region of which Standard Oil's John Archbold had once famously boasted that he would drink every gallon of oil produced in the West.

Sadly for Higgins, Lucas, and two other investors, J. M. Guffey and J. H. Galey, had forced him out just before Spindletop exploded. Higgins sued, winning an out-of-court settlement of $300,000.

Thanks to Higgins' perserverance and sagacity, America and the world had a new source of oil. In 1900, Texas had produced a little more than 836,000 barrels of oil. In 1902, Spindletop produced more than 17 million barrels. In addition, the success of Spindletop led to the drilling of thousands more oil wells throughout Texas.

To the Last Drop

Theodore Roosevelt's love affair with coffee made Maxwell House a huge success. One cold morning, while visiting Andrew Jackson's home in Nashville in 1912, he inspired their famed motto when after a warm gulp he said, "That coffee tastes good, even to the last drop."

AND THE WINNER IS . . .

Time and again throughout the course of our nation's history, Americans have proved their mettle and scrap. We face challenges with the intellect and hard work that our forefathers relied on to build a new nation. And, we've been recognized and rewarded for our efforts.

The Nobel Prize is an annual award given for international outstanding achievement. First awarded in 1901, Nobel Prizes recognized winners in each of five categories: physics, chemistry, physiology or medicine, peace, or literature. An additional economics category was added laer. Each prize consists of a gold medal, a sum of money, and a diploma with the citation of award. The Nobel Prize awards are not based on any particular nationality, and they can be shared by more than one person. The prizes are awarded each year on December 10, the anniversary of the death of Alfred Nobel, who established the original awards in his will. A total of 304 Americans have been named Nobel Prize recipients.

Peace
2007: Al Gore
2002: Jimmy Carter
1997: Jody Williams
1986: Elie Wiesel
1973: Henry Kissinger
1970: Norman Borlaug
1964: Martin Luther King, Jr.
1962: Linus C. Pauling
1953: George C. Marshall
1950: Ralph J. Bunche
1947: American Friends Service Committee
(The Quakers)
1946: Emily G. Balch
1946: John R. Mott
1945: Cordell Hull
1931: Jane Addams; Nicholas M. Butler
1929: Frank B. Kellogg
1925: Charles G. Dawes
1919: Woodrow Wilson
1912: Elihu Root
1906: Theodore Roosevelt

Literature
1993: Toni Morrison
1987: Joseph Brodsky
1980: Czeslaw Milosz
1978: Isaac Bashevis Singer
1976: Saul Bellow
1962: John Steinbeck,
1954: Ernest Hemingway
1949: William Faulkner
1948: T. S. Eliot
1938: Pearl S. Buck
1936: Eugene O'Neill
1930: Sinclair Lewis

Physiology or Medicine
2007: Mario R. Capecchi; Oliver Smithies
2006: Andrew Z. Fire; Craig C. Mello
2004: Richard Axel; Linda B. Buck
2003: Paul C. Lauterbur; Alexei A. Abrikosov
2002: Sydney Brenner; H. Robert Horvitz
2001: Leland H. Hartwell
2000: Paul Greengard; Eric R. Kandel,
1999: Günter Blobel
1998: Robert F. Furchgott; Louis J. Ignarro;
Ferid Murad
1997: Stanley B. Prusiner

1995: Edward B. Lewis; Eric F. Wieschaus
1994: Alfred G. Gilman; Martin Rodbell
1993: Phillip A. Sharp
1992: Edmond H. Fischer; Edwin G. Krebs,
1990: Joseph E. Murray; E. Donnall Thomas,
1989: J. Michael Bishop; Harold E. Varmus
1988: Gertrude B. Elion; George H. Hitchings
1986: Stanley Cohen; Rita Levi-Montalcini
1985: Michael S. Brown, Joseph L. Goldstein
1983: Barbara McClintock
1981: David H. Hubel; Roger W. Sperry
1980: Baruj Benacerraf; George D. Snell
1979: Allan M. Cormack
1978: Hamilton O. Smith; Daniel Nathans
1977: Roger Guillemin; Andrzej W. Schally;
       Rosalyn Yalow
1976: Baruch S. Blumberg; Daniel Carleton
       Gajdusek
1975: David Baltimore; Renato Dulbecco;
       Howard Martin Temin
1974: George E. Palade
1972: Gerald Edelman
1971: Earl W. Sutherland Jr.
1970: Julius Axelrod
1969: Max Delbrück; Alfred Hershey; Salvador
       Luria
1968: Robert W. Holley; Har Gobind
       Khorana; Marshall Warren Nirenberg
1967: Haldan Keffer Hartline; George Wald
1966: Charles B. Huggins; Francis Peyton
       Rous
1964: Konrad Bloch
1962: James D. Watson
1961: Georg von Békésy
1959: Arthur Kornberg; Severo Ochoa
1958: George Beadle; Joshua Lederberg;
       Edward Tatum,
1956: Dickinson W. Richards; André F.
       Cournand
1954: John F. Enders; Frederick C. Robbins;
       Thomas H. Weller

Chemistry
2006: Roger D. Kornberg
2005: Robert H. Grubbs; Richard R. Schrock
2004: Irwin Rose
2003: Peter Agre; Roderick MacKinnon
2001: William S. Knowles;
       K. Barry Sharpless
2000: Alan Heeger; Alan MacDiarmid

1999: Ahmed H. Zewail
1998: Walter Kohn
1997: Paul D. Boyer
1996: Richard E. Smalley; Robert F. Curl Jr.
1995: Mario J. Molina; F. Sherwood Rowland
1994: George Andrew Olah
1993: Kary B. Mullis
1992: Rudolph A. Marcus
1990: Elias James Corey
1989: Sidney Altman; Thomas R. Cech
1987: Charles J. Pedersen; Donald J. Cram
1986: Dudley R. Herschbach; Yuan T. Lee
1985: Jerome Karle; Herbert A. Hauptman
1984: Bruce Merrifield
1983: Henry Taube
1981: Roald Hoffmann
1980: Walter Gilbert, Paul Berg
1979: Herbert C. Brown
1976: William Lipscomb
1974: Paul J. Flory
1972: Christian Anfinsen; Stanford Moore;
       William H. Stein
1968: Lars Onsager
1966: Robert S. Mulliken
1965: Robert B. Woodward
1961: Melvin Calvin
1960: Willard F. Libby
1955: Vincent du Vigneaud
1954: Linus C. Pauling
1951: Edwin M. McMillan; Glenn Theodore
       Seaborg
1949: William Giauque
1946: Wendell M. Stanley; James B. Sumner;
       John H. Northrop
1934: Harold C. Urey
1932: Irving Langmuir
1914: Theodore W. Richards

Physics
2006: John C. Mather; George F. Smoot
2005: John L. Hall,
       Roy J. Glauber
2004: David J. Gross;
       H. David Politzer;
       Frank Wilczek
2003: Anthony J. Leggett
2002: Raymond Davis Jr.; Riccardo Giacconi
2001: Eric A. Cornell;
       Carl E. Wieman
2000: Jack Kilby

383

1998: Robert B. Laughlin; Daniel C. Tsui
1997: Steven Chu; William D. Phillips
1996: David M. Lee; Douglas D. Osheroff;
Robert C. Richardson
1995: Martin L. Perl; Frederick Reines
1994: Clifford G. Shull
1993: Russell A. Hulse; Joseph H. Taylor Jr.
1990: Jerome I. Friedman; Henry W. Kendall
1989: Hans G. Dehmelt; Norman F. Ramsey
1988: Leon M. Lederman; Melvin Schwartz;
Jack Steinberger,
1983: Subrahmanyan Chandrasekhar; William
A. Fowler
1982: Kenneth G. Wilson
1981: Nicolaas Bloembergen; Arthur L.
Schawlow
1980: James Cronin; Val Fitch
1979: Steven Weinberg; Sheldon Glashow
1978: Robert Woodrow Wilson; Arno Penzias
1977: Philip Anderson, John H. van Vleck
1976: Burton Richter; Samuel C. C. Ting
1975: Ben R. Mottelson; James Rainwater
1973: Ivar Giaever
1972: John Bardeen; Leon N. Cooper; Robert
Schrieffer
1969: Murray Gell-Mann
1968: Luis Alvarez
1967: Hans Bethe
1965: Richard P. Feynman; Julian Schwinger
1964: Charles H. Townes
1963: Maria Goeppert-Mayer; Eugene Wigner
1961: Robert Hofstadter
1960: Donald A. Glaser
1959: Owen Chamberlain, Emilio Segrè
1956: William B. Shockley; John Bardeen;
Walter H. Brattain
1955: Willis E. Lamb; Polykarp Kusch
1952: E. M. Purcell; Felix Bloch
1946: Percy W. Bridgman
1944: Isidor Isaac Rabi
1943: Otto Stern

Economics
2007: Leonid Hurwicz; Eric S. Maskin; Roger
B. Myerson
2006: Edmund S. Phelps
2005: Robert Aumann; Thomas Schelling
2004: Edward C. Prescott
2003: Robert F. Engle
2002: Daniel Kahneman; Vernon L. Smith

2001: Joseph E. Stiglitz; George A. Akerlof;
A. Michael Spence
2000: James J. Heckman; Daniel L. McFadden
1997: Robert C. Merton; Myron Scholes
1996: William Vickrey
1995: Robert Lucas, Jr.
1994: John Charles Harsanyi; John Forbes
Nash
1993: Robert W. Fogel; Douglass C. North
1992: Gary S. Becker
1990: Merton H. Miller; William F. Sharpe;
Harry M. Markowitz
1987: Robert M. Solow
1986: James M. Buchanan
1985: Franco Modigliani
1983: Gerard Debreu
1982: George J. Stigler
1981: James Tobin
1980: Lawrence R. Klein
1979: Theodore Schultz
1978: Herbert A. Simon
1976: Milton Friedman
1975: Tjalling C. Koopmans
1973: Wassily Leontief
1972: Kenneth J. Arrow
1971: Simon Kuznets
1970: Paul A. Samuelson

START OF WWI

On June 28, 1914, when a nineteen-year-old Serbian nationalist named Gavrilo Princip fired his pistol into the 1910 Gräf & Stift Double Phaeton automobile transporting Archduke Franz Ferdinand, heir to the Austro-Hungarian throne, he wanted to strike a blow for Serbian nationalism. But Princip set in motion what would become known as the First World War, which would result in the deaths of more than 10 million people.

Princip belonged to a Serbian secret society known as the Black Hand. When the archduke came to Sarajevo to inspect army manuevers, the Black Hand resolved to assassinate him. The motorcade containing the archduke and his wife, Sophie, was attacked by a Princip co-conspirator, who threw a hand grenade, but the driver of the car the archduke was riding in sped away and the grenade exploded underneath a following car, injuring its occupants and some onlookers. Princip got his chance to make history later in the day when the lead car in the archduke's motorcade took a wrong turn on the way to the hospital where the grenade victims had been taken. The archduke's driver stopped the car a few feet from Princip, who drew his pistol and fired twice, hitting Francis Ferdinand in the neck and Sophie in the stomach. Both died later that morning.

The two murders were all the spark needed to ignite a worldwide conflagration. Europe had been on the brink of war for some time. Imperialistic aims of European countries with an eye on expanding their empires had caused friction with other countries. A complicated series of military alliances meant that, once begun, any isolated military action would be answered with widespread action. Russia, Serbia, Germany, Austria-Hungary, Great Britain, France, Belgium, and Japan were all involved in various and sundry alliances. Strong nationalist feelings ran through many groups, not just the Black Hand.

On July 28, Austria-Hungary declared war on Serbia. Germany declared war on Russia on August 1, declared war on France August 3, then declared war and invaded Belgium on August 4. Austria-Hungary declared war on Russia on August 6. On August 22, more than 27,000 French soldiers were killed in an offensive during the Battle of the Frontiers. The world was truly at war.

THE AEF AND THE MEUSE-ARGONNE OFFENSIVE

Although America officially entered the war in 1917, it was not in a position to immediately meet the enemy in battle.

The nation had to mobilize and train its forces, and the battlefields were an ocean away. Although its allies were desperate for the manpower and industrial might America could provide, it would be more than a year before U.S. forces would play a major role in the conflict.

General John "Black Jack" Pershing was named commander of the war effort in France. His troops, the American Expeditionary Forces (AEF), began arriving in France in June 1917, and saw action on a limited scale. In October, the U.S. Army's newly created 1st Infantry Division, which became known as "The Big Red One" for its shoulder insignia of a red numeral one on an olive-green field, entered the war at Nancy, France. America was now fully involved in the war.

New to the battlefields, the AEF was at first used to support the more seasoned British and French units. But the AEF was soon taking the lead role in battles, including the Meuse-Argonne Offensive, a 47-day battle that ended the war.

The AEF had already helped turn the tide of the war during the Battle of Belleau Wood, when it stopped German forces that had been sweeping toward Paris. British and French forces were re-energized by the AEF's success, and the Allies began pushing back the Germans.

On the afternoon of September 26, 1918, the Big Red One attacked the German line between the Meuse River and the Argonne Forest. To the north of the American offensive, British forces began their own attack, opening up two fronts that German general Erich Ludendorff had to contend with. Although the AEF was unable to break through the Argonne Forest, they were able to hold their position, and while the Germans were contending with the AEF, more Allied forces were being added to the battle.

The end of the Meuse-Argonne Offensive was the end of the war. On November 11, Germany and the Allies signed the Armistice and the war ended.

TRENCH WARFARE

One of the defining characteristics of World War I was the horrific nature of trench warfare. Troops spent long periods of time in trenches dug into the ground, with their constant companions being gunfire, artillery fire, sickness, rats, lice, and death.

Although soldiers had long sought protection from holes in the ground, trench warfare became particularly important during World War I. The advent of the machine gun and its ability to cover large amounts of battlefield with deadly force, meant that advancing soldiers faced almost insurmountable challenges.

Trench warfare allowed troops some measure of protection, although that protection came at a cost. Water collected in the trenches, and the wet conditions bred infections like trench foot, which could result in gangrene and necessitate amputation of limbs. The close contact and lack of hygiene resulted in widespread infections of lice, which caused constant itching and could spread diseases like trench fever, a painful affliction that beset a soldier for three months.

Trenches were perfect environments for rats, and they bred in the millions, spreading disease and eating up food supplies, as well as feasting on the dead bodies of fallen soldiers.

The area between trenches was called "no man's land" in respect of its deadliness. In addition to gunfire and artillery fire, the areas were protected by barbed wire. The amount of wire varied, but usually measured between fifty and a hundred feet. Repairs to the wire, as well as to the covering sandbags or any other protection, had to be completed at night.

Trenches also had an all-pervasive stench. Latrines overflowed or were poorly constructed. Men went weeks (or months) without bathing. Thousands of dead and decaying bodies lay in the open or barely buried. Not without reason did the poet Ezra Pound describe trench warfare as being "eye-deep in Hell."

CHEMICAL WARFARE

The use of machine guns led to the use of trenches in World War I, and the use of trenches led to the use of chemical warfare. Troops dug into a trench could be killed with lobbed-in artillery shells or sniper fire, but chemicals—specifically, gases—offered a new, terrifying and far-reaching method of killing or removing a soldier.

Several different types of gases were used, all of which had horrific effects. Tear gas was used to disrupt and harass enemy troops, although the coughing and eye irritation it caused were survivable. Chlorine gas forms hydrochloric acid in the presence of moisture, so inhalation of the gas destroyed lung tissue and caused asphyxiation. Phosgene gas has the same effect, but at much lower concentrations. In addition, phosgene gas victims sometimes suffer from initial exposure, then appear to recover, only to have their symptoms return.

Mustard gas, the most feared chemical weapon of the war, wasn't usually fatal. Instead, it blistered flesh, both internally and externally. It was heavier than air, so it sank into trenches, and it was so persistent that it remained toxic for weeks. In addition, it took as many as six hours for symptoms of mustard gas exposure to manifest themselves, so a solider could unknowingly take position in a contaminated trench.

Although the use of chemical warfare methods had greatly decreased by the time America entered World War I, American casualties from gas attacks topped 72,000, and more than 1,200 died from gas attacks. Total casualties among both sides in the war topped 1.24 million, with more than 91,000 deaths.

CRASH COURSE
JOHN HEISMAN

John Heisman's name is associated with the best of college football, the revered Heisman Trophy. Heisman was also associated with college football's worst; namely, a 222-0 beating that is the worst example of piling-on ever recorded in college football.

Heisman had experienced coaching success in locations like Auburn and Clemson. But it was at Georgia Tech that he would reach the heights of both fame and infamy. In sixteen seasons, Heisman's teams posted 102-29-6 record, including three undefeated seasons, a 32-game winning streak, and a national championship.

Heisman also coached Tech's baseball and basketball teams, and it was the baseball diamond where the seeds of the 222-0 thrashing were sown. Tennessee's Cumberland College had defeated Tech 22-0 in 1915. So when Cumberland's football team came to Atlanta in 1916, Heisman took his revenge.

Only Cumberland didn't have a team, having disbanded its football program before the season started. However, their contract with Tech specified a $3,000 fee to forfeit. So, a student manager recruited fourteen students to fulfill the contract and play Tech.

The game was a slaughter from the onset. Tech led 63-0 at the first quarter's end. By halftime, they had doubled that lead to 126-0. Reportedly, Heisman's halftime talk included this gem of unsportsmanlike wisdom, "We're ahead, but you just can't tell what those Cumberland players have up their sleeves. They may spring a surprise. Be alert, men."

His players took heed. Heisman's team added 54 points in the third quarter and 42 points in the fourth.

But if onlookers were shocked by the thrashing, they shouldn't have been. The esteemed icon of college football had coached Clemson to a 122-0 shellacking of Guilford in 1901. And in 1903, Georgia Tech had taken notice of Heisman when he coached Clemson to a 73-0 win over Tech.

MAJOR AMERICAN PAINTERS AND SCULPTORS

Albert Bierstadt (1830–1902) After an 1859 expedition to Western territories, Bierstadt painted a series, including *Looking Down Yosemite Valley, California,* that secured his reputation as a "western" artist.

Roy Lichtenstein (1923–1997) Pop Artist Lichtenstein is known for works derived from comic strips, such as *Preparedness,* that reflect modern typographic and printing techniques.

Grandma Moses (1860–1961) A farmer's wife who began painting in her seventies, Moses achieved popularity with her primitive, colorful paintings of farm life, such as *Sugaring-Off.*

Georgia O'Keeffe (1887–1987) O'Keeffe created powerful abstract images, incorporating flowers, rocks, shells, and animal bones from the Southwestern landscape, as in *Cow's Skull, Red, White and Blue.*

Jackson Pollock (1912–1956) Abstract Expressionism pioneer Pollock painted to express, not illustrate, feeling. His "action painting" works are typically large, of dripped and thrown paint.

Norman Rockwell (1894–1978) A *Saturday Evening Post* illustrator, Rockwell's style of realism portrayed scenes of everyday small-town America, featuring great detail.

John Singer Sargent (1856–1925) Widely known for celebrity portraits, Sargent also produced impressionistic watercolor landscapes and painted murals.

George Segal (1924–2000) Pop Art sculptor Segal was known for plaster life-sized figures of ordinary people in everyday situations, such as *Bus Driver.*

Andy Warhol (1930–1987) The Pop Art movement leader, Warhol was one of the most influential artists of the late twentieth century. His works are notable for repetition of everyday images, such as Campbell's soup cans.

Grant Wood (1891–1942) Best known for "American scene" landscapes of the rural Midwest, Wood featured stern people in rigid images, as in *American Gothic.*

GENERAL JOHN J. PERSHING

Many figures made their mark on American history during World War I. Alvin York went from backwoods Tennessee woodsman to fabled hero, capturing a German machine gun nest, taking 132 German soldiers prisoner and earning a Medal of Honor and movie portrayal by Gary Cooper in "Sergeant York." Billy Mitchell became America's best pilot, earning the Distinguished Service Cross and the Distinguished Service Medal, and went on to become the father of the U.S. Air Force. But no American's World War I legacy could top that of John Joseph "Black Jack" Pershing. Curiously, although Pershing's fame persists, his role in black history, which gave him his name, isn't nearly as well-known.

Pershing was a Laclede, Missouri native who became a teacher before he became a soldier. He taught at the local black school when he was only seventeen, then earned a college degree while teaching at an elementary school. He entered West Point in 1882, when he was already twenty-two years old.

The future military leader graduated in 1886. From 1895 to 1897, Pershing served with the Army's 10th Cavalry. The 10th was one of the legendary Buffalo Soldiers, comprised of black soldiers. Pershing returned to West Point as an instructor in 1897. Owing to his service with the Buffalo Soldiers, Cadets gave Pershing the derogatory nickname "Nigger Jack," which was later modified to "Black Jack."

When America entered World War I in 1917, Pershing was given the unenviable task of creating a fighting force to aid the British and French who were already fighting the war. In a year, he had made the Allied Expeditionary Force into a formidable weapon, one strong enough to not only aid the British and French, but come to their rescue. Pershing's AEF was the military shot in the arm the American allies needed, and the German war effort was doomed.

PIGGLY WIGGLY AND CLARENCE SAUNDERS

The next time you visit your local grocer and stroll through the aisles, easily picking out your desired nourishment, give a thanks to Clarence Saunders. His name isn't well-known today, but the concept he embraced and spread—self-service grocery shopping—is emblematic of America's sprawling bounty.

As a teenager, Saunders worked at a Clarksville, Tennessee, general store. In his twenties, Saunders headed to Memphis for a sales position in a grocery company there.

At the time, grocery shopping was a convoluted, slow affair. Shoppers presented their shopping lists to clerks, and the clerks then retrieved the desired items for the shoppers. Saunders saw the process's inefficiency and decided to open a grocery store where shoppers would procure their own items. Under the name Piggly Wiggly, Saunders opened America's first self-service grocery in Memphis in 1916.

Business exploded at the store with the silly name but brilliant sales ploy. Customers loved the convenience, cutting out the clerks meant a higher profit margin, and Saunders could also benefit from that most American of inventions, the impulse buy.

Saunders began selling franchises and by 1923, 1,268 Piggly Wiggly stores operated across America, and Piggly Wiggly stock was traded on the New York Stock Exchange. But an abortive attempt by Saunders to corner the company's stock in 1923 cost Saunders his fortune. He was forced into bankruptcy, and resigned from Piggly Wiggly.

The grocery entrepreneur wasn't finished. He opened the less euphonious Clarence Saunders Sole Owner of My Name Stores, which also sold groceries, and which were also a success. But the Depression cost Saunders his business again.

Saunders spent the rest of his days working on a new grocery concept—the Keedoozle, a key-operated, automated grocery store. But, sadly for those who like whimsical names, the Keedoozle never caught on.

TREATY OF VERSAILLES

The hostilities of World War I ended on November 11, 1918, but it took several months for the victorious countries to hammer out the treaty that formally ended the war. However, far from serving as a document of peace, the Treaty of Versailles instead enflamed tensions and would be one of the major causes of World War II.

The treaty's negotiations were mainly carried out by David Lloyd George, British prime minister; Georges Clemenceau, French prime minister; and President Woodrow Wilson. Germany had no part in the negotiations. The finished product was a gargantuan example of government by committee. It contained more than 400 articles and stretched for more than 200 pages. Some of its more memorable points included the return of the Alsace-Lorraine region to France, the demilitarization of the Rhineland, and the abolition of the German general staff. But it was Article 231 that would become infamous. Known as the war guilt clause, it said that Germany and the other Central Powers were solely responsible for the war. An interim fine of $5 billion was assessed, with a final figure slated to be handed down on May 1, 1921.

The treaty was presented to the Germans on May 7, 1919. The conquering powers gave Germany a three-week period to consider the treaty. Although furious at what it considered the overly punitive terms of the treaty, a defeated Germany was in no position to refuse, and accepted. On June 28, five years to the day after Gavrilo Princip assassinated Archduke Franz Ferdinand and set in motion what would become World War I, German representatives signed the treaty.

The treaty that was supposed to quiet the contentious continent instead laid the groundwork for the next world war. In his 1920 book, *The Economic Consequences of the Peace,* economist John Maynard Keynes wrote, "The Treaty includes no provisions for the economic rehabilitation of Europe—nothing to make the defeated Central Empires into good neighbors, nothing to reclaim Russia; nor does it promote in any way a compact of economic solidarity amongst the Allies themselves; no arrangement was reached at Paris for restoring the disordered finances of France and Italy, or to adjust the systems of the Old World and the New."

Who Said What, WWI

- "The lamps are going out all over Europe; we shall not see them lit again in our lifetime." -Sir Edward Grey
  This British statesman recognized the threat of German aggression and worked behind the scenes to prevent war, but fell short in his efforts, partially because of their behind-the-scenes nature. Some believe that if Great Britain had made public its support for France, war could have been avoided. He made this famous remark in 1914, at the start of the war.

- "I hope we may say that thus, this fateful morning, came to an end all wars." -David Lloyd George
  The British prime minister during World War I, George made this overly optimistic comment to the House of Commons on the morning of November 11, 1918, the day the armistice ending the war was signed. Ironically, George was one of the architects of the Treaty of Versailles, which became a major cause of World War II.

- "We will get everything out of her that you can squeeze out of a lemon and a bit more.... I will squeeze her until you can hear the pips squeak." -Sir Eric Geddes
  Geddes held several positions during the war, including First Lord of the Admiralty, but became most famous for this comment that he made concerning getting reparations from Germany. ("Pip" is British English for "seed.")

- "We are fighting in the quarrel of civilization against barbarism, of liberty against tyranny. Germany has become a menace to the whole world. She is the most dangerous enemy of liberty now existing." -Theodore Roosevelt
  Roosevelt made this comment during an April 1917 speech.

- *"Gott strafe England!"* -German slogan
  In English, it means "May God punish England!" Germany printed it on propaganda labels for placement on envelopes.

WORLD WAR I SONGS

With the "Great War" involving the whole globe, Americans needed some comfort and levity in song, as well as a heaping slab of patriotism, and thanks to songwriters like Irving Berlin and George M. Cohan, they didn't lack for such song fodder.

Berlin, who himself served in the 77th Division of the U.S. Army, crafted a hit when he wrote down his sentiments about the early-rising Army life in "Oh! How I Hate to Get Up in the Morning."

> *Oh! how I hate to get up in the morning,*
> *Oh! how I'd love to remain in bed;*
> *For the hardest blow of all, is to hear the bugler call;*
> *You've got to get up, you've got to get up*
> *You've got to get up this morning!*
> *Some day I'm going to murder the bugler,*
> *Some day they're going to find him dead;*
> *I'll amputate his reveille, and step upon it heavily,*
> *And spend the rest of my life in bed.*

Berlin may have been the only songwriter in history to rhyme anything with "reveille," so he earns creativity points for that. But simplistic rhymes were more common, as in the 1919 song "And He'd Say Oo-La-La! Wee-Wee."

> *Willie Earl met a sweet young girl*
> *One day in France.*
> *Her naughty little glance*
> *Put Willie in a trance.*
> *Willie Earl said, "This little girl*
> *Is meant for me.*
> *No more I'll cross the sea,*
> *I'll stay in gay Paree."*
> *Ev'ry day you would hear him*
> *Say to his babee,*
> *"Your talk I do not know,*

But I will manage to get by,
With my oo-la-la and wee-wee."

Perhaps the most famous song of the WWI era, "Over There," had no small amount of lyrical hooks, as well as everything from seeking divine guidance to warning the enemy.

Over there, over there
Send the word, send the word over there
That the Yanks are coming, the Yanks are coming
The drums rum tumming everywhere.
So prepare, say a prayer
Send the word, send the word to beware
We'll be over, we're coming over
And we won't come back till it's over, over there.

Last Dance with Ellen Wilson

Famous for his role in ending World War I and overseeing three popular amendments to the Constitution, Woodrow Wilson seemed unstoppable. But just a few months into his term, his beloved wife, Ellen, died and left a depression so deep that he sat stunned by her cold body for two straight days. His sullen demeanor would not heal until after he married his second wife, Edith Bolling Galt, the next year.

However, by that time, Wilson's health had deteriorated significantly. A stroke in 1906 had left him blind in one eye, and he had high blood pressure and frequent headaches. Another stroke in 1919 left him paralyzed on one side. With that, Edith decided it was her turn to step up to the political plate. She took over many of her husband's responsibilties, serving as a middleman between him and other government officials. She reviewed important documents and made decisions she didn't consider serious enough to bother her husband about. In fact, her leadership earned her the nickname the "Secret President" and the "first woman to run the government."

WORLD WAR I TRIVIA

Aerial warfare was of course a new development, and the rules of that warfare were still being written. German air ace Oswald Boelcke wrote one of the first set of rules for aerial combat, the "Dicta Boelcke," which included guidelines like putting yourself between the sun and the enemy, and the admonition not to be brave to the point of foolhardiness.

One of Boelcke's pupils was Manfred von Richthofen, better known as the "Red Baron." Richthofen shot down eighty planes in his career, including twenty-one planes in April 1917. Until the German silver supply became scarce, he commemorated each kill with a silver cup. Richthofen's brother, Lothar, himself scored forty kills.

America's top World War I flying ace, Eddie Rickenbacker, left a racecar cockpit for a war plane cockpit. "Fast Eddie" had set a world speed record of 134 miles per hour in 1914, and had raced in the second Indianapolis 500 in 1912. He enlisted in the Army when America entered the war, and for a while was a driver for Colonel Billy Mitchell, who headed the U.S. Air Services. Rickenbacker was twenty-seven, and the upper age limit for pilots was twenty-five, but he convinced Mitchell to let him go to flight school. It was a good decision. Rickenbacker scored twenty-six kills (six more than any other U.S. pilot) and won nine Distinguished Service Crosses, becoming America's "Ace of Aces."

Once America entered the war, anti-German sentiment led to the renaming of many things associated with Germany. The word "hamburger" was linked to Hamburg, Germany, so hamburgers became "Liberty Sandwiches." Sauerkraut became "Liberty Cabbage" or "Victory Cabbage." Even diseases received a verbal retrofitting. "German measles" became "Liberty Measles."

World War I Slang

The pressure of wartime usually creates some verbal gems in the form of slang, and World War I was no exception. Here's a list of a few slang terms, some of which have stuck around to the present day.

- Ack-ack: The then-new phenomenon of anti-aircraft fire.
- Big Bertha: Named, presumably without her knowing, for Bertha Krupp, wife of armament manufacturer Alfred Krupp, the Big Bertha was a monstrous howitzer with a bore of 16.5 inches that could fire a 2,200-pound shell more than nine miles.
- Coal scuttle: A German field helmet (which was also used in World War II), so named because it resembled a coal bucket.
- Cooties: Long before it was a playground term for imaginary creatures, it was soldier slang for an all-too-real affliction: lice.
- Funk: A "funk hole" was a dugout in a trench that soldiers could enter and rest.
- Potato masher: A German hand grenade with long throwing handle, it resembled a common kitchen utensil.
- Shell-shock: Although the concept of a soldier being traumatized by war had long existed, WWI was the first time the phenomenon received a proper psychological term.
- Whizz-bangs: A masterpiece of onomatopoeia, this term referred to artillery shells, which went "whizz" through the air, then went "bang" once they impacted the ground.

Ailments and Maladies

The son of a Presbyterian minister, Woodrow Wilson seemed too plagued by ailments to have any future in politics. He struggled with dyslexia as a child. He also suffered from such severe heartburn that he often pumped water into his stomach to equalize the acid build-up.

However, by the time he was in his late forties, Wilson covered the sickly façade with charm, and he became a shoe-in for the presidency.

CRASH COURSE
CHARLES PONZI

Evidently, no one ever told Charles Ponzi's victims that if something appears too good to be true, it probably is. Before his chicanery caught up with him, the con man managed to bilk unsuspecting investors out of millions.

Ponzi immigrated to America from Italy when he was twenty-one. He knocked around the Eastern Seaboard for a few years, ending up in Montreal, where he was imprisoned for three years for check forgery.

After his release from prison, the young schemer went back to America, where he would wreak his legendary levels of financial havoc. In 1919, Ponzi founded the Securities Exchange Company in Boston, and promised outlandish returns—reportedly, 50 percent in forty-five to ninety days—on investments deposited there. Investments began selling like hotcakes, if hotcakes were made of gold with diamond filling and in a platinum carrier. People literally lined up to deposit money in Ponzi's "company."

The particulars of Ponzi's SEC aren't that important. (They involved something called *postage coupons*.) The structure of Ponzi's organization was the important thing, because Ponzi had hit on the "pyramid scheme." In a nutshell, money from new recruits paid off the original investors. Pyramid operators rob from Peter to pay Paul, then pay Mary, Ernesto, Wendell, and everybody else stupid enough to invest money with them. The scheme looks foolproof, but the investor requirements increase exponentially, and eventually, there aren't enough investors on Earth to keep it running, and it collapses.

Which is what happened to Ponzi. He was forced to flee. Although he had amassed mountain ranges of money, he ended up on the run, was imprisoned and deported, and died, penniless in Rio de Janeiro in 1949. While his wealth was gone, the phrase *Ponzi Scheme* outlives him, memorializing a charismatic scoundrel.

PHILO T. FARNSWORTH

How did a man with as blazingly American a name as Philo T. Farnsworth, who grew up in a log cabin, rode a horse to school and who conceived the television—the television!—when he was only fourteen and invented a working television at twenty-one end up a footnote to history? Bad timing, rough business practices and the general injustice of history. Even though he finally made it onto a postage stamp in 1983, by then, Farnsworth had been dead twelve years and had almost faded away from the American consciousness.

Born in Beaver, Utah in 1906, Farnsworth devoured *Popular Science* magazines and science books in general. He developed that interest under the tutelage of Justin Tolman, his chemistry teacher, and at fourteen hit on the concept of a scanning television tube. He was inspired by the back-and-forth action farmers used in plowing a field.

Farnsworth entered Brigham Young University in 1922, and had to leave after two years due to the death of his father. But he continued to develop his vision of television. He snagged investment money from friends in 1926, and a year later, he demonstrated his "image dissector" television with help from his brother-in-law.

He won a patent for his invention in 1930, but it was then that his problems started, specifically a patent battle with Vladimir Zworykin, a Russian émigré inventor connected to the giant Radio Corporation of America (RCA). Of the situation, RCA head David Sarnoff allegedly remarked, "RCA doesn't pay royalties; we collect them."

Farnsworth won his patent battle in 1934, and eventually received $1 million from RCA, but continued public relations battles, the expiration of his patents and other problems led to depression and an eventual nervous breakdown.

The genius inventor from Utah did manage to get a last laugh from his invention. In 1957, he appeared on the television show "What's My Line?" As the celebrity panel attempted to determine why Farnsworth was on the show, he was asked if his creation was ever painful. Farnsworth replied, "Yes, sometimes it's most painful."

PRESIDENTIAL BIOS 5

Woodrow Wilson, 1913–1921

Wilson overcame a reading difficulty (possibly suffering from dyslexia, he still couldn't read when he was ten years old) to become a university president and two-term U.S. president. In 1912, Wilson, then New Jersey governor, ran for president as a Democrat and defeated a Republican effort split between incumbent William Howard Taft and Theodore Roosevelt's "Bull Moose" Party. Wilson, who had run on a "New Freedom" platform, immediately began his reforming efforts. In Wilson's first term, the Federal Reserve and Federal Trade Commission were created, and child-labor restrictions were enacted. Wilson won re-election in 1916, running on the claim that he had kept the nation out of World War I. The war continued, however, and Wilson would ask Congress for a declaration of war in 1917. After the war ended, Wilson would help craft the Treaty of Versailles, although many of his goals for the treaty were rejected.

Warren G. Harding, 1921–1923

Harding is largely forgotten today, and that's probably a good thing, considering his legacy. While in the White House, he hosted boozy poker parties with his "Poker Cabinet," and was known to surreptitiously visit burlesque shows. He was chosen as the Republican candidate in the original, literal, "smoke-filled room." He was a former newspaper publisher who, at least judging by the way he mangled it, appeared to have a seething hatred for the English language. Consider this gem he uttered: "Progression is not proclamation nor palaver. It is not the perturbation of a people passion-wrought, nor a promise proposed." Even Harding knew he wasn't presidential material. He once remarked, "I am not fit for this office and never should have been here." Harding died in 1923, officially from a heart attack, although it was rumored that his wife, Flossie, who refused an autopsy on the president, had poisoned him in order to protect him from the scandals that came to light after his death.

Calvin Coolidge, 1923–1929

Coolidge became president upon Harding's death, then won re-election in 1924. While Coolidge is sometimes referred to as "Silent Cal," the nickname isn't really accurate. The Vermont native had little use for small talk, but also held many press conferences and often spoke on the radio. (First Lady Grace Coolidge, on the other hand, was so gregarious and friendly that she referred to herself as "the national hugger.") Coolidge's administration was marked by a hands-off approach toward business, reflecting his famous sentiment that "the business of America is business." Coolidge was a popular president when he chose not to run for re-election in 1928, but his popularity plummeted in 1929, when the Great Depression hit and his administration was blamed for not preventing it.

Herbert Hoover, 1929–1933

Hoover took office amidst the prosperity of pre-Depression America, and won election by promising even more prosperity, in the form of "a chicken in every pot and two cars in every garage." Only eight months into his administration, however, the Great Depression began, and Hoover was forced to deal with its effects. Although Hoover had experience in handling disasters—head of the Food Administration during World War I, he had kept food flowing to the Allies without rationing food in America, had helped feed millions in Soviet Russia during a 1921 famine, and had overseen the government's relief efforts during the 1927 Mississippi River flood—he had little success handling the Depression. In the 1932 presidential election, Hoover lost to Franklin Delano Roosevelt by seven million votes.

Franklin Delano Roosevelt, 1933–1945

The fifth-cousin of President Theodore Roosevelt, "FDR" became the only person to win four terms in the White House, and he will most likely hold that record forever. The Twenty-Second Amendment limits presidents to two terms of office. A 1921 polio infection left Roosevelt confined to a wheelchair. Although he was rarely photographed in his wheelchair, his paralysis was no secret. Roosevelt became president during the Great Depression, and greatly expanded the federal government's powers in an effort to lead America out of its problems. The Tennessee Valley Authority, Civilian Conservation Corps, Public Works Administration, and other programs and entities were all creations of FDR's administration. Roosevelt also led the country during World War II, making his famous "a date which will live in infamy" request for a declaration of war following the Japanese attack on Pearl Harbor on December 7, 1941. Roosevelt suffered a fatal stroke while sitting for a presidential portrait by Elizabeth Shoumatoff, and died from a cerebral hemorrhage on April 12, 1945.

Harry S Truman, 1945–53

The Missouri Democrat replaced Henry Wallace as Franklin Delano Roosevelt's vice president during the 1944 campaign, then became president on April 12, 1945, following Roosevelt's death. Truman was then faced with overseeing the end of World War II for the U.S., including the bombing of Hiroshima and Nagasaki. He won re-election in 1948 over Thomas Dewey, although an early edition of the *Chicago Daily Tribune* famously erred and printed the headline "Dewey Defeats Truman."

Dwight D. Eisenhower, 1953–61

Eisenhower used his military leadership reputation—he was Supreme Commander of the Allied invasion on D-Day, then became chief of the staff of the U.S. Army—to win two terms as president. During his eight years in the White House, Eisenhower was faced with the increasing tensions of the Cold War, the Soviet Union's launch of Sputnik in 1957 and the U-2 incident of 1960, when pilot Gary Powers' spy plane was shot down in the Soviet Union.

EXTRA CREDIT: Eisenhower played football in college and was injured trying to tackle Jim Thorpe.

HANDS-ON HISTORY
RADIO

The telegraph had provided the means of communication as America spread west, but while the telegraph's dots and dashes conveyed information, they were sorely lacking in the ability to convey entertainment. That entertainment vacuum began to be filled on November 2, 1920, when KDKA in Pittsburgh, Pennsylvania, began broadcasting and became America's first commercial radio station.

Radio had been around for many years before KDKA went on the air. Guglielmo Marconi had sent radio waves across the Atlantic in 1901, and experiments in radio transmission dated back further than that. But commercial radio, with the goals of providing entertainment and generating revenue, began because radio manufacturer Westinghouse wanted to sell more units. Westinghouse reckoned that transforming the radio from a one-to-one, telegraph-like communication method to a one-to-many model of mass communication would convince more Americans to splurge on a radio. The company worked with Dr. Frank Conrad, a local amateur radio operator, and unknowingly kicked off a revolution that November day.

The day had been chosen because it was presidential election day. KDKA broadcast the news that Warren G. Harding had defeated James M. Cox to take the White House, and the radio revolution began.

In four years, the number of American radio stations had gone from one to 600. The number of American households with a radio skyrocketed from 60,000 to 400,000 in the same period. The first national radio network, the National Broadcasting Company, was founded in 1926. When pioneering aviator Charles Lindbergh returned from Paris to America, on June 11, 1927, an estimated 30 million Americans across the country listened to radio coverage of the event. The first transcontinental radio broadcast was the 1927 Rose Bowl, heard on the NBC network. Stanford and the University of Alabama played to a 7-7 tie.

BOSTON MOLASSES FLOOD

The phrase "slower than molasses in January" is often used to denote something lacking in speed. But while usually accurate, the phrase isn't always. Under the right conditions, even in January, the thick syrup produced from sugar refining can in fact move with alarming speed. Deadly speed, even, as the Boston Molasses Disaster proved.

The first large-scale death by molasses occurred in Boston's North End in January 1919. A molasses-storage tank owned by United States Industrial Alcohol that measured fifty feet high and ninety feet in diameter held about 2.3 million gallons of molasses. The day was unexpectedly warm for January, with the temperature at about forty degrees Fahrenheit. At 12:30 in the afternoon, a sticky hell was unleashed on Boston's citizens.

The tank ruptured, spilling 14,000 tons of molasses in a wave fifteen feet high. The molasses spread at an estimated thirty-five miles per hour, enveloping humans and animals in a death grip as it crushed houses and anything else in its path. In all, twenty-one people were killed, 150 injured. Several horses were also killed.

In addition to the area directly affected by the flood, workers, gawkers, and others spread the molasses throughout Boston by tracking through the muck. The city smelled of molasses for decades.

Although an official examination of the disaster never determined what caused the tank's collapse, a Massachusetts court held United States Industrial Alcohol liable for damages owing to insufficient inspections, rejecting the company's claims that an anarchist bomb had caused the catastrophe. In addition, it was determined in court that USIA had responded to tank leaks by painting the tank brown, the better to hide oozing molasses. After 300 days of hearings that included testimony from more than 3,000 witnesses, the company was ordered to pay almost $1 million in damages.

CRASH COURSE
WOMEN'S SUFFRAGE

The wheels of politics can sometimes grind slowly, and that was the case for women's suffrage in America. Women didn't receive the right to vote until 1920, fifty-seven years after Abraham Lincoln issued the Emancipation Proclamation.

The battle for women's suffrage in America can be traced back to 1776, when Abigail Adams wrote to her husband John, then attending the Continental Congress in Philadelphia and crafting the Declaration of Independence. Abigail wrote, "I long to hear that you have declared an independancy—and by the way in the new Code of Laws which I suppose it will be necessary for you to make I desire you would Remember the Ladies, and be more generous and favourable to them than your ancestors." Unfortunately for Abigail, her husband and the rest of the drafters turned a deaf ear to her pleas.

Progress toward women's suffrage was slow. In 1848, the first national convention for women's rights was held in Seneca Falls, New York. In 1872, women's rights crusader Susan B. Anthony was arrested for trying to cast a vote for Ulysses S. Grant in the presidential election. The Nineteenth Amendment, which gave women the right to vote, was introduced in Congress. When Wyoming was admitted to the Union in 1890, it became the first state with women's suffrage. In 1912, Theodore Roosevelt ran for re-election as president on the Bull Moose/Republican ticket, whose platform included women's suffrage.

Many women's rights activists postponed their work when America entered World War I in 1917, but resumed their activities once the war ended. Finally, on August 26, 1920, 144 years after Abigail Adams' letter, Secretary of State Bainbridge Colby certified the ratification of the Nineteenth Amendment was adopted, and women had the right to vote.

PROHIBITION

While American law was heading toward giving women the vote, it was also heading toward taking away the use of alcohol. A prohibition movement that had begun in the 1800s achieved its goals on January 16, 1920, when the Eighteenth Amendment to the Constitution went into effect. The amendment made the "manufacture, sale, or transportation of intoxicating liquors" illegal in the United States Coupled with the Volstead Act of 1919, which provided for the amendment's enforcement and specified that "intoxicating liquors" were any beverage with more than 0.5 percent alcohol, the laws began the Prohibition Era.

Although Prohibition hardly accomplished the goal of stamping out alcoholic beverages, every chronicler of American history owes it a debt, because it produced some enduring images. "Moonshiners" who had been producing untaxed (and therefore illegal) liquor from hidden stills for decades saw a boom in their business once legal liquor sales were suspended. Enforcement of Prohibition was at first handled by the Internal Revenue Service, so still-busting "revenuers" became the bane of the clandestine distillers.

While moonshiners became famous for rural activities, urban areas became known for things like illegal saloons called "speakeasies" and gangsters. In Chicago, Al Capone took in a reported $100 million annually from illicit activities including speakeasies. Treasury Department agent Eliot Ness and his "Untouchables" became famous for successfully pursuing Capone and other Prohibition ignorers. In New York City, agents Izzie Einstein and Mo Smith conducted raids using disguises, until a raid on the city's 21 club had the side-effect of ensnaring some prominent citizens. Through it all, Americans who wanted to drink, got to drink.

Support for Prohibition waned through America, until Utah became the thirty-sixth state to ratify the Twenty-First Amendment on December 5, 1933. With that ratification, the so-called "Noble Experiment" of Prohibition was over.

MISSISSIPPI RIVER FLOOD OF 1927

On an average day, the Mississippi River discharges 612,000 cubic feet of water per second. That's not too surprising, considering the Mississippi drains about 41 percent of the continental United States. But on April 16, 1927, the river carried more than 3 million cubic feet per second in places. The Mississippi River flood of 1927 had begun.

The numbers related to the flood are staggering. The heavens appeared to have had the goal of obliterating the entire Mississippi Valley. New Orleans, Louisiana, received fifteen inches of rain in eighteen hours. The Mississippi, which had historically been two miles across at its widest point, eventually stretched seventy miles from side to side. In all, 27,000 square miles of land were flooded.

While the rain would have caused catastrophic damage under any circumstances, the flood's effect could have been mitigated if the U.S. Army Corps of Engineers had listened to James Buchanan Eads. In 1879, the great engineer had proven narrowing and straightening the Mississippi increased its flow rate and caused it to scour a thirty-foot deep channel through a section of the river called South Pass. But the Corps relied on levees for flood control, and no system of levees ever conceived could contain the 1927 waters.

Levees failed on their own. On April 16, 1,200 feet of levee gave way in Illinois. On April 21, the levee failed at Mounds Landing, Mississippi. That gaping hole half a mile wide let through enough water that in ten days, a million acres were ten feet deep in floodwaters.

Levees failed through human intervention. To prevent the flooding of New Orleans, officials dynamited a hole in levees south of the city. As a May 9, 1927, *Time* magazine article put it, "Engineers believed that water drained through the Poydras cut would lower the Mississippi flood crest two to three feet, so that levees protecting New Orleans would not give way when high-water reached the city. When Oramel Hinkley Simpson, Governor of Louisiana, wrote his official announcement: 'I do hereby declare that a public emergency exists and an artificial break in the levee of the Mississippi River is hereby ordered to be created . . .,' he wrote also a death-sentence for two Louisiana parishes, St. Bernard and Plaquemines."

Thousands of black Americans were forced to work shoring up the levees during the flood for very little pay, and were prevented from leaving at gunpoint. In Greenville, Mississippi, 13,000 black refugees were left, homeless and hungry, on a levee, while boats, capable of evacuating them all, removed only thirty-three white women and children. After the flood, many black people left the South for the North, never to return. The Mississippi Delta lost 50 percent of its black population in a year.

Estimates of the flood's economic impact range from $1 to $11 billion when adjusted for inflation.

Silence of the Man

Not a man of many words, Calvin Coolidge was nicknamed "Silent Cal" by some. He was once so rudely quiet at his own White House dinner party that a female guest made a bet that she could get him to say more than two words. Upon hearing about the wager, the president looked her in the eyes and said, "You lose." Coolidge and his family were often so discreet about the conversations they did have in public that they would use sign language so as not to be overheard. "If you don't say anything, you won't be called on to repeat it," Coolidge said.

BLACK TUESDAY AND THE GREAT DEPRESSION

On October 24, 1929, esteemed Yale economist Irving Fisher remarked, "The nation is marching along a permanently high plateau of prosperity." Five days after Fisher made his spectacularly ill-timed remark, what became known as Black Tuesday hit, and the Great Depression had a convenient historical reference point.

Although Black Tuesday is often cited as the beginning of the Depression, the Depression had been a smoldering fire for quite a while. Black Tuesday was just that fire's big flash point. It had been preceded by the "Black Thursday" on October 24 and "Black Monday" on October 28. On Black Thursday, panic on the New York Stock Exchange had been stemmed by Richard Whitney's judicious application of $130 million (roughly $1.5 billion in modern dollars) in funds pooled from Wall Street Bankers. On Black Monday, the Dow Jones Industrial Average lost 12.8 percent of its value.

Wall Street's edginess quickly manifested itself on Black Tuesday. Panicked selling caused the Dow Jones Average to drop from 299.6 at opening to 230.7 at closing, a loss of 23 percent.

There were many causes of Black Tuesday and the Great Depression that followed. For one, many Americans had bought stocks "on margin," using money borrowed from brokerages. Buying stocks on margin was fine as long as stocks were going up. When they plummeted, many investors found themselves unable to answer the "margin call."

The stock market wasn't the only place Americans were using borrowed money. The ending of World War I and the ensuing economic boom had whetted Americans' appetite for shiny new things, and many bought those things on credit.

Banks also failed in record numbers. More than 9,000 banks went under during the 1930s, taking individual fortunes with them. The banks were uninsured, so there was no recourse for the investors who had lost their money.

Congress didn't help matters, either. In 1930, it passed the Hawley-Smoot Tariff Act, and President Herbert Hoover signed it into law. (If that sounds familiar, it's probably because Ferris Bueller's history teacher mentioned it.) The act dramatically raised tariffs on many imported goods in an attempt to protect American industry. But instead of propping up native industry, the act led to retaliatory tariffs from foreign countries and decreased American exports.

Added to all the financial upheaval was a natural one. A drought struck the Great Plains, affecting 100 million acres and spurring the flight of "Okies" to California in search of jobs.

The Great Depression affected more than America. Across the globe, the financial downturn hit with devastating consequence. In Germany, 6 million were unemployed when an Austrian-born veteran of World War I named Adolf Hitler came to power and set Germany on the road to rearmament. Six years later, Germany invaded Poland, beginning World War II.

A Chicken in Every Pot and a Car in Every Garage

Talking his fellow countrymen into the notion that they would be economically sound and secure if he were president in 1928, Herber Hoover told voters that they would have "a chicken in every pot and a car in every garage." Little did he know that his staff would face the worst depression the country had ever seen.

1920s Inventions

Commercial radio wasn't the only big development that took place in the 1920s. Here are a few more groundbreaking inventions from that decade.

- Clarence Birdseye took inspiration from Eskimos in frigid Labrador and revolutionized food preservation. Birdseye had moved his family to northeast Canada to trade in furs. As part of that adventure, Birdseye noticed that Eskimos would flip fresh-caught fish onto the ice. The fish would freeze quickly, and be eaten later without a decrease in quality. He realized that the flash-freezing prevented the formation of large ice crystals, which damaged the cellular structure of foods. Armed with that knowledge, Birdseye started General Seafoods to create and sell frozen food in 1924, and food preservation was changed forever.

- If you've ever nicked yourself and scampered to the first-aid kit for a prepackaged, sterile, easily dispensed Band-Aid instead of a roll of gauze, a scissors and some tape, thank Earle Dickson. In 1921, Dickson noticed his wife Josephine frequently cut herself while preparing food in the kitchen, and also noticed that the gauze bandages she applied wouldn't adhere very long. Dickson, a cotton-buyer for Johnson & Johnson, developed a bandage from tape, gauze and a roll of crinoline that kept the tape from sticking to itself. He showed his invention to company officials, and J&J began producing Band-Aids. For his creativity, Dickson was made a J&J vice president.

- What's better than sliced bread? The machine that slices bread, of course. And the credit for that machine goes to Otto Frederick Rohwedder, an Iowa jeweler. Rohwedder began working on a machine that would automatically slice loaves of bread in 1912, but between trial and error and a fire that destroyed his blueprints, it would take him to 1927 to finalize his machine. The first loaf of machine-sliced bread from Rohwedder's machine was sold on July 7, 1928.

FDR AND THE NEW DEAL

Although he had won the hearts of Americans for his aid efforts during the 1927 Mississippi River flood, Herbert Hoover didn't retain those hearts for very long. The Great Depression hit in 1929, early in Hoover's administration, and the nation was soon disenchanted with him. (How much blame Hoover deserved and how much he could have done to lessen the effects of the depression is debatable, but the public has never been known for its patience.) A turned-out (and empty) pocket was a "Hoover flag," and a group of shacks inhabited by unemployed workers was a "Hooverville." In the 1932 presidential election's popular vote, Franklin Delano Roosevelt crushed Hoover 22,829,501 to 15,760,684.

Whereas Hoover had been reluctant to involve the federal government in recovery efforts, FDR took the opposite tack of intense federal involvement. Immediately after taking office in 1933, FDR called a "bank holiday" that shut down banking activities and helped settle financial jitters. That same week, he called special session of Congress in order to deal with the Depression. With public support for Roosevelt obvious, Congress quickly took action. The Emergency Banking Act, which greatly increased the federal government's role in banking, was introduced, voted on, passed, and signed into law in one day.

That act was just the beginning of Roosevelt's activism. Under his "New Deal," a flurry of new policies and agencies were created, sometimes on shaky legal foundations. The National Industrial Recovery Act suspended antitrust laws and forced industries to create "codes of fair competition" in which prices and wages were set. The National Recovery Administration was created shortly after passage of the NIRA, and companies that met NIRA standards displayed the blue eagle logo of the NIRA. (The NIRA was effectively stripped of power in a 1935 when the Supreme Court decision of *Schechter Poultry Corp. v. United States* ruled it unconstitutional.)

The New Deal created the Federal Deposit Insurance Corporation to insure financial deposits and limit damages caused by bank failures. The Agricultural Adjustment Act paid farmers to decrease production and stabilize prices. (The AAA was ruled unconstitutional in 1936, but Congress reinstated many of its provisions in 1938) Creation of the Civilian Conservation Corps put three million young men to work on public works projects. The Tennessee Valley Authority began electrifying and modernizing the Tennessee Valley. The Securities and Exchange Commision, Federal Communications Commission and Social Security administration were all begun during the New Deal.

It's not debatable that FDR and the New Deal forever changed America. What is debatable is how much good was done by the New Deal. While the New Deal is often credited with lifting the country out of the Depression, others believe the industrial buildup during World War II should get the credit. In her 2007 book *The Forgotten Man: A New History of the Great Depression*, author and economic commentator Amity Shlaes posited that the federal government actually worsened the Depression with its heavy intervention during the New Deal.

Ready, Aim, Misfire

When it came to protecting Franklin Roosevelt's wife, Eleanor, from any harm, he simply was not able to overcome her stubborn independence. Eleanor refused to be escorted by Secret Service agents, so government officials gave her lessons on how to use a personal handgun. But after a trip with her to the FBI firing range, then-FBI Chief J. Edgar Hoover had his doubts. "Mr. President," he said, "if there is one person in the U.S. who should not carry a gun, it's your wife. She cannot hit a barn door."

LINDBERGH KIDNAPPING

On March 1, 1932, someone kidnapped a twenty-month-old boy from his Hopewell, New Jersey, home. Kidnappings always grab headlines, and child kidnappings are even more shocking. But this was no ordinarily tragic kidnapping. The infant was the son of famed aviator and American hero Charles Lindbergh, and his abduction would become one of the most infamous crimes in U.S. history.

Charles Augustus Lindbergh Jr. was suffering from a cold that March night, and his nurse, a Scottish girl named Betty Gow, had applied congestion medication to the boy's chest about 8:30 p.m., then left him to sleep. When Gow returned to the nursery at 10 p.m. to check on the boy, he was gone. On the window sill, a poorly written ransom note read:

> Dear Sir,
> Have 50,000$ redy 25000$ in 20$ bills 15000$ in 10$ bills and 10000$ in 5$ bills. After 2-4 days will inform you were to deliver the Mony.
> We warn you for making anyding public or for notify the Polise the child is in gut care.
> Indication for all letters are singnature and 3 holds.

A New Jersey State Police colonel named H. Norman Schwarzkopf was placed in charge of the investigation. Fifty-nine years later, the colonel's son would become famous as the leader of the 1991 Iraq War.

The advent of radio networks in the 1920s had brought instantaneous national communication to America, and news of the kidnapping was broadcast across the country by 10:30 p.m. On March 2, countless newspapers made the kidnapping their lead story. Americans reacted with reported sightings of the infant, calls for public prayer, and offers of help. From an Illinois jail, gangster Al Capone was quoted as saying, "It's the most outrageous thing I've ever heard of!" and offered a $10,000 reward for the boy's return.

On March 6, the Lindberghs received a second ransom note, which increased the ransom amount to $70,000. A third note on March 8 told the Lindberghs that their appointed intermediary wasn't acceptable to the kidnappers. On the same day, a retired New York City school principal named Dr. John F. Condon offered to serve as intermediary. Condon received a note from the kidnappers the next day that he was an acceptable intermediary, and eventually met several times with someone calling himself "John" several times at a cemetary.

Condon gave a negotiated ransom of $50,000 to "John" on April 2, and received a note stating that the child was on a boat near Martha's Vineyard, Massachusetts. Two searches were conducted, but the child wasn't found.

On May 12, 1932, the child's partially decomposed body was found in woods about 4.5 miles from the Lindbergh house. A coroner's investigation showed that the boy had been dead for about two months.

Marked bills used to pay the ransom began showing up in New York City, and eventually the trail of bills led to Bruno Richard Hauptmann, a carpenter. Hauptmann's home was searched and found to have $14,000 of the ransom money. Hauptman was arrested on September 19, 1934.

Beginning on January 3, 1935, Hauptmann's trial lasted five weeks and brought 60,000 people to Flemington, New Jersey. The case against Hauptmann rested on circumstantial evidence. The ladder that had been left leaning against the Lindbergh house had tool marks that matched tools Hauptmann owned, and wood in Hauptmann's attic matched wood in the ladder. Investigators had found Condon's phone number and address written on a door frame in Hauptmann's house.

The Flemington jury returned its verdict on February 13. Hauptmann was found guilty of first-degree murder, and sentenced to death. Appeals by his lawyers failed, and Hauptmann was executed in the electric chair on April 3, 1936.

EMPIRE STATE BUILDING AND CHRYSLER BUILDING

Two American icons were completed in New York City during the 1930s, and both endure as landmarks today. The Chrysler Building and Empire State Building are epic monuments to big-thinking America.

Auto tycoon Walter P. Chrysler began construction on a headquarters building for the Chrysler Corporation on September 19, 1928. The building was located at the intersection of 42nd Street and Lexington Avenue. The building's design, by architect William van Alen, was an Art Deco triumph of style. It featured a tower with metal sunbursts and gargoyles, simulated car hubcaps, and a lobby mural titled "Energy, Result, Workmanship and Transportation."

Construction of the building took 21,000 tons of steel and almost 4 million bricks. At the height of construction, some 2,000 workers labored on the building and managed to add four floors a week to the building's height.

Although publicly, the Chrysler Building was designed to be 925 feet tall, Chrysler and Van Alen secretly planned a sneaky architectural masterstroke. The Bank of Manhattan Tower reached 927 feet in height, and Chrysler wanted his building to be not only taller than the bank tower, but the tallest building in the world. So to keep the bank's builders from taking that title, Chrysler and Van Alen waited until the Bank of Manhattan building was almost complete. Then, in only ninety minutes, workers erected a 180-foot spire that had been secretly shipped to the building and assembled inside. The building that was completed on May 28, 1930 reached 1,047 feet into the air and gave Chrysler his "world's tallest" title. He wouldn't keep it long.

Construction on the Empire State Building, located at the intersection of Fifth Avenue and West 34th Street, had begun shortly before the Chrysler Building's completion, on March 17, 1930. Like the Chrysler Building, the Empire State Building was the child of an automotive magnate. John Jacob Raskob, former CFO of General Motors, had conceived the building, along with Alfred Smith, a former governor of New York.

Architect William Lamb at the firm of Shreve, Lamb & Harmon designed the building. For such a monumental project, Lamb's design inspiration was a simple one: a pencil.

From the beginning, the newcomer outdid the Chrysler Building. Construction of the Empire State Building required 60,000 tons of steel. Ten million bricks were used, as well as 200,000 cubic feet of limestone and granite. Workers managed to add 4.5 floors per week. Some three thousand workers completed the building in only a year and forty-five days.

On May 1, 1931, the Empire State Building opened to the public. It was 1,250 feet tall, surpassing the Chrysler Building by 203 feet. The new building was the tallest in the world, and it held that title for forty-one years, until the completion of New York City's World Trade Center in 1972.

Smokin' Shoulders

Woodrow Wilson once described Franklin Delano Roosevelt as "the handsomest young giant I have ever seen." The quote was a friendly tease. Although FDR was 6-feet-2-inches tall and weighed 190 pounds, he lost the use of his legs to polio. Soon after he was confined to a wheelchair, he buffed up his upper body to build some impressive muscle. "Maybe my legs aren't so good, but look at these shoulders! Jack Dempsey would be green with envy," he once said.

The president was known to make light of his disability. When Madame Chiang Kai-shek visited the White House during his term, she politely asked him not to bother with standing out of respect as she rose to leave the room. "My dear child," he laughed, "I couldn't stand up if I had to!"

NEW LONDON SCHOOL EXPLOSION

A nation already in the clutches of the Great Depression was inured to bad news, but even the most jaded observers were shaken by the stories coming from New London, Texas. Shortly after 3 p.m. on March 18, 1937, an explosion at the New London High School leveled the building and killed almost 300, most of them schoolchildren.

The explosion occurred when an instructor of manual training named Lemmie R. Butler turned on a sanding machine. Odorless natural gas had been leaking from pipes beneath the school and accumulating through the building. When Butler turned on his machine, the gas ignited violently, destroying the school and entombing many. The explosion was audible four miles away, and the force of it threw a 4,000-pound concrete slab 200 feet away, crushing a car.

A PTA meeting had been in progress at the school's gymnasium, and frantic parents rushed to the school scene. Boy Scouts, Texas Rangers, the Red Cross, doctors and oil company workers were among the volunteers who worked to recover bodies and treat the wounded. Twenty-five embalmers from the Texas Funeral Directors Association were sent to deal with the bodies.

Investigators later determined that, in order to stop paying $300 a month in gas fees to the United Gas Company, school officials had tapped into a "green" gas line belonging to the Parade Gasoline Company. A faulty connection allowed the odorless gas to escape, collect and then explode.

Today, at the London Museum Tea Room and Gift Shop, a sympathy telegram received after the explosion is the most popular display. In German, a young chancellor named Adolf Hitler had written to President Roosevelt, "On the occasion of the terrible explosion at New London, Texas, which took so many young lives, I want to assure your excellency of my and the German people's sincere sympathy."

Hands-on History
1939 Movies

The toughest circumstances can sometimes produce the best results, and that was the case for Hollywood in 1939. Even though the world was still fighting a depression and a new European war was beginning, the film industry managed to turn out two all-time classics: *Gone with the Wind* and *The Wizard of Oz*.

Gone with the Wind was the film adaptation of author Margaret Mitchell's Civil War and Reconstruction Pulitzer Prize-winning novel of the same name. Producer David O. Selznick paid $50,000 for the film rights to the book shortly after it was published in 1936, but bringing the book to the screen took three directors (Victor Fleming, George Cukor, and Sam Wood all worked on the film), a massive casting call to find a suitable Scarlett O'Hara in Vivien Leigh and an estimated $3.9 million in production costs. But the effort was worth the result, as GWTW won eight Academy Awards and became, after inflation is accounted for, the most successful movie ever.

The Wizard of Oz was another film adaptation of a successful book, this one L. Frank Baum's 1900 fantasy *The Wonderful Wizard of Oz*. The film transformed the book into a musical, and, like GWTW, was filmed in Technicolor (except for the opening and closing). Technicolor gave the film's colors an incredibly rich depth, particularly to audiences used to black-and-white movies.

"Oz" had the misfortune of being released the same year as GWTW, so it only managed to win two Academy Awards, for Best Music, Original Score and Best Music, Original Song for "Somewhere Over the Rainbow."

POP QUIZ #6

1) What do all of these have in common: Mount Vernon, the Hermitage, Monticello, Cypress Grove, Sherwood Forest, Highland, Polk Place?

2) Who wrote *The Adventures of Tom Sawyer* and *The Adventures of Huckleberry Finn*?

3) What was the world's first national park?

4) Match the Presidential campaign slogan with its candidate.
   1. William Henry Harrison a. 54-40 or Fight
   2. James K. Polk b. Cox and Cocktails
   3. Abraham Lincoln c. He Kept Us out of War
   4. Woodrow Wilson d. Tippecanoe and Tyler, Too
   5. Warren G. Harding e. Vote Yourself a Farm

5) Who implemented the concept of self-serve grocery stores?

6) Is it possible for 14,000 tons of molasses to ooze at 35 miles per hour?

7) Match the state with its trivial information.
   1. Nebraska a. Most counties
   2. New Hampshire b. Northern-most point in the Contiguous States
   3. Texas c. Largest number of legislators
   4. Kentucky d. Most Coastline
   5. Alaska e. Unicameral legislature
   6. Minnesota f. Commonwealth

8) Norman Rockwell was an American artist known for his illustrations in what magazine?

9) What do Edward Albee, Arthur Miller, and Eugene O'Neill have in common?

10) Who designed the Washington Monument?

ANSWERS:

1) They are all homes of presidents.
2) Mark Twain
3) Yellowstone
4) 1-d; 2-a; 3-e; 4-c; 5-b
5) Clarence Saunders
6) Yes, especially if daytime temperatures are warmer than usual for January.
7) 1-e; 2-c; 3-a; 4-f; 5-d; 6-b
8) *The Saturday Evening Post*
9) They are all famous American playwrights.
10) Robert Mills

LEND-LEASE

Officially, America entered World War II on December 8, 1941, after the bombing of Pearl Harbor. But America had a great impact on the war long before that. Beginning in March 1941, the U.S. had pumped billions into the war effort as part of the Lend-Lease Act.

The impetus for the Lend-Lease Act came in July 1940, in the form of the Destroyers for Bases Agreement. German naval forces had sunk eleven British destroyers in ten days, and Prime Minister Winston Churchill asked President Franklin Delano Roosevelt for help replacing them. The two leaders worked out a deal: England got fifty American-built destroyers, and America got long-term leases on British bases in the Caribbean and Newfoundland.

The war continued, without American participation, and Churchill again appealed to Roosevelt for help, telling him, "Give us the tools, and we'll finish the job." Roosevelt planned for America to serve as the "great arsenal of democracy," and with the passage of the Lend-Lease Act on March 11, 1941, that plan was put into action. That act, and additional legislation passed later with the same goal, allowed America to supply arms and other supplies to "any country whose defense the President deems vital to the defense of the United States."

Although the act was called "Lend-Lease," the terms of the act allowed the president wide leeway in determining what payment the United States received in return for its help, stating "the benefit to the United States may be payment or repayment in kind or property, or any other direct or indirect benefit which the president deems satisfactory." In all, some $50 billion in 1940s dollars was transferred under terms of the Lend-Lease Act.

JAPANESE INTERNMENT

More than six decades removed from the events, the U.S. government's internment of thousands of Japanese and German Americans seems too preposterous to grasp. But that's exactly what President Franklin Delano Roosevelt did, imprisoning more than 130,000 in fenced camps.

Internment began when Roosevelt signed Executive Order 9066 on February 19, 1942. The order stated that "the successful prosecution of the war requires every possible protection against espionage and against sabotage," and authorized the secretary of war (at the time, Henry Stimson) and any military commanders he designated to create "military areas" and also determine the people who could enter, leave or remain in those areas.

On March 2, Military Areas Nos. 1 and 2 were created and included all of California, Oregon, Washington, and Arizona. Later that month, sixteen "Assembly Centers" had opened to hold 92,000 people until permanent camps were built. By the end of the war in 1945, 120,000 Japanese-Americans would be interned in camps, or what the government called "relocation centers," located in remote and harsh land. Half those interned were children. Those sent to camps could bring with them only what they could carry. Everything else, including pets, had to be left behind.

Although Japanese-Americans were the largest group affected, some 11,000 German-Americans and 1,500 Italian-Americans were also interned.

When the war ended in 1945, internees received $25 and a ticket home. In 1988, President Ronald Reagan signed a law that apologized to detainees and authorized payments of $20,000 to surviving internees.

Rosie the Riveter

She's one of the most enduring WWII images, and rightly so. A determined woman with a red bandanna on her head stares into the camera, flexes a muscular right arm that sports a rolled-up sleeve and declares, "We can do it!" Rosie the Riveter symbolized the thousands of American women who entered the industrial world and kept the war effort running.

The familiar image of Rosie began as an unnamed subject created by J. Howard Miller, an artist with the Westinghouse company, in 1942. Geraldine Doyle, a worker at an Ann Arbor, Michigan, plant, was the model for the image.

In 1943, Kay Kyser released a hit song, "Rosie the Riveter," which included inspiring lyrics like:

> *All the day long,*
> *Whether rain or shine,*
> *She's a part of the assembly line.*
> *She's making history,*
> *Working for victory,*
> *Rosie the Riveter.*
> *Keeps a sharp lookout for sabotage,*
> *Sitting up there on the fuselage.*
> *That little girl will do more than a male will do.*

The legend that would become Rosie picked up momentum when the May 29 issue of *The Saturday Evening Post* featured a Norman Rockwell cover image of a muscular female war worker. A riveting machine on her lap, the woman grasps a ham sandwich in one hand while resting her feet on a copy of Adolf Hitler's *Mein Kampf.* An American flag flies behind her. The name "Rosie" is painted on the woman's lunchbox. The woman who had posed for the picture was nineteen-year-old Mary Keefe. Rockwell had based her on Michelangelo's painting of the prophet Isaiah on the Sistine Chapel, and had even painted a halo over the woman's head.

Rosie became a true American icon when actor Walter Pidgeon

toured Ford Motor Company's Willow Creek plant, which had been converted to aircraft production for the war. Pidgeon noticed a young Kentucky native named Rose Will Monroe, who did indeed work as a riveter. Monroe was tapped to perform in a motivational film for the war effort, and the Rosie legend was secured.

Rosie hit a nerve with the public. The propaganda effort aimed at getting women involved in the war effort succeeded in the millions. The number of women employed outside the home soared from 12 million when the war began to 18 million by the end of the war. Women worked in aircraft factories, ammunition plants, shipyards, offices, the service industry, and countless other occupations.

To commemorate the WWII role of the Rosies, and the men who worked on the homefront, the Rosie the Riveter/World War II Home Front National Historical Park was opened in Richmond, California, which had been home to four shipyards during the war.

The story of the two major Rosie images is a divergent one. Since Miller's image wasn't copyrighted, it's appeared on posters, t-shirts, bumper stickers, mouse pads, and seemingly any number of other surfaces. Rockwell's painting, however, was copyrighted. In 2002, the original painting, for which Mary Keefe had received a $10 posing fee, sold for almost $5 million.

General Patton

George S. Patton was known for turning out gems like:

"No sane man is unafraid in battle, but discipline produces in him a form of vicarious courage."

"Untutored courage is useless in the face of educated bullets."

"An Army is a team; lives, sleeps, eats, fights as a team. This individual heroic stuff is a lot of crap."

Although he fought all over Europe, Patton died from injuries suffered in a car crash after the war was over.

MILITARY BATTLES

Americans in World War II fought in countless military battles, all of which, particularly to the people fighting in them, were memorable. But three—D-Day, the Battle of the Bulge and Midway—have received the lion's share of attention over the years. Here's a look at all three, with one extra bit of information thrown in at the end.

D-Day

On the morning of June 6, 1944, the English Channel between Great Britain and France was clogged with five thousand ships. Nine battleships, twenty-three cruisers, 104 destroyers, and an armada of LSTs (landing ship, tank), mine sweepers, and various other craft bobbed in the water. It took that many ships to convey the 150,000 men and thirty thousand vehicles that the Allies planned to use to retake Europe from the Nazis. In addition, the pilots of more than eight hundred planes were preparing to drop more than thirteen thousand paratroops.

The Allies had designated five landing points: American forces were to take Utah and Omaha, Great Britain was to take Gold and Sword, and Canadian forces were to take Juno. At 6:30 a.m., the first of those forces, the 4th U.S. Division, came ashore on Utah beach. The fighting was savage. By the time night fell, the Allies had suffered nine thousand casualties, but more than 100,000 had made it ashore. The freeing of Europe had begun.

The Battle of the Bulge

The Allied offensive that had begun with D-Day received another test beginning on December 16, 1944. More than 200,000 German troops attempted to turn back the Allies along a front in the Ardennes forest that stretched seventy-five miles from southern Belgium into Luxembourg. The German offensive through the Ardennes created a bulge in Allied lines as German forces advanced toward the Meuse River. But General Dwight Eisenhower sent reinforcements, Lieutenant General George Patton began a counterattack and other American forces first held their ground and then began to advance. By January, there were more than seventy-six thousand American casualties, but the German offensive was turned back.

Midway

On June 4, 1942, almost six months after Pear Harbor was attacked, Japan's progress in the Pacific Ocean was stopped in the Battle of Midway. U.S. Admiral Chester Nimitz's fleet of seventy-six ships defeated Admiral IsorokuYamamoto's fleet of 160 ships. When the battles ended, the United States had lost 150 planes and 307 men, but the Japanese had lost 253 planes and 3,500 men.

What's the story behind that flag-raising?

One of the most enduring images from WWII is that of U.S. Marines raising an American flag at Iwo Jima. But the story behind that picture isn't often told. Let's correct that.

The flag was actually raised on Mount Suribachi, which is the highest point on Iwo Jima, an island 760 miles south of Tokyo. Suribachi was a dormant volcano at the time, although the ground was hot from volcanic activity in places. On February 21, 1945, at around 10:30 a.m, an American flag was raised on Suribachi, but that's not the flag in the picture. The flag in the picture was larger, and was raised later that day by five Marines and one Navy corpsman: Sgt. Michael Strank, Cpl. Harlon H. Block, Pfc. Franklin R. Sousley, Pfc. Rene A. Gagnon, Pfc. Ira Hayes and John H. Bradley, USN. Strank, Block, and Sousley later lost their lives in battle on the island. For capturing the moment, photographer Joe Rosenthal won a Pulitzer Prize.

WWII Trivia

- Theodor Seuss Geisel, aka Dr. Seuss, was more than just a children's book author. Between 1941 and 1943, he drew more than 400 political cartoons for New York magazine *PM*. According to Art Spiegelman, one of the co-authors of *Dr. Seuss Goes to War*, The Cat in the Hat's striped top hat is a take-off on Uncle Sam's hat.

- Many an e-mailer has read or passed on the story of how actor Lee Marvin lauded children's show host Captain Kangaroo for his fearless fighting on Iwo Jima. According to the oft-circulated story, Marvin told talk-show host Johnny Carson that Bob Keeshan, who played the captain, was "the bravest man I ever saw." But while Marvin did indeed fight (although at Saipan, not Iwo Jima), receiving the Purple Heart for a wound he suffered, Keeshan was a captain on television only. Although he enlisted in the Marines after graduating from high school in 1945, he never saw any combat.

- Pearl Harbor wasn't the only American location to be attacked during WWII. A Japanese sub shelled an oil refinery near Santa Barbara, California, on February 23, 1942, although it did little damage. In April, another Japanese sub attacked Oregon's Fort Stevens, although the major came in the form of a damaged backstop on a baseball field. The most damage done came late in the war, when a desperate Japan launched 9,000 balloon bombs over a five-month period. One of the balloons landed in a tree in Oregon, and on May 5, 1945, a group of picnickers found it. When they pulled it from the tree, it exploded, killing six people.

CRASH COURSE
MILITARY LEADERS

While FDR led the homefront, the military had a plethora of leaders during WWII. Here's a look at a few of the most notable.

George Catlett Marshall

Marshall achieved his greatest fame following WWII, when, as secretary of state, he proposed rebuilding Europe in what became known as the Marshall Plan. But Marshall also served with distinction during the war. He had become chief of staff in September 1939, and became General of the Army in 1944. His wartime duties included planning and organizing Operation Overlord, the Allied invasion of Europe that began with D-Day. British Prime Minister Winston Churchill said, "There are few men whose qualities of mind and character have impressed me so deeply as those of General Marshall."

George S. Patton

The personification of a blood-and-guts soldier, Patton was almost ubiquitous during the war. He commanded the all-American Western Task Force during Operation Torch, the Allied invasion of North Africa. From there, he went to Sicily to lead the Seventh Army. He took control of the Third Army in France in 1944, sweeping through France, Belgium, Luxembourg, Germany, Austria, and Czechoslovakia. Patton had a rough eloquence to his speech.

Audie Murphy

When the Texas-born Murphy applied to the Marines, he was turned down for being too light and too short. (Murphy was a thin 5-foot-5-inches.) He made it into the military in 1942, joining the Army in 1942. The Army made a good choice. Murphy would go on to become the most-decorated combat soldier of WWII, winning twenty-four medals including the Medal of Honor, Distinguished Service Cross, Silver Star with First Oak Leaf Cluster, Legion of Merit, and Purple Heart.

TUSKEGEE AIRMEN

In March 1942, five aviation cadets completed nine months of instruction and became pilots in the Army Air Corps. That fact wasn't remarkable, as the United States had entered the war a few months earlier and so needed pilots and every other manner of fighter. But the makeup of this small class of pilots was remarkable. They were black men, and they were the first Tuskegee Airmen.

Black men had not been allowed to even receive flight training until 1941, when the War Department, under pressure from the National Association for the Advancement of Colored People and other forces, had established the 99th Pursuit Squadron of the Army Air Corps. (The AAC was the forerunner of the U.S. Air Force.) The squadron was to be trained at Tuskegee Army Air Field in Tuskegee, Alabama. That location was chosen for its proximity to historically black Tuskegee University.

That first class included Captain Benjamin O. Davis Jr., who became squadron commander. Over the course of the war, 940 pilots graduated from the school. Of those 940, 450 served overseas, flying P-40 Warhawks in North Africa, Sicily, and Italy. Later, three more squadrons were added to the 99th to form the 332nd Fighter Group. That group became the only AAF escort group to not lose a bomber to the enemy.

Captain Charles B. Hall became the first Tuskegee-trained pilot to shoot down an enemy plane on July 2, 1943. For his feat, Hall received only a Coca-Cola.

To commemorate the actions of the airmen, the Tuskegee Airmen National Historic Site at Tuskegee's Moton Field was established in 1998.

GI Bill

The Marshall Plan funded the rebuilding of western Europe, but closer to home, there was another group that faced a monstrous need for funds and training: millions of men and women who had left the armed services when the war ended. For those people, there was the Servicemen's Readjustment Act of 1944, better known as the G.I. Bill.

During the war, Department of Labor estimates predicted 15 million men and women would be unemployed when their armed forces service ended. The country had seen the catastrophic economic effects caused by WWI veterans returning from the war, untrained and unfunded, and had also just come out of a worldwide economic depression. Steps had to be taken, in advance of the war's end, to provide for the people who had fought for their country.

The legislation that would become the G.I. Bill was largely crafted by the American Legion. When presented to Congress, it sailed through both the House and Senate unanimously. President Franklin Roosevelt signed the act into law on June 22, 1944, just sixteen days after the D-Day invasion.

The bill's stated goal was "to provide federal government aid for the readjustment in civilian life of returning World War II veterans." Eventually, more than 8 million received educational and training benefits, from a disbursement of $14.5 billion. More than 4.3 million home loans were granted, with a total value of $33 billion. The bill had such an impact that historian Stephen Ambrose said the G.I. Bill was "the best piece of legislation ever passed by the U.S. Congress, and it made modern America."

EXTRA CREDIT: Franklin Delano Roosevelt's mother forced him to wear dresses until he was five years old.

Manhattan Project

The Manhattan Project, the massive effort to harness the power of the atom, was an epic scientific undertaking. Relating that story is too much for a bathroom reader (author Richard Rhodes won a Pulitzer Prize for his book *The Making of the Atomic Bomb*, which covers more than nine hundred pages), so here are a few trivia facts, in more digestible form.

The history of the Manhattan Project owes a debt to college football coach Amos Alonzo Stagg. One of the most successful college football coaches ever, Stagg coached at the University of Chicago from 1892 to 1932. In 1913, the university named its football stadium Stagg Field in his honor. On December 2, 1942, as part of the Manhattan Project, a team led by Italian physicist Enrico Fermi demonstrated the world's first man-made, self-sustaining nuclear chain reaction. Such a demonstration was vital to proving that atomic energy could be harnessed. The location of the historic reaction? Underneath the abandoned west stands of Stagg Field.

Fermi's team had proven that creating a chain reaction was possible, but attempting to use atomic power in a weapon and on a large scale was another realm of difficulty and danger. On July 16, 1945, before Fermi, Edward Teller, Robert Oppenheimer and other scientists detonated the innocuously named "Gadget," the first atomic weapon ever exploded, Fermi was concerned that it might create a runaway chain reaction that could ignite the Earth's atmosphere and destroy the world.

FDR the Trendsetter

Besides being known for his bulging shoulder muscles, FDR was also quite the trendsetter when it came to clothes that were easy for his personal assistants to dress him in. Because putting on a heavy overcoat was so difficult, he became known for his trademark navy cape, which kept him warm during the winter.

THE ATOMIC BOMB

On August 6, 1945, less than a month after America exploded the world's first atomic bomb in the New Mexico desert on July 16, Brigadier General Paul Tibbets' plane, the *Enola Gay*, dropped an atomic bomb known as Little Boy on Hiroshima, Japan. Three days later, Brigadier General Charles W. Sweeney's *Bockscar* dropped a second bomb, Fat Man, on Nagasaki. Japan surrendered six days later, on August 15.

Tibbets had named the plane after his mother, whose maiden name was Enola Gay Haggard. In 2002, Tibbets told author Studs Terkel he did so because she had supported him in his flying efforts, while his father hadn't. "When I told them I was going to leave college and go fly planes in the Army Air Corps, my dad said, 'Well, I've sent you through school, bought you automobiles, given you money to run around with the girls, but from here on, you're on your own. If you want to go kill yourself, go ahead, I don't give a damn.' Then Mom just quietly said, 'Paul, if you want to go fly airplanes, you're going to be all right.' And that was that."

Physicist J. Robert Oppenheimer, who headed the research station at Los Alamos, New Mexico, that created the first atomic bombs, is one of America's tragic scientific figures. Although he was lauded for leading the project, after the war, Oppenheimer was accused of being a Communist and lost his security clearance.

What's in a Name

Thirty-third President Harry S Truman's middle name is just that—S. After a family feud about whether the new baby should be named after his paternal grandfather, Shippe, or his maternal grandfather, Solomon, Truman's mother threw up her hands and settled with what would please both sides.

TEXAS CITY DISASTER

On the morning on April 16, 1947, at the port of Texas City, Texas, a ship was burning. But attitudes toward industrial dangers were still quaint in 1947, so the fire on board the *SS Grandcamp* caused not panic, but interest. Word-of-mouth and a strange, orange-red smoke spread news of the fire among Texas City residents, a town of 18,000 located about forty miles southeast of Houston, and interested residents made their way to the waterfront to take in the spectacle. They watched the Texas City Volunteer Fire Department spray water on the fire, only to have the water they sprayed turn into steam from the heat of the fire.

The onlookers didn't know it, but the *Grandcamp* held 2,300 tons of ammonium nitrate. Ammonium nitrate is an excellent oxidizer, meaning that it enhances combustion. The load the ship contained had been created during WWII for use in explosives. The steam from the fire department's water hoses had begun liquefying the ammonium nitrate, releasing nitrous oxide, another oxidizer.

At 9:12 a.m., the *Grandcamp* exploded. The force of the explosion lifted the 7,176-ton ship twenty feet into the air. Residents in Port Arthur, Texas, one hundred miles away, felt the concussion. A fifteen-foot wave pushed a 150-foot barge out of the harbor and two hundred feet inland. Every firefighter on the scene was killed immediately, as were many spectators. More than 1,000 buildings in Texas City were destroyed. Flying debris ignited fires throughout the city.

A nearby ship, the *High Flyer*, caught fire and was towed one hundred feet from the docks. It carried one thoudand tons of ammonium nitrate, which exploded at 1:10 a.m. April 17, destroying more buildings and causing more fires.

In all, 576 people died as a result of the explosions—398 confirmed dead, 178 missing. Sixty-three victims were still unidentified when they were buried. In addition to the human loss, $67 million in property damage was done.

POLITICAL SCIENCE 101
MARSHALL PLAN

The Allies had defeated the Axis, but now Europe lay in shambles. Rebuilding Europe was crucial in order to alleviate the suffering of the European people and to avoid the continued economic turmoil that had helped precipitate World War II. That rebuilding effort would become known as the Marshall Plan, and would result in the U.S. investing $13.3 billion in western Europe over the course of four years.

The seeds of the plan were planted on June 5, 1947, when George C. Marshall gave the commencement address at Harvard University. Marshall, who had served as Army chief of staff during the war and who had become secretary of state in 1947, began his address by stating, "I need not tell you, gentlemen, that the world situation is very serious. That must be apparent to all intelligent people."

Marshall went on to urge western European nations (the ones not under the control of the Soviet Union) to form a plan of recovery, and for the U.S. to help with the recovery's funding. After an endorsement of Marshall's proposal by President Harry Truman, Congress passed the Economic Cooperation Act of 1948, although history would remember it as the Marshall Plan.

The plan worked to perfection. Millions of Europeans' lives were lifted out of an economic abyss, building projects provided hope and employment and laid the groundwork for the creation of the North Atlantic Treaty Organization in 1949. For his efforts, Marshall won the 1953 Nobel Peace Prize.

EXTRA CREDIT: Unsuccesful assassination attempts were made on the lives of Andrew Jackson, Theodore Roosevelt, Franklin D. Roosevelt, Harry Truman, Gerald Ford, and Ronald Reagan.

COLD WAR

Although the United States and the Soviet Union were allies during WWII, that changed before the war ended. Joseph Stalin's Soviet forces had forced Hitler's forces from Poland and then established a provisional government that was pro-communist. The United States wasn't pleased with this, and became concerned about the post-war fate of other eastern European nations. Their concern was well-founded, as Bulgaria, Romania, and Hungary turned communist after the war ended.

On March 12, 1947, President Harry Truman addressed a joint session of Congress. Truman stated that the United States had received pleas for financial and economic aid from the government of Greece, and said, "The very existence of the Greek state is today threatened by the terrorist activities of several thousand armed men, led by Communists, who defy the government's authority at a number of points, particularly along the northern boundaries."
Truman added that Turkey was also facing difficulty, and asked Congress for $400 million in economic aid to Greece and Turkey, and for America civilian and military to be sent to the two countries.

In his closing statements, Truman said, "The free peoples of the world look to us for support in maintaining their freedoms." That was the crux of what would become known as the Truman Doctrine, in which the United States would work to prevent the spread of Communism. The Cold War, the struggle between the Soviet Union and Communism on one side and the United States, its allies, and capitalism on the other, had begun. Although it never erupted into a shooting war between the two sides, the Cold War would consume billions of dollars in defense spending, lead to worldwide tension, the creation of the North Atlantic Treaty Organization and the Warsaw Pact and would last until the fall of the Soviet Union in the early 1990s.

LEVITTOWN

The Great Depression had ended, millions of men and women had returned from military service, and the G.I. Bill provided vast reserves of money for their education and housing. Then the chance intersection of a visionary building company with a tiny worm combined to reshape and redefine American housing forever in the form of Levittown.

The story of Levittown began in 1941, when Nassau County, New York's potato farms were attacked by a worm known as the Golden Nematode. Despite having a name better suited to a rock band or fairy tale, the nematode devastated the potato crop and the potato farmers. A real estate investor named Abraham Levitt saw a bargain in one former potato field and bought it on the cheap.

During the war, Levitt and his sons Alfred and William built houses for shipyard workers as Levitt & Sons in Norfolk, Virginia. The war meant time was of the essence, and Levitt & Sons became proficient in quickly turning out houses.

When the war ended and the post-war housing shortage began, the company subdivided the former potato farm into small lots suitable for new homes. The homes were to be mass-produced, uniform in design, close together and, most importantly, affordable.

Using the techniques they'd learned during the war, Levitt & Sons began turning out houses at a breakneck pace, sometimes as many as thirty a day. Demand was so great that the company decided to build four thousand more houses. Although the first houses were rentals, in 1949 the company began selling houses for $7,990. A $90 deposit and monthly payments of $58 put new homeowners in an eight-hundred-square-foot ranch house with stove and refrigerator.

The fame of Levittown put William Levitt on the cover of *Time* magazine in 1950. By 1951, the company had built 17,447 houses on the former potato field, and had inspired the construction of countless subdivisions across the country.

FIFTIES TV

Although electronic television had been invented in the 1920s, it wasn't until the 1950s that the flickering eye really became a standard part of American life. Delivery of entertainment right into the home was the perfect addition to a nation enjoying a postwar economic boom.

One of the biggest American television stars of the 1950s actually got his television start in 1948. Milton Berle had hosted *The Texaco Star Theater* on radio, and when the show added a television version in 1948, he was hired as a one of several rotating hosts for the show. Berle was soon named permanent host of the show, which became the first incarnation of "must-see TV" with its blend of broad humor and variety acts. Ed McMahon once remarked of Berle's show, "There was a time ... when people didn't go out of their house on Tuesday night at 8 o'clock because Milton Berle was on."

In 1951, CBS began broadcasting the situation comedy *I Love Lucy*, starring Lucille Ball. Ball had been a successful movie actress, and had starred on the radio comedy *My Favorite Husband*. But when she took on the role of ditzy redhead Lucy Ricardo, she stepped into television history. The show quickly jumped to number one in the ratings, and was at the top for four of its six years. In 1953, 44 million Americans watched the episode in which Lucy gave birth to her son, Little Ricky.

EXTRA CREDIT: President Eisenhower was initially named after his father, David Dwight Eisenhower. However, the two men tired of being confused with the other, so Eisenhower decided to call himself Dwight David instead.

STATE ORDER TIMELINE

Sure, the U.S. Mint released all those state quarters in the order of each state's statehood, but who wants to line up fifty quarters as a reference? Use this handy list instead, with the order and date of statehood.

Delaware—December 7, 1787
Pennsylvania—December 12, 1787
New Jersey—December 18, 1787
Georgia—January 2, 1788
Connecticut—January 9, 1788
Massachusetts—February 6, 1788
Maryland—April 28, 1788
South Carolina—May 23, 1788
New Hampshire—June 21, 1788
Virginia—June 25, 1788
New York—July 26, 1788
North Carolina—November 21, 1789
Rhode Island—May 29, 1790
Vermont—March 4, 1791
Kentucky—June 1, 1792
Tennessee—June 1, 1796
Ohio—March 1, 1803
Louisiana—April 30, 1812
Indiana—December 11, 1816
Mississippi—December 10, 1817
Illinois—December 3, 1818
Alabama—December 14, 1819
Maine—March 15, 1820
Missouri—August 10, 1821
Arkansas—June 15, 1836
Michigan—January 26, 1837
Florida—March 3, 1845
Texas—December 29, 1845
Iowa—December 28, 1846
Wisconsin—May 29, 1848

California—September 9, 1850
Minnesota—May 11, 1858
Oregon—February 14, 1859
Kansas—January 29, 1861
West Virginia—June 20, 1863
Nevada—October 31, 1864
Nebraska—March 1, 1867
Colorado—August 1, 1876
North Dakota—November 2, 1889
South Dakota—November 2, 1889
Montana—November 8, 1889
Washington—November 11, 1889
Idaho—July 3, 1890
Wyoming—July 10, 1890
Utah—January 4, 1896
Oklahoma—November 16, 1907
New Mexico—January 6, 1912
Arizona—February 14, 1912
Alaska—January 3, 1959
Hawaii—August 21, 1959

Card Sharks and Link Lovers

During their two-term stay at the White House, Dwight and
Mamie Eisenhower were obsessed with playing cards. In
fact, they would regularly fly friends in to Washington, D.C.,
to make sure they had enough gamers for bridge night.
Their addiction, however, never matched Old Ike's
obsession with hitting the links. During his two-term
presidency, he spent an incredible 150 days a year playin g
golf and even had a putting green built on the White
House lawn.

STATE TRIVIA

Admit it: You only memorized those state facts to get out of tenth grade civics, then you immediately consigned them to the nether regions of your brain, right next to the lyrics to the *Gilligan's Island* theme song and maybe the ideal gas law. But you never know when an offspring or compatriot might ask you about state trivia, so here's some mental ammunition for you.

Largest state: Everything might be bigger in Texas, but that claim doesn't extend to total area. Texas covers about 268,581 square miles, Alaska 663,267. Just don't tell any Texans that.

Smallest: Rhode Island covers only 1,214 square miles, or what a Texans call a backyard. (Alaskans call it a foyer.) Rhode Islanders feel better if you also point out that their state has the longest official name: State of Rhode Island and Providence Plantations.

Most counties: Here's where Texas takes the title. The Lone Star State has 254 counties, a roster that includes Crockett, Throckmorton, Jim Hogg, and Deaf Smith counties. Georgia comes in second, with 159 counties, none named Deaf Smith.

Fewest counties: Some sources say that belongs to Delaware, with a total of three: New Castle, Kent, and Sussex. But those sources are wrong, because zero is less than three, and two states have no counties. Alaska is divided into sixteen boroughs and eleven geographical census areas (but no counties), while Louisiana has sixty-four parishes (but zero counties).

Total number of states after August 21, 1959: 46. Yeah, this one's a little cutesy, but technically, Hawaii became the forty-sixth state on August 21, 1959. Four of what are generally called states are officially commonwealths. Kentucky, Massachusetts, Pennsylvania, and Virginia mess up that whole "fifty states" thing.

Total of unicameral legislatures: One. Nebraska bucks the trend of all the other states (and commonwealths) by having only one house in its legislature. Instead of a House of Representatives and a Senate, all Nebraska's legislature members are referred to as senators. The state changed from a bicameral to a unicameral legislature in 1937.

442

Largest number of legislators: 424. Nope, it's not Texas or California or New York that holds the biggest legislature title, but New Hampshire. The state that only has ten counties has four hundred representatives and twenty-four senators in its General Court of New Hampshire. About the only thing more surprising than the number of legislators is their salary: $200 a year plus mileage.

Smallest number of legislators: Forty-nine. One of the benefits of halving the size of your legislative branch is that you cut out a lot of politicians, and that's what Nebraska did in 1937 when it went to a unicameral legislature. The state slashed the number of legislators from 133 to forty-nine.

Most miles of coastline: Alaska has more coastline than all the other states combined. Bordering the Pacific and Arctic Oceans, Alaska's shore coastline totals 6,640 miles. In contrast, Hawaii's total coastline is 750 miles long, and New Hampshire's Atlantic coastline is only thirteen miles long.

Extreme eastern, western, southern, and northern points: In the entire United States, Alaska has the distinction of having the most extreme points in three of the four directions. The most northern point, of course, is a given, and so is western. Alaska also boasts the most eastern point because its Aleutian Islands stretch into the Eastern Hemisphere. Hawaii, obviously, has the most southern point.

Extreme eastern, western, southern, and northern points in the "Lower 48:" Angle, Minnesota, is the most northern point; East Cape, Florida, is the most southern; West Quoddy Head, Maine, is most eastern; and Cape Alva, Washington, is farthest west.

THE BEAT GENERATION

The combination of free time and spending money usually results in some form of rebellion, and the fifties were no exception. The Beat Generation postured itself as a free-wheeling counterpoint to what it saw as an overly straight-laced culture, and American society (and hygiene) has never been the same.

Beat Generation writer Jack Kerouac coined the term "beat" in the late 1940s to describe himself and like-minded individuals. Determining exactly what the term was derived from is difficult. Various interpretations include the beaten state of individualism in society, or being "on the beat" in a musical sense.

Whatever the derivation of the term, the rule of thumb for Beat Generation members, or beatniks, was to be interested in whatever their parents weren't. Their parents were clean-cut, so beatniks wore sloppy clothes and grew facial hair. Their parents wrote and read books that fit a classical mold, so beatniks like Kerouac, Allen Ginsberg, and William S. Burroughs wrote prose and poetry that didn't fit any mold. Ginsberg's *Howl* is a collection of poetry that includes lines like "yacketayakking screaming vomiting whispering facts and memories and anecdotes and eyeball kicks."

The problem with rebelling is that sometimes, rebellion becomes so popular it's accepted into society. That's what happened to the beatniks in 1959, when the sitcom *The Many Loves of Dobie Gillis* premiered. The show featured Maynard G. Krebs (the G stood for Walter), a young beatnik played by future Gilligan Bob Denver. Suddenly, beatniks were mainstream, and nothing takes the buzz off rebellion like being accepted.

FIFTIES CIVIL RIGHTS

The Allies had set Europe free from Nazi aggression and stopped the advancement of the Japanese in the Pacific, but at home, many Americans faced a more entrenched enemy in the form of racism. The civil rights movement that would eventually remake American society found its legs in the 1950s.

In 1955, Rosa Parks was a forty-two-year-old seamstress for the Montgomery Fair department store in Montgomery, Alabama. At the time, the Montgomery bus system was segregated. Black riders were forced to enter the bus through the front door, pay the bus driver, then exit the bus and re-enter through the back door. Black riders also had to give up their seats to white riders. On December 1, 1955, Parks was ordered to give up her seat to a white rider. She refused. Told that she would either move or be arrested, she told the driver that she would be arrested. Parks was arrested, and her arrest set off a bus boycott by black riders.

After Parks' arrest, trial and conviction, black Montgomery residents formed the Montgomery Improvement Association. The minister at Dexter Avenue Baptist Church named Martin Luther King Jr. was elected as president. With King as leader, the bus boycott lasted 382 days and ended when the U.S. Supreme Court declared bus segregation laws unconstitutional.

King was elected president of the Southern Christian Leadership Conference in 1957. For the next eleven years, King traveled the world to spread the civil rights gospel. He spoke to 250,000 in Washington, D.C., giving his historic "I Have a Dream" speech. He won the 1964 Nobel Peace Prize when he was only thirty-five.

King was assassinated on April 4, 1968, but the revolution he, Parks, and others had ignited lives on. Today, the Lorraine Motel where King was assassinated is the home of the National Civil Rights Museum.

BABY BOOMERS

Once WWII ended and the service men and women returned, Americans began to attend college, build new houses, enjoy a strong economy, check out this new "rock and roll" music that was most definitely not Glenn Miller-esque and many other activities. But mostly, they made more Americans. Americans proved to be as reproductive, post-war, as they had been productive during the war. The Baby Boom began in 1946, peaked about 1957 (4.3 million babies were born that year) and lasted through 1964. In all, more than 77 million babies were born during the Baby Boom.

Kathleen Casey-Kirschling is known as the first baby born during the Baby Boom. She was born in a Philadelphia hospital at one second past midnight on January 1, 1946.

The February 9, 1948 issue of *Time* magazine included a mention of the Baby Boom, stating, "Manufacturers of children's clothing and toys, obstetricians and hospitals are immediately affected."

They had no idea how true that statement was. When the Boomers got old enough to spend their parents money, they attracted the attention of marketers, and everything from Hula Hoops to rock and roll was pitched to them. The American economy felt the impact of millions of boomers.

That impact is still being felt, and will only increase. Casey-Kirschling became the first Baby Boomer to apply for Social Security benefits on October 15, 2007. The addition of Baby Boomers to the Social Security rolls, and the subsequent cost of providing for those boomers, has been called a "Silver Tsunami."

ROCK AND ROLL

One of the travesties of American pop culture is the location of the Rock and Roll Hall of Fame in Cleveland, Ohio. It makes as much sense as locating the Sailing Hall of Fame in Fargo, North Dakota. Sure, Cleveland was the home of Alan Freed, who popularized the term "rock and roll," but he stole that from blues musicians. Memphis, Tennessee, gave birth to rock and roll, and it should be the home of the hall, with a special satellite wing in Clarksdale, Mississippi.

Clarksdale deserves a mention because that Mississippi Delta town is the center of blues music, and rock and roll was mainly blues played up-tempo and, usually, by white musicians. Without blues, there would have been no rhythm and blues, and without rhythm and blues, there would have been no rock.

But it was in Memphis that record producer Sam Phillips turned out the first rock record, 1951's "Rocket 88," by Jackie Brenston. Phillips followed that up by launching the recording careers of Jerry Lee Lewis, Johnny Cash, Roy Orbison, Carl Perkins, Howlin' Wolf, and Elvis Presley. Phillips' Sun Records turned out seminal rock songs like Presley's "That's All Right," Carl Perkins' "Blue Suede Shoes," and Jerry Lee Lewis' "Whole Lotta Shakin' Going On."

In a 1997 interview, Phillips said of his role in rock history, "God only knows that we didn't know it would have the response that it would have. But I always knew that the rebellion of young people, which is as natural as breathing, would be a part of that breakthrough."

CRASH COURSE
KOREAN WAR

On August 10, 1945, five days before Japan's surrender ended WWII, the United States made a decision that, five years later, would lead them into another war. Japan had annexed Korea by force in 1910, then had remained there. The Soviet Union had entered the situation earlier that month, fighting with the Koreans against the Japanese in north Korea. America, concerned that the Soviets would take over all of Korea, decided to occupy the southern half of the country. Colonel Charles H. Bonesteel and Major Dean Rusk, both members of the State/War/Navy Coordinating Committee, chose the thirty-eighth parallel as the dividing line between the two areas. Joseph Stalin, then still in control of the Soviet Union, accepted their proposal.

The United States remained in Korea until 1949, backing anti-Communist and American-educated Syngman Rhee over the Communist Kil Il Sung. In 1948, the Republic of Korea, led by Rhee, emerged in the south, while the Democratic People's Republic of Korea emerged in the north.

On June 25, 1950, North Korea invaded South Korea. By June 28, the capital city of Seoul had been taken by North Korean troops. On June 30, President Harry S Truman, who had put forth the 1947 Truman Doctrine of containing Communism, gave General Douglas MacArthur the go-ahead to use ground troops in support of South Korea.

The U.S. involvement in the Korean War would last until 1953. (*M*A*S*H*, the sitcom about the Korean War, lasted eleven seasons, from 1972 to 1983, on CBS.) Almost 55,000 American soldiers lost their lives, and another 103,000 were wounded. The two Koreas remain divided, separated by a 2.5-mile-wide, 155-mile-long "demilitarized zone." North and South Korea each have more than 1 million troops amassed along the DMZ, and the U.S. has 80,000 troops in South Korea.

WHO SAID WHAT, 1950s

- "We will bury you!" Nikita Khrushchev
  Kruschev, then-premier of the Soviet Union, did make this
  statement about Communism replacing capitalism. However, he
  made it in 1956, not 1960, and at the Polish Embassy in Moscow,
  not the United Nations headquarters in New York. The November
  26, 1956, edition of *Time* quoted Kruschev: "Nikita plunged on,
  turning to the Western diplomats. "'About the capitalist states, it
  doesn't depend on you whether or not we exist. If you don't like
  us, don't accept our invitations, and don't invite us to come to see
  you. Whether you like it or not, history is on our side. We will
  bury you!'"

- "Klaatu barada nikto." Patricia Neal in *The Day the Earth Stood
  Still*
  In this 1951 science fiction film, an alien named Klaatu lands a
  spaceship in Washington and tries to convince Earthlings to
  contain their warrior ways to Earth or face the consequences.
  Klaatu is shot and killed, and his powerful robot Gort is about to
  wreak robotic havoc on Earth when Neal says her now-famous
  line, which Klaatu had told her to say before he was shot, stopping
  Gort's revenge.

- "Beep, beep, beep." Sputnik 1
  It wasn't much to listen to, but the beeps proceeding from the first
  manmade satellite sent a strong message in 1957: America was
  behind in the space race. The Soviet Union launched Sputnik on
  October 4, 1957. Spurred on by the Soviets' success, the United
  States created the National Aeronautics and Space Administration
  (NASA) in 1958.

HIPPIES

In the fifties, it was the Beat Generation that symbolized rebellion. But the beatniks were mostly a big-city, coastal phenomenon. The only beatnik most Americans ever saw came in the form of television's Maynard G. Krebs, the token beatnik of *The Many Loves of Dobie Gillis*. In the sixties, the beatniks were joined by another, more widely dispersed and larger group of rebels. The sixties was the decade of the hippies.

The hippies (and the more radical and smaller in number Yippies) became more widespread than the beatniks ever were for several reasons. The first wave of kids born during the Baby Boom entered their teens, bringing their spending money, free time and sense of entitlement with them. Televisions were in more households, and pop culture was more easily spread by pictures than it was by words. The 1960 advent of the combined oral contraceptive, better known as "The Pill," lessened the consequences of sex. And the United States was becoming involved in another war, one without a clearly defined objective. Nothing makes a counterculture more attractive than a culture that's tied up in a shooting war.

San Francisco was the center of the tie-dyed, long-haired, and laid-back hippie movement, specifically the area around the intersection of Haight and Ashbury streets. Haight-Ashbury was where rock groups like Jefferson Airplane and the Grateful Dead began to spread the hippie message of rebellion, especially against middle-class traits like corporate America, traditional clothing and haircuts, and (apparently, judging by the pictures) the use of soap. It was also the site of the Summer of Love, a gathering of some 100,000 hippies that made people across the country aware of the hippie movement.

BRITISH INVASION

What do Frank Gorshin, Fred Kaps, Wells and the Four Fays, McCall & Brill, the cast of *Oliver!* and Tessie O'Shea have in common? They all had the misfortune to be on *The Ed Sullivan Show* the night the Beatles debuted on American television. That night, they received about as much attention as one of Elvis Presley's scarf wranglers.

In early 1964, America was still reeling from the assassination of President John F. Kennedy on November 22, 1963. It needed a diversion from its troubles, and it got that diversion in the form of a musical force from across the Atlantic known as the British Invasion. That invasion began on February 9, when the Beatles played on *The Ed Sullivan Show.* John, Paul, George, and Ringo played five songs— "All My Loving," "Till There Was You," "She Loves You," "I Saw Her Standing There," and "I Want to Hold Your Hand."

The Beatles were already established stars when they obliterated Gorshin and the others. "I Want to Hold Your Hand" had reached the top of the American music charts in January. But just as Johnny Carson's *Tonight Show* would later become the place for a young comedian to make a name for himself, Sullivan's show was *the* place for Mr. and Mrs. America to get their entertainment.

The pop sounds of the Beatles were quickly joined by the equally pop Dave Clark Five ("Glad All Over," "Catch Us If You Can"), the soulful Gerry and the Pacemakers ("Don't Let the Sun Catch You Crying," "You'll Never Walk Alone") and the brooding The Animals ("House of the Rising Sun," "We Gotta Get Out Of This Place"). Later, The Who, the Rolling Stones, The Moody Blues, and a raft of other British bands would join the invasion. Every American rock singer who's ever affected a fake British accent since then owes Ed Sullivan a thank-you.

SIXTIES TELEVISION

The same current of change that made the British Invasion and the San Francisco music scene the talk of the music world swept the television world during the 1960s. An anarchic comedy show, a science-fiction juggernaut, and a black woman raising her son were symbolic of the changes television experienced.

Rowan and Martin's Laugh-In premiered on January 22, 1968 on NBC as a mid-season replacement. Hosted by dapper Dan Rowan and goofy Dick Martin, the show didn't just turn American comedy on its ear, it spun it at high revolutions, dipped it in frenzy, and slapped it with farce. *Laugh-In* packed as many as three hundred jokes and gags into a one-hour show. At that rate, not all of them could be winners. "A myth is an effeminate moth" for example. But show catchphrases like "Sock it to me!" "You bet your sweet bippy" and "Look that up in your Funk & Wagnalls" became national catchphrases, and the show's gravitational pull was strong enough to snag guest stars evangelist Billy Graham, Orson Welles, and presidential candidate Richard Nixon. (Nixon appeared on September 16, 1968, and won the presidential election November 5) *Laugh-In* ended its run in May 1973.

Star Trek was the creation of a decorated WWII pilot and former Los Angeles policeman named Gene Roddenberry. Although it only ran from September 8, 1966 to June 3, 1969, William Shatner's opening voiceover of, "Space...the final frontier" turned many a wide-eyed television watcher into a "Trekkie." The show was set in the twenty-third century, and was described by Roddenberry as " *Wagon Train* to the stars," after the fifties western series. Shatner played Captain James T. Kirk, aided by the supremely logical First Officer Commander Spock (Leonard Nimoy), and the supremely hot-headed Chief Medical Officer Dr. Leonard H. "Bones" McCoy played by DeForest Kelley. NBC originally planned to cancel the show after only two seasons, but a letter-writing campaign by fans convinced the network to run a third season. But "Trek" began running in syndication during the seventies, and became a bona fide cultural force as a result, spawning five additional TV series (including an unsuccessful animated series), ten movies and countless books, magazines, and Internet sites.

Like *Star Trek*, the situation comedy *Julia* only ran for three seasons, but its impact on television lasted far beyond its three-year run. The show was groundbreaking in several respects. Julia Baker was a single mother, not a common quantity for the times. She was the widow of a Vietnam War helicopter crash victim, at a time when America was still coming to grips with that war. And Julia was portrayed by actress Diahann Carroll, making her the first black woman to have her own show. *Julia* entered the ratings top ten during its first year and remained successful the rest of its run, and earned Carroll a Golden Globe award for Best Actress and an Emmy nomination for Best Actress. Although *Julia* never explicitly dealt with racism as subject, it did help break down racial barriers in Hollywood.

Peyton Place

When author Grace Metalious wrote a manuscript about life in a fictional New England town, she titled it *The Tree and the Blossom*. Luckily for her, the publishing company of Julian Messner, Inc., insisted on a title change. It's doubtful that *The Tree and the Blossom* would ever have become a metaphor for soap opera-style life the way that Peyton Place did.

In 1955, Metalious was a thirty-year-old mother of three living a threadbare existence in Gilmanton, New Hampshire, in a cottage she named "It'll Do." But her novel, in which the town of Peyton Place is a swirling maelstrom of sin, hypocrisy, and drama, became an instant smash when it was published in 1956, remaining atop the bestseller lists for more than a year. Americans lapped up the story of protagonist Allison MacKenzie and a cast of scandalous townspeople.

The book was made into a 1957 movie starring Lana Turner and Lee Phillips, then became a television series in 1964. The series ran for five years, airing twice a week on ABC except for the final season, when only one episode ran per week.

MOON LANDING

On March 25, 1961, newly-inaugurated President John F. Kennedy addressed a joint session of Congress. The Soviet Union had put the first man-made satellite in space in 1957, and had made Yuri Gagarin the first man to orbit the earth on April 12, 1961. America was badly lagging in the space race. Kennedy's speech dealt with more than space, touching on the condition of the dollar, the budget deficit, the North Atlantic Treaty Organization, and other issues. But it was Kennedy's remarks about space exploration that are most remembered, particularly the statement that "First, I believe that this nation should commit itself to achieving the goal, before this decade is out, of landing a man on the moon and returning him safely to the earth." It took eight frenetic years of activity, but the United States finally achieved that goal in 1969, when the Apollo 11 mission landed on the moon's surface and then returned to earth.

The Apollo program, NASA's effort to put a man on the moon, didn't start out promisingly. On January 27, 1967, three astronauts— Virgil Grissom, Edward White, and Roger Chaffee—were killed on the launchpad of Apollo 1 during a preflight test fire. Manned space missions were put on hold while the cause of the fire was investigated. Eventually, a combination of factors including combustible wiring and inadequate excape provisions was blamed for the astronauts' deaths, and changes were made to future command modules.

Apollo 7, America's next attempt at manned flight in the Apollo program, was more successful. Walter "Wally" Schirra Jr., Donn F. Eisele and Walter Cunningham blasted off on October 11, 1968, then spent eleven days in orbit before returning to earth.

The wait for another manned Apollo mission wasn't long. On December 21, Frank Borman, James A. Lovell Jr., and William A. Anders, the Apollo 8 astronauts, left earth. Three days later, they entered the moon's orbit and circled the moon for twenty hours. The astronauts also read the Book of Genesis to television viewers on earth.

Apollo 9 flew from March 3 to March 13, 1969 with astronauts James A. McDivitt, David R. Scott, and Russell L. Schweickart. From May 18 to May 26, Apollo 10 flew Thomas P. Stafford, John W.

Young, and Eugene A. Cernan to within nine miles of the moon's surface.

America reached one half of Kennedy's goal at 4:17 p.m., when Neil Armstrong landed the "Eagle" Lunar Module from Apollo 11 on the surface of the moon. Six hours later, Armstrong became the first man to set foot on the moon. He was joined by Edwin "Buzz" Aldrin Jr. Astronaut Michael Collins had stayed behind on board the command module "Columbia."

For decades, the quote Armstrong uttered when his boot touched lunar soil was reported as being, "That's one small step for man, one giant leap for mankind." That would have been an error on Armstrong's part, because the line, which Armstrong said he had thought of in the six hours between touchdown and his step, was, "That's one small step for a man, one giant leap for mankind." But in 2006, a British computer programmer named Peter Shann Ford announced that his analysis of the radio transmission from the moon showed that Armstrong had in fact said "for a man," but that the missing article "a" was drowned out by transmission static.

Armstrong and Aldrin spent twenty-one hours on the moon before returning to Columbia. The three astronauts safely splashed down in the Pacific Ocean on July 24, completing the goal Kennedy had set.

Cuban Cigar Crisis

President John F. Kennedy loved the smell and taste of Cuban cigars so much that he commissioned a friend to buy and stockpile 1,500 premium Havanas just before the signing of the Cuban Trade Embargo, legislation that would have prevented him from buying his beloved stogies in the future.

WOODSTOCK

The three-day rock festival that took place near Woodstock, New York, from August 15 to August 18, 1969, was the pinnacle of the counterculture. What was supposed to be a very large festival of 50,000 to 100,000 ended up being an epic festival of some 500,000. (No one knows exactly how many attended, since keeping an accurate count of hippies over three days is like taking a census at a hyperactive prairie dog colony.) But that countercultural high point actually took place on a dairy farm—not a pig farm, despite what the Internet might tell you—of a man described by his son as a "conservative Republican."

Officially, the festival now known as just "Woodstock" was "The Woodstock Music and Art Fair." (Despite the title, the festival was actually held in Bethel, New York, not Woodstock.) It was the brainchild of Michael Lang, Artie Kornfeld, John Roberts and Joel Rosenman. The four rented a field belonging to Max Yasgur, a successful dairy farmer and began planning their festival.

The Woodstock organizers knew they had a giant happening on their hands on the Thursday before the festival began, when so many would-be festival attendees were heading toward Bethel that traffic jams miles long had piled up. Faced with that crush of humanity, they wisely decided to waive the admission fee rather than attempt to collect.

Folk singer Richie Havens kicked off the festival Friday afternoon. He was followed by a laundry list of heavyweight acts including Janis Joplin, Creedence Clearwater Revival, The Who, Jefferson Airplane, The Band and Jimi Hendrix, who closed out the festival Sunday night with "Hey Joe." Although Woodstock was supposed to only last through Sunday, by the time Hendrix took the stage, it was Monday morning.

ALL IN THE FAMILY

In the sixties, *Rowan and Martin's Laugh-In* used quick-hitting camera shots, one-liners and an anarchic sense of humor to change the shape of American television comedy. In the seventies, *All in the Family* used a grumpy middle-aged resident of Queens, New York, named Archie Bunker to change America.

Archie lived in a house with his ditzy wife, Edith, the couple's daughter, Gloria, and Gloria's husband, Mike Stivic. The show mined humor from Archie's mangling of the English language ("Your honor, may I encroach the bench?" "Present company suspected") and his self-important and misguided words of wisdom ("Well, in the words of Harry S Truman, if it's too hot in the kitchen, stay away from the cook.")

But the true focus of the show was the contrast between the ultra-conservative Archie with the ultra-liberal Mike and Gloria.

Gloria: "Do you know that 60 percent of all deaths in America are caused by guns?"
Archie: "Would it make you feel any better, little girl, if they was pushed out of windows?"

The show pushed more buttons than a clearance at a fabrics superstore. Archie spouted every bigoted viewpoint possible, inevitably leading to a shouting match with his son-in-law. And while the two were arguing, American television was changing from pure entertainment to an inseparable combination of entertainment and agenda. It was now not only acceptable for even sitcoms to spend airtime addressing issues like racism, it was expected.

All in the Family (and a reworking of the show, *Archie Bunker's Place*) would run for 204 episodes, win nine Emmy awards and spawn the spinoffs *Maude* and *The Jeffersons*.

WHO SAID WHAT, 1960S

- "We'll win Sunday. I guarantee you." Joe Namath
  The cocky quarterback for the upstart New York Jets made this
  remark to a heckler at the Miami Touchdown Club three days
  before Super Bowl III. The Jets were champions of the American
  Football League (AFL), which merged with the National Football
  League in the late 1960s. The Jets were heavy underdogs to the
  NFL champion Baltimore Colts, but Namath backed up his
  statement, leading the Jets to a 16-7 upset of the Colts in 1969.

- "I have a dream." Martin Luther King Jr.
  Civil rights leader King made his most famous speech at the March
  for Jobs and Freedom in Washington, D.C. on August 28, 1963.
  Speaking to 200,000 on the Lincoln Memorial steps, King made a
  stirring speech that included several "I have a dream" segments,
  including, "I have a dream that my four little children will one day
  live in a nation where they will not be judged by the color of their
  skin but by the content of their character."

- "We're more popular than Jesus now." John Lennon
  Beatle Lennon made this comment to English journalist and friend
  Maureen Cleave in 1966. Lennon's statement reached America
  when *Datebook* magazine published an article that included it. Two
  Birmingham, Alabama, radio personalities named Tommy Charles
  and Doug Layton called for a boycott of the Beatles on
  Birmingham radio station WAQY. National media got wind of
  Charles's and Layton's idea, and the boycott spread. Eventually,
  both Beatles manager Brian Epstein and Lennon issued an apology
  for his comment.

CRASH COURSE

OLEG PENKOVSKY AND THE CUBAN MISSILE CRISIS

On October 15, 1962, an American U2 spy plane took pictures of nuclear missile bases being built in Cuba by the Soviet Union. The Cuban Missile Crisis had begun. President John F. Kennedy ordered a naval blockade of Cuba in order to prevent Soviet completion of the bases. The world wondered if this event would begin World War III. Thirteen days after the standoff began, it ended. America pledged not to invade Cuba, and the Soviets agreed to dismantle the missile sites. The young president had stared down the Soviet Union.

Kennedy did indeed stare down the Soviet Union. But he had help. A disenchanted Soviet military intelligence officer and spy named Oleg Penkovsky had been giving Soviet military secrets to the British and Americans since 1961. Included in Penkovsky's treasures was the knowledge that the Russians' intercontinental ballistic missiles based in the Soviet Union couldn't reach America. Armed with this knowledge, as well as the assessment of Secretary of Defense Robert McNamara, Kennedy was able to call the Soviets' bluff, avert disaster, and add to his reputation as a skilled and brave politician.

Penkovsky wasn't as lucky as Kennedy. The man now referred to as "the spy who saved the world" was arrested by KGB on October 22, 1962, the same day Kennedy gave a speech in which he stated, "It shall be the policy of this nation to regard any nuclear missile launched from Cuba against any nation in the Western Hemisphere as an attack on the United States, requiring a full retaliatory response upon the Soviet Union." Penkovsky was executed in May 1963.

JFK ASSASSINATION

It was the ultimate "Where were you?" moment in a decade that had many. The assassination of President John F. Kennedy during a November 22, 1963 visit to Dallas, Texas, drove a dagger into the heart of the innocent fifties and created the mother of all American conspiracy theories.

Kennedy was a symbol of the hopeful sixties. WWII and the Korean War were over, and U.S. involvement in the Vietnam War wasn't yet a hot-button issue. Kennedy had become America's youngest president when he won the 1960 election at the age of forty-three. He was handsome, with a beautiful fashion plate of a wife, Jacqueline, and two adorable children, John Jr. and Caroline.

The young president had a history to go with his handsomeness. He was a decorated U.S. Navy veteran of World War II. He had energy. In his inauguration speech, the charismatic Kennedy had said, "Ask not what your country can do for you—ask what you can do for your country."

But all of Kennedy's promise, and a lot of Americans' hope, ended on that November morning. Kennedy, a Democrat, had barely won the state of Texas during the 1960 election, and he wanted to shore up Democratic support in the state, as well as prepare for a 1964 re-election bid.

In Dallas, the president, his wife, Texas Governor John Connally, and Connally's wife, Nellie, were traveling in an open Lincoln convertible through a city park named Dealey Plaza. The presidential motorcade was heading to the Trade Mart, where Kennedy was to address a crowd of 2,600 guests at a luncheon.

At about 12:30 p.m., as the motorcade passed the Texas School Book Depository, a seven-story brick building, both Kennedy and Connally were shot. Connally was injured, but survived. Kennedy was hit twice, with one of the bullets striking him in the head. Secret Service Agent William Greer, the driver of the limousine, slowed the car and turned around to see what had happened. Secret Service Agent Roy Kellerman screamed at Greer, "Step on it, we're hit!"

The presidential limousine sped to Parkland Hospital. At the Trade

Mart, an announcement was made that there had been a delay, and that the guests should go ahead and eat.

At 1 p.m. Dallas time, the announcement was made that the president was dead. The luncheon attendees found out mid-meal.

Vice President Lyndon B. Johnson, who had been riding in the motorcade, three cars behind Kennedy, was sworn in as president aboard Air Force One. The plane was on the runway at Love Field airport in Dallas. Jacqueline Kennedy was one of the witnesses to the swearing-in. She still wore the blood-stained clothes she had been wearing when her husband was shot. Air Force One departed for Washington seven minutes later.

The official government investigation into the assassination, commonly called the Warren Commission after Chief Justice of the United States Earl Warren, who led the investigation, concluded that former U.S. Marine Lee Harvey Oswald had been the lone gunman. Oswald had been working at the Book Depository the day of the shooting, and was arrested for killing J. D. Tippit, a Dallas Police Department officer, shortly after the Kennedy shooting. Oswald was later accused of assassinating the president, but on November 24, while being transported from police headquarters to the county jail, Oswald was shot and killed by Dallas nightclub owner Jack Ruby while television camera broadcast the event to the nation.

The sixties would hold more tragedy for the Kennedy family. On June 5, 1968, Robert Kennedy, John's brother, was shot and killed by an assassin in Los Angeles.

Inquiring Photographers Want to Know

Jacqueline Lee Bouvier, future wife of President John F. Kennedy, once won first place in a *Vogue* magazine Prix de Paris contest, in which she submitted a composition and was quizzed in an interview with the publication's editors. However, instead of accepting their offer to work for the magazine, she accepted a job at the *Washingon Times Herald*, where she put together the "Inquiring Photographer" column for $42.50 per week.

CRASH COURSE
MLK ASSASSINATION

Frank Holloman, then director of Memphis police and fire departments, made the announcement: "I and all the citizens of Memphis regret the murder of Dr. King and all resources at our and the state's command will be used to apprehend the person or persons responsible." It was April 4, 1968, and the Reverend Martin Luther King Jr., in Memphis to lead a protest march supporting striking garbage workers, was dead. The civil rights movement had lost a leader, but gained an icon.

King had first come to prominence as a civil rights leader during the Montgomery Bus Boycott that began in December 1955, lasted 382 days and ended when the U.S. Supreme Court declared bus segregation laws illegal. He was elected president of the Southern Christian Leadership Conference in 1957, named *Time* magazine's Man of the Year in 1963, and won the Nobel Peace Prize in 1964.

On April 3, King had spoken at Memphis' Mason Temple, telling the crowd that he had seen the promised land, then going on to say, "I may not get there with you. But I want you to know tonight that we as a people will get to the promised land."

King and some associates were staying at the Lorraine Motel in Memphis. A famous Associated Press photograph shows Hosea Williams, Jesse Jackson, King, and Ralph Abernathy standing on the hotel balcony. As the party was leaving the motel at 6 p.m. April 4 to go to dinner, a bullet from a .30-caliber rifle struck King, severing his jugular vein and spine. He was rushed to St. Joseph's Hospital, where he was prononounced dead at 7 p.m.

VIETNAM WAR, PART 1

In 1941, political decisions in Asia led to the United States' involvement in a war. That May, Vietnamese communist Ho Chi Minh returned to his native land for the first time in thirty years and organized the Viet Minh, the League for the Independence of Vietnam. Ho's return set in motion a conflict that would eventually cost almost 58,000 American lives.

Vietnam had been part of French Indochina (along with Cambodia and Laos) since the 1880s. In 1940, Japan invaded and occupied French Indochina, spurring the creation of the Viet Minh in 1941. At first, the goals of the United States and the Viet Minh were at least partially the same. Both wanted Japanese forces removed from Vietnam. To that end, the Office of Strategic Services (the forerunner of the Central Intelligence Agency) worked together, and Ho was even made a special agent of the OSS.

The conflict between the United States and Ho began after WWII ended. In 1945, Ho declared that Vietnam was independent, and called it the Democratic Republic of Vietnam. The French and the Viet Minh would battle for control of the country until 1954, when the Viet Minh defeated French forces at the Battle of Dien Bien Phu on May 7. Some 2,200 French died in the battle, along with two Americans. Wallace Buford and James "Earthquake McGoon" McGovern Jr. were two civilian pilots taking part in efforts to resupply the French garrison when they were shot down. They were the first Americans killed in the fighting that would eventually become known as the Vietnam War.

Representatives from France, the Soviet Union, the People's Republic of China, Vietnam, and other countries then crafted the Geneva Accords, which specified the terms of France's withdrawal and dealt with the future of Vietnam. Like Korea, Vietnam was split into two separate countries, with the north Communist and the south non-communist.

France was now out of the picture, but the wheels were in motion for America to enter. One month before Dien Bien Phu fell, President Dwight D. Eisenhower had given his "Domino Theory" speech. Eisenhower said, "You have a row of dominoes set up. You knock over the first one, and what will happen to the last one is the certainty that it will go over very quickly." For Eisenhower, Vietnam was the first domino in what could be a row of countries that would turn Communist.

In 1959, North Vietnam began using the Ho Chi Minh Trail (actually a sprawling web of trails, paths, and roads) to infiltrate South Vietnam. The first American military deaths occurred when Major Dale R. Buis and Master Sergeant Chester M. Ovnand were killed by North Vietnamese guerillas.

Five years later, on August 2, 1964, the destroyer *U.S.S. Maddox* was fired on by North Vietnamese gunboats in the Gulf of Tonkin, off the coast of Vietnam. Two days later, the *Maddox* and another ship, the *U.S.S. Turner Joy*, reported that they were fired on by North Vietnamese boats. (Documents released by the National Security Agency in 2005 quote NSA historian Robert Hanyok, who stated that the attacks never happened. The NSA goes on to state, "This article does not dispute Mr. Hanyok's ultimate conclusion—an attack did not occur.")

The night of August 4, President Lyndon B. Johnson appeared on television to speak about the Gulf of Tonkin incidents. On August 7, Congress passed the Gulf of Tonkin Resolution, which authorized Johnson to take "all necessary steps" to protect the United States and its allies. For the United States, the Vietnam War now began in earnest.

White Supremacy Stupidity

Once engaged to the daughter of a Texas Ku Klux Klan leader, Lyndon B. Johnson called off the wedding when he found out his future father-in-law called his family a bunch of "shiftless dirt farmers and grubby politicians." "None of them will ever amount to a damn," he said, unaware that Johnson would one day become vice president under John F. Kennedy and later the thirty-sixth president of the United States.

PRESIDENTIAL BIOS 6

John F. Kennedy, 1961–1963

When he took office at 43, Kennedy became the youngest president in history, as well as the first Roman Catholic to hold the office. A decorated World War II veteran who had also won a Pulitzer Prize for his book *Profiles in Courage*, Kennedy faced down the Soviet Union in the Cuban Missile Crisis of 1962, persuading them to cease the construction of ballistic missile bases in Cuba. He was assassinated on November 22, 1963, while visiting Dallas, Texas.

Lyndon B. Johnson, 1963–1969

Johnson had the delicate and demanding task of taking over as president following Kennedy's assassination. The cagey Texan wisely stuck to the course Kennedy had been following, including a civil rights bill and a tax cut. Johnson won re-election in 1964, then oversaw enactment of the Medicare program and continued civil rights legislation. But he was also burdened by the ongoing conflict in Vietnam. In 1968, with the war increasingly unpopular, Johnson declined to run for reelection.

Richard Nixon, 1969–1974

Nixon, who had served as vice president under Eisenhower, barely missed out on the presidency in 1960, losing to JFK by just 118,000 votes. He won the office in 1968, defeating Hubert Humphrey. He became an active international president, visiting China and Russia and crafting a nuclear-weapons treaty with Russia in 1972. His administration ended America's involvement in Vietnam in 1973. But Nixon's tenure will always be remembered for the Watergate scandal, in which members of the Committee to Re-elect the President had broken into Democratic National Committee offices in the Watergate complex in 1972. Because of the scandal, Nixon became the only president to resign while in office on August 9, 1974.

Gerald R. Ford, 1974-77

Ford became Nixon's vice president on December 6, 1973, after his confirmation by Congress. He had been chosen by Nixon to replace the departing Spiro Agnew, who had resigned due to an income tax scandal. Just eight months later, Ford was sworn in to replace Nixon, declaring, "My fellow Americans, our long national nightmare is over." Ford's tenure was marked by his pardoning of Nixon shortly after taking office, a move that instantly earned him the scorn of many. Ford survived two assassination attempts (one by former Manson family member Lynette "Squeaky" Fromme) to run for the presidency in 1976, but lost to Jimmy Carter.

Jimmy Carter, 1977–1981

Despite Ford having the stigma of being associated with the Nixon presidency, Carter only defeated Ford by 1.6 million votes, or 50.1 percent to 48 percent of the popular votes. During his administration, he oversaw the Camp David Accords between Israel and Egypt and established U.S. diplomatic relations with the People's Republic of China. Carter ran for re-election in 1980, but, saddled with the Iran hostage crisis and a weak American economy, lost to Ronald Reagan.

Not Just Peanuts

Jimmy Carter may have made a fortune working on the family peanut farm in Georgia, but he had other qualifications, too. During his campaign, Carter felt the need to plead with America (inconspicuously, or course) to consider the fact that he did have talents other than the ones related to his homegrown farmboy image. He passed out a T-shirt featuring his face and the line "Not Just Peanuts" to prove his point.

OPERATION PAPERCLIP

After Neil Armstrong became the first human to set foot on the moon on July 21, 1969, a jubilant group of Huntsville, Alabama, city officials hoisted Wernher von Braun on their shoulders at a celebration in front of the Madison County Courthouse. Von Braun, the director of Marshall Space Flight Center in Huntsville, was one of about 500 German scientists who had been working on V-2 rocket development when they surrendered to American forces in 1945. Under the auspices of a government operation dubbed Project Paperclip, von Braun and his rocket team were brought from Germany to Fort Bliss, Texas, to develop ballistic missiles under the auspices of the U.S. Army. Five years later, the scientists were moved to Huntsville. In 1960, von Braun and company became part of the new organization known as NASA, and were tasked with building the Saturn rockets that would eventually put man on the moon.

But von Braun and his fellow scientists wouldn't have come to America without the intervention of an American Army officer. Major Robert Staver deserved a shoulder ride of his own.

Staver's role in space-exploration history began in 1945. Germany's war effort was dying, and although war had made the two countries allies, both America and the Soviet Union had begun efforts to harvest for themselves the tremendous brainpower that had been concentrated in Germany. Staver, who had earned an engineering degree at Stanford before the war, was given the job of locating the German rocketeers who had developed the V-2 rockets that had been launched toward western Europe.

The first V-2 engineer Staver located was Karl Otto Fleischer, followed by Walther Riedel, who had been the chief designer at the German rocket research facility at Peenemünde, on the Baltic Coast. Riedel urged Staver to remove the leading V-2 engineers and bring them to America.

Von Braun and some one hundred Peenemünde scientists fled the rocket facility and headed south to Bavaria. There, von Braun sent his brother Magnus on a bicycle to tell the Americans the scientists were ready to surrender.

Now, America had the scientists, but they needed the scientists' documentation. They had been hidden, on von Braun's instructions, in an abandoned mine near Nordhausen. Staver tricked Fleischer into revealing the documents' location by telling him von Braun wanted the Americans to know where they were. On May 27, Staver found the documents.

But Staver's ordeal wasn't over yet. The mine was located in an area that was to be under British control, starting May 27. England was an ally, but these were potentially world-changing documents. Better to evaluate them first, then decide whether or not to share them with an ally. Staver and his men had to get the documents out.

Staver accomplished his mission. In just six days, he and his men loaded out fourteen tons of documents, just ahead of the British.

The success of Operation Paperclip meant that America, not the Soviet Union, was the beneficiary of the German's rocket efforts. Without Staver's efforts, America might never have found the Peenemünde documents, von Braun and his team might never have come to Huntsville, and the Soviet Union could have been the first nation to put a man on the moon.

Straight from the AP (Annoying Press, That Is)

Lyndon B. Johnson wasn't going to put up with any crap from nosy members of the press looking to pry into his personal life and political agenda. When a reporter once asked a question Johnson didn't feel like answering, he replied, "Why do you come and ask me, the leader of the Western world, a chicken-shit question like that?"

VIETNAM WAR, PART 2

President Lyndon B. Johnson won reelection in 1964, soundly thrashing Republican candidate Barry Goldwater. His inauguration took place on January 20, 1965. Seven days later, he receives a memo from National Security Advisor McGeorge Bundy and Defense Secretary Robert McNamara. In the memo, Bundy and McNamara tell Johnson that American efforts in Vietnam are not succeeding, and that the U.S. should either increase its efforts or withdraw.

On February 24, the United States began Operation Rolling Thunder, a bombing campaign against North Vietnam that would last until October 1968. On March 8, 3,500 Marines landed at Da Nang, Vietnam, joining the 23,000 American military advisors already there.

President Johnson gave his first major speech on the war on April 7, at Johns Hopkins University in Baltimore, Maryland. Known as the "Peace Without Conquest" speech, it includes the lines,

- "Tonight Americans and Asians are dying for a world where each people may choose its own path to change."

- "This is the principle for which our ancestors fought in the valleys of Pennsylvania. It is the principle for which our sons fight tonight in the jungles of Vietnam."

- "Vietnam is far away from this quiet campus. We have no territory there, nor do we seek any. The war is dirty and brutal and difficult. And some four hundred young men, born into an America that is bursting with opportunity and promise, have ended their lives on Vietnam's steaming soil."

Johnson went on to announce plans for a $1 billion development program in Vietnam and unconditional discussions with North Vietnam if they would stop their movement on South Vietnam. After the speech, while making the short flight back to Washington, Johnson remarked that "...old Ho [Chi Minh] can't turn me down." Johnson was wrong. Ho's goal was a Communist, united Vietnam, not a development program. He rejected Johnson's offer the next day.

In July, Johnson announced that he would be sending an additional forty-four combat battalions to Vietnam. The number of U.S. military personnel would now total 125,000. By the end of 1965, that number would reach 200,000.

As America's military efforts continued, public support for the war waned. Protests against U.S. involvement were commonplace. In 1966, Arkansas Senator J. William Fulbright published *Arrogance of Power*, a book critical of American involvement in the war. In it, Fulbright wrote, "The cause of our difficulties in southeast Asia is not a deficiency of power but an excess of the wrong kind of power which results in a feeling of impotence when it fails to achieve its desired ends. We are still acting like boy scouts dragging reluctant old ladies across the streets they do not want to cross."

The turning point of the war came on January 30, 1968. A ceasefire had been called in honor of Tet, the Vietnamese celebration of the lunar new year. But an estimated 80,000 North Vietnamese simultaneously attacked some one hundred cities and military installations in South Vietnam. Communist forces occupied the U.S. embassy in Saigon for eight hours before they were repelled by U.S. soldiers.

Although some locations were retaken by U.S. and South Vietnamese forces quickly, other areas took weeks to retake. During the fighting, the United Stesand South Vietnamese lost more than 3,000 men, while North Vietnamese lost an estimated 40,000 men.

The Tet Offensive was a military loss for the North Vietnamese. But it was a psychological victory. The American public, which had watched the Saigon fighting on television, largely turned against the war.

On March 31, Johnson announced that he would not seek reelection. The Vietnam War would become the next president's problem.

Hands-on History
Seventies Fads

Picking cheesy fads to represent the seventies is a hard task. There are just so many options. There was macramé, in which millions of homes were "decorated" by knotted monstrosities holding spider plants. There was harvest gold and avocado green, two colors that were so ubiquitous they appeared to have been mandated by federal law. And streaking made running around nude fashionable, even though not everybody looks good naked.

The Pet Rock was the brainchild of a California (of course) advertising executive named Gary Dahl. In 1975, Dahl and his friends were complaining about the high cost of having pets, when Dahl remarked that his pet was inexpensive, since it was a rock. A light went off in Dahl's head. A very stupid, but lucrative, light. He spent months writing *The Pet Rock Care and Training Manual*, then began selling Pet Rocks, manual included, in a box, for $5. He sold 1.5 million in five months, and probably hasn't stopped grinning since.

Have you ever wanted to know what your mood was, but had no way of determining it? Neither has anybody else, ever, but that didn't stop Americans from buying millions of mood rings during the mid-1970s. The rings were just cheap jewelry with liquid crystals that reacted to changes in body temperature. A blue reading on your ring was supposed to mean you were happy, but it could also mean you'd worked up a sweat pushing your Chevrolet Vega to the shop.

Earth Shoes came in many styles, but they all had the unifying characteristic of the heel being lower than the toes, or a "negative heel." This was supposed to have several benefits, although nobody really knew what they were. What's scarier is that you can still buy Earth Shoes. (Mood ring not included.)

PUNK AND DISCO

Several music trends came and went in the seventies. Peter Frampton made live albums and creepy talk box sounds trendy. Progressive rock like King Crimson and Yes made pretension cool to millions of would-be rock snobs. But the seventies' main musical forces were the polar opposites of disco and punk.

Disco can be summed up in one image: John Travolta as *Saturday Night Fever*'s white leisure suit-clad Tony Manero underneath a glittering disco ball, glaring sultriness at the camera. But it's his pose that sells the image. Right leg far in front of the left, he thrusts his right arm into the air while pointing up with his index finger. It's not so much dancing as it is posing as dancing. And for most of America, that was disco.

The disco-themed *Fever* was released in 1977, and overnight made disco a craze. Anywhere two dance partners and a disk jockey got together became a disco, spinning airy confections of repetitive music that anybody could dance to. Not everybody could dance well to disco, but it was the seventies and nobody cared.

The counterpoint to the fluffiness of the Bee Gees, Donna Summer, and K.C. and the Sunshine Band came in the form of four surly Englishmen who weren't so much musicians as they were an upraised finger. Johnny Rotten, Sid Vicious, Steve Jones, and Paul Cook called themselves the Sex Pistols. The band only released one album, "Never Mind the Bollocks, Here's the Sex Pistols." They toured the United States for just two weeks in January 1978. While they were by no means the first punk band, or the best, the Pistols were for punk what the Bee Gees were for disco. When Middle America heard "punk," the mental image that symbolized frenetic pacing and a distaste for harmony for them was the Pistols.

1973 Oil Crisis

In 1973, an embargo against the United States by the Organization of Petroleum Exporting Countries (OPEC) caused long lines at gas pumps and a major energy crisis for America. Only it didn't. The true story of the 1973 Oil Crisis actually involves Richard Nixon and the television series *Bonanza*.

Faced with rising inflationary pressure in 1971, President Nixon met with advisors at the presidential retreat at Camp David, Maryland. During three days of weekend meetings from August 13 to August 15, Nixon and his team crafted his New Economic Policy, which called for a ninety-day freeze on wages and prices, a 10 percent import tax on many goods as well as repeal of excise taxes and other tax breaks to stabilize the economy.

The decision had been made, but now Nixon had to tell the country. And Sunday night was when NBC aired the blockbuster Western series *Bonanza*. Nixon didn't want to interrupt the show, but his advisors convinced him he needed to announce the policy as soon as possible.

Nixon got lucky. The American public liked the concept, and Wall Street jumped on the news. But the program's benefits were shortlived and inflation returned to the American economy.

OPEC is blamed for the shortages because in October 1973, it imposed an embargo on the U.S. and other allies of Israel, which was fighting with Syrian and Egyptian forces. But Nixon's 1971 price controls were the real reason for the shortages. With the price of oil artificially limited, consumption went up and supplies began drying up. Then OPEC further limited supplies by their embargo, and thus got the blame for the shortages.

In a 2002 *Wall Street Journal* article, authors Jerry Taylor and Peter Van Doren quoted Saudi oil minister Sheikh Yamani, who said the embargo "did not imply that we could reduce imports to the United States ... the world is really just one market. So the embargo was more symbolic than anything else."

PATTY HEARST

The main thing on America's minds on April 15, 1974, was the same thing it was every April 15—paying income taxes. But the news from San Francisco, California, was enough to shock even the most harried taxpayer from his financial plight. Patricia Hearst, daughter of publishing heir Randolph Hearst, who had been kidnapped on February 4, was photographed holding a gun as part of a bank robbery.

Hearst's saga began on February 4, when three men had broken into her Berkeley, California apartment and kidnapped the nineteen-year-old college student. Two days after the kidnapping, radion station KPFA received a letter from a group calling itself the Symbionese Liberation Army (SLA). The letter said that the SLA had "served an arrest warrant" on Hearst, and included her credit card.

On February 12, KPFA received a tape of Hearst telling her parents she was alright. In April, radio station KSAN received a tape in which Hearts swore her allegiance to the SLA and had taken the name "Tania." Hearst was then photographed robbing the bank on April 15.

A year and six days after the 1974 bank robbery, Hearst took part in another one. The SLA robbed a bank in Carmichael, California. During the robbery, a bystander was killed by SLA member Emily Harris.

Hearst was arrested in September in San Francisco. During her 1976 trial, Hearst was represented by famed attorney F. Lee Bailey, who argued that Hearst had been abused and brainwashed by the SLA. Hearst was found guilty of armed bank robbery and sentenced to seven years in prison, although she served less than two years before President Jimmy Carter commuted her sentence.

WALT DISNEY WORLD

When entertainment giant Walt Disney opened California's Disneyland on July 18, 1955, he proved that the Disney magic could be transferred from movies and television to the real world. But the perfectionist Disney had made one mistake. While the park was a smash (after a bumpy patch when it first opened), its four hundred acres were surrounded by plain old property, which could be developed by plain old developers. Disneyland was soon surrounded by developments cashing in on the park's pull and fouling up the Disney aura. There would be no such mistake when the Walt Disney Company built a second park in Florida. In fact, Walt Disney World, which opened in central Florida in 1971, is actually the center of a quasi-state known as the Reedy Creek Improvement District.

In the early sixties, the Disney Company began surreptitiously buying up 28,000 acres of Florida land. The company then went to the Florida Legislature and expressed its desire to develop the land, albeit with some autonomous powers. In 1967, the Legislature created the RCID. Disney had its autonomy.

Disney owns a vast majority of the district's 25,000 acres. Among a long list of services and functions, the district is responsible for providing roads and bridges, fire protection, emergency medical services, utilities, and mosquito control. In his book *Married to the Mouse: Walt Disney World and Orlando*, author Richard E. Foglesong called the RCID "the governmental arm of the Disney Co."

The Orlando Sentinel says the RCID "has powers typically reserved for city and county governments, such as the ability to regulate building codes, issue bonds and even levy property taxes."

Most visitors to Walt Disney World don't know about the RCID, but they also don't notice any urban sprawl around the Disney parks. Walt made sure of that.

VIETNAM WAR, PART 3

In the seventies, as America grew steadily more disenchanted with the war, Nixon was under increasing pressure to achieve the "peace with honor" that he had promised. The United States and the North Vietnamese had begun negotiations in 1968, while Johnson was still in office, but little progress was made. In addition to the public talks, Nixon's national security advisor Henry Kissinger had secretly begun negotiating with North Vietnam's Le Duc Tho in 1970. Again, there was little progress.

Tensions between the United States and the North Vietnamese increased in March 1972, when the North Vietnamese began the Easter Offensive. Some 200,000 forces under General Vo Nguyen Giap attempt to take over South Vietnam. The United States responded with massive air bombardment of North Vietnamese positions.

In October, the two sides reached a peace agreement. A cease-fire was to begin twenty-four hours after the agreement was signed. But the peace process was sidelined again, this time by America's ally. South Vietnamese President Nguyen Van Thieu protested the fact that the agreement allowed thousands of North Vietnamese soldiers to remain in South Vietnam. The talks collapsed in December.

Nixon reacted with force. On December 18, the United States began Operation Linebacker II. For eleven days and nights, American planes dropped more than 35,000 tons of explosives on North Vietnamese positions.

North Vietnam signaled its willingness to negotiate on December 26, and agreed to meet with the United States and South Vietnam in January. The Paris peace talks resumed on January 8, 1973. A new peace agreement, which was little changed from the previous one, was signed on January 27. For America, the war was over. North and South Vietnam would continue fighting until April 30, 1975, when the North captured the South Vietnam capital of Saigon. If the nation building process is taken into account, fighting did not stop until after the nations merged into the Socialist Republic of Vietnam on July 2, 1976.

American involvement in Vietnam began in 1945 and lasted thirty-eight years. In all, 58,000 Americans lost their lives in the conflict.

WATERGATE

Before adding the suffix "gate" to any term became an indicator for scandal, Watergate was just a Washington, D.C., complex of buildings that held offices, hotel rooms, and apartments. But that changed forever on Sunday, June 18, 1972, when *The Washington Post* ran the headline "Five Held in Plot to Bug Democratic Offices Here." That story ran at the bottom of page one, but the scandal it heralded would become the top story nationwide, and would result in a president resigning from office.

The story began on May 28 of that year, when five men working for the Committee to Re-elect the President (CRP, although it became known as "CREEP") broke into the national headquarters of the Democratic National Committee and installed electronic spying devices, or "bugs." The five returned to the DNC offices that June to adjust the devices. At 2:30 a.m. on June 17th, they were arrested.

Although the *Post* break-in story that ran the next day was written by Alfred E. Lewis, Bob Woodward, and Carl Bernstein, two young reporters at the *Post*, were assigned to investigate the story. The trail they followed began leading toward the Nixon White House. One of the burglars had received $25,000 from the CRP. The five burglars were indicted, along with former White House staff members E. Howard Hunt and G. Gordon Liddy. The FBI linked the break-in to the CRP.

Despite the trail, Nixon won re-election in a landslide in November, crushing the Democratic nominee, George McGovern, by more than 20 percent. But things started unraveling for Nixon in January 1973.

Hunt, a former CIA spy, plead guilty to six counts of burglary and wiretapping. Liddy and James W. McCord Jr., another former Nixon aide, were convicted of conspiracy, burglary, and wiretapping.

In April, Nixon fired White House counsel John Dean. Nixon had hired Dean to investigate the scandal, but Dean had begun cooperating with prosecutors. In addition to Dean's firing, advisors H. R. Haldeman and John D. Ehrlichman and Attorney General Richard G. Kleindienst resigned.

The Senate Watergate committee began televised hearings in May. In June, Dean testified that he told Nixon of the Watergate cover-up at least thirty-five times, and that the Nixon White House had long been involved in political espionage. The Senate committee asked for access to presidential documents in July, but Nixon refused, citing executive privilege. Former Nixon aide Alexander Butterfield testified on July 16 that Nixon had taped all conversations in his office since 1971.

Nixon's downward spiral now began in earnest. The committee and special prosecutor Archibald Cox demanded tapes and documents from the president. He refused, again claiming executive privilege. The committee subpoenaed the tapes, but Nixon continued to refuse to turn them over. Judge John Sirica then ordered Nixon to turn over some of the tapes.

In November, during a press conference at Florida's Walt Disney World, Nixon stated, "People have got to know whether or not their president is a crook. Well, I'm not a crook."

The investigation continued into 1974. In July, the Supreme Court ruled 8-0 that Nixon must surrender the subpoenaed tapes. The House Judiciary Committee passed three articles of impeachment against Nixon for obstruction of justice, abuse of power, and defiance of subpoenas.

On August 5, the White House released transcripts of conversations between Nixon and Haldeman that showed the president's obstruction of justice. Three days later, Nixon announced his resignation. He left office on August 9.

Nixon was replaced by Vice President Gerald Ford. On September 8, Ford granted Nixon a "full free and absolute" pardon.

BICENTENNIAL

In retrospect, the 1976 Bicentennial came at just about the right time. America was dealing with a scandal that had brought down a president, U.S. involvement in Vietnam had just ended, and the economy was still digging out of a recession. So throwing itself a big, red-white-and-blue party was just the thing to give the country a boost.

The Bicentennial commemorated the passage of the Declaration of Independence on July 4, 1776, but celebratory events began long before the actual bicentennial date. CBS Television began airing "Bicentennial Minutes" on July 4, 1974. The sixty-second segments aired nightly in primetime and described important events in American history. They were often narrated by movie stars like Charlton Heston, and ended on December 31, 1976.

The United States Mint released commemorative quarters, half-dollars, and dollars with special designs and the dates "1776-1976" on them. Bicentennial-themed commercial products ranged from soda bottles to candy bars. Disneyland replaced its Main Street Electrical Parade with "America on Parade," which included patriotic songs and historical figures like Betsy Ross and Benjamin Franklin. And the American Revolution Bicentennial Association even chose an official Bicentennial theme song, "Get Into America."

Praying Playboy

Jimmy Carter was open about his religious duties during his presidency, often juggling cabinet meetings with Bible studies and teaching Sunday School at First Baptist Church in Washington, D.C. For some reason, however, the evangelical Christian agreed to an interview with *Playboy* in 1976.

In his discussion with the reporter, Carter admitted that he had lust in his heart and, from time to time, felt attracted to other women. "I've looked at a lot of women with lust," he said. "This is something that God recognizes I will do ... and God forgives me for it."

SEVENTIES CARS

Sure, they look goofy now, but back in the seventies, cars like the AMC Gremlin were downright…okay, they were goofy then, too. But so was everybody and everything back then, and when everybody's goofy, it means nobody is. Or something like that. So while it's not really fair to poke fun at some of the iconic cars of the seventies, it's most definitely fun.

AMC Gremlin, 1970–1978

Ahh, the Gremlin. Where to begin? The grotesquely bobtailed vehicle was named for what Webster's defines as "a cause of error or equipment malfunction." A gremlin on an airplane wing is what drove William Shatner to craziness in that *Twilight Zone* episode. So this car was doomed from the start. It might as well have been named the Vapor Lock, or the Busted Crankshaft.

The Gremlin was AMC's attempt to beat the other American manufacturers to the subcompact market, and the company didn't care if they sacrificed things like quality, styling, and performance to do it. Which, come to think of it, were the things the other carmakers sacrificed, too. With space-age technology like a 128-horsepower engine and "three on the tree" manual transmission, the Gremlin logged a space-warping 0-to-60 time of under twelve seconds.

How quintessentially seventies was this car? In 1973, AMC released a special "Levi's" edition, including—really—a blue jean interior with copper rivets for upholstery buttons. You had to supply your own Emerson, Lake, and Palmer 8-tracks.

AMC Pacer, 1975–1980

The only car that can rival the Gremlin for sheer, unmitigated dorkiness, the Pacer looked like the answer to a question no reasonable person would ask: What if we took a fish bowl, turned it upside-down, and put wheels on it? The Pacer carried (roughly) a metric ton of glass, making it the perfect car for seventies sun worshippers who never wanted to stop working on that melanoma.

The Pacer oozed weirdness. The passenger door was four inches longer than the driver's door. (Ostensibly to allow for easier entry to the rear seats, but more likely somebody forgot to carry the "2" during design.) The car was supposed to be fuel-efficient, but, glass being heavy, that went out the window. (Bad pun intended.) And plans called for the Pacer to come with a Wankel rotary engine, but none were ever built. That's a shame, because the only way to make the Pacer more ridiculous would be to make a Wankel Pacer.

Ford Pinto, 1971–1980

This really happened: In 1968, an official memo from Ford Motor Company included calculations in which the Blue Oval guys calculated that cost of fixing a known fault on its new Pinto car—it had the nasty habit of bursting into flames when rear-ended—versus the cost of litigation over burn deaths and burn injuries if the fault was left in the car. Ford calculated 180 burn deaths at $200,000 per death, 180 serious burn injuries at $67,000 per case, and 2,100 burned vehicles at $700 per car. Total costs, which were listed as "Benefits," were $49.5 million.

Under "Costs," Ford calculated the price of fixing the cars and light trucks that would be built on the Pinto chassis. The fix cost $11 per vehicle, and 12.5 million vehicles would be built. Total cost? $137 million. That's $87.5 million more than letting the fault stay in, so Ford decided to do just that. "We cut the safety out and pass the death on to you!" So the Pinto and its sister, the Mercury Bobcat, wasn't just ugly. It was ugly *and* sinister.

CRASH COURSE
IRAN HOSTAGE CRISIS

Mohammad Reza Shah Pahlevi, then ruler of Iran, fled his country as a result of widespread rioting and unrest on January 16, 1979. The story was reported in America, but few paid very much attention to the power struggle taking place a world away from them. Many more would have paid much more attention if they'd known that the shah's fleeing would result in an American crisis.

Pahlevi had ascended to the Peacock Throne (once a literal, peacock-themed throne but later used to symbolize the ruler of Iran) in 1941. Twenty-two years later, in 1963, Pahlevi quashed an Islamic uprising and sent its leader, Ruhollah Khomeini, into exile in neighboring Iraq. Pahlevi continued to rule until 1979, but economic grumblings, revolt against heavy-handed tactics by the Pahlevi, and continued opposition from Muslim clerics led to his being overthrown in 1979. Khomeini returned to Iran in February.

In addition to being deposed, Pahlevi was also suffering from lymphatic cancer. When he left Iran, he lived in Egypt, Morocco, the Bahamas, and Mexico, then came to the United States in September 1979 for cancer treatment. In response to his entering the United States, a crowd seized the American Embassy in Tehran, Iran and took its staff hostage. The captors released some hostages, but held fifty-three. (One more was later released after developing multiple sclerosis.) In response, President Jimmy Carter stopped Iranian oil imports, froze Iranian assets and began negotiations to free the hostages.

The crisis captivated America. Continuing television coverage beamed images from Iran into homes across the country. ABC started a late-night news show that would eventually become *Nightline* to provide daily updates on the crisis.

Carter faced the dual dilemmas of an international hostage crisis and a re-election campaign. Every day that went by without resolution was another day that, rightly or wrongly, increased the view that his administration was weak or misguided.

In April, Carter approved "Desert One," a military rescue mission

that ended in failure and the deaths of eight servicemen. The failure was another black mark on Carter's efforts.

The Iranians began to soften their position following Pahlevi's death in Egypt in July, and further softened when Iraq invaded Iran on September 22. Working through Algerian intermediaries, the Carter administration began negotiations with the Iranians that month.

The change came too late for the Carter administration. In November, with the hostage crisis, inflation, and high unemployment hanging over the White House, Republican Ronald Reagan trounced Carter in the presidential election by more than 9 million votes.

Working even while preparing to leave office, Carter agreed to release $8 billion in frozen Iranian assets and grant immunity from future lawsuits relating to the situation in exchange for the hostages' release. But despite Carter's efforts to free the hostages during his administration, the actual release didn't happen until January 21, 1981, minutes after Reagan was inaugurated.

At his inaugural luncheon, Reagan gave a toast that included, "And now, to conclude the toast, with thanks to Almighty God, I have been given a tag-line, the get-off line that everyone wants for the end of a toast or a speech or anything else. Some thirty minutes ago, the planes bearing our prisoners left Iranian airspace and are now free of Iran."

Early Entrepreneur

Jimmy Carter may have been nuts about nuts, but he sometimes took the passion a bit too far. Sure he became a millionaire when he improved production at the family peanut farm in Georgia, but who would have a giant peanut-shaped balloon at his inauguration? Well, Carter did. But those who mocked his wacky escapade could learn a thing or two from the country-boy politician with a knack for making a buck. Before his peanut fame, at just nine years old, Carter bought a few bales of cotton for just five cents per pound and stored them until inflation caused the price to more than triple.

WHO SAID WHAT, 1970s

- "It was a fairly robust-looking rabbit who was swimming, apparently with no difficulty." -Jimmy Carter
  In 1979, all President Jimmy Carter wanted was a little peace and relaxation. Nothing beats fishing when it comes to quiet contemplation and blood-pressure-lowering solitude, so Carter set off in a small boat in a pond near his home in Plains, Georgia. While fishing, he noticed something coming toward him in the water. It was a rabbit. Since the presidential handbook contains nothing about dealing with waterborne rabbits, Carter improvised a reaction and splashed water at the rabbit, scaring him away.

- "We're gonna need a bigger boat." -Roy Scheider
  Scheider played Police Chief Martin Brody in the 1975 Steven Spielberg movie *Jaws*, about a ravenous great white shark that was killing people off the coast of the fictional town Amity Island. Scheider makes the remark after the shark surfaces just feet from him. *Jaws* is regarded as the first summer blockbuster movie.

- "Houston, we've had a problem." -Astronaut Jack Swigert
  Although the phrase is usually given as "Houston, we have a problem," Swigert didn't say it that way. On April 11, 1970, a fuel cell tank on the Apollo 13 Command Module *Odyssey* exploded, cutting off the main power supply. The crew—Swigert, James Lovell and Fred Haise Jr.—were forced to abort a planned moon landing and return to Earth in a Lunar Module designed to hold only two astronauts.

YUPPIES

In the eighties, Yuppies (from "Young Urban Professionals") showed that being cool doesn't mean ignoring your stock portfolio. A legion of hard-charging, upwardly mobile, and taste-conscious men and women rebelled against the rebels of previous generations and traded tie-dye for Brooks Brothers. Even former radical Jerry Rubin, one of the co-founders of the too-radical-to-be-hippies Yippies (Youth International Party), cut his hair, put on a suit and tie and became a Yuppie.

Newsweek commemorated the Yuppie when it proclaimed that 1984 was the "Year of the Yuppie." Movies like *Bright Lights, Big City* helped spread the Yuppie lifestyle. On television's *Family Ties*, Michael J. Fox played aspiring Yuppie Alex P. Keaton, proving even high-school kids could dream the Yuppie dream.

The Yuppie lifestyle began to fall from favor beginning with the 1987 stock market crash. (At least, the overt aspect of Yuppie-ness fell from favor. Folks still want to get rich today; they just don't want to appear as if they want to get rich.) In addition, the Young Urban Professionals that had led the eighties started to become less young, slowing down their drive to thrive. Still, wherever there's a college student poring over an economics textbook while simultaneously dreaming of one day strolling into a BMW dealership, the Yuppie spirit lives on.

Sworn Into the Skulls

Born in 1924 to a wealthy banker named Prescott Bush, George H. W. Bush went on to become the youngest pilot in the Navy when he was just eighteen years old. After his plane was shot down during a WWII bombing mission, Bush returned home to Connecticut and married sweetheart Barbara Pierce, who once said Bush was the first man she had ever kissed. The couple had six children (one died of leukemia at just three years old), and Bush enrolled at Yale University, where he played baseball and became a member of an elite secret society known as Skull and Bones.

RISE OF ELECTRONICS

Two devices broke open the electronics revolution in the 1980s. One, the Betamax videocassette recorder, is now a synonym for failed technology. The other, the personal computer, has become a ubiquitous part of modern life.

In 1976, the Sony Corporation began importing its Betamax videocassette recorders into the United States. Americans could now record television programs for future watching, rather than being bound to the television networks' broadcast schedules. They could also record broadcast movies, and, not surprisingly, some movie studios had a problem with that. Universal Studios and Walt Disney Productions sued Sony, claiming that the Betamax technology allowed consumers to infringe on the studios' copyrights.

The case was filed in 1976 and eventually made it to the Supreme Court, which ruled in January 1984 that taping of programs was fair use, and therefore legal. Americans could keep their VCRs, and the newfound control over their entertainment ramped up the demand for electronics in the home. (Ironically, Betamax would lose the videocassette format war to the VHS format invented by JVC.)

Personal computers began their conquest of the American home on August 12, 1981, with the release of the IBM PC. The little pioneer started with a monstrous sixteen kilobytes of memory and started at $1,565. Computers were no longer the exclusive possessions of corporations and universities, and *Time* magazine named the computer "Man of the Year" for 1982.

In 1983, personal computing took another quantum leap when Apple Computer released Lisa. The new computer's innovation came in the way users interacted with it. Where the IBM PC required clunky, unintuitive text commands, the Lisa had a GUI, or graphical user interface, that allowed users to control the computer via easily navigated icons and menus. Now, not only could the average person own a computer, he could also use it. The computer revolution had begun.

I WANT MY MTV

It's no longer a trivia fact to be proud of, since Google rendered all trivia common knowledge, but for many years, rock music fans considered it the equivalent of a password into the cool club: The Buggles' "Video Killed the Radio Star" was the first video played on MTV. And while it might come as a shock to anyone watching the network today, MTV once played nothing but videos, and in fact those videos changed American television and movies.

MTV began broadcasting at midnight on August 1, 1981. MTV co-creator John Lack said, "Ladies and gentlemen, rock and roll," then the Buggles' video rolled. Pat Benatar's "You Better Run" was the second video played, and the video revolution had begun.

The new network tapped into three lucrative aspects of American life: the love of television, the love of rock music, and the desire to be cool. Throw in true artistry in videos like Peter Gabriel's stop-motion animation for his "Sledgehammer" video, the creepy 14-minute mini-movie for Michael Jackson's "Thriller" and the computer animation for Dire Straits' "Money for Nothing" video, and the result was earth-shattering.

MTV's influence on television was exemplified by *Miami Vice*. The story of two supremely cool Miami policemen premiered in 1984 and was shot, MTV-style, with short cuts, dramatically framed shots ,and a rock soundtrack. *Vice* was a smash, and slow-paced, traditionally shot television shows and movies soon went the way of the 8-track tape.

REAGAN REVOLUTION

When Republican Ronald Reagan defeated Democrat Jimmy Carter in the 1980 presidential election, it was obvious that things were not going to be the same in America. But few people could have predicted that the election was the beginning of a revolution. The Reagan Revolution turned federal policy to the right, helped bring about the final fall of the Soviet Union, and re-energized a flagging American economy.

Tax and budget cuts were the cornerstones of Reagan's economic policy. In his first inaugural address, he had said, "In this present crisis, government is not the solution to our problem; government *is* the problem." Accordingly, once he took over the Oval Office, he began cutting back government. In the Economic Recovery Tax Act (ERTA) of 1981, personal, marginal tax rates were cut 25 percent across the board. In the Tax Reform Act of 1986, maximum marginal tax rates were lowered from 50 percent to 28 percent, beginning in 1988.

Reagan also increased the U.S. military budget by 40 percent. The combination of an expanding economy and an expanding military was noticed around the world. As economist Robert A. Mundell, winner of the 1999 Nobel Prize in Economics, noted, "The 1982-90 expansion was the second longest up to that time and, along with the arms buildup, helped to convince the leaders of the Soviet Union to leave Eastern Europe free to choose its own system."

No presidential administration is perfect, and that includes Reagan's. The federal budget deficit almost tripled under his administration, and the Iran-Contra scandal permanently scarred his legacy. But during his eight years in office, America changed from a nation seemingly stumbling in the dark (during a 1979 speech, President Carter had said, "It's clear that the true problems of our nation are much deeper—deeper than gasoline lines or energy shortages, deeper even than inflation or recession) to the one remaining world superpower.

ECONOMICS 101
REAGANOMICS

Economist Arthur Laffer sketched what would become known as the Laffer Curve on a cocktail napkin during a dinner with Donald Rumsfeld, Dick Cheney, and others in 1974. The principle behind the Laffer Curve—that a reduction in tax rates can in fact increase tax revenues—was one of the Reagan administration's economic principles.

The theory behind the curve was called "supply-side economics" (although when he was running against Reagan in 1980, George H.W. Bush had called it "voodoo economics"). Put simply, if a government taxes its citizens at zero percent, it will obviously receive zero revenue. However, if a government taxes its citizens at 100 percent, it will also collect zero revenue, since no one wants to work for no gain. The curve merely showed that in-between those two points, although not necessarily at 50 percent, there is a rate that will generate maximum revenue.

The Reagan administration wasn't even the first to use the principle. In the sixties, President Kennedy had lowered the highest federal marginal tax rate from from 91 to 70 percent, and the highest marginal corporate tax from 52 percent to 47 percent.

Reagan's tax cuts dropped the highest personal income tax rate from 70 percent to 28 percent. Even with the cuts, federal tax revenues went up from $517 billion to $1.3 trillion, and supply-side economics became as much a staple of eighties culture as skinny ties and Members Only jackets.

EXTRA CREDIT: Ronald Wilson Reagan was the oldest president inaugurated. He became president at age 69 and left office at 77 years of age. Reagan was also the first president to have been divorced.

IRAN-CONTRA

Ronald Reagan became known as the "Teflon president," because controversy slid off his reputation the way food slid off a Teflon-coated pan. And no episode demonstrated Reagan's non-stick coating like the Iran-contra Affair. The biggest political scandal since Watergate exploded while he was in office, but it had little effect on his popularity.

The story behind the scandal was a complicated one that began during Reagan's first year in the White House. In December 1981, he authorized action by the Central Intelligence Agency to support the contras, a group that was fighting a guerilla war against the leftist Sandinista government in Nicaragua. These efforts were stymied when a Democratic-controlled Congress enacted restrictions against actions in Nicaragua by the CIA or the Department of Defense.

Reagan would not be stopped. He told National Security Advisor Robert McFarlane, "I want you to do whatever you have to do to help these people keep body and soul together." The National Security Council had not been specifically prohibited from intervening in Nicaragua, so the NSC replaced the CIA in aiding the contras.

The story took another twist in 1985. Iran, which was fighting its neighbor Iraq, wanted to buy arms from the United States, in violation of a U.S. trade and arms embargo against Iran. McFarlane lobbied Reagan to okay the deal, arguing that it might improve relations between the United States and Iran, and that Iran might persuade Lebanon to release American hostages it now held. Reagan sided with McFarlane, and the United States began secretly selling arms to Iran.

On November 3, 1986, a Lebanese newspaper broke the story of the U.S.-Iran dealings. Reagan went on television and denied the allegations. A week later, he returned to television to admit that there had been arms sales, but he claimed that there had not been an arms-for-hostages deal.

The link between Iran and the contras was discovered during investigations that followed. Although Iran had paid the administration $30 million, only $12 million had been deposited. The other $18 million had been diverted by Lieutenant Colonel Oliver North of the NSC. North was also in charge of the NSC's aiding of the contras.

Just as Archibald Cox had been named to investigate the Watergate scandal, Lawrence E. Walsh was named special prosecutor to investigate the Iran-contra scandal. North testified he believed Reagan and vice president George H.W. Bush had known about the arrangement, although both men denied knowledge, and no evidence linking them to any crime was discovered.

In 1989, North was convicted on three felony charges, including altering and destroying documents related to the scandal and illegally accepting an expensive home security system. He was acquitted of nine other charges.

McFarlane attempted to commit suicide in 1987, but survived. He later pleaded guilty to withholding information from Congress, but was pardoned in 1992 by President George H.W. Bush.

Walsh's investigation lasted eight years. When it was released in 1994, one of its conclusions was, "The underlying facts of Iran/contra are that, regardless of criminality, President Reagan, the secretary of state, the secretary of defense, and the director of central intelligence and their necessary assistants committed themselves, however reluctantly, to two programs contrary to congressional policy and contrary to national policy. They skirted the law, some of them broke the law, and almost all of them tried to cover up the president's willful activities."

These Are a Few of My Favorite Things

The oldest man to ever serve as president, Ronald Reagan caused quite a stir when he announced both his guilty pleasures and his medical provisions. When he purchased a hearing aid during his White House reign, sales for the product went up a whopping 40 percent in the United States. When he joked with the press about his sweet tooth and obsession with the bowl of jelly beans in the Oval Office, sales of jelly beans also skyrocketed (some records say the White House purchased twelve tons of the candy during his term).

CHALLENGER EXPLOSION

It was a testament to the faith Americans had in the nation's space program that by 1986, sending personnel and equipment into space and back was almost routine. But that faith was severely shaken on January 28, 1986, when the space shuttle *Challenger* exploded shortly after leaving the launchpad at Cape Canaveral. All seven crew members on board were killed.

This *Challenger* mission had faced miscues and setbacks before it ever left the ground. Originally scheduled to begin January 22, the mission had been pushed back due to delays in a *Columbia* space shuttle mission that had ended on January 18. Next, bad weather at the Transoceanic Abort Landing site in Senegal, an emergency landing site, pushed the date to January 25. Bad weather at Cape Canaveral and a problem with a malfunctioning hatch sensor pushed the launch date to January 28.

Challenger was finally launched at 11:38 a.m. Eastern Standard Time. It exploded seventy-three seconds later. An investigation later revealed that the seven crew members had survived the explosion, but were killed two minutes and forty-five seconds later, when the shuttle's cabin landed, hitting the water off Cape Canaveral with a force of 200g. Astronauts Francis R. Scobee, Michael J. Smith, Ronald E. McNair, Ellison S. Onizuka, Judith A. Resnik, and Gregory B. Jarvis, as well as schoolteacher Christa McAuliffe, all died.

Investigations into the explosion revealed that the combination of a badly designed O-ring seal on the shuttle's right solid-fuel rocket and extremely cold temperatures the morning of the launch had doomed the *Challenger*. The cold had shrunk the O-ring, worsening the design flaw. During the shuttle's flight, the O-ring allowed hot gases to escape, causing the explosion.

FALL OF COMMUNISM

When President Ronald Reagan, speaking in front of the Berlin Wall's Brandenburg Gate in 1987, told Soviet Union leader Mikhail Gorbachev, "Mr. Gorbachev, open this gate. Mr. Gorbachev, tear down this wall!" the Berlin Wall actually falling seemed as likely as the Kremlin turning into a disco. But a little more than two years after Reagan made his speech, the Berlin Wall fell, taking Eastern European Communism with it.

After Germany was defeated by the Allies in World War II, the country was divided into four zones, with the United States, Great Britain, France, and the Soviet Union each controlling one zone. In addition, the city of Berlin was also divided into four sectors, each controlled by one of the Allies. In 1949, the three non-Soviet zones became the capitalist and democratic Federal Republic of Germany, or West Germany, while the Soviet-controlled zone became the communist German Democratic Republic, or East Germany. In addition, Berlin was divided into democratic West Berlin and communist East Berlin.

In 1961, East Germany and the Soviet Union erected first a barbwire fence and then a concrete wall to separate East and West Berlin. The Berlin Wall soon became a worldwide symbol for communist oppression.

But changes began to rumble through Eastern Europe in the eighties. In Poland, the anti-Communist union and social movement Solidarity began striking against the Communist government there. In the Soviet Union in 1985, Gorbachev came to power as a reformer. In early 1989, the Communist governments in Hungary and Poland began ceding power and allowing competitive elections.

The success of the reforms in other countries led East Germans to agitate for reforms of their own, and they conducted protests asking for freedom to visit the West and other rights. When the Soviet Union, which for decades had operated under the "Brezhnev Doctrine" of maintaining Communist power by force, refused to intervene in East Germany, the protestors knew their cause had hope.

Erich Honecker, the Communist leader of East Germany, was

against the reforms that were taking place in other Eastern European countries. He was removed office in October 1989.

On the night of November 9, 1989, the East German government opened its borders. Televisions around the world showed joyous residents of both East and West Berlin climbing on top of the wall and smashing it with hammers.

The fall of the Berlin Wall led to the reunification of Germany in 1990, then to revolution in the Soviet Union. The Communist Party was dissolved and the democratic Commonwealth of Independent States created. The Cold War between the Soviet Union and the United States was over.

Reagan's speech became part of history, but he was not the first American president to make a speech in front of the Berlin Wall. In 1963, President John F. Kennedy had made his "I am a Berliner" speech after visiting Checkpoint Charlie, a crossing point in the wall. An urban legend says that Kennedy mangled his German and instead of saying "I am a Berliner," he actually said, "I am a jelly doughnut." ("Berliner" being German slang for a jelly doughnut.) But a 2006 *International Herald Tribune* article quoting Heinz Weber, who translated Kennedy's speech that day in 1963, said that the doughnut story was "nonsense."

Do the Bush Thing

In 1992, President George H. W. Bush visited Japan for a state dinner with dignitaries including Japanese Prime Minister Kiichi Miyazawa. After turning white as a sheet and nearly sliding out of his seat in pain, he threw up in Miyazawa's lap. Ever since, the Japanese have honored Bush with the word *bushusuru*, which literally means "to do the Bush thing," or to vomit.

THE INTERNET

It's as crucial a part of modern life as electricity, but it wasn't all that long ago that the Internet was just a gleam in some techies' eyes. What began with a small government grant in the sixties eventually grew into a world-spanning, and world-changing, ubiquitous force. And anyone who's ever sent an e-mail or viewed a web page has a small Russian satellite to thank for it. Sputnik helped create the Internet.

In 1957, the Soviet Union launched Sputnik, the first manmade satellite. The Cold War had the world on edge, and the fact that the Soviets had begun conquering space was a frightening how-do-you-do to America. One of the nation's responses was the creation of ARPA, the Advanced Research Projects Agency of the Department of Defense, whose mission was to "assure that the U.S. maintains a lead in applying state-of-the-art technology for military capabilities and to prevent technological surprise from her adversaries." (ARPA later became DARPA, the Defense Advanced Research Projects Agency.)

Seven years after ARPA was created, in 1965, Thomas Merrill and Lawrence G. Roberts connected a computer in Massachusetts to another computer in California via a telephone line, and the wide-area computer network was born. It had been proven that computers could work with each other over long distances, and could "pool resources" between.

On December 6, 1967, the Defense Department issued a contract for "a study related to the design and construction of a computer network." The contract ran for four months and was for $19,800. Cheaply and without much notice, ARPANET was born.

Researchers at ARPA and other locations developed a "packet switching" system of transferring information. In this system, information is broken down into discrete units, each of which can be transferred over any number of different routes and then reassembled at another point. The original idea came from an Air Force project that would allows the U.S. telecommunications to continue even after a nuclear strike.

ARPA awarded another contract in 1968, this one for $563,000 to network computers at four locations (three in California and one in Utah) via what were clunkily named Interface Message Processors

(IMPs). The ARPANET had its "Mr. Watson—come here!" moment, ninety-three years after Alexander Graham Bell invented the telephone. On October 15, 1969, ARPANET transmitted its first message: "log in." It wasn't exactly quotation-book material, but it was significant.

Work on networking computers continued, both within ARPA/DARPA and outside the organization. Problems arose when different systems using different standards of transmitting data tried to communicate. Two computer scientists, Robert E. Kahn and Vinton Cerf, created TCP/IP, or Transmission Control Protocol/Internet Protocol, which allowed different networks to communicate via a common standard. Today, Cerf is often referred to as "the father of the Internet" for his work developing the protocols.

The Internet became supercharged in 1989, when computer scientist Tim Berners-Lee invented the World Wide Web. (You did know that the Internet and the Web were two things, didn't you? Quick analogy: The Internet is the truck that delivers the Web to your computer.) Berners-Lee's invention used the Internet to transport information via hypertext transfer protocol, or HTTP. Users of HTTP could create "websites" containing text, images, and eventually, sound and video. With the ramped-up impact of the Web, being online became much more attractive, and the public outside universities and organizations jumped on the Internet.

Commercial development followed, surfing the web" became a common phrase and what had started with "log in" being sent from one computer to another now allowed millions of computers to interact. All because of a Soviet satellite.

Napster

In 1998, Shawn Fanning, a college student at Northwestern University, put together a program called Napster for exchanging music files over the Internet. The program became wildly popular across the county, but was shut down in July 2001 because the recording industry was losing money. Since Napster, other peer-to-peer (P2P) programs like Gnutella and KaZaa have emerged that allow music and even movies to be traded online.

Presidential Bios 7

Ronald Reagan, 1981–1989

The Reagan administration was marked by a more conservative philosophy that cut taxes and government programs and raised defense spending. Reagan, a former actor and California governor, was shot by John Hinckley Jr. on March 30, 1981. When wife Nancy Reagan appeared at the hospital, he told her, "Honey, I forgot to duck." With his nomination of Sandra Day O'Connor in 1981, he became the first president to nominate a woman to the Supreme Court. His administration was tarred by the Iran-Contra investigations, in which money from illegal arms sales was diverted to anti-Communist rebels in Nicaragua.

George H. W. Bush, 1989–1993

Bush, a former director of the Central Intelligence Agency, served as Reagan's vice president for eight years, then defeated Democrat Michael Dukakis in the 1988 presidential election. Bush's administration ratified the START I and START II treaties that reduced strategic weapons and the defeat of Saddam Hussein's Iraqi forces in Operation Desert Storm. Bush, who had won election in 1988 by pledging, "Read my lips—no new taxes," ratified Congress' Omnibus Budget Reconciliation Act of 1990 which raised taxes, hampering his re-election chances.

William Jefferson Clinton, 1993–2001

Clinton became the second Southern governor to take the White House in sixteen years, following in the footsteps of Georgia Governor Jimmy Carter. Clinton defeated incumbent George H. W. Bush, and as a result the phrase, "It's the economy, stupid" became part of American political history. Clinton's administration included a deficit-reduction package, low unemployment, a 1998 federal budget surplus of $70 billion, and the beginning of normal trade relations with China.

George W. Bush, 2001–2009

Bush, the son of the forty-first president, a Yale graduate and a former Texas governor, took office only after one of the most contentious elections in modern history. He lost the popular vote to Al Gore, but won the electoral vote, a conflict that took until December 2000 to sort out. He then defeated Massachusetts Senator John Kerry in 2004 to win re-election. His administration has included the passage of the No Child Left Behind Act of 2001 and a $1.35 trillion tax cut, among other unprecedented tax cuts.

Bush in Uniform

In December 2004, George W. Bush became the first U.S. president to wear a uniform when he sported a traditional military jacket to address the troops in Marine Corps base Camp Pendleton. Even former Presidents Eisenhower and Grant never donned military garb when they ceased to be generals and switched to civilian clothes (as would be expected from Bush). Traditionally, only dictatorial nations wear uniforms.

WHO SAID WHAT, 1980s

- "Just say no." Nancy Reagan
  The First Lady made this three-word campaign her slogan against drug use. She even appeared on the sitcom *Diff'rent Strokes* in 1983 to promote the slogan.

- "My fellow Americans, I'm pleased to tell you today that I've signed legislation that will outlaw Russia forever. We begin bombing in five minutes." Ronald Reagan
  Reagan was sometimes known as "The Great Communicator," but on August 11, 1984, he communicated a little too much. While preparing for his weekly radio address, Reagan, a former radio broadcaster and actor, forgot that a prudent person considers every mic as "hot," and made this gaffe. Reagan had called the Soviet Union the "Evil Empire" the year before.

- "Senator, you're no Jack Kennedy." Lloyd Bentsen
  In 1988, Texas Senator Bentsen was the vice presidential running mate of Democrat Michael Dukakis. During a televised debate with Republican vice presidential nominee Dan Quayle, Quayle defended his inexperience by saying, "I have as much experience in the Congress as Jack Kennedy did when he sought the presidency." Bentsen, who at sixty-seven was twenty-six years older than the forty-one-year-old Quayle, replied, "Senator, I served with Jack Kennedy. I knew Jack Kennedy. Jack Kennedy was a friend of mine. Senator, you're no Jack Kennedy."

Vulgar Veggies

Regardless of any charm President George H. W. Bush may have communicated on camera, he was less polite while dining, both at home and in public. He refused to eat broccoli, pitching a little fit and saying, "I am the President of the United States, and I don't have to eat it!" Southern vegetable farmers were so upset at his pronouncement that they delivered truckloads of broccoli to the White House in protest.

FIRST GULF WAR

The modern world revolves around oil. Cut off the supply of oil
and you cut off food, transportation, materials, and energy for billions
of people. So when Saddam Hussein's Iraq invaded its neighbor
Kuwait, a major oil producer, on August 2, 1990, the world took
notice. A coalition of nations under United Nations authority began
assembling in the Persian Gulf. In November, the UN approved the
use of force to remove Iraqi forces from Kuwait and set a deadline of
January 15 for Iraq to withdraw from Kuwait. In January 1990,
Congress authorized the use of force by the U.S. military. On January
17, at 2:38 a.m., American helicopters attacked Iraqi radar
installations, beginning the First Gulf War.

The war was largely fought in the air. In forty-three days, coalition
aircraft flew 109,876 sorties, or an average of 2,555 per day. Coalition
forces dropped 60,624 tons on enemy positions. In addition, 297
Tomahawk missiles, each carrying either 1,000-pound warheads or 166
wide-scattering bomblets, were launched.

Air strikes considerably "softened" Iraqi positions before the ground
war started on February 24. Coalition forces moved so quickly and
devastatingly that they were at times overwhelmed by numbers of Iraqi
soldiers anxious to surrender. Iraqi troops began to retreat on February
26. On February 28, a hundred hours after the ground offensive began,
a temporary cease-fire took effect. On March 3, Iraq and the coalition
agreed to a permanent cease-fire.

Some 500 coalition forces had been killed, while estimates of Iraqi
deaths vary from 20,000 to 100,000. Although Hussein's forces had
been repelled from Kuwait, he remained in power, a fact that many
Americans resented and which allowed him to crush uprisings by
Kurds and Shia Muslims in his country shortly after the war. Between
30,000 and 60,000 Shias were killed, and 450,000 Kurds fled into
Turkey.

1992 ELECTION

George H. W. Bush had served eight years as Ronald Reagan's vice president, then surfed into the Oval Office on a wave of Reagan popularity in 1988. He then presided over the successful and politically popular Gulf War of 1991, turning Saddam Hussein's Iraq back from Kuwait. He appeared to be a favorite to win reelection in 1992, but was defeated by Arkansas Governor Bill Clinton. Ironically, it was one of Bush's own campaign slogans that helped sink his bid for another four years in the Oval Office.

During his 1988 campaign for the Republican nomination, Bush had begun to promise no new taxes. When he accepted the nomination at the Republican Convention in New Orleans, he said, "My opponent, my opponent won't rule out raising taxes. But I will. And the Congress will push me to raise taxes and I'll say 'No.' And they'll push, and I'll say 'No.' And they'll push again, and I'll say to them, 'Read my lips: no new taxes.'"

The phrase "Read my lips: no new taxes" resounded with the public, and Bush defeated Democratic candidate Michael Dukakis in the 1988 election. But once he took office, when Bush was faced with a widening budget deficit and pressure from Congress, Bush signed the Omnibus Budget Reconciliation Act of 1990 (OBRA-90), which raised a number of taxes.

By signing OBRA-90, Bush also signed away his chances at re-election. Both Republicans and Democrats hammered him for breaking his promise, and one of the catchphrases of Clinton's 1992 campaign was "It's the economy, stupid." Bush lost the 1992 election to Clinton by 5.8 million votes.

CLINTON-LEWINSKY SCANDAL

It became one of the enduring images of the nineties. During a January 26, 1998 press conference, the day before his scheduled State of the Union Address, President Bill Clinton, his voice shaking, said, "I did not have sexual relations with that woman, Miss Lewinsky. I never told anybody to lie, not a single time. Never. These allegations are false."

"These allegations" were rumors that Clinton had had an illicit affair with Monica Lewinsky, a former White House intern, and then told her to lie about the affair to investigators. The story had broken on the website Drudgereport.com on January 19, and the possibility of a presidential sex scandal had captured the nation's attention.

The rumors of Clinton having an affair had begun because of a 1994 sexual harassment lawsuit brought against him by Paula Jones. Jones alleged Clinton had sexually harassed her in 1991, when he was governor of Arkansas and she was an Arkansas state employee. Jones' lawyers had included Lewinsky's name in a list of women they'd like to depose as part of their case.

On August 17, the president went before a federal grand jury investigating his conduct during depositions in the Jones case. That night, he went on national television, saying, "Indeed, I did have a relationship with Miss Lewinsky that was not appropriate. In fact, it was wrong." But while he admitted the relationship, Clinton went on to say, "But I told the grand jury today and I say to you now that at no time did I ask anyone to lie, to hide or destroy evidence or to take any other unlawful action."

Other Presidential Sex Scandals

The Oval Office has seen many presidential scandals over time. In 1802, rumors of Thomas Jefferson's alleged rendezvous with slave Sally Hemings were published in capital newspapers. Ten years before Grover Cleveland became president in 1885, a store clerk named Maria publicly named him the father of her illegitimate son. Twenty-ninth president Warren G. Harding fathered a child out of wedlock in 1919 while he served on the Senate.

WHO SAID WHAT, 1990S

- "...the mother of all battles." Saddam Hussein
  This quote has come to be applied to just about any situation
  needing amplification: "Mother of all football games," "Mother of
  all kidney stones," "Mother of all earnings before interest, taxes,
  depreciation, and amortization." But it began with Iraqi dictator
  Saddam Hussein. After he invaded Kuwait in 1990, he was quoted
  as saying, "Prepare for war with the United States. Let everybody
  understand that this battle will become the mother of all battles."
  Later, the United States developed the 21,000-pound GBU-43/B
  Massive Ordnance Air Blast Bomb, nicknamed the "Mother of All
  Bombs."

- "And just think: nobody thought this would last," Michael Jackson
  Jackson appeared at the MTV Video Music Awards on September
  8, 1994 with his new wife Lisa Marie Presley, whom he had
  married on May 26 of that year. He made this statement, then
  grabbed Presley and kissed her awkwardly. The marriage did
  last...eighteen months. The two divorced in January 1996.

- "You double-dipped the chip!" Timmy
  The sitcom *Seinfeld* ran for nine years on NBC and contributed a
  wealth of phrases to popular culture: close talkers, the Soup Nazi,
  the kiss hello. One of the most famous phrases was created when
  Jason Alexander (as George Costanza) lowers a chip into a bowl of
  dip, eats the dip off the chip, then dips the chip again. He's
  confronted by "Timmy" (no last name given), who accuses him of
  "double-dipping."

- "I love California; I practically grew up in Phoenix." Dan Quayle
  This gem of political misspeak was brought to you by Vice
  President Dan Quale. His other greatest hits include "It isn't
  pollution that's harming the environment. It's the impurities in our
  air and water that are doing it," "For NASA, space is still a high
  priority," and "One word sums up probably the responsibility of
  any vice president, and that one word is "'to be prepared.'"

2000 ELECTION

In 1876, Republican Rutherford B. Hayes ran for president against Democrat Samuel J. Tilden. The election was a close one, with Tilden defeating Hayes by only 250,000 votes out of more than 8.3 million votes cast. But Hayes, not Tilden moved into the White House, because Hayes had lost the popular vote, but won the Electoral College vote, 185-184.

Except for a detail here or there, the controversy of the 1876 election was repeated in 2000. Republican George W. Bush ran against Democrat Al Gore. Gore defeated Bush in the popular vote, 50,999,897 to 50,456,002. But Bush defeated Gore in the Electoral College, 271-266.

So what is this "Electoral College"? Put simply, as specified in the Constitution, it's a group of representatives from each state (and the District of Columbia, since the twenty-third Amendment was passed in 1960) that actually elects the president.

The use of electors rather than popular votes arose from the Constitutional Convention of 1787. Delegates were faced with two choices: have the president chosen by the legislature or by popular vote. If the legislature chose the president, he might be likely to favor the legislators who voted for him. If popular vote chose the president, the more populous states would have more power.

The Convention delegates finally reached compromise that made the presidential election process resemble the way Congress operates. Just as each state had two senators in Congress, each state received two electors. And just as the number of representatives each state received was determined by population, each state also received an elector for each representative it had. For the most part, whichever candidate receives the majority of the popular vote in each state receives all that state's electors.

Economics 101
Dotcom Bubble

People who have money—even people who have lots and lots of money—don't always have the smarts to spend that money wisely. Furthermore, people with money like shiny new things and alluring new concepts just like everyone else. So when terms like "Information Superhighway" and "Internet" began to float around the business world and elsewhere in the mid-1990s, attempts to make a financial killing also began.

The dotcom bubble began to inflate in earnest following the initial public offering (IPO) of web-browser developer Netscape in 1995. On August 9, the stock opened at $28 a share. By December 5 of that year, it was $174 per share, and had made Chairman James H. Clark a billionaire.

Investors soon pumped millions into concepts that would have been laughed out of pitch meetings just a few years earlier. The investors behind Flooz.com decided that credit cards and gift cards weren't good enough. What consumers needed was another means of paying for things, with an added layer of complexity. Customers bought Flooz, then spent it, adding another step to online purchases that could just as easily be completed with a credit card alone. It didn't take long for even the densest consumer to figure out that the concept was laughably useless, and the company went bankrupt despite having raised $35 million in investments.

Flooz.com wasn't alone. Online startups like Webvan, Kozmo and Pets.com burned bright but didn't burn long, taking multiple millions of investment dollars when they went belly-up.

The burning desire to burn away hard-earned assets couldn't last, and it didn't. The dotcom bubble began to lose internal pressure on March 10, 2000. The tech-heavy NASDAQ stock index peaked at 5,048.62 that day. It closed at 3361 on October 5. Investors sobered up and began investing more wisely (at least for a while) and the dotcom bubble was soon well and truly burst.

SEPTEMBER 11, 2001

At 8:46 a.m. Eastern Daylight Time on September 11, 2001, American Airlines Flight 11, a hijacked Boeing 767 carrying ninety-two people, smashed into the north tower of New York City's World Trade Center. At 9:03 a.m., another hijacked 767, United Airlines Flight 175, hit the south tower of the World Trade Center. Flight 175 held sixty-five people. The most devastating attack on American soil since December 7, 1941 had begun.

As a shocked nation dealt with the images of destruction from the Twin Towers, it received news of more destruction. At 9:37 a.m., American Airlines Flight 77, a Boeing 757 carrying sixty-four people, slammed into the Pentagon in Washington, D.C.

Weakened from the impact of the crash and the burning of thousands of gallons of jet fuel, the south tower of the World Trade Center collapsed at 9:59 a.m., killing emergency workers who had rushed to the scene. At 10:10 a.m., United Airlines Flight 93, carrying forty-four people, crashed southeast of Pittsburgh, Pennsylvania. It was later determined that Flight 93 had also been hijacked, and that passengers on the plane had attempted to retake the plane when the hijackers had crashed the plane. At 10:28 a.m., the north tower of the World Trade Center collapsed.

In all, 2,948 people were confirmed dead as a result of the four hijackings and crashes, with twenty-four reported dead and twenty-four missing.

On September 14, the Federal Bureau of Investigation released the names of nineteen suspects in the 9/11 hijackings. Fifteen of the hijackers were from Saudi Arabia, two were from the United Arab Emirates, one from Egypt, and one from Lebanon. In addition, it was determined that the terrorist group al-Qaeda, led by Osama bin Laden, had been responsible for the attacks.

WHO SAID WHAT, 2000s

- "All your base are belong to us." CATS villain
  CATS was (evidently; nobody is really sure) an evil organization that planned to do serious harm in the 1989 Japanese video game "Zero Wing." The opening sequence to the game, which included horrifically translated English versions of Japanese comments ("Take off every Zig!!" "Somebody set up us the bomb") was eventually animated using Flash, and it permeated the Internet in 2001. Soon, "All your base..." was common Internet jargon.

- "Let's roll." Todd Beamer
  Beamer was one of the passengers on United Airlines Flight 93, which crashed south of Pittsburgh September 11, 2001. The plane had taken off from Newark, New Jersey and was on its way to San Francisco when it was hijacked by accomplices of the World Trade Center and Pentagon attackers. The attackers had turned the plane toward Washington, D.C., possibly to hit the Capitol Building. Beamer made a phone call using the plane's in-flight phone system and was routed to GTE supervisor Lisa Jefferson. He told Jefferson that he and some of the other passengers were planning to rush the hijackers, made Jefferson promise to call his family, then asked her to pray with him. They recited the 23rd Psalm together, then Beamer dropped the phone, leaving the line open for Jefferson to hear Beamer say "let's roll" before the passengers rushed the hijackers.

- "This race is shakier than cafeteria Jell-O." Dan Rather
  As the 2000 presidential election dragged on into the night, the CBS anchor began spouting down-home Texas aphorisms like this one to describe the action. Other Rather gems included, "If a frog had side pockets, he'd carry a handgun" and "These returns are running like a squirrel in a cage."

FINAL EXAM

1) What is the oldest permanent European settlement in North America?

2) What was the name of Sir Walter Raleigh's Lost Colony settlement?

3) What was the first permanent English colony in America?

4) What was so special about Virginia Dare?

5) What document did the Pilgrims adopt that established self-government?

6) When did the first Africans arrive in Jamestown?

7) What village staged a witch hunt in 1692 and 1693?

6) African slaves taught their colonial owners the things they knew about raising which cash crop?

7) What religious movement of the 1740s united colonists in their democratic tendencies and sense of American nationality?

8) Who won the French and Indian War?

9) The First Continental Congress met on September 5, 1774, to discuss a response to what acts, which were themselves Parliament's response to the Boston Tea Party?

10) Who put forth a two-step government growth process?

11) What governmental assembly adopted the Declaration of Independence on July 4, 1776?

12) Fill in the blanks. Thomas Jefferson wrote in the Declaration of Independence, "We hold these truths to be self-evident, that all men are created equal, that they are endowed by their Creator with certain unalienable Rights, that among these are Life, Liberty and the _____ _____ _____."

13) The Age of Reason, a time when long-held beliefs about the basic rights guaranteed by government, was also called by what other name?

14) The beginning of the battle for America's independence is famously signified by what phrase written by Ralph Waldo Emerson in his poem, "The Concord Hymn?"

15) America declared war against Britain on June 18, 1812, because Britain had retaliated against Americans for ignoring the British blockade of European ports. This was called the War of _____.

16) What did Mary Pickersgill do that Betsy Ross probably did not?

17) Choose the selection below that is NOT an actual political party in early American history.
a) Whigs
b) Tories
c) Know-Nothings
d) Free Soil Party
e) Barn Raisers

18) Match the President with the correct biographical detail.

1. George Washington	a. Father of the Constitution
2. John Adams	b. Elected by the House of Representatives
3. Thomas Jefferson	c. Shortest inauguration speech
4. James Madison	d. First president to live in the White House
5. John Quincy Adams	e. Author of the Declaration of Independence

19) Match the President with the correct biographical detail

1. Andrew Jackson	a. Acquired California from Mexico
2. Martin Van Buren	b. Called "Old Kinderhook"
3. William Henry Harrison	c. Relied on his Kitchen Cabinet friends
4. John Tyler	d. The first president to die in office
5. James K. Polk	e. Known as "The Accidency"

20) The Civil War began in 1861 when Confederate forces fired on Ft. Sumter. Where is Ft. Sumter located?
   a) Savannah, Georgia
   b) Charlottesville, Virginia
   c) Charleston, South Carolina

21) Charles Mason and Jeremiah Dixon surveyed and marked the boundary line between what two states?
   a) Maryland and Pennsylvania
   b) Virginia and New Hampshire
   c) Massachusetts and Pennsylvania
   d) Florida and Georgia

22) What tragic event began in the year after Herbert Hoover won the presidential election with the campaign slogan, *A Chicken in Every Pot and a Car in Every Garage*?

23) Name the largest state and the smallest state.

24) Which states do not have any counties?

25) What president had to take his oath of office secretly, in the Red Room of the White House?
   a) William Jennings Bryan
   b) Rutherford B. Hayes
   c) Millard Fillmore

26) When did the United States enter World War I?

27) What treaty ended WWI?
   a) Treaty of Caravazzio
   b) Treaty of Versailles
   c) Treaty of Oscarmeyerstan

28) What constitutional amendment gave women the right to vote?

29) The _____ Amendment began the Prohibition era. The _____ Amendment ended it.

30) What act allowed America to aid Great Britain militarily, even before December 7, 1941?

31) German rocket scientists were brought to the U.S., where they eventually helped land a man on the moon, as part of Operation:
a) Paperclip
b) Mockingbird
c) Redbug

32) The Truman Doctrine was the U.S. policy of fighting the spread of:
a) poverty
b) Communism
c) rock and roll

33) Rosa Parks refused to give up her bus seat to a white bus rider in 1954, leading to the _____ _____ Boycott.

34) What was notable about the birth of Kathleen Casey-Kirschling in 1946?
a) She was the first test-tube baby
b) She was the first baby born on an airplane in flight
c) She was the first child of the Baby Boom

35) Who were Wallace Buford and James "Earthquake McGoon" McGovern?
a) The last American soldiers killed in WWII
b) the first American soldiers killed in the Korean War
c) the first Americans killed in the Vietnam War

36) True or False: "Blue Suede Shoes" by Carl Perkins is regarded as the first rock and roll record.

37) True or False: Nikita Kruschev made his remark about Communism replacing capitalism, "We will bury you!" at the United Nations.

38) How many songs did the Beatles sing the first night they appeared on "The Ed Sullivan Show" in 1964?
a) 1
b) 3
c) 5

39) In 1987, President Ronald Reagan made a famous statement while in Germany. Reagan said, "Mr. Gorbachev, tear down ____ ____."

40) When was the first message sent via what would become the Internet?
a) 1954
b) 1963
c) 1969

ANSWERS:

1) St. Augustine
2) Roanoke
3) Jamestown
4) She was the first child born to English parents in America
5) The Mayflower Compact
6) 1619
7) Salem, Massachusetts
6) Rice
7) The Great Awakening
8) The British
9) The Intolerable Acts
10) John Locke
11) The Second Continental Congress
12) Pursuit of Happiness
13) The Age of Enlightenment
14) "The shot heard 'round the world"
15) 1812
16) Sew the American flag that inspired Francis Scott Key to write a poem that became our national anthem.
17) e
18) 1-c; 2-d; 3-e; 4-a; 5-b
19) 1-c; 2-b; 3-d; 4-e; 5-a
20) a
21) a
22) The Great Depression
23) Alaska and Rhode Island
24) Alaska has boroughs and geographical census areas, and Louisiana has 64 parishes.
25) b—Hayes lost the 1876 popular election but won the Electoral College votes, a process that took until January 1877 to sort out.
26) 1917
27) b
28) Nineteenth
29) Eighteenth and twenty-first
30) The Lend-Lease Act
32) b
33) Montgomery Bus
34) c
35) c
36) False
37) False
38) c
39) this wall
40) c

512